MW00721129

Computer users are not all alike.
Neither are SYBEX books.

We know our customers have a variety of needs. They've told us so. And because we've listened, we've developed several distinct types of books to meet the needs of each of our customers. What are you looking for in computer help?

If you're looking for the basics, try the **ABC's** series. You'll find short, unintimidating tutorials and helpful illustrations. For a more visual approach, select **Teach Yourself**, featuring screen-by-screen illustrations of how to use your latest software purchase.

Mastering and **Understanding** titles offer you a step-by-step introduction, plus an in-depth examination of intermediate-level features, to use as you progress.

Our **Up & Running** series is designed for computer-literate consumers who want a no-nonsense overview of new programs. Just 20 basic lessons, and you're on your way.

We also publish two types of reference books. Our **Instant References** provide quick access to each of a program's commands and functions. SYBEX **Encyclopedias** provide a *comprehensive reference* and explanation of all of the commands, features and functions of the subject software.

Sometimes a subject requires a special treatment that our standard series doesn't provide. So you'll find we have titles like **Advanced Techniques, Handbooks, Tips & Tricks**, and others that are specifically tailored to satisfy a unique need.

We carefully select our authors for their in-depth understanding of the software they're writing about, as well as their ability to write clearly and communicate effectively. Each manuscript is thoroughly reviewed by our technical staff to ensure its complete accuracy. Our production department makes sure it's easy to use. All of this adds up to the highest quality books available, consistently appearing on best-seller charts worldwide.

You'll find SYBEX publishes a variety of books on every popular software package. Looking for computer help? Help Yourself to SYBEX.

For a complete catalog of our publications:

SYBEX Inc.
2021 Challenger Drive, Alameda, CA 94501
Tel: (415) 523-8233/(800) 227-2346 Telex: 336311
Fax: (415) 523-2373

UNDERSTANDING
PC TOOLS™ 7

UNDERSTANDING
PC TOOLS™ 7

Peter Dyson

SYBEX ®

San Francisco ■ Paris ■ Düsseldorf ■ Soest

Acquisitions Editor: Dianne King
Developmental Editor: Gary Masters
Editor: Stefan Grünwedel
Technical Editor: Sharon Crawford
Word Processors: Ann Dunn and Susan Trybull
Chapter Art and Layout: Charlotte Carter
Technical Art: Delia Brown
Screen Graphics: Delia Brown and Cuong Le
Typesetters: Winnie Kelly and Elizabeth Newman
Proofreaders: Rhonda Holmes and Catherine Mahoney
Production Assistant: Thomas Goudie
Indexer: Anne Leach
Cover Designer: Thomas Ingalls + Associates
Cover Photographer: Michael Lamotte

Library of Congress Card Number: 91-75001
ISBN: 0-89588-850-5
Manufactured in the United States of America
10 9 8 7 6 5 4 3 2

To my mother and father

Give us the tools and we will finish the job.

Sir Winston Churchill

ACKNOWLEDGMENTS

Once again, I have enjoyed my part in writing this book, but as always, many people have worked on the project, providing technical assistance, advice, and many other services.

I want to thank everyone at SYBEX, particularly Dianne King, Acquisitions Manager, for her constant encouragement and good spirits. Thanks to developmental editor Gary Masters, copy editor Stefan Grünwedel, technical editor Sharon Crawford, and screen-graphics supervisor Delia Brown. Thanks also to word processors Ann Dunn and Susan Trybull, typesetters Winnie Kelly and Elizabeth Newman, proofreaders Rhonda Holmes and Catherine Mahoney, screen-graphics artist Cuong Le, artist Charlotte Carter, production assistant Thomas Goudie, and indexer Anne Leach.

At Central Point Software, thanks to Debbie Hess for providing beta copies of PC Tools 7, and thanks to Ken Dietz and Doug Whitney of Technical Support for answering my questions quickly and completely.

Thanks to Nancy for her continuing support, patience, and encouragement as I worked on this manuscript. Now that it's done, I'll have to make good on my promise to paint the bathroom. Thanks also to Gene Weisskopf for his advice and for going to Comdex so I didn't have to, Tom Charlesworth for information on data-compression techniques, Bob Jungbluth for information on modems and data communications, and Russell McFall for the temporary use of his partition table.

... AT A GLANCE

TABLE OF CONTENTS

FOREWORD

No matter how you tally the votes—in the press or on the best-seller list—PC Tools has emerged as the clean choice for PC utility software. Whether you're running DOS or Windows, on a network or stand-alone, no single package can help you protect and manage your data as completely as PC Tools.

Now in its seventh major release, PC Tools gives you a complete collection of system-management tools in one integrated package:

- Hard-disk backup (DOS and Windows applications)
- Data protection and disk maintenance
- Data recovery (DOS and Windows applications)
- DOS shell and file manager with viewers
- Comprehensive desktop organizer with electronic-mail support
- Remote PC access and file transfer
- System and network information on over 160 items
- Disk cache and optimizer (defragmenter)
- Data security and encryption

When Peter Dyson's *Mastering PC Tools Deluxe* first came to our attention, we were pleased to see a book we could recommend as a companion reference to our product. It is intuitively organized and clearly written, and it contains helpful examples and summary tables that help you get the most from our software.

Now *Understanding PC Tools 7* incorporates the same attention to detail as the previous editions. What's more, it helps you get the most from more than 100 new features and improvements in Version 7. May it speed you along to more productive computing.

Corey Smith
President
Central Point Software, Inc.

INTRODUCTION

There are many reasons for using the programs in PC Tools. They present many essential capabilities in a compact, cost-effective package. They also present alternatives that are easier to use than the equivalent DOS commands, if indeed there are equivalents.

This book describes the programs in PC Tools Version 7, released in the Spring of 1991. If you have not upgraded yet, I urge you to do so, because Version 7 contains several major new programs.

WHO SHOULD READ THIS BOOK

Understanding PC Tools 7 is intended to meet the needs of a wide variety of readers. You don't have to be a computer expert to understand and use this book; every attempt has been made to minimize jargon and present the material clearly and logically.

If you are new to PC Tools, this book will serve as your guide as you learn the fundamentals of the programs. All the examples are short and concise, so you won't waste time trying to figure out a complex example. You don't have to read this book from front to back in strict sequence, either; you can plunge in anywhere, since the chapters stand alone as discussions of individual components of the PC Tools package. However, you may wish to pay special attention to Part I, which describes the installation and how to get the most out of the user interface, before moving on to the more advanced material presented in later sections.

If you already have PC Tools 7, *Understanding PC Tools 7* will help you get more out of the programs and your computer system. The book covers all aspects of PC Tools and even includes a complete reference of commands, with their respective command-line arguments. In your case, you can probably move straight to the sections describing specific problems and solutions. You may also want to brush up on your understanding of disk and directory structure by looking at Chapter 6 before using the data-recovery programs described in later chapters.

HOW THIS BOOK IS ORGANIZED

This book is divided into five parts containing a total of 20 chapters. Each chapter describes a group of PC Tools programs and provides examples on how to get the most out of your system.

Part I, "Installing and Running PC Tools 7," presents essential information about the tools and your computer; it builds a strong foundation necessary for any user. You will learn how to install PC Tools on your hard disk and use the new interface. You will learn how to configure the programs in the PC Tools package to form your own personal computing environment, specifically designed to meet your day-to-day needs.

Part II, "File and Program Management Tools," describes how to use PC Shell and to get the most out of the file-management and program-management features of the package.

Part III, "Disk Recovery and Data Protection Tools," starts with an introduction to disk and directory structure to set the stage for the discussion of the file- and disk-recovery tools later in the section. Chapter 8 includes programs that let you look into the dark corners of your PC without getting into any complex programming; the other chapters describe ways of squeezing the last ounce of performance from your hard disk by using a disk-cache program, optimizing the interleave factor, and unfragmenting your files. The Windows-only programs in PC Tools are also covered.

Part IV, "Desktop Tools," covers Notepads, Outliners, the Clipboard and the Macro Editor, Modem, Fax, E-Mail Communications, and the Desktop Database.

Part V, "Reference Tools," gives an insight into how to use the DiskFix program to track down and fix general disk, DOS, and CHKDSK error messages. It contains a full discussion of memory-resident programs and how to make them work together successfully. Part V also includes a complete reference guide to the PC Tools commands, which lists each command's program switches or parameters for ease of reference.

THE MARGIN NOTES

As you read through this book, you will come across margin notes that are prefaced by a symbol. There are three types of notes:

This symbol indicates a general note about the topic under discussion. I often use it to refer you to other chapters for more information.

This symbol denotes tips or tricks that you may find useful when running PC Tools. They might be shortcuts I have discovered or just important techniques that need to be emphasized.

Pay close attention when you see this symbol in the margins. It alerts you to potential problems and often gives you methods for avoiding them.

THE FIGURES

The figures in this book were designed for tutorial purposes only, not to show the "definitive screen." The default screen positions and sizes were used in most cases. Because you can configure PC Tools in many different ways, do not be concerned if you detect minor differences between the figures in this book and what you see on your own computer screen.

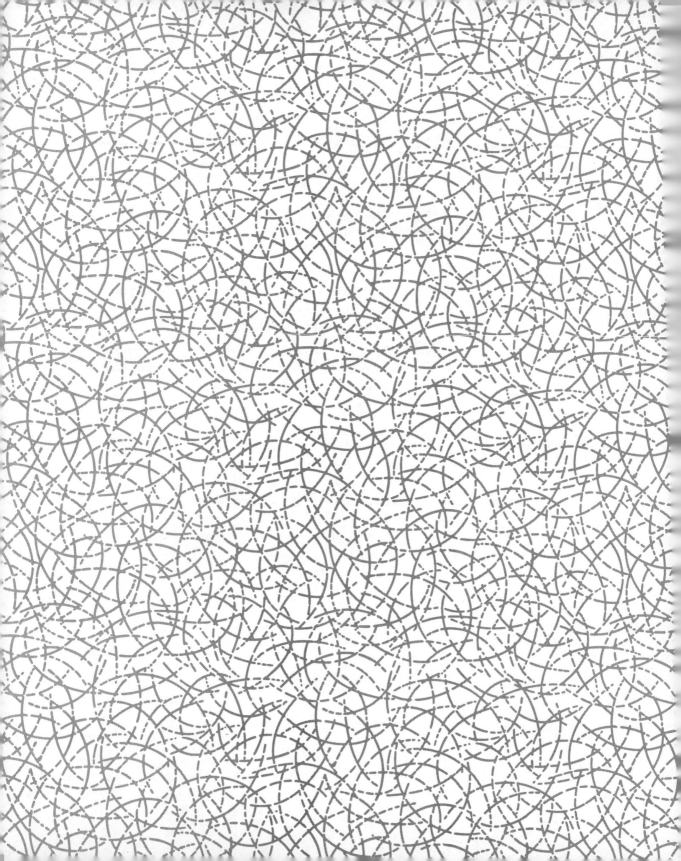

PART I

Installing and Running PC Tools

CHAPTER

1

*An Overview
of PC Tools*

PC Tools is a powerful and complete collection of programs, designed to make your computing easier and more productive. These utilities all share a common interface design—with pulldown menus and full mouse support—so once you learn how to use one program, you can work with all of them. There are very few tasks in home or office computing that you cannot accomplish with Version 7 of PC Tools.

WHAT'S NEW IN VERSION 7?

There are many completely new programs in this release of PC Tools, as well as countless enhancements to the core set of programs. Here is a short list of the major new additions:

- Microsoft Windows programs for hard-disk backup, file undelete, and applications launching
- New DOS 5-like user interface for all PC Tools DOS programs
- Greatly enhanced network support
- New System Information program, with hardware and system software and memory information
- New File Fix program to repair Lotus, Symphony, and dBASE files
- New Emergency System Recovery Disk to boot when your hard disk refuses to start
- New Commute program for remote access to your office PC or LAN
- Directory Maintenance program for managing directories
- FileFind program to locate lost files and search for text
- DiskFix for enhanced error checking, interleave testing, and optimization
- Support for detection of over 400 computer viruses

- Ability to view over 30 different types of data files in their native format

PC TOOLS IN BRIEF

This section provides a short description of each of the programs in PC Tools 7. A complete listing of all the command-line options for these programs is given in Chapter 20:

Backtalk	A memory-resident program that performs Desktop background communications
Commute	A powerful communications program that lets you take over a remote PC, transfer files, and even reboot the remote computer
Compress	A disk-optimization and file-unfragmenting program
CP Backup	Lets you back up your hard disk—in whole or in part—to another hard disk, to floppy disks, or to tape. CP Backup is available in DOS and Windows versions
CPBDIR	A small program for reading backup disks made in Central Point's proprietary format
CP Scheduler	A task scheduler linked to CP Backup, Commute, DiskFix, and Desktop E-Mail
Data Monitor	A memory-resident program that prevents unauthorized writes to your hard disk, offers two kinds of file delete protection, and displays a disk-light indicator
DeskConnect	A pair of programs that let you transfer important files from your main office PC to your laptop computer before a business trip
Desktop	Provides an easy-to-use desktop manager, including word processing, database, an

	appointment scheduler with a to-do list, and four calculators
DiskFix	Finds and fixes logical or physical problems on floppy or hard disks; it can also evaluate your current hard disk interleave factor and recommend appropriate changes
Directory Maintenance	Lets you make, remove, and rename directories, as well as move whole directory structures to new locations on your disk
FileFind	Locates lost files or groups of files, searches for text and searches by date, file size, or file attribute
File Fix	Repairs damaged files created by Lotus 1-2-3, Symphony, dBASE, and other programs that generate compatible files
Kill	A program that removes PC Tools memory-resident programs from memory
MI	A command-line memory display
Mirror	Saves a copy of the system area of your hard disk for use by Undelete or Unformat
Park	Moves your hard disk heads to a safe area of your disk before you turn off the power
PC-Cache	A disk-cache program that can improve the performance of your system by speeding up disk accesses
PC Config	Lets you change the screen colors and alter the display, mouse, and keyboard options for all PC Tools programs
PC Format	A safe alternative to the DOS FORMAT command
PC Secure	Compresses, encrypts, and hides confidential files

PC Shell	A DOS shell program that provides many useful disk, file, and applications services
System Information	Gives a detailed report on the hardware and system software installed in your computer and calculates several performance indicators
Rebuild	Recovers CMOS information and reloads the boot sector and partition table of a damaged disk
Undelete	Searches for and recovers deleted files in DOS and Windows. The DOS version also has a powerful manual undelete mode
Unformat	Lets you recover data on a hard disk after the disk has been accidentally reformatted with the DOS FORMAT command
VDefend	A memory-resident program that watches for computer virus-like activity and can protect your system against over 400 computer viruses
View	Contains over 30 viewers that let you examine the data files of applications programs without having to load the applications
Wipe	Completely obliterates deleted files so that they can never be recovered, not even by PC Tools

In the chapters that follow I will explore all of the PC Tools programs in detail, and—with examples where it is appropriate—show you how to use them to get the most out of your computer.

USING PC TOOLS WITH WINDOWS OR DESQVIEW

Microsoft Windows and DESQview (by Quarterdeck Office Systems) both bring multitasking capabilities to DOS. Multitasking means that you can run several different applications programs at once, and switch from one to another without quitting any of them. PC Tools includes several programs specifically designed to run under Windows, and most of the DOS-based programs can be run from Windows, too. All the PC Tools programs that can be used with Windows are collected together in a program group created by the PC Tools Install program.

Because many of the PC Tools programs run as DOS tasks, not as Windows or DESQview applications, they cannot observe all the protocols required for successful data interchange and multitasking operation. Therefore, the PC Tools programs contain extensive error-checking routines to avoid anything unpleasant from happening should you run the programs in either of these environments. In general, the PC Tools programs that write critical information to the disk are potential problems. For example, the disk-optimizer program Compress is not available in the PC Tools group in Windows' Program Manager, but you can still run it if you use the Run option in Windows' File Manager. If you start Compress in this way, you will see a screen similar to the one shown in Figure 1.1.

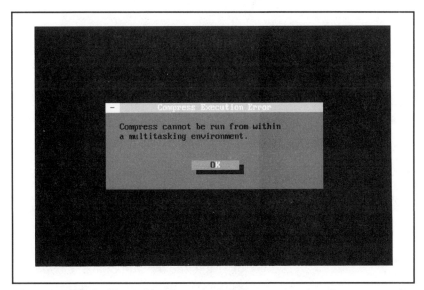

Figure 1.1: You will see this error window if you try to run Compress under Microsoft Windows

If you run the CPU benchmark test in System Information in a multitasking environment, your system will seem slower than if you run System Information under DOS. This is due to all the extra work the processor is doing to keep track of the concurrent activities. All the other PC Tools programs work as you would expect.

USING PC TOOLS ON A NETWORK

You can run PC Tools on a networked drive, and you can use many of the more important programs on the file server itself. However, as with the multitasking environments described in the previous section, those PC Tools programs that are capable of modifying the File Allocation Table should not be run on the file server. Installing PC Tools on a network should only be done by your network supervisor; this is covered in detail in Chapter 2.

HARDWARE AND SOFTWARE REQUIREMENTS FOR PC TOOLS

PC Tools is designed to work with all the IBM PCs, including the PC/XT, PC/AT, all models of the PS/2, and PC-compatible computers. You should have 640K of RAM and one or two floppy disks; a hard disk is required. To use Desktop Modem Communications or E-Mail and the Commute program, you need a modem.

Windows applications programs require Microsoft Windows 3.0 or higher, a 1.2MB high-density 5¼-inch floppy disk drive, and 2MB of RAM.

If you use 5¼-inch disks, note that the PC Tools Windows applications are distributed on a 1.2MB high-density floppy disk; all the other PC Tools programs are on 360K double-density disks.

PC Tools, with its menus and dialog boxes, works best with a mouse. If you have a Microsoft mouse, you should be using Version 6.14 or higher of the mouse driver. If you have a Logitech or Dexxa mouse, check that you have Version 3.4 or higher of the device driver. You must have one of the following fax cards installed in your computer to send Desktop Faxes: Intel Connection CoProcessor, Intel SatisFaxion board, or SpectraFax board.

PC Tools runs on DOS 3.0 or higher. To take full advantage of all the features of PC Tools, including the Commute program, however, you should use DOS 3.3 or higher. PC Tools is completely compatible with DOS 5.

You can install PC Tools on an IBM PC LAN server or on a Novell file server running NetWare 286 or 386.

CHAPTER

2

Installing
PC Tools

In this chapter, I describe how to install PC Tools onto your hard disk. As a preliminary to this installation process, you should make floppy-disk backup copies of the distribution disks; this protects you in case you accidentally damage the original disks. The last part of this chapter describes installing and configuring PC Tools on a network.

EXAMINING THE DISTRIBUTION PACKAGE

The PC Tools 7 distribution package consists of either fifteen 5¼-inch floppy disks, one of which—the Windows Utilities disk—is a 1.2MB high-density disk, or eight 3½-inch floppy disks, and six manuals: *Getting Started/Tips for Windows*, *Data Recovery and System Utilities*, *DOS Shell/File Manager*, *Hard Disk Backup*, *Desktop Manager*, and *Windows Utilities*.

Check to see whether there is a README.TXT file on disk 1. Since the README.TXT file contains the latest information about the package—information that may not be in the program manual—you should read it before installing the package. To do this, place disk 5 (3½") or disk 9 (5¼") in drive A and type

DIR A:

The DIR command lists all the files on the disk on your computer screen; there should be one called README.TXT. You can display the contents of the file on your computer screen by typing

TYPE A:README.TXT

or you can send the file to your printer by typing

PRINT A:README.TXT

MAKING THE FLOPPY-DISK BACKUPS

You should back up any software package immediately after taking it out of the box. Do this even if you plan to install the software on your hard disk. If the original disks are lost, damaged, or destroyed, your backup copy ensures that you can still use the software.

The easiest way to make a floppy-disk copy of the distribution disks is to use the DOS command DISKCOPY. Use DISKCOPY rather than COPY because DISKCOPY makes an exact duplicate of the original disk; it even copies the volume label—and you won't be able to install PC Tools from these duplicates if the volume labels are not identical to the original disks. If you have two disk drives of the same size and type, place the first distribution disk in drive A and a formatted blank disk in drive B, and enter:

DISKCOPY *.* B:

If you want to use just one drive, type

DISKCOPY A: A:

instead. When the first copy is complete, you will be asked whether you want to copy another disk. Answer Yes and repeat this procedure with each of the other distribution disks in the package. Label each disk to match the original distribution disk. Store the original disks in a safe place and from now on work with the copies rather than the originals.

Now that you have backed up the original distribution disks, you are ready to install the package on your hard disk.

INSTALLING PC TOOLS ON YOUR HARD DISK

If you bought PC Tools to help you recover an erased file or directory, do not install the programs on your hard disk yet. Instead, use PC Tools from your floppy-disk drive to recover the file and then continue with this installation procedure. The disk labels on the original disks list the programs contained on each disk; check disk 3 if you use 3½″ disks, and either disk 5 or disk 6 if you use 5¼″ disks. If you install PC Tools without first recovering the file, the installation program may overwrite the area of the disk occupied by the erased file, making its recovery impossible. Chapter 7 describes in detail what actually happens when you delete a file and how to perform file recovery.

USING THE INSTALL PROGRAM

The Install program installs PC Tools on your hard disk. Many files on the distribution disks have been "compressed" to save space and will not run as they are. Install "decompresses" the files so that they can run properly.

PC Tools includes an installation program called Install that guides you through the installation procedure step by step, explaining the choices available at each stage. Install also lets you make a Recovery Disk that you can use in the event that your hard disk refuses to start. To make a Recovery Disk, you need a blank floppy disk of the same size as the disks you will use to make the PC Tools installation. Format this blank floppy disk by typing:

FORMAT A: /S

at the DOS prompt. Set this disk aside for now; we will use it later.

To start Install, insert PC Tools disk 1 into drive A and type **INSTALL**.

Help is always available in the Install program; just press the F1 key.

Install opens a dialog box that allows you to choose the best display options for your computer: color, monochrome, LCD if you use a laptop with a liquid crystal display, or black-and-white. Enter the first letter of the monitor type to make your selection; as you choose a letter the screen changes to show you what PC Tools will look like if you decide on that option. You can also choose to load the graphic fonts used to make screen icons by clicking on the checkbox at the bottom of the screen, or by typing **G**. A warning screen then appears to remind you not to install PC Tools on your hard disk if you want to recover an erased file. Choose OK to continue with the installation (or choose Exit to return to DOS). Next, you can choose one of three installation options:

- Install on a Personal Computer
- Install on a Network Server
- Customize for this Network Workstation

Most people will choose the first selection. The network options will be discussed at the end of this chapter.

If you choose the option for installing on a personal computer, the next dialog box asks you to choose the directory where you want PC Tools to be installed. If the directory does not exist yet, Install will create it for you. This book uses the sample directory PCTOOLS, so go ahead and use this name for the directory. You can install all the PC Tools files into the same directory, or you can have Install locate the system and data files in separate subdirectories below the main directory. Choose OK to create separate subdirectories for these files. If you decide to use the Desktop in PC Tools when you configure your system, Install makes several more directories regardless of what you choose here. Install creates several directories to hold your electronic-mail files: INBOX, OUTBOX, and SENT—and another directory called APPT if you install PC Tools on a network.

If you want to install the PC Tools Windows programs, you must tell Install where your main Windows directory is located on your hard disk. Either select OK or type in the drive and directory name you used for Windows. Select Skip if you don't want to install the Windows programs.

The next screen offers four choices:

- Install all of PC Tools, for which you will need 6.9MB of free disk space

- Install Windows applications only, for which you will need 1.7MB of free disk space

- Install selected PC Tools applications. Here you can choose to install just the parts of PC Tools that you know you need.

- Install help files. This is always a good idea, so be sure and check this box.

Choose the first selection to install the complete PC Tools package, then select OK to begin copying files from the floppy disk to your hard disk. If you wish to install only a few applications, see "Installing Selected Programs" later in the chapter.

Install copies all the files from the floppy disk into the newly created directories on your hard disk, displaying each file name on the screen as it is copied and prompting you to insert the next disk when it has finished copying the first one. If you are updating from an earlier version of PC Tools, any user files you have—such as configuration files, phone files, and so on—are automatically copied into a subdirectory below the PCTOOLS directory called OLDPCT so that they are not overwritten by the new files. Then all the old program files are deleted from your system.

Install guides you through the rest of the installation, asking you to insert each disk in turn. The program even checks that you load the disks in the correct sequence; it will not let you use the wrong disk. Install also decompresses several large files that were in compressed form on the distribution disks to save space. The percentage complete is shown on the horizontal bar graph at the bottom of the window. If you are installing from a 360K 5¼-inch disk drive, Install is smart enough to know that it cannot install the Windows programs from the 1.2MB floppy, so it doesn't even try.

MAKING A RECOVERY DISK

Install assumes that you want to make the Recovery Disk using drive A, because drive A is the drive you will boot from; you cannot use drive B.

Once all the files are decompressed and loaded onto your system, Install asks whether you want to make a Recovery Disk. A Recovery Disk is a floppy disk that contains essential information about your system, as well as the DOS files needed to boot your system from a floppy disk. It is an excellent insurance policy against the day when your hard disk refuses to boot, so I strongly recommend that you take the time to make one now. Select OK and in the next window specify the drive that contains your current AUTOEXEC.BAT file. This is the drive you boot your system from, usually drive C. Next insert the blank floppy disk that you formatted earlier with the /S option. Alternatively, if you didn't prepare a disk earlier, type **F** to choose the Format button and let Install format the disk for you, or type **D** to return to DOS to format the disk yourself. Type **EXIT** to return to Install when the format is complete and select OK to continue. Install copies all the files needed to start your computer as well as specific recovery information. A dialog box informs you of your progress and indicates when the Recovery Disk is complete. Remove the floppy disk from drive A, label the disk with the special Recovery Disk label that came with the PC Tools package, and put the disk in a safe place. You should test the Recovery Disk after you have finished installing PC Tools.

If you installed PC Format, Install asks whether you want to rename the DOS FORMAT command to a new name, FORMAT!-.COM, so that you cannot run the DOS version by accident. That way, if you *do* type **FORMAT**, PC Format will run instead.

If you installed the Windows applications in PC Tools, the next dialog box asks if you want to open CP Launcher and CP Scheduler each time you start Windows. Type **C** to select the Launcher, or **S** for the Scheduler, and your Windows configuration files will be updated.

The next dialog box asks whether you want Install to convert any setup files you may have on your system for Norton Backup or Fast-Back into a form that can be used by the PC Tools backup program, CP Backup. If you have setup files made by these programs that you want to convert, select OK; otherwise select Skip to advance to the next screen, which asks if you want to configure PC Tools. Configuring PC Tools may result in changes to your AUTOEXEC.BAT or CONFIG.SYS files, so to avoid any problems, Install makes copies of them before changing them. The copies are called AUTOEXEC.SAV and CONFIG.SAV.

INSTALLING SELECTED PROGRAMS

If you chose to install selected PC Tools applications rather than the complete package, Install asks you to choose the programs you want in the Select Applications window, as Figure 2.1 shows. Here you can choose to install all the PC Tools programs, just the parts of PC Tools that you know you need, or none of the PC Tools programs.

The programs are divided into eight choices in this window. The list on the left side represents complete applications programs, while the list on the right side represents groups of programs, as follows:

Data Recovery (Recover)	Undelete, DiskFix, Unformat, File Fix
Data Protection/ Security (Prot)	Mirror, Data Monitor, Wipe, PC Secure, VDefend, PC Format

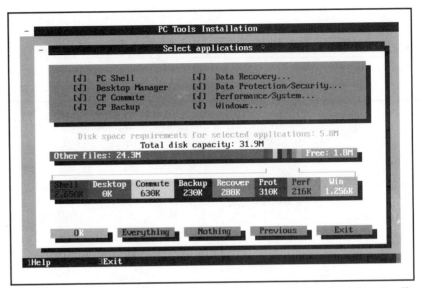

Figure 2.1: Select the PC Tools programs you want to load in the Select Applications window

Performance/ System (Perf)	Compress, PC-Cache, System Information, FileFind, Directory Maintenance, View
Windows (Win)	CP Backup, Scheduler, CP Launcher, TSR Manager, Undelete

The total amount of disk space needed for the chosen programs is shown under this selection box. Next on the screen is a bar representing the total disk capacity. The amount of space already occupied by files is shown on the left of this bar. The amount of space that the selected PC Tools programs will take is indicated by small colored bands, one band for each of the eight groups of programs. The amount of free space remaining after the installation is complete is shown at the right end of the bar. Below the bar you can see details of the space requirements for each of the selected PC Tools programs.

This whole window is dynamic: as you change your selections among the eight groups at the top of the window, the amount of disk space needed changes, and so do the colored bands on the disk-space requirements bar.

All the applications in this dialog box that have a check mark beside them will be installed on your system. In fact, Install initially assumes that you want to install all the PC Tools programs until you tell it otherwise by unselecting programs or groups.

Choose the programs you want to install by typing the highlighted letter in each program or group name, or by clicking on the checkbox with the mouse. Alternatively, you can hit the Tab key to activate the list of programs, then press the arrow keys to move the highlighted bar up or down the list. Press Enter to select or unselect a program or group.

To install all the programs, or all the programs in a group, select Everything. Use Nothing to unselect all programs and groups. When you are happy with your selections, choose OK to continue with the installation.

CONFIGURING PC TOOLS

After all the files have been copied onto your hard disk, the next screen lets you configure the various PC Tools programs on your computer for your own way of working. If you change your mind about any of these choices in the future, just run Install again and change your setup. The PC Tools Program Configuration window is shown in Figure 2.2.

If a program name is grayed out, you did not choose to load it when you selected certain PC Tools programs.

Down the left side of this window, you will see a list of all the PC Tools programs that can be configured as memory-resident programs. These are programs that are automatically loaded by AUTOEXEC.BAT or CONFIG.SYS each time you start your computer. As you choose a program from the list on the left, the right window shows you the installation options you have chosen, and also the amount of memory that each of the selections takes up. Type the highlighted letter to make or change a setting; if you are a mouse user, click the left mouse button.

PC SHELL   PC Shell is a powerful program that lets you do many DOS operations in an easy-to-use way; you can manage files and directories, even transfer files to another computer. You can load PC Shell memory-resident, in which case it takes 10K of memory.

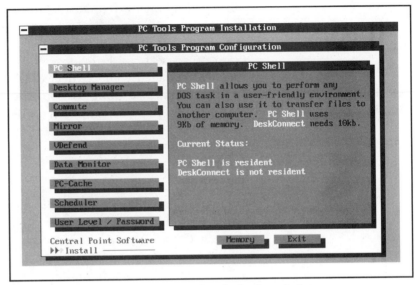

Figure 2.2: The PC Tools Program Configuration window

You can add PC Shell to your AUTOEXEC.BAT file so that each time you start your computer, you will find yourself in PC Shell. DeskConnect is a program that runs with PC Shell and lets you transfer files to another computer over a serial line. DeskConnect takes 10K of memory.

Click the Applications button to make Install look in all the directories on your hard disk for popular programs from other vendors to add into the PC Shell Applications menu system.

Do Not Search Network Drives tells Install not to look for applications on the network drives you are logged onto. It can take a long time to search through a large file server. Similarly, Do Not Create Separate Network Workgroup tells Install not to make a separate submenu in PC Shell for any applications found on the network file server.

DESKTOP MANAGER The Desktop Manager gives easy access to many important features, including word processing, a dBASE-compatible database, four calculators, modem, fax, electronic-mail, a clipboard, and an appointment scheduler. Choose Load Desktop to make Desktop memory-resident. Desktop takes 24K. To use background communications, select Load Backtalk; if you want to use a fax board, select Load Fax Support.

If you choose Load Fax Support, Install reminds you that you should have loaded your fax device driver software first, and then asks for the name of the directory you want to use to hold faxes before they are sent to your fax board. Finally, choose whether the fax board is installed in your own local computer or whether it is installed in a remote network workstation.

Install the fax board and the fax-specific software on your PC or network before choosing this option.

COMMUTE Commute is a program that lets you take over a remote computer. Choose Commute if you want to load it memory-resident; it will load into the upper memory blocks on a 386 or 486 computer if they are available. Choose Commsml to load a smaller version of Commute to occupy less memory. Finally, choose None if you don't want to load Commute.

MIRROR Mirror saves an image of the system area of your hard disk every time you start your computer. This is an excellent way to safeguard your system against accidents, so choose Run Mirror.

VDEFEND VDefend is memory-resident virus protection. You can choose to add VDefend to your AUTOEXEC.BAT file or to CONFIG.SYS.

DATA MONITOR Data Monitor protects your files against accidental erasure. It also features a screen blanker and displays a small indicator when you access your hard disks. Choose one of the methods of delete protection:

- **Delete Sentry** saves deleted files in a directory and is the best way to ensure that you will be able to recover accidentally deleted files.

- **Delete Tracking** saves information about deleted files so you can recover them, but it does not save the actual files, as Delete Sentry does.

- **None** provides no protection.

There are several other choices you can make in Data Monitor. Choose Screen Blanker to blank your screen after a period of inactivity so that the display is not burned onto the screen. Select Directory Lock if you want to keep confidential files in an encrypted directory. Write Protection can prevent files from being overwritten, deleted, or damaged. Disk Light displays a disk access indicator on your screen so that you don't have to look under your desk to see whether the disk drive is working. Before some of these options can actually take effect, you must complete the Data Monitor configuration by running the Data Monitor program when Install is complete. This is described in full in Chapter 9.

PC-CACHE   PC-Cache is a disk-cache program that acts as an intermediary between your hard disk and DOS. It can speed up disk accesses by keeping the most recently used information in memory.

You should never use more than one disk-cache program at a time.

You will see the greatest speed increase if you choose the Enable Write Delay option. This combines several disk-write commands and makes them all at the same time.

SCHEDULER   The Scheduler lets you run Commute and CP Backup in unattended mode, so you can transfer files or back up your hard disk when you are away from your PC. Since both the Scheduler and the Desktop Manager can schedule tasks, it is not necessary to load both of them.

USER LEVEL/PASSWORD   In PC Tools, you can choose a password, as well as configure your user level to suit your needs. You can choose your user level to be Beginner, Intermediate, or Advanced. These different levels are available in PC Shell and in CP Backup only. All the examples in this book are created using the advanced user level to show you all the options available in these programs, but you don't have to use them all. If you decide to use a password, you will have to enter it here twice to confirm it.

MONITORING MEMORY USAGE   As you make your selections from the list on the left of the configuration window, type **M** for Memory to see a display of the memory in your computer and how it is being used by the PC Tools programs. This way you can balance the needs of the PC Tools programs against the amount of memory you have available in your system. If you load too many of the PC Tools programs as memory-resident programs, and the amount of free conventional memory falls below 470K, you will see a warning message from Install. This is because some of the other PC Tools programs need a minimum of 470K of conventional memory in order to run properly.

SAVING YOUR CONFIGURATION   When you are happy with your choices from the list on the screen, choose OK in the configuration window. To save your changes to AUTOEXEC.BAT and CONFIG.SYS automatically, choose Exit. If you want to examine these changes before they are saved, select View Configuration. A window opens showing you your AUTOEXEC.BAT file with highlighted lines that have been added or changed. You have the following options in this screen:

> If at any time you want to change the way PC Tools is installed on your system, you can run Install again and select a different configuration.

- **Save** keeps the file as your new AUTOEXEC.BAT file; it will be loaded the next time you boot your computer. Your current AUTOEXEC.BAT file will be renamed to AUTOEXEC.SAV.

- **Delete Line** removes the highlighted line from the file.

- **Discard** lets you review CONFIG.SYS, if necessary, and then return to the Program Configuration window.

- **Save As** lets you choose the name of this configuration file.

- **Cancel** returns you to the Program Configuration window.

The final Install window gives you the choices of rebooting your computer or returning to DOS. Take the Recovery Disk out of drive A before you reboot your computer.

TESTING THE RECOVERY DISK

After you have completed the installation and configuration of PC Tools, you should test the Recovery Disk so that you are sure that it works.

There are several files on the Recovery Disk, a simple CON-FIG.SYS, the DOS SYS file which is used to copy system files and the COMMAND.COM file to another disk, and three PC Tools programs: MI for examining memory allocations, Unformat for recovering after an accidental format of the hard disk, and Rebuild, a program to reload partition table information that Install saved in a file called PARTNSAV.FIL.

To test the Recovery Disk, insert it into drive A and press the Ctrl, Alt, and Del keys all at the same time; this will reboot your computer. When you see the date and time prompts on your screen, you know that you can boot from the Recovery Disk, and that is about all the reassurance you need at this point. If you ever have problems booting your system from your hard disk, you know that you can use this Recovery Disk to boot your system and reload a copy of your partition table. This operation is covered in Chapter 7.

INSTALLING PC TOOLS ON A LOCAL AREA NETWORK

You can run PC Tools on a Novell network using Novell Netware 286, or 386, or on an IBM token ring using IBM PC Local Area Network Program Version 1.20.

Install the PC Tools programs in a write-protected directory on the network server. Then you can run them from any station on the network that has access to the server. Make sure that the server directory is in each user's path and set an environment variable for each user to specify where PC Tools should keep all the user-specific files, such as configuration files. This directory should be specific for each user and the user should have write privileges for it.

If you are installing PC Tools on a Novell Netware network, you can make the PC Tools directory path available to all users and use a system login script to define the PC Tools environment variable for them. For example, use the SYSCON command to add a line like the following to the system login script:

```
SET PCTOOLS = "drive:\\home\\%login name"
```

where the directory below *home* has the same name as the user's login name, and the user has write privileges. Add the directory where you located the PC Tools programs to each user's search path. Add this line to the system login script:

MAP INS S*n*: = *server\volume:path*

where *n* is the search drive number and *server\volume:path* specifies the directory where you installed the PC Tools programs.

On an IBM PC LAN network, add a line like the following to each user's AUTOEXEC.BAT file before the commands that log the user onto the network:

SET PCTOOLS = *drive:\directory path*

where *drive* is the drive letter and *directory path* is the full path description of the directory where PC Tools should keep the user-specific files. Add details of the PC Tools directory to each user's AUTO-EXEC.BAT file, assuming you loaded PC Tools in the PCTOOLS directory on drive G, as follows:

PATH = G:\PCTOOLS;*existing path statement*

where *existing path statement* is the user's current path.

Install will not modify a network AUTOEXEC.BAT file, so if any changes are needed, they should be made by the network supervisor.

Finally, select Customize for this Network Workstation in the Install program to configure PC Tools for your workstation. If you have a fax board in one of the computers on your network, follow these steps to configure the fax:

You cannot install the fax card onto the network file server.

1. Install the fax board and associated software into a computer on the network.

2. Create a directory on the network to hold the fax files before they are sent by the fax software. Grant network users who will be using the fax all privileges in this directory except supervisor privileges.

3. On the computer containing the fax board, start the Install program from the network server. Use the Desktop Manager option in Program Configuration to specify that the fax board is located in this computer and to define the directory used to hold the fax files before transmission.

4. At each computer on the network, use Install to configure the Desktop Manager and select Load Fax Support. Enter the location of the fax directory and specify that the fax board is located in a remote network workstation, then choose OK.

5. Make sure these changes are saved in the AUTOEXEC-.BAT file.

If you use PC Shell to look at a network file server, PC Shell only lists the directories for which you have at least read privileges, so you will not be overwhelmed by a listing of all the directories on the file-server disk.

All of PC Shell's commands are available for use on a network except Rename Volume, Search Disk, Directory Sort, Disk Information, Disk Map, File Map, Verify Disk, View/Edit Disk, Format Data Disk, and Make System Disk. You can use the Prune and Graft function from Directory Maintenance if you are using Novell NetWare 2.10 or later. Also, Compress and DiskFix will not run on a Novell Network file server or any networked disk. You can use Undelete to recover erased files if they were protected by the Delete Sentry method of delete protection.

Finally, note that you need a network or site license to run PC Tools on a Local Area Network. Otherwise, you must purchase a copy of the package for every station on the system.

CHAPTER

3

*Using
PC Tools*

As you saw in the last chapter, PC Tools is not a single program, but a complete set of many powerful utility programs. You can run many of the PC Tools from the DOS command line in interactive, full-screen mode.

USING PC TOOLS IN FULL-SCREEN MODE

Most of the PC Tools programs have a full-screen windowed mode with pulldown menus and function-key shortcuts. To run any program in this mode, just type its name at the DOS prompt. The following programs normally run in full-screen mode:

- Commute
- Compress
- CP Backup
- Data Monitor
- Directory Maintenance
- DiskFix
- Desktop
- FileFind
- File Fix
- PC Config
- PC Format
- PC Secure
- PC Shell
- System Information
- Undelete
- Unformat
- View
- Wipe

You can use the keyboard or, better still, use your mouse to navigate through the menus in these programs.

THE PC TOOLS SCREEN LAYOUT

All of the PC Tools programs that use a full-screen display share a common user interface designed to make it easy to move from one program to another. I'll use PC Shell to illustrate this interface. Figure 3.1 shows PC Shell's opening screen.

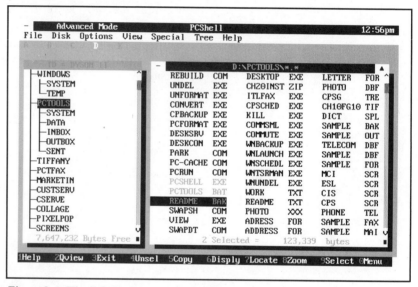

Figure 3.1: The PC Shell opening screen

The PC Tools programs use a system of windows and menus that makes choosing a command quick and easy. In this way, several different things can be shown on the screen at one time: menus, help windows, dialog boxes, and so on.

The screen in Figure 3.1 has the following components:

- The *title bar* runs across the top of the window, containing the name of the program and the close box. If you click on the close box once, you will see the System Control menu; if you click on the close box twice, you will exit the program. The System Control menu is described in detail later in this chapter. The title bar also shows the user level that the program is running in, if the user level is configurable.

- The *horizontal menu bar* runs across the top of the screen and contains the names of the menus and the current time. In PC Shell, the menu bar contains entries for the File, Disk, Options, View, Special, Tree, and Help commands. Select any of these by typing their first letter while pressing the Alt key, or by clicking on them with the mouse.

- The *drive line,* the next line in the display, contains the drive letters of all the disk drives that PC Shell can find on your system. The current drive is highlighted. You can select from these drives by simultaneously pressing the Ctrl key and the drive letter or by clicking on the drive letter with your mouse.

- Next comes the *applications window,* which changes from program to program. In PC Shell, the left side of the screen shows the Tree List window, a graphic display of the directories and subdirectories on the current drive. The current directory is highlighted. Vertical scroll bars are located on the right side of the window. The File List window on the right side of the screen lists all the files in the current directory. Scroll bars are also located at right.

- The *status line* is below the Tree List and File List windows. In PC Shell, this line shows the number of files in the directory and their total size in bytes. Other PC Tools programs show different information in the status line.

- The last line on the screen is sometimes used as a message bar to display additional information and small help messages. Commands are often shown on this line. Select these commands by pressing the appropriate function key from the keyboard, or by clicking on them with the mouse. The function keys change from program to program, with the exception of F1 (Help), F3 (Exit), and F10 (Menu); these three are always present.

You will find these elements (with some minor variations depending on the individual application) in all the PC Tools programs that use full-screen displays.

SELECTING WITH THE KEYBOARD

To select a menu, hold down the Alt key and type the menu's initial letter. For example, to open the File menu, hold down the Alt key and type **F**; to see the Special menu, type **S**. Similarly, to select an item from the menu, type the highlighted letter. For example, from the File menu, type **C** to copy a file, or **P** to print a file. As each letter can have only one meaning in each menu, and some of the menus contain many selections, the choices may be less than intuitive. You can press ↑ or ↓ to move the highlight up or down the menu items. To close a menu, press Escape.

If a menu is displayed, press ← or → to display the next menu to the left or right.

Some of the most often used commands have function-key equivalents displayed on the message bar or in the menu itself. To use one of these, just press the appropriate function key. However, no function-key equivalent will work when any menu is showing (except F1 for Help).

To scroll through the Tree List or File List, press ↑ and ↓ to move one line at a time, and PgUp and PgDn to move a whole window at a time. The Home and End keys move to the start and end of the information displayed in the window, respectively. Press Tab to move from one window to the other. The active window will be highlighted. To close a window, press Escape.

To select a file in the File List, move the highlight to the file name and press Enter. Repeat this process to select more files. To deselect a file, place the highlight over a selected file and press the Enter key again.

SELECTING WITH THE MOUSE

The PC Tools programs have been designed for the mouse user: navigating your way through the menus is fast and easy with a mouse. To open a menu, click on the menu name. To select an option from the menu list, just click on the item you want. To remove a menu from the screen, click anywhere outside the menu.

To scroll through the Tree List or File List window, press the right mouse button and drag the mouse. As it moves, the highlighted bar moves. You can also use the scroll bars: clicking on the scroll arrows moves the display in the direction of the arrow. Holding down the mouse button scrolls the display continuously.

To select a file in the File List, just click on the file with the mouse. To select several files, hold down the right mouse button while you press down the left mouse button and drag the mouse over the files you want to select. To deselect a range of files, simply repeat this process.

You can use the scroll box to move to a particular part of a display. For example, if you move the scroll box to the middle of the scroll bar, the screen displays the data from the middle section of the list.

Many of the windows have close boxes in the upper-left corner. To close the window, click on the close box with the mouse.

MOVING AND RESIZING WINDOWS

The System Control menu opens when you click on the close box, or when you press the Alt key and the spacebar at the same time. The first option in the menu is Version, which shows information about the version number of the PC Tools program you are using.

If a window has a *maximize button,* an upward-pointing triangle in the top-right corner, you can click on this to expand the window to its maximum size. The triangle now becomes downward-pointing, and if you click on now, the window shrinks back to its original size. To maximize a window from the keyboard, open the System Control menu and choose Maximize. To shrink the window back to its original size, choose Restore from the System Control menu.

If a window has a resize box in the lower-right corner, you can use it to change the height of the window. When you resize a window, the top-left corner remains in the same place on the screen and the lower-right corner moves as you move the mouse. From the keyboard, select Size from the System Control menu and then use the arrow keys to resize the window. Press Enter when the window is properly resized.

To move a window, click on the title bar of the window and drag the window to its new location. To do this using the keyboard, choose Move from the System Control menu, then use the arrow keys to move the window to the new location. Press Enter to confirm the new position.

The last selection in the System Control menu is Close (Alt-F4); this is the selection that closes your application program at the end of a session.

SELECTING FILES

All PC Tools applications that load files use the same File Load dialog box for file-name entry and directory selection. Figure 3.2 shows an example from Notepads.

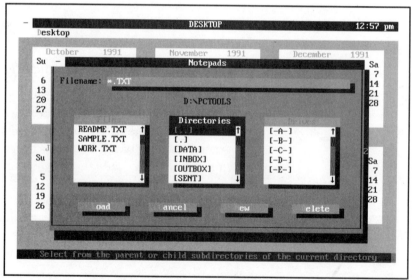

Figure 3.2: The File Load dialog box in Notepads

When the File Load dialog box opens, three lists detail your choices:

- **Files** lists all files with the appropriate file-name extension in the current directory. Notepads files all have the extension .TXT. Use the arrow keys to select the file you want to work with, or just click on the file using the mouse. If the file you want is not shown in this list, then you can use either of the next two lists to look elsewhere for the file.

- **Directories** lists all the subdirectories in the current directory. Directory names are enclosed in square brackets; [.] represents the current directory, and [..] represents the parent directory. To change directories, just select another name in the list.

- **Drives** lists all the drives that PC Tools can find on your system. Drive letters are enclosed in square brackets and dashes, like [–C–].

Once you have selected a file, select the Load command buttons at the bottom of the window to load the file.

HOW TO GET HELP

Type any PC Tools program name followed by /? to see the program's command-line help screen.

PC Tools contains an extensive online help system that you can access from almost any program; press F1 or make your selection from the Help menu, as follows:

- **Topics** lists the main help headings for the program. Entries here include Menu Commands, Function Keys, and Using Command-Line options.

- **Index** is an alphabetical list of all the help entries for PC Tools.

- **Keyboard** gives information about function-key usage in each program.

- **Basic Skills** gives instructions on how to work with dialog boxes and windows within PC Tools.

- **Commands** provides information on the various menu selections available in the program.

- **Using Help** is a guide to the help system itself.

- **About** provides general information about the program you are using.

- **DOS Advice** helps you to work out which of the PC Tools programs you should use to fix a disk problem. DOS Advice is also available inside the PC Tools program and also in DiskFix.

Key phrases and menu selections in the help text are identified by a different color or intensity on the screen. These phrases are known as *hypertext links,* which you can use as additional help topics: just click on them as you would on the normal help headings. Hypertext is a method of relating one area of text to another area of text and is especially useful in help systems, because it lets you choose the path you want to take through the help system, rather than have that path dictated to you.

Figure 3.3 shows a help screen made by the About selection in PC Shell's Help menu. Once you are inside the help system, several function keys are available to you from the message line at the bottom of the window:

- **F1 (Help)** explains how to use the help system.

- **F2 (Index)** goes directly to the help index described above.

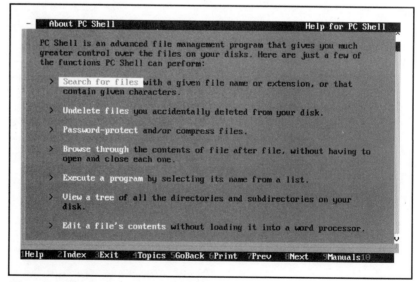

Figure 3.3: The About PC Shell help screen

- **F3 (Exit)** quits the help system and returns to the application program.

- **F4 (Topics)** goes directly to the list of help topics described above.

- **F5 (Go Back)** returns to the last help screen you looked at, retracing your steps through the help system.

- **F6 (Print)** sends the current help topic to a printer connected to the usual printer port, LPT1.

- **F7 (Prev)** shows you the previous page of information in the help system. Use F5 to look at the last page you looked at.

- **F8 (Next)** shows you the next page of information in the help system.

- **F9 (Manuals)** displays a list of help files for the other PC Tools programs. You can use this to become familiar with other programs in the PC Tools family.

RUNNING PC TOOLS IN MEMORY-RESIDENT MODE

Rather than run PC Shell and Desktop from the DOS command line every time you want to use them, you can load them in memory-resident mode so that they are available to you at all times. You can also use two small swap utilities to load the resident portion of PC Shell or Desktop into expanded memory or extended memory, or onto disk, so that the maximum amount of conventional memory remains available on your system. The swap utility for PC Shell is called Swapsh and the swap utility for Desktop is called Swapdt. You can use Swapsh to change the PC Shell hotkey, if you wish.

RUNNING PC SHELL

There are several important advantages to running PC Shell in memory-resident mode, rather than from the DOS prompt:

- You can hotkey into PC Shell from inside another application program. If you want to format a disk quickly or move some files, you won't have to leave your application to do so. When you exit from PC Shell, you return to the same place in your application program.

- You can use optional parameters to configure the amount of memory that PC Shell uses.

- You can use expanded memory with PC Shell.

To run PC Shell in memory-resident mode, enter

PCSHELL /R

You can also include this command in your AUTO-EXEC.BAT file so that PC Shell is loaded automatically each time you start your computer.

at the DOS prompt. PC Shell takes just a moment to load it into memory; then the sign-on screen shows the program name, version number, and amount of memory available to other programs.

PC Shell's default hotkey is Ctrl-Esc. Press Ctrl-Esc again to return to your original application program. You can change this hotkey combination either in your AUTOEXEC.BAT file or at the DOS prompt. Specify the new hotkey when you first load PC Shell, as follows:

PCSHELL /R /F*n*

where *n* represents the number of a function key, F1 through F10. This changes the hotkey combination from Ctrl-Esc to Ctrl plus the function key you specify. Remember, you can only use this mechanism when PC Shell is in memory-resident mode.

If you want to use SWAPSH to specify a new hotkey for PC Shell, type

SWAPSH /?

from the DOS prompt to see a list of the key codes that you can use.

REMOVING PC SHELL

You must exit PC Shell first to unload it.

If you need to recover the memory that PC Shell uses in memory-resident mode, open the Special menu and select Remove PC Shell. This selection is only available when the shell is run in memory-resident mode, and you *must* hotkey into PC Shell from the DOS prompt; you cannot remove PC Shell if you hotkeyed into it from another application. For this selection to be successful, PC Shell must be the last memory-resident program loaded. When you choose the Remove PC Shell option, a window opens to remind you of these conditions. Click the Remove button to remove PC Shell or Exit to return to the main program.

You can also remove PC Shell by entering **KILL** at the DOS prompt. Kill also removes Desktop and the background communications program called Backtalk when they are run in memory-resident mode.

RUNNING DESKTOP

PC Tools Desktop includes Notepads, Outlines, an appointment scheduler, a database, a macro editor, Telecommunications, the Clipboard, four calculators, and a set of utility programs. In addition, if you loaded PC Shell in memory-resident mode before loading Desktop, PC Shell appears in the Desktop main menu and is available at any time from any Desktop application.

To start Desktop as a memory-resident program, type

DESKTOP /R

from the DOS prompt, or include this line in your AUTOEXEC.BAT file so that Desktop is loaded automatically each time you start your computer.

Use the Ctrl-spacebar hotkey to start Desktop, and to leave it again when you have finished.

OPENING UP TO 15 WINDOWS AT ONCE

In Desktop, you can have up to 15 windows open at once; however, only one of these windows can be the *active* one. The active window is always the one at the top of the stack; the menu bar at the top of the screen always shows the menu selections for the active window. Figure 3.4 shows three windows open at once: a notepad, a database, and the Algebraic calculator; the latter is the active window.

CH. 3

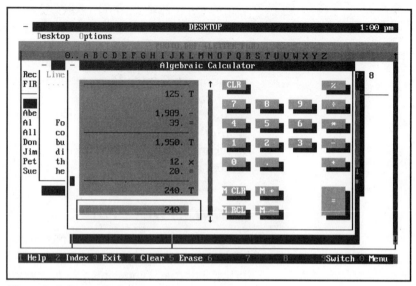

Figure 3.4: Several windows open simultaneously

You can only open one copy of the Clipboard, Modem Telecommunications, E-Mail Telecommunications, Fax Telecommunications, the Algebraic, Financial, Scientific, and Programmer's calculators, and the Utilities at once. However, you can open as many notepads, outlines, databases, appointment schedulers, and macro editors as you like until you hit the maximum number of 15 windows.

The simplest way of changing windows is to use a mouse. Just click somewhere in the window you want to make active. However, if no part of that window is visible or if you want to use the keyboard, select the Switch To option from the System Control menu or press F9.

The items in the Switch To list change, depending on which applications you have open.

If you have only two windows open, they are simply swapped— the inactive window becoming active and the active window becoming inactive. If you have more than two windows open when you choose Switch To, a dialog box shows a list of the open windows, the application associated with each, and the name of the file loaded into the window. Figure 3.5 shows the Switch Active list for the Desktop applications shown in Figure 3.4. Choose the window you want to

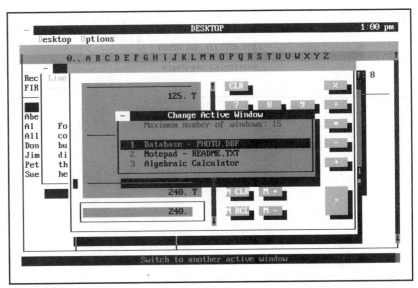

Figure 3.5: The Change Active Window dialog box

make active with ↑ and ↓, then press Enter. If you are using a mouse, you can click on the name of the window you want to make active.

A NOTE FOR DOS 5 USERS

The DOS 5 LOADHIGH command is usually abbreviated to just LH.

If you have DOS 5 on your computer, you will find that the PC Tools Install program has inserted LOADHIGH statements in your AUTOEXEC.BAT file before each of the PC Tools programs that you have requested to be installed in memory-resident mode on your system.

The DOS 5 LOADHIGH command handles the management of the Upper Memory Blocks (UMBs). UMBs are located between the normal upper limit of conventional memory at 640K and the 1MB boundary on a 386 or 486 computer. If this memory is available on your system, these changes to your AUTOEXEC.BAT will load the PC Tools programs into the UMBs. If you do not have this memory available on your 386/486, or you use a 286- or 8088-based computer, the DOS LOADHIGH command automatically loads the memory-resident programs in conventional memory instead.

USING PC TOOLS FROM THE DOS COMMAND LINE

You can run all the programs in the PC Tools package from the DOS command line, just like any other program or DOS command. You simply type the program name, add optional parameters on the command line after the program name, and press Enter.

The following list gives the file name you must type to start the PC Tools programs running.

If your monitor is having difficulty showing the graphical icons in PC Shell, use the /NF switch to turn them off.

Commute	**COMMUTE**
Compress	**COMPRESS**
CP Backup	**CPBACKUP**
CPBDIR	**CPBDIR**
Data Monitor	**DATAMON**
Directory Maintenance	**DM**
DeskConnect	**DESKSRV/DESKCON**
Desktop	**DESKTOP**
DiskFix	**DISKFIX**
FileFind	**FF**
File Fix	**FILEFIX**
MI	**MI**
Park	**PARK**
PC Config	**PCCONFIG**
PC Format	**PCFORMAT**
PC Tools	**PCTOOLS**
PC Secure	**PCSECURE**
PC Shell	**PCSHELL**
System Information	**SI**

Undelete	**UNDEL**
Unformat	**UNFORMAT**
View	**VIEW**
Wipe	**WIPE**

CONFIGURING YOUR SYSTEM

You can configure several important elements of the PC Tools package—including color, video mode, and mouse and keyboard settings—with a program called PC Config. Type **PCCONFIG** at the DOS command line to start the program. The opening screen shows four options:

- Color

- Display

- Mouse

- Keyboard

CHANGING THE SCREEN COLORS AND DISPLAY MODES

To change the colors used on the screen in the PC Tools programs, select Color from the main window; you will see the Color Options window. PC Tools programs use standard color combinations in specific ways for the different elements that make up a screen. An element is a portion of a window, such as the title bar or the message line. When all the elements of the display are assembled, you have what is called a *color scheme*. PC Config allows for several color schemes, including Monochrome, LCD (for use with a liquid-crystal display), and several other schemes specifically designed for color monitors. The easiest way to change them is to select one of these default color schemes from the Scheme drop-down box.

You can also make your own color scheme if you want to. The easiest way to do this is to start with one of the default color schemes and make the changes you want. Choose Palette to replace colors in an existing color scheme. To save the new color combination, choose Save Scheme to save an existing scheme using the current name, or use Save Scheme As to save it under a different name—both from the File menu.

Many of the color combinations that you can create on your hardware are impossible to read or very difficult to work with at best. The Edit menu contains two selections that can be life-savers: Undo Changes, which lets you abandon any changes you have made since you started PC Config this time, and Reset to Defaults, which resets the palette colors to the palette defaults.

If you are using PC Tools on a computer with an EGA or VGA monitor, you can use the Display selection from the main PC Config window to select special graphics characters for checkboxes, option buttons, and other screen elements. You can also specify how many lines of text you want to use on the screen. To specify 43 lines you must have an EGA monitor; to specify 28 lines or 50 lines, you must have a VGA monitor.

CONFIGURING THE MOUSE AND THE KEYBOARD

Choose Mouse from the main PC Config window and you will see the following options:

- **Fast Mouse Reset** optimizes the mouse performance. If your mouse doesn't seem to work after using Windows, turn this option off.

- **Left Handed Mouse** interchanges the functions of the left and right mouse buttons.

- **Disable Mouse** turns the mouse off.

- **Graphics Mouse** displays the mouse cursor as a pointer on EGA and VGA monitors. If you turn this option off, you will see a box mouse cursor.

- **Speed** sets the mouse speed; the higher the number, the faster the mouse moves across the screen.

If you choose Keyboard from the main PC Config window, you have the following options:

- **Rate** sets how fast a keystroke repeats when you hold down a key. The higher the number, the faster the key repeats.

- **Delay** specifies the length of time you must hold down a key before that key begins to repeat. The higher the number, the longer the delay.

Try adjusting these settings until your computer responds in the way that you find most comfortable.

You must check the Enable Keyboard Speed box before you exit to activate the new settings. If you don't check the box, your new settings will be ignored.

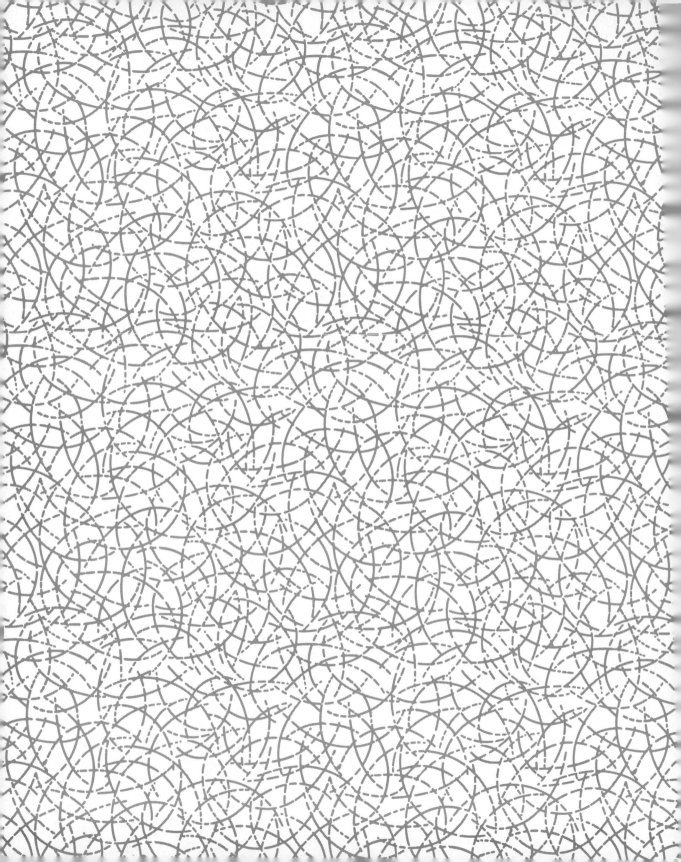

PART II

File and Program Management Tools

CHAPTER

4

Using
PC Shell

PC Shell performs two main functions: file and directory management, and program management. This chapter is concerned with the first function and describes how to get the best out of PC Shell in your day-to-day computing. Besides explaining how to configure PC Tools to give you the computing environment you want, it details some of the file-management tasks you will use every day. The next chapter, Chapter 5, concentrates on the program-management capabilities of PC Shell.

STARTING PC SHELL

To start PC Shell from the DOS prompt, type **PCSHELL**—or, if you have loaded PC Shell in memory-resident mode, type the hotkey combination. The PC Shell startup screen, showing the Tree and File Lists, is shown in Figure 4.1.

The left side of the screen, headed by the disk-volume label, shows a graphic representation of the directory structure on your disk, highlighting the currently selected directory. The right side of the screen shows the full path name of the current directory and lists the names of all files in the directory. As you select different directories in the

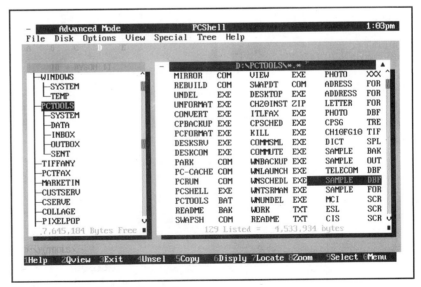

Figure 4.1: The PC Shell opening screen

Tree List on the left side of the display, the File List on the right is automatically updated to show the files contained in the new directory. Press Tab to move between the two windows or click the mouse on the screen you want to make active. The Tab key also activates the drive line and the DOS command line, if it is turned on.

Sometimes these directory or file lists are too long to fit in the window, so you have to scroll the display to see it all. You can scroll either side of the display independently: press ↑ and ↓ to move one line in the window at a time, press PgUp or PgDn to move a column at a time, or press Home to go to the top of the list and End to go to the bottom of the list.

With the mouse, scrolling is even easier. Press the right mouse button and drag the mouse up to move up the screen or down to move down the screen. Alternatively, you can move by clicking on the scroll bars. You will become familiar with these two windows very quickly, because here is where you choose the files, disks, or directories that you will work on.

Most of the PC Shell commands that deal with files require you to select the file(s) you want to work with before you choose the command. So before you can go very far in PC Shell, you must know how to select and unselect files:

- To select a file using the keyboard, press the arrow keys to highlight the file you want and press Enter to confirm your choice.

- To select a file using the mouse, position the highlight bar on a file and click the left mouse button.

- To unselect all previously selected files with a single keystroke, press F4.

- To unselect files individually using the keyboard, press the arrow keys to highlight the file(s) you want to unselect and press Enter to confirm your choice.

- To unselect a file or files using the mouse, either:

  Click on the first file you want to unselect.

  Press the right mouse button, position over the first file to unselect, and then press and hold down the left mouse button. Now drag the highlight over the additional files you want to unselect. When you have unselected all the files, release both mouse buttons.

- To select all the files in a directory, choose Select All Toggle in the File menu.

- To unselect all the files in a directory, choose Select All Toggle a second time, or press F4 (Unsel).

Now that you know how to work in the main PC Shell window, the next part of this chapter will concentrate on how you can configure PC Shell to give you the computing environment you want.

CONFIGURING PC SHELL

There are several important configuration options you can use to tailor the PC Shell user interface to your own requirements, including different user levels and user-definable function keys. If you have upgraded from PC Tools Version 6, you can even make the PC Shell 7 menus look just like those you are used to in Version 6.

CHOOSING YOUR USER LEVEL

If you specified a password to prevent unauthorized changing of your user level when you first installed PC Shell, you must enter the password before you can change your user level.

You can choose your user level in PC Shell to be either Beginner, Intermediate, or Advanced. Open the Options menu and choose Change User Level to bring up the Change User Level dialog box. Choose Beginner User Mode to have access to basic DOS-type commands for finding and copying files; choose Intermediate User Mode if you want more complex functions, such as deleting and editing files and sorting directories; and choose Advanced User Mode to have access to the entire range of PC Shell's capabilities. The selections available in the File, Disk, and Special menus are determined by your user level. The System Control, Options, View, Tree and Help menu selections do not change. Information displayed in windows, such as the program list, do not change with the user level. All of the examples in this book assume that you are using the Advanced User Level.

DEFINING FUNCTION KEYS

You can make the function keys in PC Shell perform the commands you use most often, except for F1 (Help), F3 (Exit), and F10 (Menu), which always stay the same. You can assign your favorite functions to the other keys. Select Define Function Keys from the Options menu and you will see the Define Function Keys dialog box shown in Figure 4.2.

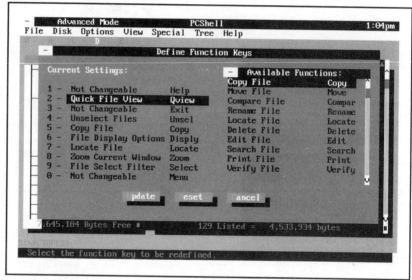

Figure 4.2: The Define Function Keys dialog box

Press ↑ and ↓ or the mouse to locate the function key you want to use, then press Enter to select it. Press Tab to move to the other side of the display where the available functions are listed, then use the arrow keys or PgUp or PgDn to select the PC Shell command you want to have associated with that key. Press Enter to confirm your choice. When you have made all your selections, select Update to save your choices and close the dialog box. If you change your mind and decide you don't like the new function-key assignments you just created, select Reset to return to the settings you had at the start of this PC Shell session. Select Save Configuration File from the Options menu to save your changes for all future PC Shell sessions.

USING VERSION 6 MENUS

If you have upgraded from PC Tools 6, you can stay with the Version 6 menus and short-cut keystrokes. Select Version 6 Menus from the Options menu and a check mark appears next to the menu selection to show you that it is turned on. Now the entries in the File, Disk, and Special menus show their Version 6 commands, and the View menu disappears completely. Select Version 6 Menus a second time to return to Version 7-style menus.

MANAGING PC SHELL WINDOWS

You can maximize or zoom the currently active window to fill the whole screen by pressing F8. Pressing F8 a second time returns the window to its usual size.

There are several commands in the View menu that you can use to configure the PC Shell windows to your own requirements. Select Custom List Configure from the View menu and you will see the following options:

- **Tree List** toggles the Tree List Window on and off. A check mark by the menu item indicates that it is selected. When you choose this selection, PC Shell removes the Tree List to reveal the underlying screen. If you have two Tree Lists on the screen at the same time, both are removed by this command. You can also close the window if you click on the close box in the upper-left corner of the window.

- **File List** toggles the File List window on or off, just like the Tree List.

- **Program List** toggles the Program List window on or off.

- **View Window** toggles the View window on or off. When it is turned on, the View window is displayed across the bottom half or the right side of the PC Shell window, depending on the setting you choose in Viewer Config (described below).

- **Background Mat** shows the pattern behind the PC Shell windows. Turn Background Mat off if you want to see what is displayed on the screen by the underlying application program.

- **DOS Command Line** accesses the DOS prompt while you are using PC Shell. When DOS Command Line is turned on, you can enter any DOS command as though you were right at the DOS prompt. The command runs, and when it has finished a short message tells you to press any key or a mouse button to re-enter PC Shell. Use the Tab key, or click the mouse to activate the DOS command line, then just type in the DOS command as you would normally, followed by the Enter key. Select DOS Command Line a second time to turn this feature off again.

- **Viewer Config** specifies whether the Viewer will use a horizontal (Horiz) or vertical (Vert) window when you turn on the View window.

- **Window Style**: choose either Tiled or Cascaded windows. Tiled windows are the default for PC Shell: they divide the screen up between the open windows and show them side-by-side. You can zoom tiled windows, but you cannot move or resize them. You can resize and move cascaded windows anywhere on the screen, and they can even over-lap each another.

To turn all the PC Shell windows off with a single command, select Hide All Lists from the View menu. As its name suggests, this command closes all the open list windows and removes the menu bar, leaving only the message bar and the DOS command line, if it is turned on. If you also turn off the background mat, you will be able to see the underlying application program's screen. To access the PC Shell menu, click on the part of the screen where the menus used to be, or press the Alt key followed by the first letter of the menu name. (For example, press Alt-V to access the View menu.)

You can use any of the PC Shell commands when all the windows are hidden, but some of the commands work a little differently, especially those that work with items you normally select using the Tree or File Lists. Instead of selecting items from the Tree or File Lists, you must use dialog boxes to specify the files or directories you want to work with. These commands are listed below:

Attribute Change	Compare
Copy	Delete

Edit File	Hex Edit File
Move	Print
Rename	Show Information
View File Contents	Verify

The Wait on DOS setting in the Options menu determines whether PC Shell pauses after completing a DOS command invoked from the DOS command line, and waits for you to press a key or click a mouse button, or whether you return to PC Shell immediately. If you plan to use DOS commands that output information to the screen, like DIR or CHKDSK, make sure you select this setting so that you have a chance to read the information on the screen. If you plan to use the DOS command line only for running programs, you can turn this option off.

If you choose Colors in the Options menu, PC Shell loads PC Config so that you can change your PC Shell colors. As this program was described in Chapter 3, it will not be described again here.

ONE- OR TWO-SCREEN LISTS

PC Shell usually displays one Tree List and one File List at a time. If you need to see a second set of Tree and File Lists, select Dual File Lists in the View menu. This can be especially useful if you are copying or moving files from one directory to another on your hard disk. Now two Tree Lists and two File Lists are shown on the screen. You will get the same result if you press the Insert key on the keyboard. When the second set of lists open, it shows the same directory and files as the first set, but you can select a different drive from the drive line and then choose a new directory to look at. To go back to a one-list display, select Single File List from the View menu, or press the Delete key. When you close the second set of lists, make sure that the list you want to keep open is the active list.

If you want to open the Program List and keep the File Lists open at the same time, select Program/File Lists from the View menu. The Tree and File Lists shrink to make room for the Program List across the bottom of the PC Shell window, and these three windows replace whatever was on the screen before they were opened.

Program List Only turns off all the other windows and opens the Program List. You can use this as a way to start programs, rather than using the Open command or using the DOS command line in PC Shell. Press F10, or click on Shell on the message bar to return to the main PC Shell display.

The Viewer/File List command opens the File List, the Tree List, and the View Window all at once, replacing the windows that were open previously. You can also use the File List, Tree List, and View Window commands in Custom List Configure in the View menu to open or close these windows individually.

LISTING AND SELECTING FILES

Once you have decided on the number of Tree and File List windows you want to have open, you can use the File Display Options command in the Options menu to choose what information is displayed for each file. The Filters command in the View menu allows you to choose which files are displayed.

When you select File Display Options, or press F6, the Display Options dialog box opens, as shown in Figure 4.3. Make your choice from the following sort options:

- Name
- Extension
- Size
- Date/Time

When you have chosen a sort option, select the type of sort you want to make:

- **Ascending** lists the files in ascending order of the options you have chosen. File names and extensions are listed in alphabetical order, from small to large, and from oldest to newest file (first by date, then by time).
- **Descending** lists the files in descending order.
- **None** lists the files as they occur. This is the default setting.

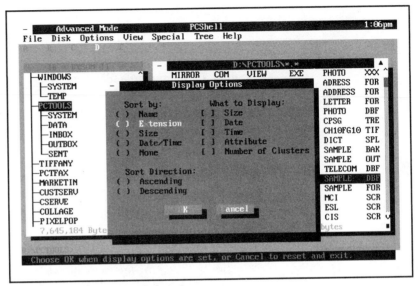

Figure 4.3: The Display Options dialog box

You can also choose from the following display options:

- **Size** to display the file size

- **Date** to display the file-creation date

- **Time** to display the file-creation time

- **Attribute** to display the file's attributes: read-only, system, hidden, and archive

- **Number of clusters** to display the number of clusters that the file occupies

I often sort the files on my hard disk according to the file-name extension in order to group files according to their function. This also sorts by file name within each extension.

Use the Filters selection from the View menu to choose which files are displayed in the File List. This opens a submenu containing two items:

- **File List** lets you enter the names and extensions you want to see listed in the File List.

- **File Select** lets you specify the files you want to select from the files shown in the File List.

You can use a ? to replace a single character or a * to replace all subsequent characters in a file name. For example, *.* lists all the files in the directory, but *.COM only lists those with the .COM extension. Select Display to return to the File List and see the files you specified in the display.

Once you have used a filter to screen out certain files, you must remove the filter to look at all the files in that directory. Choose the Reset button to reset the Name and Extension boxes to the equivalent of *.* and thus show all the files in the directory.

USING THE TREE MENU

The Tree Menu lets you decide how many directory levels are shown in the Tree List at one time by expanding or collapsing the directory structure display. The actual directories on the disk are, of course, unchanged, only the Tree List display changes. There are four options in the Tree menu:

- **Collapse Branch** (–) hides all subdirectories of a directory.
- **Expand One Level** (+) displays the next level of subdirectory after it has been collapsed.
- **Expand Branch** (*) lets you see all levels of subdirectory for a directory after it has been collapsed.
- **Expand All** lets you see everything, all subdirectories of all directories.

CHOOSING THE CONFIRMATION

PC Shell often opens a dialog box to confirm an operation, especially a potentially dangerous one, like deleting a file. If you don't want to see these dialog boxes, you can turn them off by selecting Confirmation from the Options menu. There are three selections:

- **Confirm on Delete** opens a dialog box when you delete files or directories. Leave this option selected.

- **Confirm on Replace** opens a dialog box when you replace files.
- **Confirm on Mouse Operations** opens a dialog box when you use the mouse to move or copy files.

A check mark indicates that the option is selected.

SAVING THE CONFIGURATION FILE

Now that you have completed your PC Shell configuration, don't forget to select Save Configuration File from the Options menu to store your changes in the PCSHELL.CFG file. Also, if you try to exit PC Shell without saving your changes, a dialog box opens asking whether you want to save your changes.

WORKING WITH FILES AND DISKS

So far, we have looked at the PC Shell commands you use to configure the program. Now we'll review the commands that work with files and disks: Copy, Move, Delete, and Compare. You need to be familiar with these operations to manage your hard disk effectively.

COPYING AND COMPARING FILES

You use the Copy command from the File menu to make additional copies of a file or group of files. You can copy files to a different directory, to a different disk, or to the same disk with a different name.

Select the directory you want to copy files from in the Tree List, highlight the files you want to copy in the File List display, and then choose Copy from the File menu. Select the drive and, from the Tree List, select the directory into which you want to copy the files.

If there are files with identical names in the group you want to copy and in the destination directory, you have five options:

- **Replace All** replaces all the files in the destination directory that have the same names as files in the selected group, without asking for confirmation each time.

- **Replace File** replaces each file with the same name, but asks for confirmation on each file replacement.

- **Skip File** moves to the next file. The current file is not copied.

- **Skip All** skips any of the selected files that already exist on the target directory and copies all of the others.

- **Cancel** returns you to the main PC Shell screen.

You can also use the mouse to copy files by dragging them from one directory on your disk to another. Both directories must be visible at the same time in the Tree List for this to work, as you cannot scroll the Tree List and copy a file at the same time. To use the mouse to copy a file from one directory to another, follow these steps:

1. Select either a one-tree list or a two-tree list, depending on where the source and target directories are located.

2. Click the file with the left mouse button and hold the button down as you drag the file to the target directory. A small dialog box opens, showing the number of files being copied. This box moves with the mouse cursor as you drag the file.

3. Release the mouse button over the target directory to start the copying.

The Compare File command compares the contents of two or more files, usually to see whether two files located in different directories are identical. You can also use Compare File to verify whether two programs on two different disks with different dates are just replicas of one another, created at different times.

Suppose you want to see whether the copy of AUTOEXEC.BAT in your root directory is identical to the file in your word processing directory:

1. Select the root directory in the Tree List and then select the AUTOEXEC.BAT file in the File List.

2. Choose the File menu and the Compare command.

3. From the File Compare dialog box, select drive C as the second drive, since all the files for comparison in this example are on drive C.

4. PC Shell asks how you want to compare files. In this example, choose the Matching option.

5. Select the directory that contains the second copy of AUTOEXEC.BAT. If you chose Matching, the files are compared. If you chose Different, PC Shell asks you for the name of the file to compare to.

6. Type the name and extension and select Continue to proceed. If you selected more than one file, the files are processed in turn.

If Compare File finds a difference between the two files that are identical in size, it displays the sector number and a byte offset of the position of the difference, as well as the ASCII value of each difference. If the files are different in size, it shows the original file name and the path to the comparison file. Then Compare File states that the comparison was unsuccessful because the files were of different sizes.

MOVING AND RENAMING FILES

When you copy a file, an exact replica of the file is made in the destination directory and the original is preserved. That is, after the copy operation, there are two copies of the file in two different places. Sometimes you may want to move rather than copy a file. The Move command is designed for exactly this purpose. At other times, you may want to change the name of the copy by renaming the file with the Rename command.

Moving a file is much like copying a file, except that the original file is deleted when the operation is complete. First, select the files you want to move from the Tree List and the File List, then select Move from the File menu. Choose the destination drive and directory. PC Shell moves the files to the destination directory and deletes the original source files. If you try to move files to the same directory that the originals occupy, PC Shell responds with a dialog box containing the message

File already exists.

You may then choose Replace All, Replace File, Next File, Skip All, or Exit.

You can also move files by just using the mouse. As with copying files with the mouse, both source and target directories must be visible in the Tree List. To move a file, hold down the Ctrl key while you click on and drag the file to its new directory. The Ctrl key tells PC Shell that you are moving a file, rather than copying it. As you drag the file(s), a dialog box opens to detail the number of files you are moving. Release the mouse button over the directory you are moving the file(s) to.

Renaming a file is even easier than moving it. Select the file(s) you want to work with from the file list and select Rename from the File menu. If you selected one file, its current name is shown in the File Rename window and you are asked to enter the new name and extension. If you selected several files, you can change their names or extensions globally, or one at a time:

- **Global**: enter the new file name or extension. For example, to change all your file extensions from .DOC to .TXT, put the wildcard character * in the Name box, **TXT** in the Extension box, and select Rename.

- **Single**: enter the file name and extension to use and select Rename. Choosing Next File displays the next file from the list of selected files.

VERIFYING FILES AND DISKS

You can verify a file to ensure that it is readable after a copy or move operation. Select the files for verification from the File List and choose Verify from the File menu. Verify reads each sector in the file to ensure that the whole file can be read without errors. If you specified a group of files, each file is checked in turn for errors. If Verify finds an error, the sector number containing the error is displayed.

You can also verify a complete disk to make sure that all the files and directories are readable. Select the disk to verify from the drive line in PC Shell, then choose Verify from the Disk menu. If PC Shell finds a bad sector not marked as bad in the FAT by DOS, Verify displays the sector number and indicates whether the sector is in the DOS system area, part of an existing file, or in the data area and available for use. If the sector is available, Verify marks it as bad in the FAT, so it will not be used for files at any time in the future. If the sector is in use by a file, a dialog box recommends that you run the DiskFix Surface Scan program on this disk as soon as possible to move the data to a safe area of the disk.

DELETING FILES

Be very careful that you do not delete a system file or device driver with the extensions .COM or .SYS by accident. Your system may refuse to boot after such a file is deleted.

At some point, you will want to throw away a file or group of files. Use the Delete command in the File menu for this. Unlike the DOS DEL or ERASE commands, Delete can erase files that have the hidden, system, or read-only bits set in their attribute byte.

If you want to delete more than one file, first choose your victims in the File List and then select Delete from the File menu. The File Delete dialog box is displayed for the first file in the list. If you chose one file, two options are offered: Delete and Cancel. If you selected more than one file, you have four options:

- **Delete** erases the file.
- **Next File** skips over this file and displays the next file.
- **Delete All** erases all the files you selected without any further dialog.
- **Cancel** ends the deletion and returns you to the main PC Shell display.

When all the files have been deleted, you return to the main PC Shell screen.

COPYING AND COMPARING DISKS

Often it is preferable to copy a whole disk in one operation than to copy all the files individually. The Copy option in the Disk menu is

Both source and
target drives must
be of the same drive and
media type when you are
copying an entire disk.

designed for this. First, select the source and target drives. PC Shell prompts you to change disks if you are making a copy using a single drive. As the copy proceeds, a display indicates its progress. A character is displayed opposite each track: *F* shows that the disk is being formatted, *R* indicates that the disk is being read, and *W* shows that the data are being written to the disk. When the copy is complete, you return to the PC Shell main screen.

To confirm that the disk is an exact copy, you can use Compare to check the copy against the original. This works much like Copy. The main difference is that *R* indicates that the disk is being read and *C* indicates that the comparison is taking place. If a dot appears in the track window, then that track has been compared successfully.

PRINTING FILES

Often you will want to print a file without using a word processor, or—with a binary file—you might want to dump it to the printer in ASCII and hexadecimal. Print File can handle both of these tasks; it can also print a directory listing. Choose the file or files you want to print in the File List and then choose Print from the File menu. You can then use one of these three options to print the file:

- **Print as a Standard Text File** prints a simple ASCII text file.

- **Print File Using PC Shell Print Options** formats the output according to the settings shown in the File Print dialog box.

- **Dump Each Sector in ASCII and Hex** displays the decimal and hexadecimal equivalents.

Try running README.TXT through the Print command, selecting a different option each time to see how the output varies:

- If you select the first option, the file is printed as a long piece of text without any page breaks or any other formatting.

- When you use the second setting, the file is divided into numbered pages and is much nicer to look at.

- If you select the third option, each sector is numbered sequentially with the count starting at sector zero at the beginning of the file. On the left side of the printout, the decimal-byte offset count is shown next to the hex-byte offset count. This is the byte number starting with zero at the beginning of the file. In the center of the printout, the file's data are listed in two columns of eight bytes each, separated by a hyphen for easier reading. On the right, the data are shown again, this time in ASCII.

USING SHOW INFORMATION

The File List shows you the file name and its position in the directory, but doesn't tell you very much about the file itself. To find out more about a file, use Show Information from the Options menu. I'll use the README file as an example.

Use the mouse or the cursor keys to make PCTOOLS the current directory, then select README.TXT. Select Show Information from the Options menu. Figure 4.4 shows the More File Information dialog

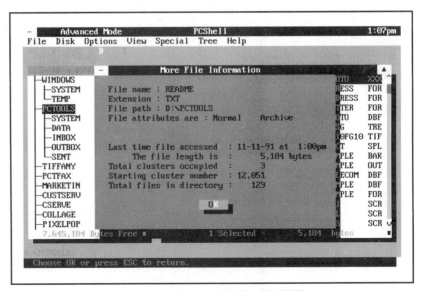

Figure 4.4: More File Information for README.TXT

box for the README.TXT file. The display lists the file name, extension, path name, file attributes, time the file was last accessed, file length in bytes, total number of clusters and the starting cluster number, as well as the total number of files in the directory. You will see a different starting cluster number on your system.

Show Information gives you much more useful information than the DOS DIR command does, but what if you want to display and print this information for all the files in the directory? Select the directory you want to print and use Print File List from the File menu. I chose the DOS directory, and Figure 4.5 shows the result. The disk's volume label is printed in the upper-right corner of the printout, followed by the full path name of the directory. The files are arranged in columns, with file name and extension, size in bytes and clusters, last access date and time, and file attributes. (Note that the starting cluster is not listed in this display.) The summary information given at

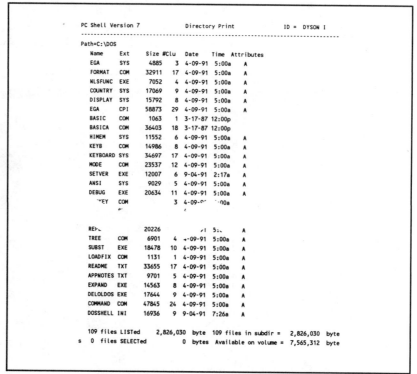

```
PC Shell Version 7                    Directory Print              ID = DYSON I
-----------------------------------------------------------------------------------
Path=C:\DOS
     Name      Ext    Size #Clu   Date      Time  Attributes
     EGA       SYS    4885     3   4-09-91   5:00a    A
     FORMAT    COM   32911    17   4-09-91   5:00a    A
     NLSFUNC   EXE    7052     4   4-09-91   5:00a    A
     COUNTRY   SYS   17069     9   4-09-91   5:00a    A
     DISPLAY   SYS   15792     8   4-09-91   5:00a    A
     EGA       CPI   58873    29   4-09-91   5:00a    A
     BASIC     COM    1063     1   3-17-87  12:00p
     BASICA    COM   36403    18   3-17-87  12:00p
     HIMEM     SYS   11552     6   4-09-91   5:00a    A
     KEYB      COM   14986     8   4-09-91   5:00a    A
     KEYBOARD  SYS   34697    17   4-09-91   5:00a    A
     MODE      COM   23537    12   4-09-91   5:00a    A
     SETVER    EXE   12007     6   9-04-91   2:17a    A
     ANSI      SYS    9029     5   4-09-91   5:00a    A
     DEBUG     EXE   20634    11   4-09-91   5:00a    A
     ᵛEY      COM             3   4-09-0ʳ    ˙00a


     REᵏᵊ            20226        ⸝1  5:ᵥ         A
     TREE      COM    6901     4  ⸝-09-91   5:00a    A
     SUBST     EXE   18478    10   4-09-91   5:00a    A
     LOADFIX   COM    1131     1   4-09-91   5:00a    A
     README    TXT   33655    17   4-09-91   5:00a    A
     APPNOTES  TXT    9701     5   4-09-91   5:00a    A
     EXPAND    EXE   14563     8   4-09-91   5:00a    A
     DELOLDOS  EXE   17644     9   4-09-91   5:00a    A
     COMMAND   COM   47845    24   4-09-91   5:00a    A
     DOSSHELL  INI   16936     9   9-04-91   7:26a    A

     109 files LISTed     2,826,030  byte  109 files in subdir =   2,826,030  byte
  s    0 files SELECTed            0  bytes  Available on volume =   7,565,312  byte
```

Figure 4.5: Print File List for the DOS directory

the end of the printout includes number of files listed, number of files selected, total number of files in the subdirectory, their total size in bytes, and remaining free space on the disk.

FINDING TEXT WITHIN FILES

You may remember that a particular piece of text exists in a file, but not remember the name of the file that contains the text. You can use the Search command in the File menu to search selected files. You can also use the Search command from the Disk menu to extend the search across an entire disk.

USING FILE SEARCH Search allows you to look through one or more of your files for text known as a *search string*. This search string can consist of any words or letters up to a maximum of 32 characters, and you can enter the search string in ASCII or in hexadecimal.

Select the file(s) you want to examine before you start Search. Remember that the ASCII search is not case-sensitive, so upper- or lowercase letters are treated the same. The hexadecimal search, on the other hand, matches the characters you enter exactly. So that you can check your hex entry, the corresponding ASCII characters are displayed on the line below as you enter the hex text for the search.

There are three search options:

- **All Files** extends the search to include all the files in the current directory.

- **Selected Files** searches only the files you selected before starting Search.

- **Unselected Files** searches all the files you didn't select before starting Search.

Select one of the options. Once the text is found there are two options:

- **Select File and Continue** marks the file containing the match for the search string as a selected file. When you return to the File List window, the file will be selected. This option allows you to collect all the files containing the search string together at the same time.

- **Pause Search** suspends the search when a match for the search string is found.

Now press Enter or click on OK to start the search. When a match for the search string is found, the file is added to the list of selected files if you chose Select File and Continue. If you chose the Pause Search option, the screen shows the following selections:

- **Edit** loads the Hex Editor and displays the file in sector format. The cursor indicates the position of the first byte of the search string.

- **Next File** continues the search with the next file.

- **Cancel** returns to the PC Shell window.

USING DISK SEARCH   If you know that the text is on the disk somewhere, but you don't remember the file name, you can use Search from the Disk menu to help find the file.

Choose Search from the Disk menu and enter up to 32 ASCII or hex characters to search for. Again, the text is not case-sensitive. As the search proceeds, a small horizontal display indicates its progress.

Each time that Search finds a match, it displays the following options at the bottom of the window:

- **OK** continues to search the disk for more matches.

- **Name** displays a small dialog box containing the name of the file. This allows you to go back and look at the file in detail when the search is complete.

- **Edit** loads the Hex Editor in sector mode, with the cursor indicating the starting character of the search string. You can view or edit the contents of the sector and save your work when you have finished.

- **Cancel** returns you to the PC Shell window.

CHANGING FILES

The Change File command in the File menu lets you use a small submenu to look at and change the ASCII or hex contents of a file, to obliterate a file, and to look at or change a file's attributes.

EDIT FILE   When you select Edit File from the File menu, PC Shell opens a Desktop Notepads window so you can use all the text-editing features available in Notepads to edit the file. Chapter 13 describes how to use the Desktop Notepads in detail. Using Edit File you can only work with text files; you cannot edit binary files of any kind. For that you must use the next selection in the Change Files submenu, Hex Edit File.

HEX EDIT FILE   If you want to look at and perhaps change the contents of a backup, executable, hidden, system, or read-only file, select the file in the File List and choose Hex Edit File. The leftmost column of figures shows the decimal offset of the data from the beginning of the sector. The next column of numbers in parentheses shows the hex equivalents of these decimal offsets. The central area of the display shows the data in the file as 16 two-digit hex numbers. On the right side of the window, these same data are displayed as ASCII characters.

There are several function keys you can use in the Hex Edit File window. Press F5 to change from an ASCII display to a hex display and back again. Select a different sector with F6 (Sector). You can look at the next selected file with F9 (Next). When you press F7 (Edit), the window title changes to Sector Edit and you can now edit the information in the file, as long as you know exactly what you are doing. You can edit in ASCII or in hex; press F8 (ASC/hx) to move from the hex side of the window to the ASCII side of the window and press F5 (Save) save any changes you make. F3 (Exit) takes you back to the Hex Edit File window.

CLEAR FILE   When you choose Clear File, PC Shell loads the stand-alone Wipe program. Wipe is described in detail in Chapter 9.

ATTRIBUTE CHANGE   You can change a file's attributes to prevent it from being changed, deleted, or even seen. There are many reasons you might want to do this. You might want to hide a file so others don't know that it exists. If you are not the only person working on your computer or you are working on a local-area network, you may want to restrict access to files containing sensitive data, such as payroll information or personnel records. You may also want to make important files read-only so that you cannot erase then accidentally.

Choose Attribute Change to see the window shown in Figure 4.6. To change an attribute, click on the letter in the File Attribute window, or type the appropriate letter from the keyboard: *H* for the hidden attribute, *S* for the system attribute, *R* for the read-only attribute, and *A* for the archive attribute. Each time you type the letter, the attribute is toggled on or off. To change the time or date, move to the field you want to change and type in the new number.

IDENTIFYING YOUR DISKS WITH VOLUME LABELS

Each disk has an entry in the root directory called the *volume label.* It is most often used to add a global title that applies to the whole disk.

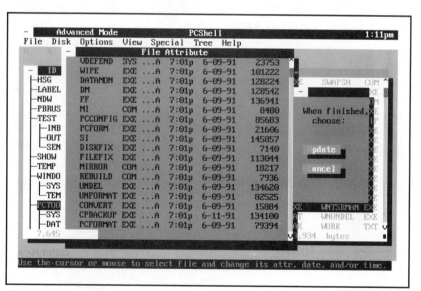

Figure 4.6: The File Attribute window

For example, you might call a floppy disk that contains word-processing work MEMOS, or a disk containing Lotus 1-2-3 spread-sheets BUDGETS.

You can use Rename Volume in PC Shell to review or change a disk's volume label. A window opens showing the text of the current volume label. Enter the new volume label and then select Rename to write the new label to the disk, or choose Cancel to ignore the new label.

SORTING FILES WITHIN DIRECTORIES

Even on a well-organized disk, the accumulation of directories and files often forces you to look through long directory listings to find the desired directory or file. You can improve this situation by sorting directory entries into groups based on certain criteria.

By using Sort Files in Directory from the Disk menu, you can sort the files in a directory by name, extension, date, time, or the order in which they were selected, in ascending or descending order. The Sort options are shown in Figure 4.7.

If you select files in the File List before using Directory Sort, the files are each assigned a number. You can then sort the files in the directory

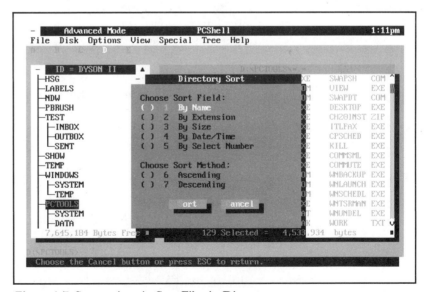

Figure 4.7: Sort options in Sort Files in Directory

by arranging the files in the exact order you require. This is completely independent of their file name or extension.

To sort the files in a directory, choose the sort field first from by name, by extension, by size, by date/time or by select number, then choose the direction of the sort, either ascending or descending. PC Shell performs the sort and then asks you to choose from the following:

- **View** allows you to look at the results of the sort before they are written to your disk. Use this option to ensure that the sort performed as expected.
- **Cancel** allows you to change your mind and unsort the files.
- **Update** allows you to write the sorted directory to your disk.
- **Resort** allows you to specify new sort options and re-sort the directory using these criteria.

PARKING YOUR HARD-DISK HEADS

If you are going to move your computer, it is a good idea to park your hard-disk read/write heads first. Parking the heads positions the read/write heads over an unused portion of your hard disk, usually over the highest-numbered cylinder on the disk. On a hard disk with more than one partition, the heads are placed at the end of the last partition. Parking the heads prevents any data loss caused by the heads accidentally touching the disk surface.

In PC Shell, choose Park Disk Heads from the Disk menu. PC Shell opens a dialog box to confirm that you want to park the heads and reminds you to turn your computer off immediately. Do not use your computer for anything else after parking the heads, otherwise the heads will move to access information and will no longer be parked.

LOADING OTHER
PC TOOLS PROGRAMS FROM PC SHELL

Several of the menu selections available from the File, Disk, Options, and Special menus actually load other stand-alone programs in the PC Tools family. Using these programs and adding other applications programs to PC Shell are described in the next chapter.

CHAPTER

5

*Using the
Program Manager*

There are several ways you can run other programs from inside PC Shell: from the Program List, the File List, or the DOS command line. In fact, there are several menu selections right inside PC Shell that are used to invoke other parts of the PC Tools package. For example, when you choose Undelete from the File menu, PC Shell actually loads the stand-alone Undelete program, so when you have finished using Undelete and you exit, you return to PC Shell rather than DOS.

Considerable space is devoted to these programs in later chapters, so they will not be discussed in detail here. Table 5.1 lists the PC Shell command used to invoke each program, along with the stand-alone PC Tools program name and the chapter where you will find a detailed description of the program.

Table 5.1: PC Tools Programs That Can Be Started from PC Shell

PC SHELL COMMAND	PROGRAM NAME	CHAPTER
Colors	PC Config	3
Clear File	Wipe	9
DeskConnect	Deskcon/Desksrv	18
Directory Maintenance	Directory Maintenance	8
Format Data Disk	PC Format	8
Locate	File Find	8
Make Disk Bootable	PC Format	8
Memory Map	System Information	8
Park Disk Heads	Park	4
Secure	PC Secure	9
System Info	System Information	8
Undelete	Undelete	7
View File Contents	View	8

RUNNING OTHER PROGRAMS INSIDE PC SHELL

There are several ways of running a program from inside PC Shell: from the Program List, from the DOS command line, using Quick Run, from the View window, and with PCTOOLS.BAT.

RUNNING A PROGRAM FROM THE PROGRAM LIST

Install looks for other Central Point products like CP Anti Virus and includes them in the Program List.

When you used Install to load and configure the PC Tools package, a dialog box asked whether you wanted Install to search your hard disk for applications programs and add them to the PC Shell Program List.

If you chose not to do this during the original installation, you can do so now. Run Install from the PCTOOLS directory, choose PC Shell in the PC Tools Program Configuration window, and click on the Applications command button. Install searches your hard disk and loads all the applications programs it can find in the PC Shell Program List.

Now to run a program from this list, you can use one of these methods:

You can even run programs from the Program List if you run PC Shell in memory-resident mode and hotkeyed into PC Shell when you were running another program.

- Click on Menu (F10) in the PC Shell screen, then double-click on the program name to start the program running.

- Find the right directory in the Tree List and the correct file in the File List, then double-click on the file you want. The file must have the extension .BAT, .COM, or .EXE. A dialog box opens, asking whether you want to use any command-line parameters when you start the program.

- Locate the right directory and file in the Tree List and File List, then select the file in the File List. Choose Open from the File menu and a dialog box opens asking for any command-line parameters.

- Find the file you want to run, select it in the File List, then press the Ctrl and Enter keys together. Again, the Open File dialog box asks for any command-line parameters you want to use.

- Double click or press Ctrl-Enter on a data file that is associated with a particular program and PC Shell launches the applications program for you. These associations, and how to establish them are described later in this chapter under ''Adding Your Own Programs to PC Shell.''

When you have finished with the application program, exit as you would normally; you will see a message asking you to press a key or click a mouse button to return to PC Shell.

STARTING A PROGRAM FROM THE DOS COMMAND LINE

When the DOS command line is turned on in Custom List Configure from the View menu, you can use it to start programs just as if you were at the real DOS prompt. If you want to use a DOS command that writes information to the screen, remember to choose Wait on DOS Screen from the Options menu to pause the DOS command before returning to PC Shell.

USING QUICK RUN

Quick Run is not available when PC Shell is run in memory-resident mode.

Quick Run in the Options menu tells PC Shell whether or not to free up memory before launching another program from PC Shell.

When Quick Run is on, PC Shell does not free up memory before starting another program. PC Shell occupies approximately 380K of conventional memory when you use it as a shell, which does not leave much room for other programs.

When Quick Run is turned off, PC Shell saves a memory image as a disk file and shrinks down to about 10K. This leaves much more space for other programs, but is relatively slow because of the extra disk accesses involved in creating the memory image file.

RUNNING A PROGRAM FROM THE VIEW WINDOW

If you are not sure whether a given data file is the one you want to work with, you can use the View window to look at the file's contents before starting the application program. This way you can be sure you have found the correct file.

This technique requires that the data files are associated with the correct program file. Once this has been done, select the file you want to view, then choose View Window from the Custom List Configure menu in the View menu to display the file contents. Now choose Open from the File menu to start the application program running. PC Shell displays an error message if it cannot find an application association for the file you chose.

STARTING PC SHELL WITH PCTOOLS.BAT

You can start PC Shell in Program-List–only mode if you type **PCTOOLS** from the DOS command line. This command invokes a small batch file that starts PC Shell with just the program list in the center of the window. None of the other familiar PC Shell screen elements are in view, except the line of function keys at the bottom of the window. When PC Shell is in this mode, you can press F2 (Description) to toggle a wider display on and off. This wide display includes a description of each of the main menu entries. For example, the PC Tools menu entry Recovery Tools lists all the appropriate PC Tools programs by name, along with a short summary of what each program can do, as Figure 5.1 shows.

If you use an EGA or VGA, you will see that different icons are used to distinguish between groups and individual programs.

The Program List can contain two different kinds of items: programs and groups. Programs are individual programs, like CP Backup or Commute in Figure 5.1. Groups are collections of programs, often with similar functions, collected under a common heading.

Groups may also contain other groups.

For example, Figure 5.1 shows a group called Recovery Tools, which includes DiskFix, File Fix, Undelete, and Unformat as individual programs. Double-click on the Recovery Tools item in the menu and another menu opens listing these programs.

All the stand-alone PC Tools programs are contained in these menus, either in groups or as individual programs. The groups are Recovery Tools, System Tools, Security Tools, Windows Tools, and Setup Tools, and these main groups form the structure for the rest of this book. Individual items include CP Backup, Commute, and Desktop.

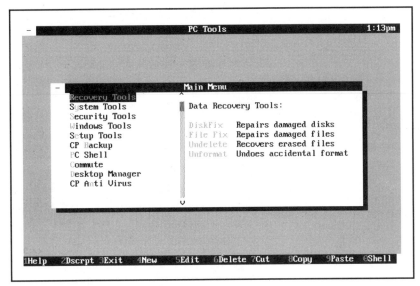

Figure 5.1: Opening PC Shell with PCTOOLS.BAT

In Program List mode, the Main Menu group is always shown first. Each time you open another group from this menu, the name of that group moves up to the menu title bar and the name of the previous group is shown preceded by two dots, on the line below the title bar. These two dots indicate that it is the parent of the current group. When it is time to close the current group and move back up the menus, double-click on the entry opposite the dots to return to that group. This makes it very easy to navigate your way through the Program List menu system. You can also press Escape to perform the same function.

Click on Shell (F10) to toggle to PC Shell in its normal mode, and use Menu (F10) in PC Shell to return to the Program-List–only mode.

ADDING YOUR OWN PROGRAMS TO PC SHELL

You can use the techniques I described in the last section to start your applications from the File List, but if you use these programs very often you can save a lot of time by installing them into the Program List. You can also define application associations, so that you can load a program by clicking on one of its data files—and you can associate programs in groups.

USING THE PROGRAM LIST WINDOW

Not all these options are available at the Beginner user level.

The easiest way to observe the process of adding new programs or groups to the Program List is to select Program/File Lists from the View menu; this opens a small Program List window at the bottom of the screen. When the Program List window is active, different function keys appear at the bottom of the screen and some of the entries in the File menu also change:

- **New** (F4) lets you add a new program or group entry.
- **Edit** (F5) allows you to edit or change an existing item in the Program List.
- **Copy** (F8) makes it easy to copy an item from the Program List to another location.
- **Cut** (F7) lets you move an item or items from one place in the Program List to another.
- **Paste** (F9) allows you to paste a copied or cut entry to a new location in the Program List.
- **Delete** (F6) removes an item or group of items from the Program List.

Using these commands makes it very easy to add new programs or groups to the Program List.

ADDING A NEW PROGRAM TO THE PROGRAM LIST

When you add a program to the Program List, you must define several important characteristics that tell PC Shell how to start the program, including command-line parameters, names of directories where you want to keep specific files, and so on.

To show an example of how to add a new program to the Program List, we will add a word processor as a separate item to the Main Menu. Follow these steps:

To add a new entry at a lower level, highlight the group to which you want to add your new entry.

1. Select New (F4) from the File menu.

2. In the New Menu Item dialog box, choose Item, then choose OK.

3. Enter the appropriate information into the next window, the Program Item Information window, as follows:

You can enter up to 256 characters into each of the text boxes in the Program Item Information and Advanced Program Item Information windows, even though you cannot see all of them at once.

- **Program Title** is the entry that will appear in the Program List window. Enter a title appropriate for your word processor.

- **Commands** includes the name of the executable file, along with any command-line parameters you want to use with the word processor. If the file is in a directory not available in the current PATH statement, include the full path name here.

- **Startup Directory** is the drive and directory containing the program files for your word processor.

- **Password** lets you specify a password, if you wish.

- **Pause after Exit** waits for you to press a key before returning to PC Shell.

4. Choose Description to open a Notepads file for a description of the program or to contain any notes you have about the program. When you have finished, save this file and leave Notepads.

5. Choose Advanced to configure the following:

- **User Prompt** contains any text you want PC Shell to display before starting the word processor. PC Shell pauses until you press a key.

- **File Associations** defines the types of file that you want to associate with this program. You can specify files individually, or you can use the DOS wildcards to include several files: if your word processor uses

.DOC as the file-name extension, you can specify
*.DOC to associate all such files.

- **Keystrokes** lets you start the application program in a specific way, as though you had used a macro. There are three different ways of entering keystrokes:

  Type a key and the key appears in the Keystrokes display.

  Type a sequence of letters contained within angle brackets, such as <esc>. Because of the angle brackets, PC Shell interprets this as Escape rather than *e*, followed by *s* and *c*. Alternatively, you can use Litkey (F7) before you type anything from the keyboard to tell PC Shell to interpret your next keystroke literally, then press the Escape key. PC Shell inserts the escape keystroke into a set of angle brackets.

  Use Keywrd (F8) to see a list of keywords on the screen. Use the arrow keys or the mouse to make your selection, then choose Insert. These keywords are listed in Table 5.2.

- **Quick Run** lets you select the Quick Run setting for each program individually, rather than making a global setting for all programs.

- **Exit to DOS after Application** lets you specify that you want to exit to DOS when you quit the program rather than return to PC Shell.

- **Force Launch with Selected File** starts the program running with the first selected or highlighted file in the File List, even though this file may have nothing to do with the application program.

- **Don't Clear Screen before Launch** lets you instruct PC Shell not to clear the computer screen before starting the program.

- **This is a PC Tools Application** lets you tell PC Shell that the program you are adding is a PC Tools program. Leave this selection off if it is not a PC Tools program.

6. When you return to the Program Item Information window, select OK to go back to the Program List.

7. Choose Save Configuration File in the Options menu to make sure that your changes are saved.

Now when you look at the Main Menu level, you will see a new menu entry for your word processor.

Table 5.2: Keyword Selections

KEYWORD	EXPLANATION
\<Path\>	Full path and file name of file
\<Drive\>	Drive letter associated with file
\<Dir\>	Path of file without drive information
\<Dir\\>	Path of file without drive information, but including \
\<File\>	Full file name with extension
\<Filename\>	File name without extension
\<Ext\>	Extension only
\<Delay*N*\>	Delays passing the characters in keystrokes to application program; replace *N* with the length of delay in seconds or tenths of seconds: \<Delay3\> indicates a delay of three seconds, while \<Delay.3\> indicates a delay of 0.3 second
\<Typein\>	Stops passing characters to application program and waits for you to type something from keyboard

ADDING A NEW GROUP TO THE PROGRAM LIST

Now that you know how to add a program to the Program List, you will find it easy to add a new group; just follow these steps:

1. Double-click on the menu item in which you want to create the new group.

2. Select New from the File menu.

3. Choose Group in the New Menu Item dialog box and select OK.

4. When the Program Group Information window opens, enter the following information:

    - **Title** lets you enter the group name that you want to see in the Program List.

    - **Password** lets you protect the group from unauthorized access; the password is optional.

5. Click on Description to open a Notepads file to associate with this new group. The information from this file is displayed on the right side of the Program List when it is in wide mode. You cannot resize or scroll the description window in the Program List; you are limited to the number of lines displayed in the window.

6. When you return to the Program Group Information dialog box, select OK to return to PC Shell.

If you want to change the order of items in the Program List, you can use the Cut, Copy, or Paste selections from the File menu to move items around. To remove an item completely, use Delete—but be aware that if you delete a group, you will erase all items and groups contained in that group.

CREATING AN APPLICATION ASSOCIATION

If you use a program that assigns characteristic file-name extensions, you can create application associations that link the data files

You can associate up to 20 file names or file-name extensions with an application, but you can only associate a file name or extension to one application at a time.

back to the application program. When these links are established, you can launch programs from the View window in PC Shell—or by selecting the data file, then pressing Ctrl and Enter. This means that you can find the right data file *before* you go to the trouble of opening the application program.

If you are a heavy Lotus 1-2-3 user, you can associate data files with Lotus by using the DOS wildcard characters in file names. A specification of *.WK? associates all WK1 and WKS files, for example.

To establish an association, highlight the program to which you want to add associations and select Edit, or choose New if you are starting this process from the beginning. Select the Advanced command button and enter your file specifications into the File Associations box. As well as the DOS wildcard characters, you can use a minus sign in front of a file specification if you want to exclude a particular group of files. Click on OK to return to the Program Item Information window and click on OK again to return to PC Shell. Use Save Configuration File from the Options menu to keep your changes.

Now when you double-click on a Lotus 1-2-3 spreadsheet file in PC Shell, Lotus will start running and then load the file you clicked.

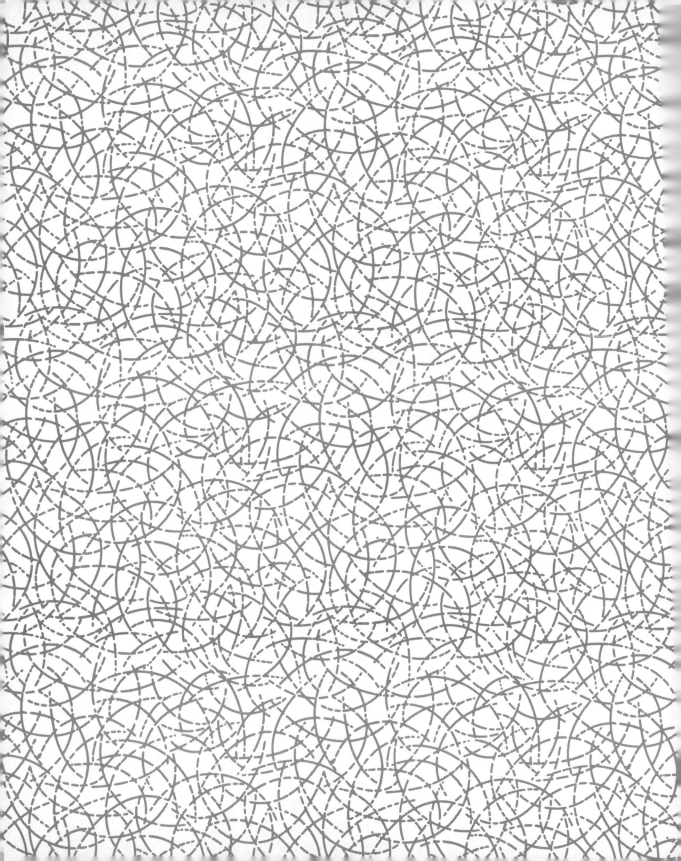

PART III

Disk Recovery and Data Protection Tools

CHAPTER

6

*An Introduction to Disk
and Directory Structure*

Before learning about file recovery and hard-disk management, you must know in detail many basic aspects of disk organization. This chapter describes floppy- and hard-disk characteristics, and gives a complete picture of the physical and logical framework of floppy and hard disks under DOS. Three PC Shell selections that you can use to explore your disks—Disk Information and the Disk and File Maps—are covered in depth in the second part of this chapter.

DISK STRUCTURE

The better you understand how the underlying hardware works, the easier it will be to understand what happens when you add or delete a file in DOS, and what procedures you must follow to recover files.

SIDES

The most fundamental characteristic of a floppy disk is that it has two sides. Data can be written to and read from either side.

In early versions of DOS, single-sided disks were common; that is, only one side of the disk was used.

The system considers the first side as side 0, and the second side as side 1. Hard disks, in contrast, may have several recording surfaces, which are called *platters*. Platters are mounted on the same spindle inside the hard disk's sealed enclosure, and each platter has two sides. The numbering scheme is as follows: the first side is 0, the next 1, the first side of the second platter is 2, and so on. Each side of a floppy disk and each side of a hard disk's platter has its own read/write head. Figure 6.1 shows a cut-away view of a hard disk. Most hard disks have between two and eight platters.

TRACKS

Each disk or platter side is divided into concentric circles known as *tracks*. The outermost track on the top of the disk is numbered track 0, side 0, and the outermost track on the other side of the disk is numbered track 0, side 1. Track numbering increases inwards towards the center of the disk (or platter).

The number of tracks on a disk varies with the media type: 360K floppy disks have 40 tracks per side, 1.2MB floppy disks have 80

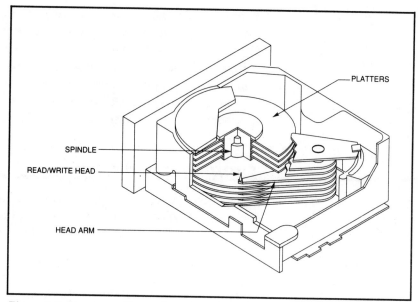

Figure 6.1: Cut-away illustration of a hard disk

tracks per side, as do 720K and 1.44MB floppy disks. Hard disks can have from 300 to 600 tracks per platter side. On a floppy disk, the tracks cover only a small area of the disk, about three-quarters of an inch. A 360K floppy disk is recorded with 48 tracks per inch, and a 1.2MB floppy disk is recorded with 96 tracks per inch (tpi).

CYLINDERS

Tracks that are at the same concentric position on the disk (or on platters) are referred to collectively as a *cylinder*. On a floppy disk, a cylinder contains two tracks (for example, track 2, side 0 and track 2, side 1); on a hard disk with four platters, a cylinder contains eight tracks. Figure 6.2 shows cylinders on a hard disk with four platters.

SECTORS AND ABSOLUTE SECTORS

Each track on a disk is in turn divided into *sectors*. Each track on the disk contains the same number of sectors.

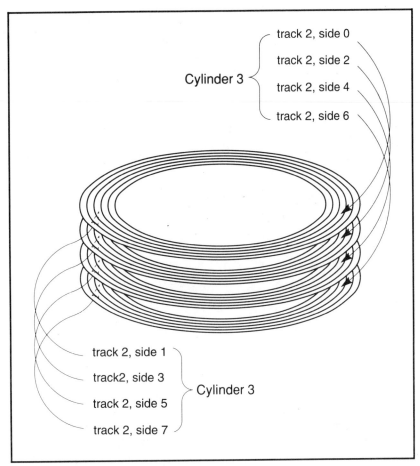

Figure 6.2: Cylinders on a hard disk with four platters

When DOS reads or writes data to a disk, it must read or write at least one complete sector.

In all versions of DOS, a sector consists of 512 bytes and is the smallest single area of disk space that DOS can read or write. Each sector has a unique sector address contained in the sector header, and is separated from the next sector by an intersector gap. The number of sectors contained in each track on the disk varies according to the media type. A 360K floppy disk has 9 sectors per track, a 1.2MB floppy disk has 15, a 720K floppy has 9, a 1.44MB floppy has 18, and most hard disks have 17 or 26. Figure 6.3 shows the relationship between tracks and sectors on a 360K floppy disk, which has 40 tracks numbered from 0 to 39, and 9 sectors per track.

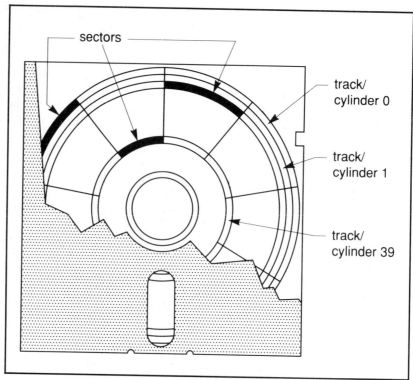

Figure 6.3: Tracks and sectors on a 360K floppy disk

In the absolute-sector numbering scheme, the first sector on a disk is identified as side 0, cylinder 0, sector 1.

DOS identifies all the sectors on a disk by numbering them sequentially. On a 360K floppy disk, for example, the sectors are numbered 0–719; a specific sector might be identified as, say, sector 317. Another way to reference a given sector is to identify it according to its disk side and cylinder and then specify its position in that cylinder. In this case, you might give a sector's location as side 0, cylinder 25, sector 7. When you use this method, you are referring to *absolute sectors*.

THE INTERLEAVE FACTOR

For several reasons, the sectors on a disk are not always numbered sequentially. One reason: A floppy disk rotates at about 200 rpm inside the disk drive and a hard disk rotates at about 3,600 rpm. DOS reads and writes data in single sectors, but by the time a sector's worth of data is read and stored in memory, and the PC is ready to read the next sector, this sector may already have passed under the head. The PC must now wait through a complete disk rotation before it can read the next sector. To minimize this delay, an *interleave factor* is introduced. Interleaving requires that logically sequential sectors are not physically adjacent to each other on the disk but are separated by some number of sectors. In this way, the performance of the disk and the layout of the sectors on the disk can be optimized. The interleave factor is discussed in more detail in Chapter 7.

CLUSTERS

The number of sectors per cluster depends on the disk media and the DOS version: 360K and 720K floppy disks have 2 sectors per cluster, while 1.2MB and 1.4MB disks have clusters of a single 512-byte sector. Hard disks have clusters of 4, 8, or 16 sectors.

Although DOS can read and write a single sector, it allocates disk space for files in *clusters,* which consist of one or more sectors. No matter how small a file is, it always occupies at least one cluster on the disk: a 1-byte file occupies one cluster, while a 511-byte file on a 1.2MB disk also occupies one cluster. Figure 6.4 shows a file of 1,025 bytes and a cluster size of 1,024 bytes, or two sectors. The file data occupy all of the first cluster and only 1 byte of the second cluster, yet the area of the second cluster not filled with data is not available for another file. This unused area is called *slack.* The next file must start at the next available cluster. If the first file increases in length, it will occupy more of the second cluster. When that cluster is filled up and more space is needed, the file will start to fill the next available cluster.

Clusters are called logical units. Tracks and sectors are *physical* units.

DOS identifies clusters by numbering them sequentially, with the first cluster labeled cluster 2. Cluster numbering begins in the data area of the disk, so the first cluster on a disk (cluster 2) is actually the *first* cluster in the data area. This is less confusing when you understand that, unlike tracks and sectors, clusters are not physically demarcated on the disk. DOS merely views groups of sectors as clusters for its own convenience.

Remember that the absolute-sector method for locating sectors locates them according to their physical position on the disk. Because clusters have no physical manifestation, however, there is no absolute method of referencing them.

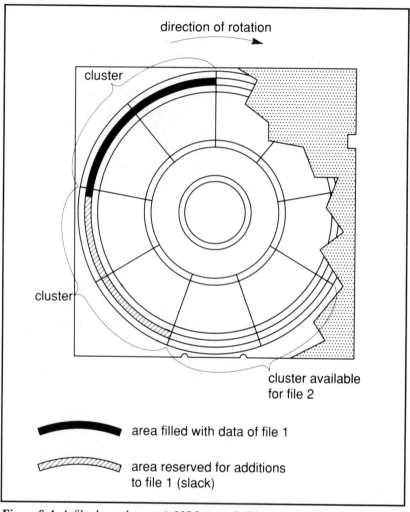

direction of rotation

cluster

cluster

cluster available
for file 2

area filled with data of file 1

area reserved for additions
to file 1 (slack)

Figure 6.4: A file that takes up 1,025 bytes of disk space is 1 byte bigger than
one cluster and so must occupy two complete clusters

Changing the num-
ber of sectors per
cluster (outside the scope
of this book) is a complicated operation that you
should only attempt
after you have made a
complete backup of
the hard disk.

The efficiency of your hard-disk storage depends in part on the
relationship between the cluster size and the most common size of
your files. Disk performance becomes a consideration when, to
access even the smallest file, DOS has to load a cluster that may contain many empty sectors.

EXAMINING THE SYSTEM AREA

> You can reference sectors in the system area with the DOS numbering system or the absolute-sector method. You cannot reference clusters in the system area because cluster numbering starts in the data area.

When you format a disk, DOS always reserves the outermost track on side 0 for its own use. This area is called the *system area* and is subdivided into three parts: the *boot record*, the *file allocation table* or FAT (of which there are usually two identical copies), and the root directory. The remaining space on the disk after the system area is called the *data area.* This is the part of the disk where applications programs and data are located. The data area is far larger than the system area. On a 360K floppy disk, the system area occupies 1.6 percent of the whole disk, and on a 40MB hard disk the system area occupies a meager 0.1 percent of the total disk space.

THE BOOT RECORD

The boot record—on all formatted disks—contains the BIOS parameter block (BPB). This block holds information about the disk's physical characteristics, which is needed by device drivers. The information contained in the BPB is shown in Table 6.1.

Table 6.1: Information Contained in the BIOS Parameter Block

INFORMATION STORED	BYTES USED	ADDITIONAL INFORMATION
Version of DOS used to format the disk	8	
Number of bytes per sector	2	
Number of sectors per cluster, per track, and per disk (or hard-disk partition)	1	
Number of reserved sectors used by the system area	2	

Table 6.1: Information Contained in the BIOS Parameter Block (continued)

INFORMATION STORED	BYTES USED	ADDITIONAL INFORMATION
Number of FAT copies and sectors used	1	
Number of root directory entries	2	112 entries on 360K or 720K floppies, 224 entries on 1.2MB or 1.44MB floppies, or 1,024 entries on hard disk
Number of sectors on disk	2	720 sectors on 360K floppy, 1,440 on 720K floppy, 2,400 on 1.2MB floppy, 2,880 on 1.44MB floppy, and thousands for hard disk
Media descriptor	1	Indicates the type of disk
Number of sectors per FAT	2	Sectors per FAT vary depending on disk's capacity (FAT references every cluster)
Number of sectors per track	2	360K and 720K floppies have 9 sectors per track, 1.2MB floppy has 15, 1.44MB floppy has 18, hard disk usually has 17
Number of heads	2	Floppy-disk drive has 2, hard disk has 4 or more
Number of hidden sectors	2	Hidden sectors in the system area

The disk space occupied by the boot record is one sector, which includes the BPB, boot program, and slack.

The boot record also contains the boot program that is used to start the computer after a system reset or after power is applied. When you first turn on your computer, it runs a set of diagnostic routines to ensure that the hardware is in good order. The ROM bootstrap program next loads the boot record from disk into the computer's memory.

The bootstrap program checks the disk for the DOS system files (IO.SYS or IBMBIO.COM, and MSDOS.SYS or IBMDOS.COM). If they are present, it loads them into the computer and passes complete system control over to DOS's COMMAND.COM. During this process, the CONFIG.SYS and AUTOEXEC.BAT files are loaded, as are any installable device drivers that a mouse or a RAM disk may need (for example, the device driver VDISK.SYS). Once everything has been loaded and you see the DOS prompt, your computer is ready for use.

However, when the computer can't find the DOS system files on the disk, it displays the error message

    Non-System disk or disk error
    Replace and strike any key when ready

and waits for you either to remove the nonsystem disk from the floppy-disk drive so it can use the hard disk, or place a system disk in your floppy-disk drive.

THE PARTITION TABLE

The DOS FDISK command establishes the partition table after low-level formatting of the disk is complete. You can use it to create or delete a DOS partition, to change the active partition, or to display the current active partition data.

The partition table, present on all hard disks, allows you to divide a hard disk into areas (called partitions) that appear to DOS as separate disks. The partition table also allows you to reserve space for other operating systems (which you can then install and use to create their own partitions). For example, DOS and XENIX can run on the same computer. A DOS disk can contain as many as four partitions, but only one of these may be active at any one time.

The partition table begins with a code called the *master boot record.* This code contains a record of which partition was the active partition—the one used to boot the system. The master boot record

Floppy disks do not have partition tables and cannot be shared between different operating systems.

also contains the locations of the boot records for the operating system of the active partition (and any other operating system installed on the disk). When the computer is started, it uses this information to boot the active partition's operating system. If you are running DOS and no other operating system, you should make the DOS partition occupy the whole hard disk.

THE FILE-ALLOCATION TABLE

The next part of a disk's system area is occupied by the file-allocation table (FAT), which is also created by the DOS FORMAT command. The FAT is part of the system that DOS uses to keep track of where files are stored on a disk. The FAT is so important that DOS actually creates two copies of it. If the first copy becomes corrupted, DOS uses the second copy. Think of the FAT as a two-column table. One column is a sequential list of the clusters in the disk's data area. The other column is another list of numbers that gives specific information about each cluster. If a cluster is being used to store file data, the second column in that row contains the number of the next cluster in that file. (Remember that data in a file are not necessarily stored in consecutive clusters.) Otherwise, the second column contains a code that indicates one of the following:

(0)000H	The cluster is available for storing data
(F)FF7H	The cluster is bad and cannot be used for storing data
(F)FF0-(F)FF6H	The cluster is reserved and cannot be used for storing data
(F)FF8-(F)FFFH	The cluster is the last cluster in a file

Figure 6.5 illustrates how FAT entries are chained together. File A starts in cluster 2, then jumps to cluster 8. The next cluster used by the file is cluster 11. Cluster 11 is followed by cluster 12, where—according to the FAT—the file ends. Thus file A is split among four clusters, two of which are not in sequence. This is called *fragmentation* and is discussed in detail in Chapter 8. File B occupies clusters 3, 4, 6, 7, 9, and 10. The sequence skips cluster 5 because it is bad, and skips cluster 8 because it is used by File A.

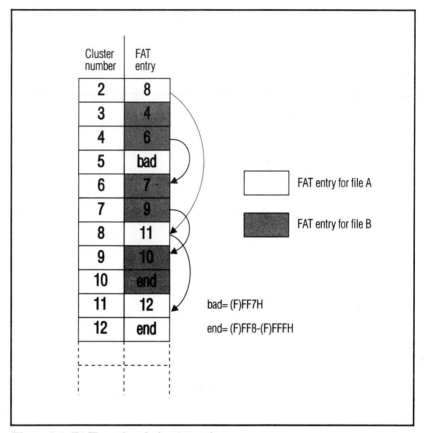

Figure 6.5: FAT entries chained together

THE ROOT DIRECTORY

Directly following the FAT is the root directory, which is the third part of the system area on a formatted disk. The size of the root directory cannot be changed, but it is proportional to the media type. For example, a 360K floppy has space for 112 entries in the root, while a hard disk has space for 512 or 1,024 entries, depending on the disk.

On a 720K floppy, the root directory takes up 7 sectors of disk space.

If the disk is a system disk, the first two files listed in the root directory are always the files containing the MS-DOS BIOS and the DOS kernel. The disk bootstrap program uses these entries when it loads the operating system into memory and starts executing DOS.

Each directory entry is 32 bytes long. The entry may contain information about a file or a subdirectory. The format of a file entry in the root directory is as follows:

Base name	8 bytes, ASCII
Extension	3 bytes, ASCII
Attribute	1 byte, each bit represents an attribute
	bit 0, file is read-only
	bit 1, file is hidden
	bit 2, file is a system file
	bit 3, entry is a volume label
	bit 4, entry is a subdirectory
	bit 5, archive bit
	bit 6, 7, unused
Reserved	10 bytes, reserved for future use
Time	2 bytes
Date	2 bytes
Starting FAT entry	2 bytes
File size	4 bytes

The file name is an 11-byte entry, divided into an 8-byte base name and a 3-byte extension, which are separated by a period. The period is not stored as a byte, but you must type it between the eighth and the ninth characters to use a file extension.

If the first byte of a file name has a value of 0, the directory entry is unused; this indicates the end of the active directory entries. If the first byte of a file name is a period (that is, the . and .. files), the file is reserved by DOS.

If the first byte of a file name is a lowercase Greek sigma (σ ASCII 229 decimal, E5 hex), the file has been erased. When erasing a file using DEL or ERASE, DOS marks the first character of the file name with the E5 hex character to show that it has been erased and then clears the

You can use letters, numbers, and any other characters except ./\{}|> < +:, =; in your files' base names and extensions.

file's entries from the FAT. As DOS leaves the starting cluster number and the file length in the directory, and leaves the data on the disk, the first cluster of a file can be found and recovered quite easily—as long as the clusters have not been overwritten by another file.

The attribute byte can have one or more of the attribute bits set at the same time. For example, a system file can also be hidden. An attribute is said to be set if the appropriate attribute bit is set to 1. If the attribute byte has no bits set, or a value of 0, the file is a normal data or program file and may be written to or erased. This probably applies to the majority of your files. Attributes are defined as follows:

- Read-only files can be used, but you can't make changes to their contents.

- Hidden files do not appear in directory listings made by DIR. You can't duplicate them with COPY or delete them with ERASE or DEL. However, you can copy them with the DOS DISKCOPY command.

- System files are read-only files.

- The volume label is a short piece of text used to identify the disk. You can specify up to 11 characters for it when you label your disk. The label's directory entry looks like a file that has no length.

- Subdirectory names have the same format as file names.

- The archive bit is used when backing up. If a new file is written to disk or an existing file is modified, this bit is set (changed to 1). After the backup program has copied the file, it resets the bit to 0. This way, the backup program knows which files need to be copied.

SUBDIRECTORIES

The root directory has a fixed size and location on the disk. By contrast, *subdirectories* can be of any size and can be located anywhere they are needed on the disk. You cannot delete the root directory, but you can create, delete, rename, expand, or contract a subdirectory as needed. Subdirectories are usually just called directories.

EXAMINING THE DATA AREA

The rest of the DOS partition (or unpartitioned hard disk or floppy disk) is the data area, which stores files and subdirectories. This is the largest part of the disk and is where all your programs are found, including spreadsheets, word processors, program-language compilers, and data files.

Figures 6.6 and 6.7 illustrate disk structure in different ways and draw together many of the concepts presented so far in this chapter. Both figures assume a 720K floppy disk.

EXPLORING YOUR DISK WITH PC SHELL

You can use several of the selections in PC Shell to explore your disks and files: Disk Information in the Disk menu, and Disk Map and File Map in the Special menu.

USING DISK INFORMATION

Disk Information provides you with a wealth of technical information about your disks that is not normally available without complex programming. From PC Shell, open the Disk menu, then select Disk Information. Figure 6.8 shows the resulting data for my hard disk, drive C.

The hard disk has 33,450,496 bytes (about 32MB) of disk space in total, of which 9,517,056 bytes (about 10MB) are available. Hidden files occupy 126,976 bytes of disk space, 1,170 user files take up 23,631,872 bytes (about 24MB), and 41 directories occupy 104,448 bytes. The formatting program sets aside 65,536 bytes of the disk as unreadable. The disk is divided into 65,494 512-byte sectors organized into 26 sectors per track or 16,333 clusters, with 4 sectors in each cluster. There are 2,519 tracks, 315 cylinders, and 8 sides or platters.

To run Disk Information on a floppy disk, click on OK to return to the main PC Shell display and insert a floppy disk into drive A. Make

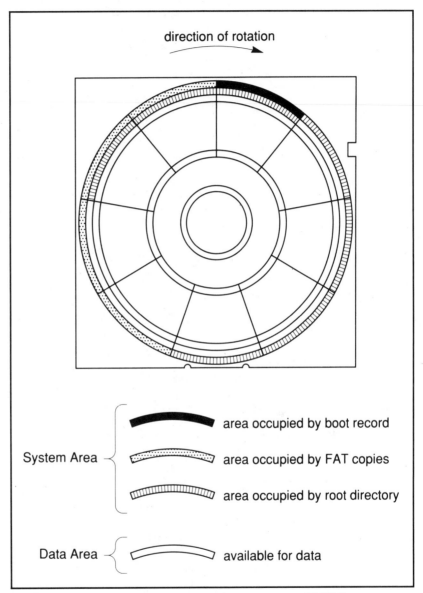

Figure 6.6: Locations of system area and data area on a 720K floppy

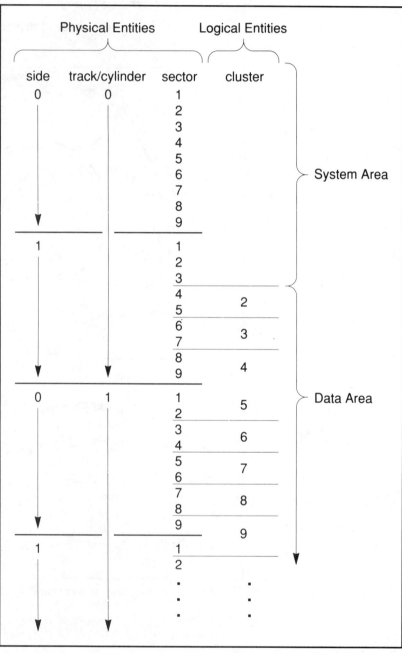

Figure 6.7: Relationships between elements of disk structure on a 720K floppy

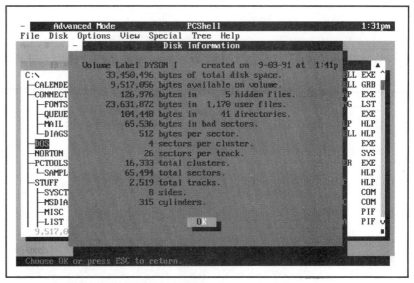

Figure 6.8: Disk Information run on drive C

that drive the current drive and notice that both the tree and the file lists change to reflect the contents of this new disk. Now open the Disk menu, choose Disk Information, and see a display similar to the one shown in Figure 6.9 if you have a 1.2MB floppy disk.

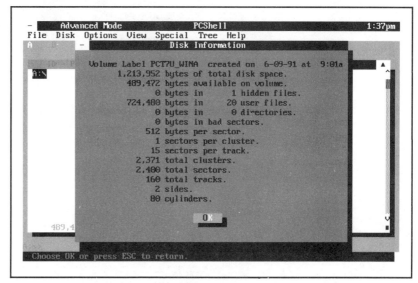

Figure 6.9: Results of Disk Information for a 1.2MB floppy in drive A

The differences in the information shown for the floppy-disk drive and the hard-disk drive have to do mostly with storage capacity—the number of sectors and the number of clusters, as you would expect.

LOOKING AT DISKS WITH DISK MAP

From PC Shell, open the Special menu and choose Disk Map. Figure 6.10 shows the Disk Map display for a hard disk.

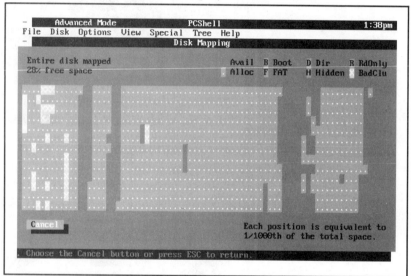

Figure 6.10: Typical Disk Map display for a hard disk

Each small square indicates several clusters of disk space occupied by your files, or $1/1000$ of the total disk space. The shaded area is the unused space on your disk. In this case, the free space is 28 percent of the whole disk.

Free space is sometimes surrounded by clusters in use. These gaps result when you delete files and the disk space is deallocated from the FAT. The space then becomes available for other files, and will eventually be used again.

The *X* represents one or more bad clusters. These were found to be damaged when the disk was formatted. A special entry in the FAT denotes that the area is bad and keeps it from being used.

An *R* on this screen indicates that a file is a read-only file, and an *H* indicates that the file is a hidden file.

Since the system area on this disk is small compared to the data area, the boot record (*B*), FAT (*F*), and root directory (*D*) cannot be shown as individual elements in the display. If you make a disk map of a floppy disk, however, these areas will be explicitly called out in the display, as shown in Figure 6.11.

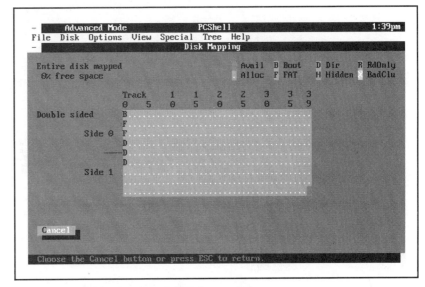

Figure 6.11: Disk map for a 360K floppy disk

USING FILE MAP

You can also look at similar information with File Map. Select the PCTOOLS directory and the file PCSHELL.EXE from the tree. Open the Special menu and choose File Map. The display for the file PCSHELL.EXE is shown in Figure 6.12.

In Figure 6.12, the file name is displayed at the top of the screen, along with explanations of the symbols used in the display. Again the FAT, boot record, and root directory are too small to show as individual elements in this display. As you can see, the PCSHELL.EXE file is recorded on this hard disk in six non-contiguous areas, starting at cluster 7,812, sector 31,401.

You can use PRIOR to show details of the previous file in your selection, or NEXT to show details of the next file. This enables you to look at several files in turn without returning to the Special menu level.

Select CANCEL when you are ready to leave File Map.

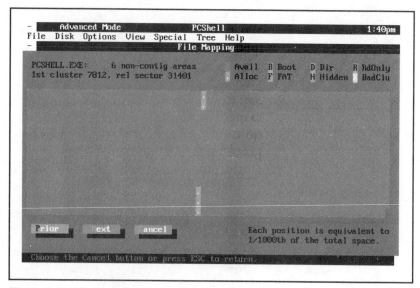

Figure 6.12: File map for the PCSHELL.EXE file

You are now familiar with the following PC Shell selections: Disk Information in the Disk menu; and Disk Map and File Map in the Special menu.

In Chapter 7, you will learn how to unerase files that have been accidentally erased and how to recover from an accidental format of your hard disk, and in Chapter 10, you will learn how to back up your hard disk.

CHAPTER

7

*Preventing Data Loss
with the Recovery Tools*

In this chapter, I discuss some of the mishaps that can befall your data and how you can recover from them. Both floppy and hard disks can be mechanically damaged by careless handling, files can be deleted accidentally, and disks can be reformatted inadvertently. The PC Tools recovery programs provide several elegant solutions to these problems and you will learn how to use all of them, including Undelete, the file-recovery program; Mirror and Unformat, which provide protection against file loss due to accidental hard-disk formatting; DiskFix, a powerful disk maintenance and repair-utility program; and File Fix, a program for rescuing damaged Lotus 1-2-3 and dBASE files. You will also learn how to use the Emergency System Recovery disk you made using the Install program in Chapter 2.

First, however, I'll give you some tips on how to prevent such problems from occurring in the first place.

TAKING CARE OF YOUR DISKS

Disks, both hard and floppy, can deteriorate through extended use. Floppy disks in particular can be easily damaged by careless handling.

Here are some suggestions for handling floppy disks:

- When you are not using a floppy disk, keep it in its jacket in a disk-storage tray or in its box.

- Do not leave floppy disks where they can get hot, such as on a window sill, on top of your monitor, or in a car parked in the sun. The disks may warp and become unusable.

- Keep disks away from devices that emit magnetic fields, such as motors, paper-clip holders, and magnetic keys.

- Do not touch the recording surface of the disk.

- Write on disk labels *before* attaching them to the disks. If you do write on a label that is on a disk, use a soft felt-tip pen, not a pencil.

- Keep backup copies of all distribution disks, and do not keep them with the original disks. If you run a small business, it may be worthwhile to store your archives at a secure off-location site. You can often find a local company that specializes in archiving data in a secure storage area. Such companies use precisely controlled temperature and humidity to preserve the media in storage. They also usually have excellent security and fire protection.

Your hard disk is not immune from problems, either. Here are some suggestions for hard-disk care:

- Do not move a computer containing a hard disk while it is turned on and you are using it.

- Use the Park Disk Heads option in the Disk menu in PC Shell before turning the computer off. This is especially important if you are going to move the computer.

RECOVERING ERASED FILES

It is easy to delete more files than you intended, especially if you use a wildcard in the command. You may even delete the entire contents of the directory. For example, both EDLIN and WordStar create .BAK files when files are modified or saved. Most people delete these files to save space, relying on their backup disks for copies of the original files. Suppose in this case you mistype

    DEL *.BAK

as

    DEL *.BAT

Instead of deleting your .BAK files, you have just deleted all your batch files!

Careful disk organization can help prevent some of these accidental erasures. To protect your batch files, for example, you should keep them in a directory separate from your EDLIN or WordStar files. No matter how good your organization is, however, sooner or later you will erase a file by accident or want to recover a file that you erased intentionally. This is where PC Tools comes into its own.

WHAT REALLY HAPPENS WHEN YOU DELETE A FILE?

Before describing how the PC Tools programs do their job, I'll explain precisely what happens when you delete a file. When you use DEL or ERASE on a file, the file's entries are cleared from the FAT. DOS also changes the first character of the file name in its directory to a lower-case Greek sigma (ASCII E5 hex or 229 decimal) to indicate to the rest of the DOS system that the file has been erased. The file's entry, including its starting cluster number and its length, remains in the directory, hidden from your view because of the sigma character. The data themselves are still in their original places on the disk. DOS does not do anything to the data until it is instructed to write another file over the same clusters. Thus, the first cluster of a file can be found and recovered quite easily as long as it has not been overwritten.

To illustrate this, make a very small text file on a blank formatted 720K floppy disk in drive B. Type

COPY CON B:TESTFILE.TXT

and press Enter. Then enter the following short piece of text (there is no prompt):

This is a short piece of text.

Press Enter, then F6 (you'll see a ^Z onscreen), and Enter again to close the file. In the main PC Shell display, you can see that the disk in drive B contains one short file. Use the View File Contents selection from the File menu to look at the details of the file, as shown in Figure 7.1.

Next, delete the file by selecting it in the main PC Shell display and then using Delete File from the File menu or returning to DOS and entering

DEL TESTFILE.TXT

Now reopen PC Shell and look at the root directory of the disk in drive B. Notice that the message

No entries found

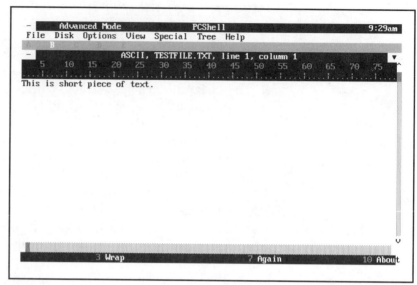

Figure 7.1: The View File Contents display for a small text file

is shown where the file was, and that the file list is empty. Select View/ Edit from the Disk menu, and look at sector 7, the original starting sector of the root directory. Note that the file name's first character has been changed to a special character, and that the rest of the file name entry is still intact, as shown in Figure 7.2.

Next, look at sector 14. The original text,

   This is a short piece of text.

is still on the disk even though the file has been erased, as shown in Figure 7.3.

WHAT HAPPENS WHEN YOU ADD A NEW FILE?

See Chapter 8 to learn how to reduce file fragmentation with the PC Tools Compress utility.

When you add a new file to your disk, DOS looks for the next available piece (cluster) of free disk space. If the file is small enough to fit into this space, DOS slots it in. If the file is larger, DOS splits it into several pieces, placing it in clusters that are not numbered consecutively. In other words, the file becomes fragmented.

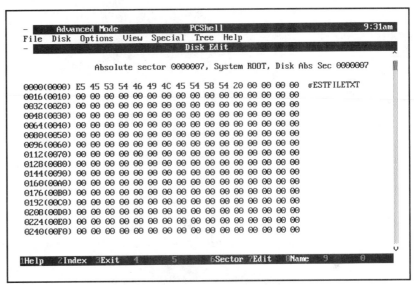

Figure 7.2: Looking at the entry for an erased file in the root directory

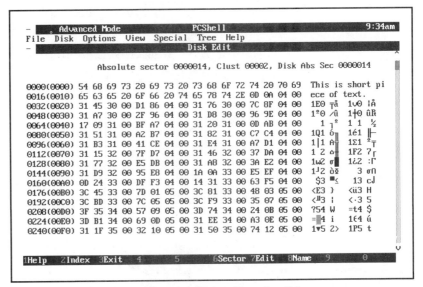

Figure 7.3: Original text of erased file is still on the disk

Thus, saving a new file onto the disk destroys the deleted file's data. If the new file is larger than the old one, the old file is completely obliterated. If the new file is smaller than the old one, some unknown

Do not save *anything* after you delete a file inadvertently, or you may be unable to recover the file.

amount of the old file will remain on the disk until it is finally over-written during another write-to-disk operation.

The most important point to remember about file recovery is that you must not save anything on the disk until you have completed the recovery operation. Do not even copy PC Tools onto the hard disk; instead, run it from a floppy disk, installing it on your hard disk only when the recovery is completely finished. By following this rule, you will not overwrite the erased file's data and will increase the chances of a complete recovery.

A NOTE FOR USERS OF DOS 5

If you have upgraded to Microsoft's DOS 5, you may have noticed that three of the new utilities contained in the upgrade were originally licensed from Central Point Software, the makers of PC Tools. These three utilities are:

- UNDELETE, which recovers erased files that have not been overwritten by new files or reorganized by a disk unfragmentation program like Compress

- UNFORMAT, which restores the FAT and directories of a recently formatted hard disk

- MIRROR, which is a memory-resident program that saves information about deleted files and directories in a hidden file for later use by UNDELETE and UNFORMAT

While these DOS 5 programs add capabilities to your computer that were completely non-existent in earlier versions of DOS, the file and disk-recovery programs available in the current release of PC Tools are far more capable and much easier to use.

THE UNDELETE FILE-RECOVERY UTILITY

I'll demonstrate how to restore erased files by using a text file rather than a program or binary file. You can examine a text file by several different methods in DOS or in PC Tools, and it is easy to see when the contents of a text file (unlike a program file) begin to make sense.

PC Tools contains two versions of the Undelete program; one runs under DOS, while the other is a Windows application. Because the way you use both programs is so similar, the following discussion can be applied equally well to either the DOS program or to the Windows version. Figure 7.4 shows the opening screen of the DOS version of Undelete, and Figure 7.5 shows the same screen for the Windows version; you can see how alike they are.

The Windows version of Undelete has a row of command buttons at the top of the window; all these options are also available from the regular menus and by keyboard shortcuts. The advanced options including the manual undelete are only available in the DOS version of Undelete; they are not available in the Windows version of the program.

Throughout the discussion that follows, I describe the DOS version of the Undelete program, and all the figures will be taken from this version.

You cannot run the DOS version of Undelete from Windows because some of the recovery methods it uses are not suitable for a multitasking environment like Windows.

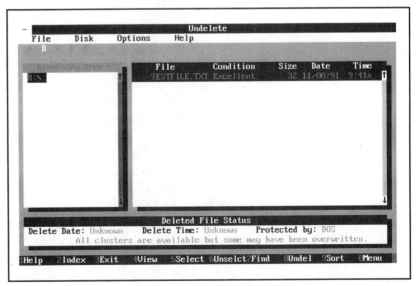

Figure 7.4: The main screen of the DOS version of Undelete

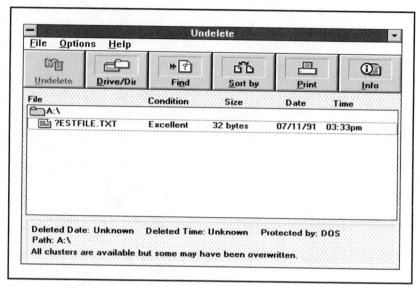

Figure 7.5: The main screen of the Windows version of Undelete

USING UNDELETE

If the deleted file is a short file or is on a floppy disk, there is an excellent chance that Undelete can restore it on the first attempt. If the file is badly fragmented, or part of it has been overwritten by another file, the chance of a complete recovery is substantially less.

To demonstrate Undelete, let's continue with TESTFILE.TXT, the small text file that you created and deleted on drive A. To start Undelete, select Undelete from the File menu in PC Shell, select Undelete from the list of programs in the Recovery Tools menu, or type **UNDEL** from the DOS prompt.

If you are using Windows, double-click on the Undelete icon in the PC Tools group in the Program Manager, or on the Undelete file name in the File Manager. You can also choose Undelete from the Central Point Launcher, if it is installed on your system.

Select drive A as the current drive and you will see the display shown in Figure 7.4.

On the left side of the window is a Directory Tree showing information for the current drive. On the right side is a list of all the erased files located by Undelete. There are five headings in this window, as follows:

- **File** lists all the deleted files found in the current directory or on the current floppy disk. If Undelete cannot find any erased files in the directory or on the disk you are working with, you will see the message No files found.

- **Condition** gives an indication of how complete a recovery you can expect, and may be one of the following:

    Perfect. This file can be recovered automatically.

    Excellent. All the clusters belonging to this file are continuous and contiguous, and recovery will be automatic.

    Good. This file's clusters are available but not contiguous, and some data may have been overwritten.

    Poor. The first cluster (and perhaps other clusters) is not available. Use the advanced methods described later under ''Manually Undeleting Files'' to recover as much of the file as possible.

    Destroyed. This file probably cannot be recovered because all the clusters have been overwritten by another file.

    Existing. This is an existing file that you can add clusters to manually with the advanced file-recovery options described later in this section.

    Recovered. You have just undeleted this file.

- **Size** gives the file size in bytes.

- **Date** shows the file-create date.

- **Time** indicates the file-create time.

The condition of a file shown in the file list may change as other files are recovered.

The Deleted File Status window across the lower portion of the screen shows you when the file was deleted, if the file is protected by either Delete Sentry or Delete Tracking protection methods, and also gives a short indication of the file's condition on the last line.

The simple example shown in Figure 7.4 contains only one deleted file. The first letter of the file name has been replaced by a ?, as it is unknown.

Select Undelete from the File menu and the Enter First Character window opens as Figure 7.6 shows. Undelete asks you to provide a suitable beginning letter for the file, so enter **T** and then choose OK. Always use the correct character if you can remember it; otherwise, use any character as the first letter. You can always use the Rename Existing File from the Advanced Undelete options in the File menu to rename the file after you have recovered it. After a moment's pause, you will see the File Condition column change to Recovered as the original file name is restored and the file is unerased.

If you want to recover several files from the same directory, you can use Search Groups to find deleted files associated with a specific application program. Choose Find Deleted files from the File menu and then choose Groups in the Find Deleted Files dialog box. Select the groups you want from the Search Groups dialog box, or use Edit to add a new group to the list; then choose OK. Now the specification for the group you selected appears in the File Specification box, and

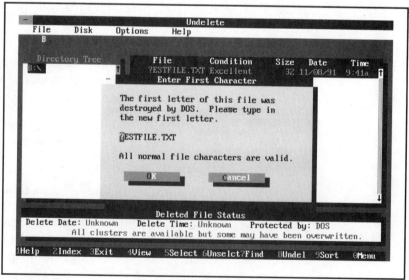

Figure 7.6: Provide an appropriate first letter for the file name

this group remains in operation until you choose another or leave the Undelete program.

There are several ways you can look at files in other directories on other disks using Undelete. To change to another disk, just click on the disk icon in the main Undelete window. The Directory Tree changes to show the current directory on the new disk and the file window now displays details of any deleted files located in that directory. To change to a specific directory, click on the directory name in the Directory Tree display.

If the main window shows a large number of deleted files, you can use the selections from the Options menu to arrange the files in the most convenient order. You can sort the files by name, extension, size, deleted date/time, modified date/time, directory, or condition. Sorting by condition moves those files in the best condition to the top of the list. Sorting by directory is only available in the expanded directory list displayed for network drives. This sorting applies only to the files shown in the main Undelete window; the order of the files on your disk remains unchanged. You may also select or unselect files by name using two selections from the Options menu: Select by Name, and Unselect by Name.

You have now completed a simple file recovery by unerasing MYFILE.TXT. As long as you start the recovery process soon after you deleted the file, and the file is not badly fragmented or overwritten, the chances for recovery are usually quite good. Unfortunately, files do become fragmented over time and DOS will eventually reuse the space formerly occupied by a deleted file. A much more certain way of recovering erased files is to use one of the PC Tools delete-protection methods that make use of the information collected by the Data Monitor program.

RECOVERING FILES USING DELETE PROTECTION

See Chapter 9 for a complete description of the Data Monitor program.

If you use the Data Monitor program to install one of the delete-protection methods, you will greatly increase the chances of recovering a deleted file. After you install delete protection, Undelete Files works in a much more powerful way. The delete-protection methods are as follows:

- **Delete Sentry** is the surest way to recover deleted files. It intercepts all requests to erase files and copies these files into a directory called SENTRY. Using Data Monitor, you select which files to save and how long you want to save them for before they are automatically purged from the system.

- **Delete Tracking** saves several pieces of information about the file before it is actually deleted, including the file's name, size, and date, and a list of the file's cluster numbers. Once this information is stored in the delete-tracking file, PCTRACKR-.DEL, the DOS DEL or ERASE operation continues and the file is actually erased. PCTRACKR.DEL is always created in the root directory of your disk and is proportional to the size of the disk media you are using.

- **DOS** indicates that no method of delete protection is being used.

The Delete Sentry method is the one likely to provide the most successful recovery of delete files, as long as you configure the program to save the appropriate file types. Delete Tracking is likely to be slightly less successful, especially if your files become badly fragmented, and DOS provides no additional protection at all.

As an example of using delete protection, you will erase and then recover a file with Delete Sentry installed. Install Delete Sentry delete protection using the Data Monitor program, or, if you do not have Data Monitor loaded, type the following from the DOS command line

You cannot use both Delete Sentry and Delete Tracker at the same time; they are mutually exclusive, so choose one of them.

       DATAMON /SENTRY +

to install Delete Sentry.

Now place a freshly formatted floppy disk in drive A. Use Copy File in the PC Shell File menu to copy the PCSHELL.EXE file from the PCTOOLS directory to drive A.

Next, select drive A and delete the PCSHELL.EXE file. Start Undelete and note that the opening screen is different from the one described in the standard DOS method of file undeletion. The Deleted File Status window at the bottom of the screen indicates the time and date that the file was deleted, as well as the message that the file was protected by Delete Sentry, and that the file can be 100 percent undeleted.

The erased file is listed on the screen with the file name shown in full. Notice that the first letter of the file name has been provided by Delete Sentry. In the example, only one file is shown on the screen, so go ahead and select Undelete (F8) from the File menu to recover it.

If you use Delete Sentry carefully, you will almost always be able to recover deleted files with complete success. The only time this may not be true is if your disk is filling up and you need the space that Delete Sentry takes for the hidden directory for your application program. Now Delete Sentry will start to purge the oldest files in the directory to make more room.

If Undelete cannot recover the file automatically, try the manual method, as explained in "Manually Undeleting Files."

UNERASING FILES ON A NETWORK

Only the Delete Sentry method of delete protection is available on networked drives; if Delete Sentry was not used on the drive, Undelete will not find or list any deleted files. If you are using Undelete on a network, in place of the Directory Tree and Files displays, you will see a single window in the center of the screen. As well as the normal listings of deleted file name, condition, size, date and time, you will see an additional column at the right of the window headed Path. This column contains the complete path for each file listed in the window.

To undelete a file on the network, highlight the file or files you want to rescue, then use Undelete to recover the file. Because the files on the network are protected by Delete Sentry, recovery will be fast and complete.

Several of Undelete's commands are not available on the network, including the Advanced Undelete options in the File menu, Show Existing Files from the Options menu, and all of the entries from the Disk menu. These options are grayed out when they are not available.

USING SEARCH GROUPS

Any search groups you establish in Undelete will also be available to you with File Find, discussed in Chapter 8.

Many applications programs make and then delete temporary files during the course of a session. These files are considered ordinary deleted files, so Undelete lists them in the main window as possible candidates for recovery. Because these files are designed to be temporary in nature, they usually do not contain meaningful information. Using search groups is one way to avoid listing these useless files in Undelete.

When you installed PC Tools, the install program scanned your hard disk looking for applications programs; when it found certain programs, it created search groups corresponding to them. You can edit these search groups or create your own from scratch if you wish. If your word processor files all have the same .DOC extension, or your Basic programs have the .BAS extension, you can create search groups to look for deleted files with these extensions in all directories on your disk.

Choose Find Deleted Files from the File menu and then click the Groups command button in the Find Deleted Files window. Now select the appropriate group from the Search These Groups dialog box; alternatively, select Edit to alter the current group or to make a new group. Then choose OK to return to the Find Deleted Files window, where you see that the group specification has been entered into the File Specification box. You can also enter a text search string to narrow the search even further. Select OK to start the search. The main Undelete window now changes to that used for undeleting files on a network; the Directory Tree display has disappeared. Any files located are listed in this window along with their complete path specifications. Highlight the file you want to recover and use the normal undelete methods to recover the file or files in the normal way. To return to the normal two-window display for Undelete, select Tree & File List in the File menu.

MANUALLY UNDELETING FILES

Now that you understand how to undelete files automatically, you are ready to learn how to undelete files manually. You should only use manual recovery methods if the automatic recovery mode does not work. Although manual recovery is considered an advanced technique, remember that context-sensitive help is always available from Undelete to help you through the steps. For the following example, we will delete the README.TXT file supplied with PC Tools and then use Undelete's Manual Undelete to recover the file. First change to the PC Tools directory on your hard disk, and type

TYPE README.TXT ¦ MORE

to display the beginning of the README.TXT file, as shown in Figure 7.7. The more you know about the contents of the file you are trying to undelete, the easier the operation becomes.

Press Ctrl-C to break out of the listing, then copy the file to a freshly formatted floppy disk in drive A. Erase the README.TXT file by typing:

DEL A:README.TXT

at the DOS prompt.

To recover README.TXT, start Undelete running from the DOS prompt by typing **UNDEL**, or select Undelete from inside the PC Tools

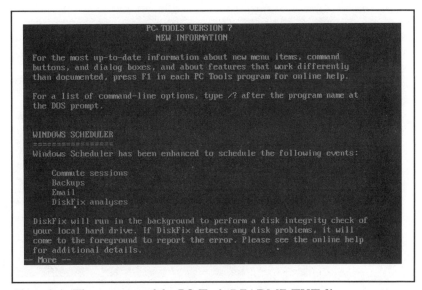

Figure 7.7: The contents of the PC Tools README.TXT file

The Advance Unde-
lete options are not
available on a network.

program. Make drive A the current drive. The Directory Tree window
shows you are using drive A and a line in the File window describes the
?EADME.TXT file.

Position the highlight over the ?EADME.TXT file, then choose
Advanced Undelete from the File menu. Choose Manual Undelete
from the small submenu, and undelete asks you to provide a character to complete the file name. Enter **R** and click on OK, and you will
see the Manual Undelete screen as Figure 7.8 shows.

At the left side of the Manual Undelete window you can see information about the README.TXT file, including the file name, size,
and create time and date. Below this, is the number of the next available cluster. On the right of the screen, the List of Added Clusters
window shows the starting cluster number for README.TXT
taken from the FAT. Below this, the Clusters Needed field reports the
number of clusters that the file occupied before it was deleted; this
represents the number of clusters that you have to recover to undelete
the whole file. Below this, the Clusters Added field keeps track of the
clusters you add to the file. This number is zero now, but it will
increase as you recover clusters and add them to the file. To the right
of these fields is the Added Clusters box.

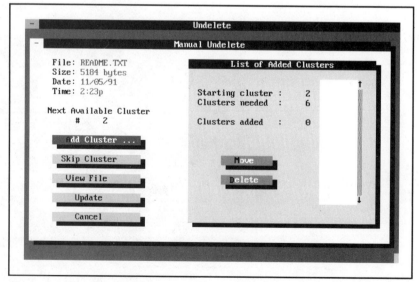

Figure 7.8: The Manual Undelete screen provides detailed information about
the erased file

From the list of commands shown at the left of the window, choose Add Cluster, and you will see the display shown in Figure 7.9. To find the file's clusters, you can choose from the following options:

- **Add All Clusters** automatically adds the most likely clusters to the file and provides the most straightforward method of recovering the file's data.

- **Add This Cluster** adds the next available cluster to the file.

- **View This Cluster** displays the contents of the next available cluster so you can examine the data that it contains to decide if you want to add the cluster to your file.

- **Scan For Contents** searches the unused data space on your hard disk for the search string you entered into the Scan For Contents option in the Disk menu from the main Undelete window. Any clusters that contain the text are added to the file.

- **Enter Cluster #** lets you add a specific cluster to the file and obviously requires you to know which cluster to add. Specify a single cluster by number. If that cluster is not available, the next free cluster will be used.

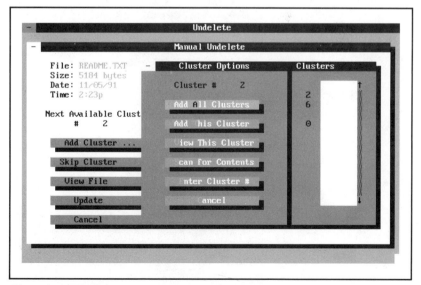

Figure 7.9: The Manual Undelete Add Clusters screen

- **Cancel** lets you change your mind and return to the Manual Undelete window.

The simplest way of finding the data for the file is to select Add All Clusters. Choose that option now. Undelete finds all the clusters that README.TXT occupied and lists them in the List of Added Clusters box. Before completing the recovery process by actually saving the file, you can examine the contents of these clusters or even remove or rearrange clusters.

VIEWING OR UNSELECTING FOUND CLUSTERS

Move the highlight to the first cluster in the List of Added Clusters display and choose View File to examine the contents of this cluster. You will see a display like the one shown in Figure 7.10, but remember that the cluster numbers may be different, depending on the type of disk you are using.

See Chapter 8 for a complete description of the View program.

Figure 7.10 shows the file contents as ASCII because README.TXT is a text file. If the file you are recovering is a program or

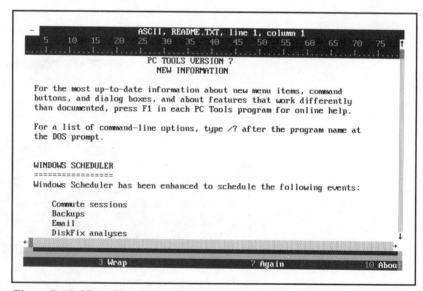

Figure 7.10: View File shows the contents of the first cluster in the README.TXT file

binary file, you will see the file's contents displayed in hexadecimal in the Binary viewer. Compare Figure 7.10 with Figure 7.6 to confirm that what you see is indeed the start of the README.TXT file.

You can move a cluster within the List of Added Clusters if you are unhappy with its current location. Move the highlight to the List of Added Clusters box and highlight the cluster you want to move; the scroll bar down the right side of the List of Added Clusters box becomes active. Use the mouse or the arrow keys to move the cluster and choose OK when the cluster is in its new location. Select View File once again to be certain that this new position is consistent with the rest of the file's contents. You can also use Delete in much the same way to remove a cluster from the file. Be careful with Delete because the highlighted cluster is deleted as soon as you choose the Delete button; there is no "Are You Sure?" dialog box.

Now that you are sure that you have chosen the correct clusters to undelete, use Update to complete the recovery process and undelete the file. This selection also restores the FAT data so that DOS can read the file again. The recovery of README.TXT is now complete.

RECOVERING PARTIAL FILES

Often, recovering files is not as straightforward as it was in the previous examples. DOS may overwrite all or part of the erased file with another file before you realize that you want to undelete the first file. Several factors determine whether recovery is possible, including the length of the new and the erased files, and the existence or nonexistence of the erased file's directory entry.

If the file has been partially overwritten, you may still be able to recover some portion of the file, but there is a good chance that its original directory entry will have been overwritten. If this is the case, you can use the Create a File option in the Advance Undelete submenu to create a new directory entry for use in the recovery process. You can now use Manual Undelete to search for clusters to add to the file; you cannot use automatic recovery techniques under these circumstances.

If you are recovering files from a badly damaged disk, you probably don't want to store the recovered clusters back on to the same disk. Select the Undelete To option from the File menu to save the file to another disk. The Drive Selection window opens for you to select the drive to undelete the file(s) to, and then asks you to enter details of the directory you want to use on this new disk. Enter the path for the directory to receive the undeleted files and choose OK. At the end of your recovery attempt, the clusters will be written to the drive you selected.

The single most important aspect of this kind of file recovery is how much you know about the contents of the erased file. If you know nothing about the file, it may be impossible to determine whether you have recovered it completely. If the file is a program file, running only the recovered portion can lead to unpredictable—and unpleasant—results. The only safe way to proceed in this case is to delete the partial file and restore the entire file from your backup set.

SEARCHING FOR LOST DATA

The Disk menu is not available if you are rescuing files on your network.

If you can't remember which directory an erased file was in, or if you are unable to recover the directory that it was in, you can use the selections in the Disk menu to locate clusters containing certain kinds of data. The Disk menu contains the following options:

- **Scan for Data Types** lets you search for normal text, Lotus 1-2-3 and Symphony, or dBASE data. Click on the appropriate box or boxes with the mouse. A horizontal bar indicates scan progress; choose Cancel to stop the search.

- **Scan for Contents** lets you enter a text search string. This search is not case-sensitive, so upper- and lowercase letters are not important. A percentage-complete display shows progress made by the search. The current cluster number and the number of matches found are shown below this display. Select Cancel to abandon the search. Each cluster that contains a match for the search string is given a unique name, CPS*nnnn*.FIL, where *nnnn* is a number starting at 0000. Use View File in the File menu to look at the contents of these clusters. When the search is complete, use Undelete from the File menu or use Manual Undelete to recover the file.

- **Scan for Lost Deleted Files** looks for inaccessible file names. Files may have been lost if the directories they were in were overwritten. Undelete first examines the SENTRY directory and the Delete Tracking file first, then it searches the rest of the disk for lost entries. Files found with this method retain their original names and have Lost File as their condition in the main Undelete window.

- **Set Scan Range** lets you specify the starting and ending cluster numbers for the search. The range of valid cluster numbers is shown in the Set Scan Range window. Use this selection to restrict the area of the disk that will be searched if you have an idea of where the missing file is located on the disk.

- **Continue Scan** resumes an interrupted search so you don't have to reenter the search criteria.

A good way of using the selections in the Disk menu is to restrict the search area first, then use one of the other selections in the menu to specify the data type you want to search for. To save any file fragments found in this way, use the Append to Existing File in the Advanced Undelete submenu. This selection adds these clusters to an existing file.

RECOVERING AN ERASED DIRECTORY

If a directory contains any files, you cannot delete it.

To recover files, you must sometimes first recover a directory. Undelete can recover subdirectories as well as files. Indeed, the process is exactly the same as recovering files. Once you have recovered the directory, all its files can be restored as long as they have not been overwritten.

DOS treats the removal of a directory as it treats the removal of a file. The first character is set to the same special character and the removed directory's entry remains in its parent directory (unseen, of course), just like a removed file's entry. Undelete identifies deleted directories by placing <dir> in the size column in the main Undelete window.

Let's look at a quick example to review this procedure briefly. Suppose you erased all of your Lotus 1-2-3 spreadsheets that were in the C drive's 123 directory, removed the directory, and then discovered that you hadn't intended to delete this directory. Undelete will not be able to find the spreadsheet files to restore them, since their names, starting cluster numbers, and file lengths are all stored in the 123 directory. You must recover the directory before you can recover the files. Select the parent directory that contained the 123 directory (the root directory in this example) and run Undelete. This displays the window shown in Figure 7.11.

Undelete asks for the first character of the file name, or uses information from Delete Sentry or Delete Tracking to complete the entry. After you have recovered the directory, you can proceed to recover the files that were in the 123 directory. Select each of the files individually, or use a group specification to include all the files if you want to recover all of them at the same time.

As you now know, file recovery is by no means certain. Many aspects of the process influence the success of any recovery attempt, most of which you have now examined. Although the file-recovery

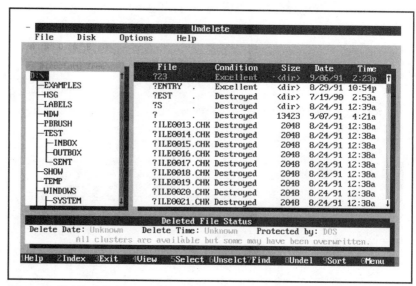

Figure 7.11: Undeleting a directory before recovering the files in that directory

process can be more difficult than was shown in this chapter (for example, recovering program files can be messy), you should have enough knowledge of the PC Tools Undelete program to attempt difficult recoveries on your own. Chances are that the file cannot be recovered if you cannot rescue it with PC Tools.

RECOVERING FROM HARD-DISK FORMATTING PROBLEMS

One of the most appalling prospects for a hard-disk user is accidentally reformatting a hard disk, an operation that destroys all data and programs. With Unformat, however, you can recover data from a reformatted hard disk.

USING MIRROR TO SAVE A COPY OF THE SYSTEM AREA

The FORMAT commands supplied with Compaq DOS up through Version 3.2, and AT&T's MS-DOS up through Version 3.1, actually erase all the data on the hard disk.

When you run the DOS FORMAT command on a hard disk, it clears the root directory and the file-allocation table (FAT) of all entries, but does not overwrite the data area on the disk. However, even though the data are still there, you normally have no way of accessing them.

Note that you cannot use Mirror and Unformat to recover data from floppy disks formatted with the DOS FORMAT command because this command overwrites all the data on the floppy.

Mirror makes copies of the FAT and the root directory of your hard disk and puts the copies into a file called MIRROR.FIL in the root directory. The size of this file is proportional to the number of files on your disk; for 25 megabytes of files, this file is approximately 50K.

If you have reformatted the disk and started to load programs onto it from your floppy-disk masters, you may have overwritten the MIRROR.FIL file, in which case complete recovery might be impossible.

You can only achieve complete recovery if the MIRROR.FIL file is absolutely accurate and up-to-date. You can run Mirror from the DOS command prompt, or install it into your AUTOEXEC.BAT file so that it runs every time you start your computer. Alternatively, you can run Mirror just before you turn your computer off to keep MIRROR.FIL up-to-date. To run Mirror from the DOS prompt, enter

MIRROR *drive parameter*

where *drive* is the letter of the drive you want Mirror to work on and *parameter* is one or more of the optional parameters you can use with Mirror. These optional parameters are

- **/1** specifies that Mirror should save only the latest FAT and root directory information in the MIRROR.FIL file.
- **/PARTN** makes a floppy-disk copy of your partition table information.

To have Mirror copy the system area of drive C, enter

MIRROR C:

Mirror normally keeps two copies of your FAT and root directory. Each time Mirror runs, it renames the old file as MIRROR.BAK and creates a new one called MIRROR.FIL that contains the latest information. This provides extra protection. If you want Mirror to keep only the latest information in a single file, enter

MIRROR C: /1

However, you should only do this when space on your hard disk is at a premium.

After Mirror creates these files, you cannot delete them by accident—they are read-only files. If you try and delete them with the DOS DEL command, you will see the **Access denied** message from DOS. The MIRROR.FIL file can also be used by DiskFix to repair serious damage to the data area of your disk.

If you run Unformat on a hard disk when the information in the Mirror file is not up-to-date, the recovery will be incomplete. If you added or deleted files and these changes were not stored in the Mirror file, Unformat will not know about them. If you deleted files, Unformat will try to assign data to them even though they no longer exist. Furthermore, data in files created since MIRROR.FIL was updated will not be recovered. After Unformat has done all it can to recover data with an outdated MIRROR.FIL file, run DiskFix to sort out any remaining file fragments.

Unlike PC Tools Version 6, Mirror is no longer used to install Delete Tracking; this is now done using Data Monitor, described in Chapter 9.

You can run Unformat from a network, but you cannot use it to unformat a network file server.

If your hard disk has been accidentally formatted with the DOS FORMAT command, insert the floppy disk that contains Unformat into drive A. This disk is labeled Data Recovery Utilities (disk 3 if you use 3½-inch disks, or disk 5 if you use 5¼-inch disks). You have to run Unformat from a floppy disk because your hard-disk copy of Unformat cannot be accessed. Do this immediately—before loading any backup copies of programs to the reformatted hard disk. If you try to load programs first, you may overwrite the MIRROR.FIL file, in which case a complete recovery will be impossible.

The Unformat program is automatic and easy to use; you don't even need to select options from menus, just choose from two or three simple alternatives shown on the screen. To run the program, select Unformat from the Recovery Tools menu in the PC Tools program, or type **UNFORMAT** at the DOS prompt. The program displays the Drive Selection window; choose the drive you want to unformat.

The next window asks whether you used Mirror to save MIRROR.FIL for the drive. Answer Yes if you did, or if you are not sure. If you answer No, the entire disk will be unformatted from scratch.

USING UNFORMAT TO RECOVER FILES AFTER AN ACCIDENTAL FORMAT

The combination of an up-to-date MIRROR.FIL file and a complete set of backup disks greatly increases the chances of a successful recovery of all the files on your reformatted hard disk. Be prepared.

The only time you should ever run Unformat is to recover your system after an accidental format.

If you previously ran Mirror regularly to save a copy of the system area of your disk, recovery after an accidental format will be fast and easy. The next window displays a warning screen that contains a list of the files in the root directory of the selected drive. These files will be lost if you unformat the disk. If you need to keep any of these files, select Cancel, copy the files to another drive, and then restart Unformat; otherwise choose OK.

Next, Unformat looks for a copy of the MIRROR.FIL file on the disk. If it finds a copy, it opens the Found MIRROR Files window, as Figure 7.12 shows. The window displays information for the most recent and also the previous Mirror files, and asks which one you want to use. If you want to use the most recent copy of the Mirror file to recover the contents of your disk, choose Last. If you want to use the previous file, select Prior; otherwise select Cancel. If damage occurred to your disk after the last MIRROR.FIL file was made,

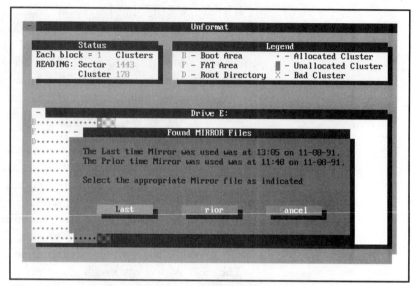

Figure 7.12: The Found MIRROR Files window displays the time and date
that the MIRROR.FIL was made

you may not always want to use the most current version of this file to
recover the hard disk. Obviously, any changes you made to the disk
after the MIRROR.FIL file was created will not be recovered.

The unformatting starts automatically, and progress is shown on
the Unformat drive map. Choose OK when you see the message
indicating that the unformatting of the drive is complete and you will
be returned to the PC Tools program or to DOS, depending on how
you originally started the Unformat program.

When Unformat completes the reconstruction of your disk, you
should run the DiskFix program as a final precaution; select the
Repair a Disk option in DiskFix to confirm that the FATs are consistent. DiskFix looks at the internal organization of your disk and
reports any remaining file fragments that it finds as unallocated clusters. If DiskFix reports errors on your disk, the errors are the result of
creating files after you last ran the Mirror utility. In other words, the
MIRROR.FIL file was not completely up-to-date.

RUNNING UNFORMAT
WITHOUT A MIRROR FILE

If you don't have a Mirror file on your hard disk, Unformat tries to recover your FAT and root directory using the information that it finds on the disk. This will be much slower and rather less reliable than recovery using a Mirror file.

In the Found MIRROR File dialog box, choose No. Unformat then shows a map of the disk and displays progress made during the unformatting process. When Unformat is finished, subdirectories will be renamed to names like SUBDIR.001, SUBDIR.002, etc. Use Directory Maintenance to rename these directories appropriately. All the files in the root directory will be missing; use the Manual Undelete techniques described earlier in this chapter to recover these files.

Unformat needs your input whenever it cannot find all the pieces of a fragmented file. Unformat asks whether it should truncate the file or delete it altogether. If you truncate the file, you can usually save at least a part of it. On the other hand, if you delete the file, you can always try the Undelete program to work on the file individually. The choice you make depends on how much you know about the contents of the file. Truncating a program file is downright dangerous and can have unpredictable results. Truncating a text file, in contrast, is much less hazardous and you *do* recover a portion of your file.

If Unformat does not ask any questions about a file, the file is probably intact and recovered.

Remember to run DiskFix to check for any remaining errors when Unformat has finished. Then check to see that all your files and directories are on the hard disk. Finally, copy any of the files you need for normal operation into the root directory. Be sure that AUTOEXEC-.BAT and CONFIG.SYS are both present. If they are not there, copy them to the root directory from your backup disks or tape.

USING THE EMERGENCY
SYSTEM RECOVERY DISK

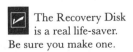
The Recovery Disk is a real life-saver. Be sure you make one.

As part of the installation of PC Tools described in Chapter 2, you made a Recovery Disk. You can use this recovery disk for the following purposes:

- Restoring the partition table and boot sector if this area of your hard disk is damaged

- Restoring your computer's CMOS data if you suffer from battery-life problems

- Booting your computer from a floppy disk in the event that the boot track on the hard disk is damaged and the disk refuses to start

- Booting your computer without loading the device drivers and memory-resident programs in CONFIG.SYS or AUTOEXEC.BAT

The Recovery Disk contains the following files:

- The DOS system files that make the Recovery Disk a bootable disk (the two hidden DOS files and COMMAND.COM)

- The file PARTNSAV.FIL, which contains information about your hard disk's partition table, boot track, and CMOS information

- A short simple CONFIG.SYS file containing appropriate values for FILES, BUFFERS, and STACKS; also, if your hard disk needs a particular device driver to start, Install copies the line that loads the driver into this CONFIG.SYS file and copies the device driver itself onto the Recovery Disk

- Rebuild, a program that can reload the information contained in PARTNSAV.FIL back into the appropriate areas in your system

- SYS.COM, a DOS program that lets you copy the DOS system files onto another disk, making it into a bootable disk

- Several of the PC Tools recovery programs, including Unformat, Undelete, and MI (see Chapter 20)

If you didn't make a Recovery Disk when you originally installed PC Tools, then take the time to make one now. The Recovery Disk can really be a life-saver; it is the disk that you wish you had the moment after you see the terrifying DOS message

Invalid drive specification

and your system refuses to boot from your hard disk.

To make a Recovery Disk:

1. Format a new floppy disk using the /S option (to copy the DOS system files onto the disk), or use PC Format to prepare the disk.

2. Place the original PC Tools Installation disk, Disk 1 (or a backup copy of Disk 1), in drive A and enter:

   INSTALL /RD

   at the DOS prompt. The /RD command-line option starts the Install program at the Recovery Disk dialog box; you do not have to repeat any of your previous installation of PC Tools.

3. Choose OK. (Demo shows you what is involved in making a Recovery Disk without actually creating one.)

4. In the Specify Installation Directory dialog box enter the drive letter and path name of the directory where PC Tools is installed on your system.

5. A warning dialog box opens, prompting you to remove the Install disk. Select OK and indicate the disk you usually boot your system from in the next window. This is so that certain files can be copied from the root directory of this disk onto the Recovery Disk.

6. You are asked to insert the blank formatted floppy disk you formatted in step 1. If you do not have a blank formatted disk ready, the Install program can use the DOS FORMAT command to make one. This process suspends the Install program and the screen commands you see are from the FORMAT program.

7. Choose OK after you have inserted the disk and you will see the Creating Recovery Disk window list several files as they are copied to the Recovery Disk.

You have now created a Recovery Disk for your system. Label the disk and keep it in a safe place.

If you change the configuration of your system at any time—add another hard disk, for example, or change to a different size floppy disk—make a new Recovery Disk immediately to record these changes to your system.

RECOVERING CMOS DATA

CMOS (pronounced *sea-moss*) is an acronym for complementary metal-oxide semiconductor. Many PCs use a small battery backed-up CMOS chip to store essential system parameters, including the date and time, and the number and type of the disks used on your system. This information is held in the CMOS chip when you turn your computer off at the end of a session, and the battery backup to the CMOS ensures that these vital data are preserved and available the next time you start your computer. CMOS devices are high speed, and consume very little power, so the battery in your computer may last for several years. Some computers even feature small recharging circuits so that the battery never needs replacing. However, if the battery voltage falls below a certain level, the data contained in the CMOS chip may be lost. You may see a message when you try to boot your computer like this:

CMOS Checksum Failure

indicating that the data held in CMOS is now inconsistent in some way. Or your computer may just refuse to boot up from the hard disk. You can reload these data using the Recovery Disk.

Place the Recovery Disk in drive A, and reboot your computer. At the DOS prompt, type **REBUILD** and enter **A** as the letter of the drive containing the Recovery Disk. You will see a screen like the one shown in Figure 7.13. This screen offers three selections; choose C to restore the CMOS data and then type **Y** to confirm that you want to reload them. When the data have been loaded into the CMOS, you can reboot your system; don't forget to remove the Recovery

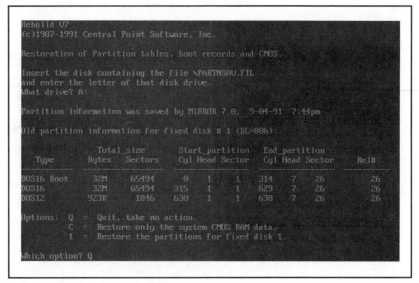

```
Rebuild V7
(c)1987-1991 Central Point Software, Inc.

Restoration of Partition tables, boot records and CMOS.

Insert the disk containing the file \PARTNSAV.FIL
and enter the letter of that disk drive.
What drive? A:

Partition information was saved by MIRROR 7.0, 9-04-91 7:44pm

Old partition information for fixed disk # 1 (DL=80h):

                  Total_size        Start_partition      End_partition
     Type        Bytes   Sectors   Cyl Head Sector     Cyl Head Sector       Rel#

DOS16 Boot        32M    65494      0    1    1         314   7   26           26
DOS16             32M    65494     315   1    1         629   7   26           26
DOS12            923K     1846     630   1    1         638   7   26           26

Options:  Q  =  Quit, take no action.
          C  =  Restore only the system CMOS RAM data.
          1  =  Restore the partitions for fixed disk 1.

Which option? Q
```

Figure 7.13: The Rebuild screen shows the time and date when the PARTN-
SAV.FILE was created

Disk from drive A. If CMOS-related problems persist on your system, you may need to change the battery.

REVIEWING PARTITION-TABLE INFORMATION

If you just want to look at the partition-table information on the Recovery Disk, place the Recovery Disk in drive A and type

A:REBUILD /L

at the DOS prompt. Rebuild lists all the partition-table information contained in PARTNSAV.FIL on the screen. There may be several screens of data here, so press Ctrl-S to pause the display so that you can read it. When you are ready, press Enter to continue scrolling.

RECOVERING THE PARTITION TABLE AND BOOT SECTOR

Every formatted hard disk contains at least one partition. Some people divide large disks into smaller partitions and may install

Restore the CMOS information before you restore the partition-table information and boot sector.

different operating systems in the separate partitions. The information on how your disk is partitioned is saved in a table on the hard disk. If this table is ever damaged or lost, DOS will not recognize the drive and you will see the Invalid drive specification error message when you try to access the drive or boot your system.

The boot sector is a small portion of all disks reserved for the DOS bootstrap loader program, a small machine-language program that loads the operating system. The boot sector also contains information that the computer needs to be able to read and write data to and from your hard disk. If the boot sector is ever damaged, your system will not be able to access your hard disk. You can restore both the partition-table information and the boot sector using the Recovery Disk.

Boot your computer using the Recovery Disk and choose A at the Recovery Disk menu to restore all partition tables for the drives on your system. Or, if you are having problems with only one drive, press 1 through 8 to indicate the drive to restore.

REPAIRING YOUR DISKS WITH DISKFIX

What do you do if your disk contains files that you cannot read? You use DiskFix to diagnose and fix the unreadable files.

DOS already provides the CHKDSK command for finding and fixing FAT errors and the RECOVER command for accessing files that contain bad sectors. However, DOS does not include programs that can find or fix physical errors on a floppy or hard disk. The diagnostic programs supplied with some computers may be able to locate errors, but they usually can't fix them. DiskFix finds and fixes any logical or high-level physical errors on your floppy or hard disks.

In fact, DiskFix finds and repairs most of the disk-related problems you are likely to encounter. It fixes bad or missing boot sectors and repairs a corrupted BPB (BIOS Parameter Block). In the area of file-structure problems, DiskFix can repair bad or corrupted FATs, reconstruct cross-linked files, and fix physical problems that prevent you from reading directories or files. This version of DiskFix can also undo or reverse any changes that were made during the repair process and return the disk to its original state.

DiskFix does not change the interleave factor on a floppy disk, as it is already optimized.

If you are having problems with your hard disk, run DiskFix from the original PC Tools floppy disk, or from the backup copy you made. DiskFix is on disk 5 if you use 5¼-inch disks or disk 3 if you use 3½-inch disks.

DiskFix can also analyze and then optimize the performance of your hard disk by changing the interleave factor.

This section does not go into great depth about the cause and nature of disk errors; suffice it to say, you should run DiskFix as soon as DOS reports a disk error.

Before you start DiskFix, remove any memory-resident programs that write to your disks, other than PC-Cache. Otherwise, you can run into problems with delayed writes to the disk while DiskFix is working.

You can run DiskFix from the DOS prompt, or from inside the PC Tools program. To run DiskFix from the DOS prompt, type **DISKFIX** with no parameters or switches. DiskFix opens a warning window with a message about using memory-resident programs at the same time as DiskFix. Choose OK and you will see the main DiskFix menu, as Figure 7.14 shows. There are six selections from the main DiskFix screen: Repair a Disk, Surface Scan, Revitalize a Disk, Undo a DiskFix Repair, Configure Options, and Advice. There is also an Exit button.

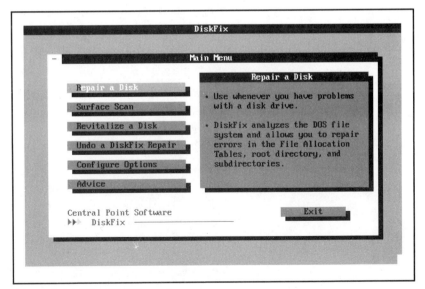

Figure 7.14: The DiskFix main menu

DIAGNOSING AND REPAIRING A DISK

Repair a Disk is probably the most important part of DiskFix; after choosing this selection, you are asked to choose a drive to work with from the Drive Selection window. Select OK to start the analysis.

DiskFix analyses the following areas of your disks:

Some of these DiskFix operations cannot be performed in Windows.

- Boot sector: DiskFix examines the boot sector to ensure it is not damaged.

- FAT integrity: DiskFix checks that both copies of the FAT are readable.

- FAT comparison: because the FAT is the index into your data and program files, DOS keeps two copies of the FAT on every disk. DiskFix compares both copies of the FAT to verify that they are identical. If there are read errors on the FAT, DiskFix uses the FAT with the fewest errors.

- Media descriptors: DiskFix checks the media descriptor byte to verify that the media-descriptor byte is correct for the type of disk in use on your system.

- FAT data analysis: both tables are checked to ensure they only contain legal DOS entries.

- Directory structure: DiskFix checks every directory entry for damage, such as illegal file names or file sizes.

- Cross-linked files: DiskFix checks for clusters that have been allocated the same space according to information contained in the FAT and tries to determine which files they actually belong to. This analysis can take several minutes.

- Lost clusters: these disk clusters are marked as "in use" by the FAT, but they are not actually allocated to a file anywhere. DiskFix converts lost clusters into files and writes them into the root directory.

If it finds an error, DiskFix describes the problem in an Error window and asks whether you want to fix the problem. Choose OK to make the repair or Cancel to move on to the next set of DiskFix tests. Figure 7.15 shows the DiskFix Error window for cross-linked files.

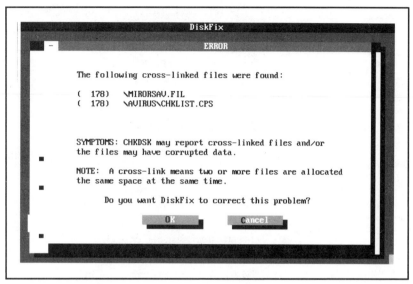

Figure 7.15: The DiskFix Error window details the problem and asks whether you want DiskFix to repair the damage

When DiskFix finds lost clusters, you have three recovery options. DiskFix asks you to choose one:

- **Save.** Use Save to convert the lost clusters into files in the root directory of the disk you are testing. Files are labeled PCT*nnnn*.FIX, where *nnnn* is a number starting at 0000. Converting the lost clusters into files means that you can examine the files to decide whether you want to keep them. If the lost cluster contains a directory, it is recovered and placed in the root directory, called LOST*nnnn*. All the original file names are intact; you can list them using the DOS DIR command.

- **Delete.** Use Delete to remove the lost clusters and recover the disk space they were occupying for use by other files.

- **Ignore.** If you choose Ignore, nothing is done to the lost clusters; they remain exactly as they were before the DiskFix analysis found them.

When the DiskFix analysis is complete, you can generate a report on your printer or send it to a file for later printing, listing the analyses performed and the steps taken to remedy any problems found. The report file is called DISKFIX.RPT. When the repairs are complete, you return to the main DiskFix window.

RUNNING A SURFACE SCAN

A cluster already marked as bad is not usually an indication of a deteriorating hard disk; most hard disks have a small number of clusters containing sectors that are marked as bad by the low-level formatting program.

Disk errors can take a variety of forms and DiskFix is especially helpful for isolating, and in some cases curing, problems associated with disk errors. Because DiskFix actually reads, or attempts to read, data from each cluster on the disk, it differs from the DOS CHKDSK command, which only tests for logical errors in the data contained in the FAT and directories. DiskFix can also repair and move damaged data to a safe location on the disk. Disk errors occur for a variety of reasons, usually at the most inconvenient moment; DiskFix is a good way to find and isolate them. Select Surface Scan from the main DiskFix window and choose the drive you want to scan from the Drive Selection window.

DiskFix reads and writes patterns to the disk to locate and repair problems. If you are scanning a hard disk, you also have the option of performing more complex read and write operations:

- **Read/Write Only** is the minimum level of testing for all types of disk. Both hard and floppy disks are tested, but no complex pattern testing is performed. Any sectors found to be defective are marked as bad in the FAT, so they will not be used by DOS for data storage in the future, and any data that were in a defective sector are relocated to a known good area of the disk. Because DiskFix actually reads and writes data to the disk, it corrects any problems associated with *track drift*, a problem produced when the disk heads drift out of alignment, making data harder and harder to read.

- **Minimum Pattern Testing** reads and writes 20 test patterns to the disk.

- **Average Pattern Testing** reads and writes 40 test patterns to the disk; this is the default setting.

- **Maximum Pattern Testing** reads and writes 80 test patterns to the disk and is the most comprehensive test in this test suite. Because it is the most rigorous test, it takes the longest to run; but it will also find the largest number of errors.

After you have chosen a pattern-testing option, the Surface Scan drive map appears on the screen and the scanning process starts running.

In the top window, the Surface Scan window, progress is indicated on the disk map. Untested disk sectors are shown as a light box and tested disk sectors as a dark box with a light center. You may see other symbols on the disk map, as follows:

- Uncorrectable errors are indicated by a *u.* An uppercase *U* indicates that the error was in a sector currently in use by a file; a lowercase *u* shows that the sector was not in use by a file. Any recoverable data in the area are moved to a known safe area on the disk and the bad area is marked as such in the FAT.

- Correctable errors are shown by a *c.* An uppercase *C* indicates that the sector is currently in use; a lowercase *c* means it is not in use.

- Bad clusters are indicated by an *X.*

- Disk defects found in an area of the disk not in use are shown by a number between 1 and 9, where the number indicates the number of defects found.

- The area being tested now is shown by the blinking character.

The Legend window at the lower left of the screen explains each of the characters seen on the screen during testing. The rightmost window, the Status window, shows the progress of the test as an analog display of percentage complete, along with the track number being tested and the current operation.

As the test progresses, if a data sector is found to be bad, but not in use by a file, DiskFix marks the sector as bad so that it will not be available for use by DOS in the future. If a data sector is bad and is being used by a file, the program copies the file to a known safe area on the disk, and the original sector is marked as bad. Select Cancel if you want to stop the scan. The program may not stop immediately, but may complete the current operation first. This is so that the program does not leave any loose ends to confuse other programs.

The errors that DiskFix locates can be listed in descending order of importance or seriousness, as follows:

1. Uncorrectable error found in a sector being used for a file.

2. Corrected error in a sector being used for a file.

3. Numbered media defect, where the number indicates the frequency of the defect.

4. Uncorrectable error in a sector not in use by a file.

5. Corrected error in a sector not in use by a file.

6. Cluster already marked as bad in the FAT.

If you see the number of errors detected by successive DiskFix analyses continue to increase rather than stay static, begin to suspect a problem with your disk or controller hardware. Make as complete a backup as you can of your important files while you still can.

DiskFix also generates a report suitable for printing or sending to a file for printing later. Figure 7.16 shows the first part of a DiskFix report. When the scan is complete, you should check the DISKFIX.LOG file to see whether any of the uncorrectable errors affected any of your files, so you can consider what action to take (such as reloading from your backups).

REVITALIZING A DISK

Sometime the address marks on a disk are so faint that they are difficult to read, and as a result DOS reports a read error whenever it tries to read that area of the disk. DiskFix reads the data in a different way, and so it can often read data that DOS cannot. In fact, DiskFix reads the data from the disk, reformats the disk, and rewrites the original data back onto the disk again.

STARTING SEVERAL TESTS Select Revitalize a Disk from the main DiskFix menu, choose the disk you want to work with from

```
                         PCTools DISKFIX
                           Version 7

                Status Report for logical drive B:
                      11/08/91 13:45:33
              -----------------------------------


    730,112 - bytes total disk space
    694,272 - bytes in 42 files and 1 directories
     35,840 - bytes available on disk

        512 - bytes in each sector
          1 - sector in DOS Boot record
          3 - sectors in each FAT (2 copies)
          7 - sectors in root directory (112 entries)
      1,440 - sectors in logical disk

        F9h - media descriptor
     12 bit - File Allocation Tables
      1,024 - bytes in each allocation unit (cluster)
          2 - sectors in each allocation unit (cluster)
        713 - total allocation units for data storage

   Logical Drive B: is accessed as bios disk 01Hex with:

          9 - sectors in each track
          2 - tracks in each cylinder (number of read/write heads)
         80 - cylinders on drive



                 AREAS TESTED AND RESULTS:

              PARTITION AND BOOT INFORMATION
              -----------------------------------
   Partition & Boot Information:      DISKFIX repaired errors found.


                    FILE ALLOCATION TABLES
              -----------------------------------
   Media descriptors:                 No errors were found
   FAT validity checks:               No errors were found


                    DIRECTORY STRUCTURE
              -----------------------------------
   Cross Linked Files:                DISKFIX repaired errors found.

       Cluster   143 x-linked in \06291816.M0A
       Cluster   143 x-linked in \06291841.M0A
       Cluster   548 x-linked in \09071123.B0A
       Cluster   548 x-linked in \06261635.N0A
       Cluster   563 x-linked in \KTEST.CFG
       Cluster   563 x-linked in \06270851.M0A
       Cluster   573 x-linked in \11281116.R0A
       Cluster   573 x-linked in \06270915.M0A

   Directory Structure and File System: DISKFIX repaired errors found.

       Found Allocation Error in file:  06291259.A0A
               Filesize is 13952 -- able to recover  7 clusters
```

Figure 7.16: The DiskFix report for a 720K floppy disk

```
Found Allocation Error in file:   KNEE    .CFG
          Filesize is 12436 -- able to recover  5 clusters

Found Allocation Error in file:   WRIST   .CFG
          Filesize is 12436 -- able to recover  10 clusters

Found Allocation Error in file:   SHLDR   .CFG
          Filesize is 12436 -- able to recover  7 clusters

Found Allocation Error in file:   06291417.B0A
          Filesize is 9728 -- able to recover  3 clusters

Found Allocation Error in file:   06291442.B0A
          Filesize is 10880 -- able to recover  5 clusters

Found Allocation Error in file:   06291504.B0A
          Filesize is 12416 -- able to recover  7 clusters

Found Allocation Error in file:   06291604.B0A
          Filesize is 10112 -- able to recover  4 clusters

Found Allocation Error in file:   06291625.B0A
          Filesize is 9728 -- able to recover  5 clusters

Found Allocation Error in file:   06291646.B0A
          Filesize is 14720 -- able to recover  13 clusters

Found Allocation Error in file:   07020859.D0A
          Filesize is 10112 -- able to recover  5 clusters

Found Allocation Error in file:   07020923.D0A
          Filesize is 9728 -- able to recover  4 clusters

Found Allocation Error in file:   07020953.D0A
          Filesize is 14336 -- able to recover  2 clusters

Found Allocation Error in file:   06270936.M0A
          Filesize is 14720 -- able to recover  14 clusters

Found Allocation Error in file:   06271059.H0A
          Filesize is 9728 -- able to recover  9 clusters

Found Allocation Error in file:   06271120.H0A
          Filesize is 11264 -- able to recover  10 clusters

Found Allocation Error in file:   06271148.H0A
          Filesize is 17024 -- able to recover  16 clusters

Found Allocation Error in file:   06290759.F0A
          Filesize is 19328 -- able to recover  18 clusters

Found Allocation Error in file:   06291210.A0A
          Filesize is 8960 -- able to recover  8 clusters

Found Allocation Error in file:   06291236.A0A
          Filesize is 8960 -- able to recover  8 clusters

Found Allocation Error in file:   06291259.A0A
          Filesize is 9216 -- able to recover  8 clusters


Lost Cluster Chains:                Errors found were ignored.
Media Surface Scan for defects:     No errors were found
```

Figure 7.16: The DiskFix report for a 720K floppy disk (continued)

the Drive Selection window, and you will see the Testing System Integrity window shown in Figure 7.17. DiskFix checks several aspects of your computer to ensure that the hardware can support the revitalization process, as follows:

When DiskFix starts, it turns PC-Cache off.

- Partition mapping: checks that the disk contains a valid DOS partition
- System RAM: tests that the memory needed for revitalization is working properly
- Controller: checks the disk controller
- Controller RAM: tests the disk on-board memory
- Timer system: makes sure your computer's timer is accurate
- Active caching: tests to see whether hardware or software disk caching is active

The progress of the test is shown as a horizontal bar graph on the screen below the list of tests. Choose OK to continue.

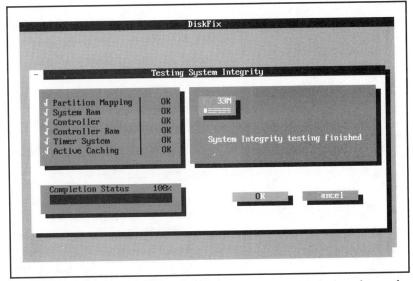

Figure 7.17: DiskFix checks several system parameters and displays the results in the Testing System Integrity window

This is the only set of tests that DiskFix performs when revitalizing a floppy disk. If you choose OK to continue, the next screen you see is the graphical display maintained during the revitalization process.

Because hard disks are rather more complex than floppy disks, several more tests must be done to evaluate the hard disk's timing characteristics and to check the physical parameters for the disk, before proceeding with the revitalization.

The next window you see is the Testing Disk Timing Characteristics window. The diagram in the center of the window represents a set of hard-disk platters and the associated read/write heads. As the timing tests are done, the diagram is animated, mimicking the movement of the disk heads. Three tests are run:

- **Track to Track** is the time it takes to move the disk heads from one track to the next.

- **Full Stroke** indicates the time it takes to move the disk heads from the first track on the disk (or partition) to the last.

- **Random Seek** calculates the time it takes to move the disk heads through a series of random movements.

All times are given in milliseconds. Select OK to continue to the last set of DiskFix tests, as shown in Figure 7.18.

Several tests are run to calculate the following:

- **Drive RPM** indicates the speed at which the disk is spinning, in rpm. Most disks revolve at about 3,600 rpm, but several high-performance disks revolve faster than this.

- **Inter-sector Angle** indicates the angular size of each sector.

- **Bits per Track** shows how many bits each track contains.

- **Data Encoding Type** identifies the actual format used to record data onto the disk from the most common types: MFM (Modified Frequency Modulation), RLL (Run Length Limited), or ARLL (Advanced Run Length Limited). RLL uses data-compression techniques to pack about 50 percent more data into the same disk space as MFM, and ARLL can store up to 100 percent more data than MFM.

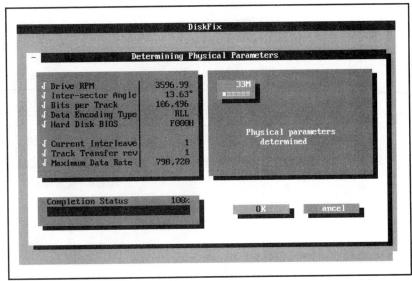

Figure 7.18: The Determining Physical Parameters window displays more information about your hard disk

- **Hard Disk BIOS** indicates the address used to access the hard disk.

- **Current Interleave** is the interleave factor in use on your hard disk. (More about the interleave factor below.)

- **Track Transfer rev** is the number of disk revolutions needed to read or write one track of data.

- **Maximum Data Rate** is the calculated maximum speed at which data can be transferred from the hard disk to the disk controller.

The interleave factor is described briefly in Chapter 2.

CHANGING THE INTERLEAVE FACTOR If your disk hardware passes all the previous tests, DiskFix next calculates the impact of different interleave factors and displays the results on the screen, as Figure 7.19 shows. The interleave factor is shown on the bottom of the graph against the calculated data-transfer rate on the left of the graph.

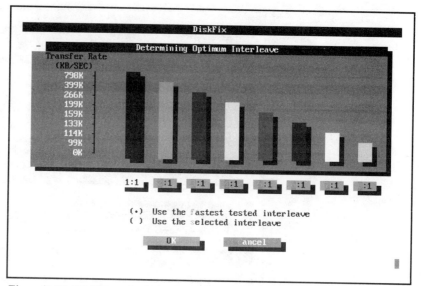

Figure 7.19: DiskFix calculates the optimum interleave factor for your system

Interleaving alternates hard-disk sectors in a pattern that increases the likelihood that when the computer is ready to read the next sector in numeric sequence, it will be the sector arriving at the head. For example, instead of being arranged on the disk in numerical order (1, 2, 3, 4,…) known as a 1:1 interleave, sectors might be arranged in a 3:1 interleave (1, 12, 7, 2, 13, 8, 3,…), in which consecutive sectors are separated by two other sectors. Figure 7.20 shows several different interleave patterns.

Interleaving thus speeds up disk access by reducing the amount of time spent waiting for the right sector to arrive at the head. Now DOS can read a sector and store the data in memory as the head passes over and ignores the next physical sector. By the time DOS is ready to read the disk again, the next logical sector is available. In this way, the performance of the disk and the layout of the sectors on the disk can be optimized.

Changing the interleave is a one-time operation, and before Disk-Fix it was a complex and time-consuming operation. First, you had to determine the optimum interleave by some method. Then you had to backup all your files from your hard disk, run a low-level format program such as Disk Manager or use Debug to access the low-level format

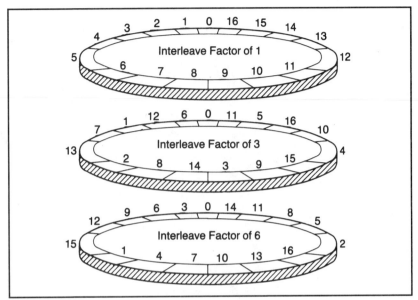

Figure 7.20: Different interleave patterns give different performance with the same hard disk and controller

firmware on your hard disk controller, and then run FDISK to partition the disk. Only after you used FORMAT to lay down a new boot track, root directory, and FAT, could you finally reload all your files and data back onto to your hard disk from the backup. DiskFix changes all that by performing a non-destructive, low-level format of your disk, changing the interleave at the same time.

If your disk was configured with the wrong interleave factor, your system may be running slower than the optimum. If your disk is already configured for the optimum interleave setting, there is no reason to change it; your disk system is working as fast as it can.

DiskFix shows both the current and the optimum interleave on the graph. The current setting is highlighted and the optimum setting is the tallest of the bars on the graph, the one giving the highest data-transfer rate. You can leave the interleave factor at the same setting, or you can change it if you wish. Fastest Tested Interleave is the default setting.

If your computer cannot display this interleave chart, DiskFix opens a dialog box telling you that the program cannot modify the interleave on your drive. DiskFix then continues to the pattern-testing portion of the program.

THE FINAL TESTS   During this final phase of the program, Disk-Fix performs several operations on your hard disk:

1. It reads the data from a track into memory.

2. It formats the track using the new interleave factor.

3. It writes a set of test patterns into each sector and rereads the data to verify that they are correct (you specify the intensity of these tests).

4. It writes the original data back onto the track.

The Pattern Testing selection screen is the same as the one used in the Surface Scan described earlier; choose from

• Read/Write Data—No Pattern Testing

• Minimum Pattern Testing

• Average Pattern Testing

• Maximum Pattern Testing

Choose the appropriate level of testing, then click on or choose OK. The more testing you do, the more secure you can feel about the integrity of your hard-disk system. When you have chosen the intensity of testing, you will see the drive-map display; this screen is similar to the drive map used in the Surface Scan analysis. The same characters are used in this display to indicate progress, and a small horizontal bar graph indicates percentage complete. This entire testing and reformatting process can take several hours, varying according to the size and speed of your disk system and the level of pattern testing you choose. Finally, DiskFix asks whether you want to generate a log report of the results of the revitalization. Select OK to make a printed report or to send the report to a file, or choose Skip to return to the main DiskFix window.

UNDOING DISKFIX REPAIRS

DiskFix contains a major advance over most disk-testing programs: the ability to reverse the repair process and remove any changes made during the repair cycle. The first time you encounter an error using DiskFix, the program asks whether you want to make a copy of the affected data before any changes are made. If you decide to save this information, make sure you save it to a floppy disk. DiskFix only asks once; if you decide not to save the data the first time, DiskFix does not ask again.

From the main DiskFix window, choose Undo a DiskFix Repair. Select the disk containing the original disk information and choose OK. DiskFix automatically restores the disk back to its original state; when it has finished, you return to the main DiskFix window.

CONFIGURING DISKFIX

To configure DiskFix for automatic operation, select Configure Options from the main DiskFix menu and you will see the screen shown in Figure 7.21. There are four main selections in this window:

- **Test Partition Information** tests the partition-table and boot-sector information before opening the main DiskFix window. This is a good check, and is the default setting for DiskFix.

- **Check Boot Sector for Viruses** tests the boot sector on your hard disk for the presence of a computer virus, and opens a message window if one is found. Several of the most insidious viruses attach themselves to the boot sector of the hard or floppy disk and therefore are loaded into memory each time you start your computer. Boot sector viruses often replace the original boot sector with their own code, so that the virus is always loaded into memory before anything else; once in memory, they can spread to other disks. This selection is also turned on by default.

- **Look for Mirror File** tells DiskFix to use the Mirror data file when determining which FAT has the fewest errors. Again, this is the default setting.

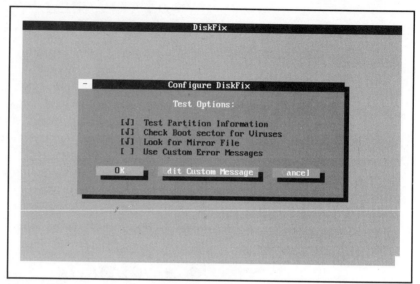

Figure 7.21: Make your selections in the Configure DiskFix window

- **Use Custom Error Messages** lets you use your own message when DiskFix finds a disk error rather than the built-in message.

If you are a network manager or are in charge of several computers in a department, you will find the Custom Message selection very useful. You can enter a message here that DiskFix displays if the program finds an error on the disk. For instance, you might not want your users to proceed with repairs on their own, so you could enter a message including your name, department, and telephone number, as shown in Figure 7.22. After you enter the text, select OK to return to the main DiskFix window. Now when DiskFix locates a disk problem that requires a decision by the user, your custom message is displayed.

GETTING DISKFIX ADVICE

DiskFix differs from the other PC Tools programs in that it doesn't have the same kind of online help available in the main window from a function key. However, it does have the Advice menu selection.

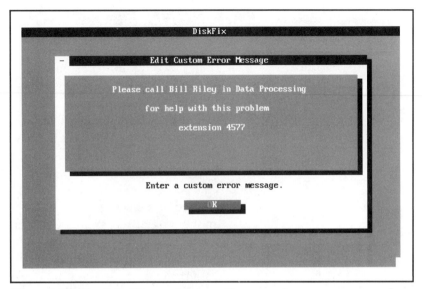

Figure 7.22: Use Edit Custom Message if you are the system manager for a group of computers

Advice works like context-sensitive help on DOS error messages, divided into the three main groups of General Problems, DOS Error Messages, and CHKDSK Error Messages. Advice is described in full in Chapter 19.

USING DISKFIX FROM THE DOS COMMAND LINE

You can run DiskFix from the DOS prompt in several different ways. To bypass the Drive Selection window, include the drive letter for analysis on the command line by typing

DISKFIX *d***:**

where *d* represents the drive you want to analyze. If you are using DiskFix as a diagnostic tool to test your disk drive, you can run a Surface Scan on drive C by typing

DISKFIX C: /SCAN

REPAIRING 1-2-3, SYMPHONY, AND dBASE FILES WITH FILE FIX

File Fix does not use menus; it has only two function keys on the message line: F1 for Help and F3 for Quit.

The File Fix program finds and fixes problems in Lotus 1-2-3, Symphony, and dBASE data files, recovering as much data as possible from the damaged file. File Fix writes this information into a new file. The original damaged file is always left intact so that you can run File Fix again using different settings. File Fix can often repair data files automatically, although occasionally the program may need your help with complex recovery operations involving dBASE file headers. File Fix can also reconstruct data files that have been collapsed or zapped by the dBASE ZAP command.

Use the Undelete program first if you want to recover erased files; then run File Fix as the second stage of the recovery process.

To run the program from the PC Tools program menu, select File Fix; from the DOS command line, type **FILEFIX**. The opening screen is shown in Figure 7.23. Select the type of file you want to repair from the three options on the screen.

You can choose from among the following selections:

- Choose **1-2-3** if you use Lotus 1-2-3 (Version 1, 1A, 2, or 3) or another program that creates Lotus-compatible files.

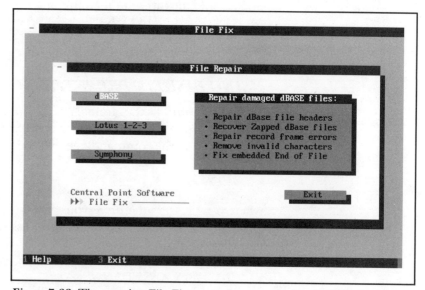

Figure 7.23: The opening File Fix screen lets you choose the file type to work with

File Fix cannot recover password-protected files made by Lotus 1-2-3 version 3.*x* because of the data-encryption scheme used.

- Choose **Symphony** if you use Lotus Symphony (Version 1.0 or 1.1).

- Choose **dBASE** if you use dBASE (III, III+, or IV), Fox-Base, Clipper, or any other program that creates dBASE-compatible files.

REPAIRING SPREADSHEET FILES

Select 1-2-3 or Symphony if you want to repair a spreadsheet file. In the following example, we will use a Lotus 1-2-3 file called GWSCREEN.WK1.

Select the 1-2-3 box and press Enter or click on the box with the mouse. Next, you will see the Select File To Fix screen.

If necessary, choose a different drive or directory. File Fix finds the files it can repair by searching for the appropriate file name extension. Enter a file name or select one from the list in the File list. Figure 7.24 shows the 1-2-3 Repair Options window.

After you have chosen the repair mode, File Fix repairs GWSCREEN.WK1 and writes the recovered information into a file

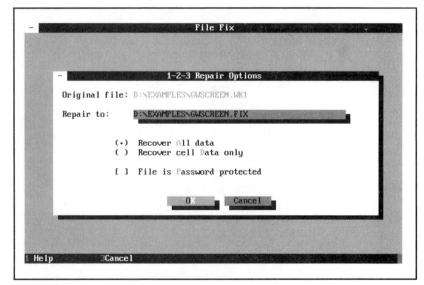

Figure 7.24: The 1-2-3 Repair Options screen

called GWSCREEN.FIX. Select one of the following modes:

- **Recover All Data.** Always try this selection first. It usually recovers the largest amount of data, including information about the spreadsheet cell ranges, column widths, and headers and footers.

- **Recover Cell Data Only.** Use this mode if the Recover All Data operation fails; you can usually recover the cell data from the spreadsheet.

- **File is Password Protected.** Select this option if the file is protected by a password in Lotus 1-2-3 or Symphony. File Fix cannot recover password-protected files made by Lotus 1-2-3 Version 3, because of the complex nature of the file-encryption scheme.

Remember that Lotus passwords are case-sensitive; you must type in the password using the right mix of upper- and lowercase letters.

The program first checks the file, then opens a window to report the percentage of the file that has been corrected. Figure 7.25 shows this screen for the GWSCREEN.WK1 file. Finally, File Fix displays

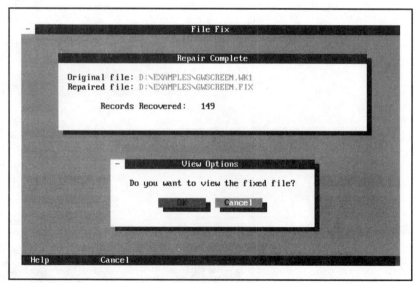

Figure 7.25: The Repair Complete window shows the number of bytes recovered

a window showing the repair statistics and asks whether you want to send a repair-report to your printer or to a file for later printing. In this case the repair-report file is called GWSCREEN.RPT.

You can make a quick check of the file if you select the View button to open the View Program. This program is described in detail in Chapter 8. Finally, check the repaired file yourself by trying to load the file into the appropriate application program—Lotus 1-2-3 or Symphony.

The report on the recovery operation contains details of the recovery operation, as well as a list of all the cells and cell types in the spreadsheet. Figure 7.26 shows the beginning of the report about the GWSCREEN.WK1 file after it was recovered. The report lists all the information recovered, along with its location in the file, length, data type, and contents. The message ∗∗∗ **DAMAGED AREA** ∗∗∗ indicates an area of the file where you will have to reenter the data.

If the attempt to recover all the data was unsuccessful, select the second mode on the 1-2-3 Repair Options screen, Recover Cell Data Only. This time, enter a different file name for the repaired file. Even if both rescue operations are not completely successful, you might be able to combine the results and reconstruct the data by hand.

REPAIRING dBASE FILES

File Fix can repair files made by dBASE II, III, III+, and IV, as well as files that use the dBASE format, such as files made by the PC Tools Desktop Database. To repair a dBASE file, select dBASE from the main File Fix menu, then select the file you want to work with from the Select File to Fix window.

File Fix can also recover files that have been deleted by the dBASE ZAP command. ZAP permanently removes all the records from an active database, but it leaves the database structure intact. It has the same effect as the dBASE commands DELETE ALL followed by PACK, but it is much faster. ZAP removes records whether they were previously marked for deletion or not.

```
                    Central Point Software File Fix

     File that was repaired:  D:\EXAMPLES\GWSCREEN.WK1
     The repaired file is:    D:\EXAMPLES\GWSCREEN.FIX
     Time of repair:          Fri Nov 08 14:00:11 1991


     Repair mode: Repairing all data

       Loc  Rec Type      Lgth  Record Description/Contents
         1  BOF              2  Version is WK1 Or WR1
         7  DIMENSIONS       8
        19  CPI             54
        77  CALCCOUNT        1
        82  CALCMODE         1
        87  CALCORDER        1
        92  SPLIT            1
        97  SYNC             1
       102  *******          6                    ***   DAMAGED AREA  ***
       108  LABELFMT         1
       113  *******         25                    ***   DAMAGED AREA  ***
       138  COLW             3  H =     8
       145  COLW             3  I =     2
       152  HIDCOL          32
       188  ADD-IN APL      10
       202  ADD-IN APL      10
       216  NRANGE          25  J47..J47      : "N_MOLES"
       245  NRANGE          25  J46..J46      : "R_FACTOR"
       274  TABLE           25
       303  QRANGE          25
       332  PRANGE           8
       344  FORMAT           1
       349  FRANGE           8
       361  SRANGE           8
       373  KRANGE1          9
       386  KRANGE2          9
       399  RRANGES         25
       428  MRANGES         40
       472  DRANGE          16
       492  PARSE           16
       512  PROTECT          1
       517  FOOTER         242
       763  HEADER         242
      1009  SETUP           40
      1053  MARGINS         10
      1067  LABELFMT         1
      1072  TITLES          16
      1092  *******        439                    ***   DAMAGED AREA  ***
      1531  EOF              0
      1535  LABEL           36  K42: '    Volume of an Ideal Gas at
      1575  LABEL           40  R42: 'C11: +$R_FACTOR*$N_MOLES*C$9/$A11
      1619  LABEL           40  K43: 'Varying Temperatures and Pressure
```

Figure 7.26: Part of the GWSCREEN.RPT report on the GWSCREEN.WK1
file after its recovery

To recover a dBASE file, you have a choice of the following repair
modes:

- **Automatic Recovery.** If your files are not badly corrupted,
  this option is probably all you need to use. It is a completely hands-off repair operation: File Fix examines the

file, extracts all the valid data, and writes those data into the repaired file. Try this option first.

- **Display Damaged Records Before Fixing.** If the Automatic Recovery mode fails to recover essential records, try this selection. File Fix starts the recovery in automatic mode until it finds a damaged record. You can then view and manually repair the record yourself.

- **Display Each Record.** This last mode lets you review every record before it is written to the fixed file. You can choose to accept, reject, or manually repair each of the records. At any point in the recovery, you can select Mode to change to another repair mode. Display Each Record is more time consuming than the other modes, but it is essential for badly corrupted databases.

Three other check boxes appear on the Repair dBASE Options screen. These offer further options in the repair process:

- **Check Data Alignment.** This selection automatically fixes misaligned data in the database as the repair proceeds. This option is on by default; if you turn it off, File Fix runs faster, but it doesn't check data alignment.

- **Check for Binary and Graphics Characters.** This selection checks the contents of the file for graphics characters. Turn this option on unless you are repairing a file that contains graphics characters.

- **File was Created with Clipper.** Use this selection only if the database was created by Clipper; otherwise, leave this selection off.

After you have made your selections from this screen, choose OK to start the repair. In this next example, we will work with the file PHOTO.DBF. In Figure 7.27, you can see that the recovery process has started and that PHOTO.DBF will be repaired as the file PHOTO.FIX.

In a dBASE file, the file header contains vital information concerning the layout of the rest of the file, including the version of

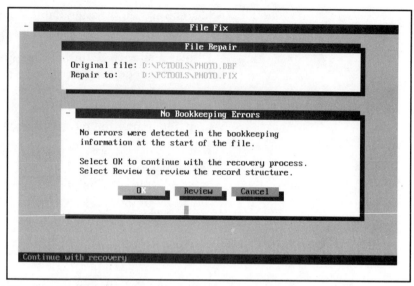

Figure 7.27: The File Repair screen shows that the header information is
intact

dBASE that made the file and the names, order, lengths, and types of
the fields in the database file. The message on the screen in Figure 7.26 indicates that this file header is intact. Choose Review to
examine the database field definitions, or select OK to continue with
the automatic recovery process.

Figure 7.28 shows the final Repairing dBASE File screen for the file
PHOTO.DBF. There were 1,032 bytes of the file recovered, and no
data were lost from the file. Select OK if you want to view the file, or
Cancel to move to the Report Options window. The repair report is
written to a file called PHOTO.RPT, in this case, and the report summarizes the repair options.

REPAIRING A DAMAGED FILE HEADER If the dBASE file
header is damaged, File Fix asks for your help in reconstructing the
data. The exact sequence of messages here depends to some extent on
how badly damaged the file header is. You may see the message:

> The file is missing its version information. What version of dBASE
> do you use?

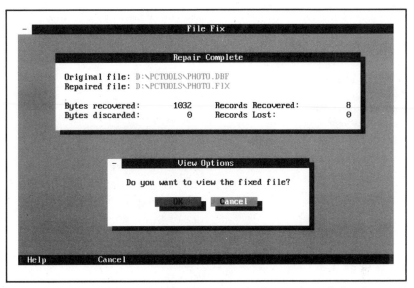

Figure 7.28: The Repair dBASE File screen indicates that all the data was recovered from the file

Select your version. Next, you may see the File Header Damaged or Missing window, showing the message:

> **The bookkeeping information at the start of the file is severely damaged or missing.**
>
> **Your assistance is required to reconstruct the database field definitions.**

Select OK to proceed with the recovery, and in the next screen select the method you want to use to rebuild the file header. There are two ways that you can make a repair to the database structure:

- **Import the Correct Structure from Another dBASE File.** If the dBASE header information is badly damaged, the easiest way to repair it is to import the header information from another undamaged file that shares the same database structure. Use a backup version of the same file for this, or load an earlier version of the file with the same structure. Choose this selection first.

- **Edit the Existing Structure.** If you cannot import a header from an undamaged file, choose this option to make the corrections by hand.

Editing the file consists of three steps:

Use a database printout, if you have one, as an aid while you manually reconstruct the file structure.

1. Find the start of the data. Use the left and right arrow keys to move the data from left to right, or enter the position directly into the File Position box. You might have to skip past some of the damaged data. Be sure that the first character of good data from the first field is aligned with the left side of the box. Also, be sure you are using real data and not one of the field names.

2. Establish the size of the record. For this part of the process, use the left and right arrows to increase or decrease the record size. Align the first character of data from the first field of every record with the left side of the box.

3. Review and, if necessary, edit the record structure. After you have aligned everything, you can edit the specific field names and their data types. Press the Insert key to insert new fields, the Delete key to remove fields, and the space-bar to *tag* fields. After you have tagged a field, use the up and down arrows to move it to its new position.

Repairing a dBASE file is a rather complex process; the following example will help to clarify the procedure.

A SAMPLE dBASE FILE REPAIR Let's assume that the file ADDRESS.DBF has a problem and dBASE has refused to process the file. Start File Fix, choose the dBASE option, and select the ADDRESS.DBF file there. Choose Automatic Recovery from the dBASE Repair Options window and select the Check Data Alignment, Check for Binary, and Graphics Characters options. Click on OK to continue. The next window alerts you that the file header is damaged because the version information is missing. Select the appropriate dBASE version, then click OK. The next window confirms that the file header is damaged or missing and that File Fix needs your help in rebuilding the header information. You can choose to import a new header from another file or edit the current one by hand.

If you choose to correct the data by hand, choose Edit the Existing Structure, which displays the screen shown in Figure 7.29.

In this example, we move the data in the central window with the left or right arrow keys until the first character of the word *Michael* is at the extreme left side of the window. This marks the beginning of the data in the record. You might have to move past some corrupted data first. In the next dialog box, as Figure 7.30 shows, make sure the record size is correct; use the arrow keys to change the size of the record. At this point, all the data in the records should be aligned correctly in neat columns.

The next screen lets you change the sizes of the individual fields. Again, use the arrow keys to adjust the data if necessary. If you make a mistake choosing the start of the data record, select the Revise button to redisplay the screen shown in Figure 7.28 so that you can establish a new starting position. In the Edit Record Structure window, you can edit the actual field name; specify the field type as

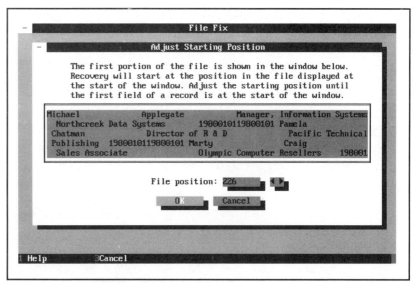

Figure 7.29: The header of the ADDRESS.DBF file is displayed in the central window

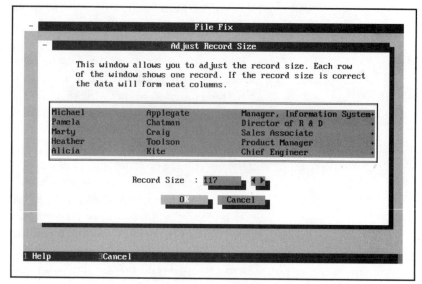

Figure 7.30: Now all the data are aligned with the left side of the window

character, numeric, logical, date, or memo; change the field width; and, if the field is numeric, alter the number of decimal places.

Use the Edit screen to change any of the field characteristics to their correct settings; then choose OK to continue with the repair. File Fix proceeds with the recovery of the rest of the file. If you are still uncertain about the file structure, select Cancel to return to the editing screens.

If you see the following messages on the screen:

The Sum of the Field Sizes Does Not Agree

or

The Field Definitions Do Not Agree

a conflict exists between the file header and the actual data in the file. You will have to repeat the previous editing steps until File Fix no longer displays these messages.

File Fix uses a percentage-complete display to show the recovery taking place. Finally, it displays a summary screen that lists the amount of data recovered and the number of bytes discarded.

Choose View if you want to review the contents of the file or Cancel to move to the Report Options window. Here you can choose to send the report to the printer or to a file for later printing. Cancel returns you to the main File Fix window.

To leave File Fix, select the Exit box on the opening screen or press Escape. Both return you to the DOS prompt.

LOADING A FILE TO FIX FROM THE DOS PROMPT

To load a file in File Fix directly from the DOS prompt, simply type

FILEFIX *file name*

in which *file name* is the file you want to repair. File Fix skips the opening screens when you load it with a file name. Since File Fix uses the file-name extension to determine which application program created it, it knows how to correct the problems in the file.

CHAPTER

8

Managing Files, Directories,
and Hardware with
the System Tools

This chapter describes all the system tools in the PC Tools package, including Compress, FileFind, System Information, Directory Maintenance, View, PC-Cache, and PC Format.

USING COMPRESS

Before using the disk-optimizing program called Compress, you should understand a little of how DOS organizes the file system on your disk. Files are written to the disk in groups of sectors called clusters. When you write a short file to disk, it occupies the first available cluster. When you write another short file to the same disk, this file occupies the next available cluster. Then, if you modify the first file by increasing its size above that of one cluster and save it under the same file name, DOS cannot push the second file up the disk to make room for the larger first file. Instead DOS *fragments* this file by splitting it into two pieces, one occupying the first cluster and one occupying the third cluster. This is the way that DOS was designed to work.

The potential problem with fragmentation is that the disk heads have to move to different locations on the disk to read or write to a fragmented file. This takes more time than reading the same file from a series of consecutive clusters. By reducing or eliminating file fragmentation, you can restore the performance of your disk and minimize any future degradation in speed.

Another benefit of unfragmenting a disk is that DOS is less likely to fragment files that you subsequently add to your disk. If you delete and then try to unerase any of these added files, your chances of success will be higher because unfragmented files are usually easier to unerase. On the other hand, unfragmenting, or *optimizing,* your disk will probably make it impossible to recover any files that were deleted before the optimization. The reason for this is that Compress "moves" data by rewriting them at a new location, and will probably write over any erased files in the process.

To remove the effects of file fragmentation, all the files on the disk must be rearranged to consist of contiguous clusters. You can do this yourself by copying all the files and directories to backup disks, reformatting the hard disk, and reloading all the files onto the hard disk,

If you have deleted files on the disk that you want to try to restore, you must rescue them before running Compress. Compress will almost always write over the deleted files at some point in its operation, practically eliminating the chances of a successful file recovery.

If there are erased files on the disk that you want to recover, do so before you unfragment the disk.

but that is a tremendous amount of tedious work. It is much easier to use a program designed for eliminating file fragmentation—the Compress program.

PRECAUTIONS TO TAKE

Before you make Compress reorganize the files on your hard disk, you must take a couple of precautions:

- Make a complete backup of your hard disk in case there is an incompatibility between your system and Compress. Problems can occur because of the enormous number of potential combinations of hard disks and disk controllers.
- Make sure that you turn off and disable any memory-resident software that might access the disk while Compress is running. For example, some programs save your work to the hard disk automatically at set time intervals. You must turn off this type of software.

If you are using the DOS FASTOPEN utility, or any other disk buffering program, you will probably have to reboot your computer after running Compress. This is because Compress changes directory and file locations when it optimizes the disk, and FASTOPEN may not find the files where it expects to. If you see the message

File not found

after running Compress, reboot your PC and try again.

Before starting Compress, you should run the DOS CHKDSK command to remove any lost clusters, and then run PC Tools Disk-Fix to find and fix any bad sectors on your disk. This will give Compress a clean system to work with.

UNFRAGMENTING YOUR HARD DISK

Select Compress from the list of programs in the System Tools menu in PC Shell, or type:

COMPRESS

Do not turn your computer off while Compress is running. If you must interrupt Compress, do so by pressing Escape; Compress may continue running until it finds a safe and convenient place to stop.

Compress should not be run under Windows, or any other multitasking system. Doing so will probably result in lost data. If you try to run Compress from Windows, you will see the message **Compress cannot be run from within a multitasking environment**.

at the DOS prompt. The program starts, performs a short analysis, and displays the window shown in Figure 8.1.

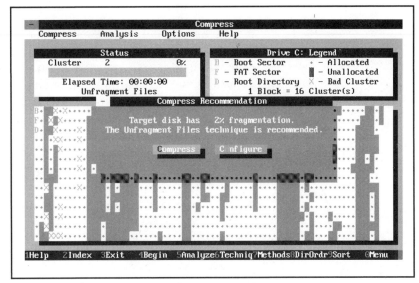

Figure 8.1: The Compress opening window

Compress does not run on a Novell NetWare file server or on any networked drive.

In Figure 8.1, Compress reports the fragmentation for the target disk and recommends a specific technique to remedy the situation. In this window, you can select Compress to proceed with the unfragmentation, or select Configure if you want to alter the unfragmentation parameters or work with a different disk drive. Select Configure so that we can look at the different settings available. The Options menu is automatically opened. The Legend box at the top right of the main Compress window defines the graphics characters used in the display, as follows:

- **Boot Sector** represents the boot sector on the disk.
- **FAT Sector** indicates the area occupied by the two FATS.
- **Root Directory** shows the space on the disk occupied by the root directory.
- **Allocated** designates the area of the disk occupied by files. It represents all the directories and files in the data area of the disk.

- **Unallocated** represents the area of the disk not in use by files. Compress can collect all the unallocated space on the disk into one single large piece at the end of the file area on the disk.

- **Bad Cluster** represents any bad blocks on the disk.

Depending on the size of the disk you are working with, each character represents a specific amount of disk space.

The Status box at the top left of the main window displays Compress's progress after you start the optimization. The current cluster number and the percentage-complete value are shown as numbers, along with the elapsed time and the optimization type selected. The horizontal bar indicates the percentage of the operation that has been completed in an analog format.

Several shortcut function keys are shown on the message bar at the bottom of the screen.

CHOOSING THE RIGHT OPTIMIZATION METHOD

Select Compression Technique (F6) from the Options menu to open the Choose Compression Technique window. The options are as follows:

Choose the method that is best suited to your disk and the way you work with your system; you don't have to use the same method every time.

- **Optimize Directories** moves directories but does not move any files. Files are not unfragmented and free space is not consolidated. Use Directory Optimization if you have added or removed directories.

- **Optimize Free Space** consolidates the free space on your disk into one single large area, but does not optimize any of the files on your system. Use this selection if you want to create a large area of free space before you install a new software package.

- **Unfragment Files** unfragments files, but it does not consolidate the free space; gaps may remain between your files. This selection does not move any of your directories.

- **Full Optimization** unfragments your files *and* collects all the free space in one place on your disk. It will give the greatest performance increase of any of the compression techniques, but it is also the slowest method because of all the work it has to do.

- **Full Optimization with Clear** does everything that Full Optimization does, but it also erases all data in the unused sectors. Recover any erased files before selecting this option, since you will not be able to recover them afterwards.

- **File Sort** rearranges the layout of files in your directories without doing any optimization. Files are sorted according to the choices you make with File Sort Options; these choices are described under the next section.

Next, choose the Ordering Methods (F7) selection from the Options menu to specify where you want your files and directories placed on the disk during the optimization. Choose from the following:

- **Standard** puts your directories at the beginning of the disk, followed by your files placed in any order. This makes Compress run faster. You can define the directory order, but if you don't, Compress uses the same sequence in your PATH statement.

Putting program files near the outer edge of the disk will help prevent future fragmentation.

- **File Placement** places directories first, in the order that you specify, followed by the files you specified using the Files to Place First command (mentioned next under "Configuring Compress"). The default is to place .EXE and .COM files first.

- **Directories First** places your directories first, followed by all files arranged by directory. This means that all the files in any given subdirectory will be kept together. This is a good selection for optimizing hard-disk performance, as data and program overlay files are kept close together.

- **Directories with Files** positions each subdirectory just before its files. Use this method if you tend to add and delete entire directories rather than single files.

CONFIGURING COMPRESS

You can use the next four selections in the Options menu to refine the directory and file choices you made when you chose a compression technique and an ordering method:

Directory Order (F8) is the first selection. It lets you choose the order in which Compress arranges the directories on your disk. You make your selections by working with the Directory Ordering window. The window is divided into two parts: the left side shows all the directories on your disk and the right side shows the sequence in which the directories are arranged. The default directory order is taken from the PATH command in your AUTOEXEC.BAT file. Press Tab and Shift-Tab to move from window to window, or click on one of the windows with the mouse to make it active. There are several buttons you can click to organize your directories:

- **Add.** First highlight a directory in the left part of the window, then choose Add to place the directory in the correct place in the right window.

- **Delete.** Once you have configured your directories, you can use Delete to remove them from the list. Position the highlight over a directory and select Delete to remove it from this list. This selection does not remove the directory from your hard disk.

- **Move.** Use Move to change the directory order. Place the highlight over the directory you want to move, select Move, then reposition the directory in its new location.

- **Cancel.** Select Cancel if you change your mind.

- **OK.** When you have arranged all your directories, select OK to return to the main Compress window.

Files to Place First lets you choose the files to place at the front or outer edge of the disk. Use this selection to place program files, which do not normally increase in size, close to the FAT. The first time this window opens, it contains two file specifications for .EXE and .COM files. You can add or remove files, and you can use the DOS wildcard characters in your file names. Position your data files, which *do* change in size, after your program files. This arrangement avoids future file fragmentation by preventing space from opening up near the front, or outer edge, of the disk. Use Delete to remove files from the list.

Unmovable Files: Compress will not move files or directories that have either the hidden or the system bit set in their attribute byte. These are often used as part of a copy-protection scheme, and Compress therefore does not move them. This window only holds up to ten entries, but you can use the DOS wildcard characters to extend protection to more than ten files.

File Sort Options (F9) specifies the order in which you want your files arranged if you chose File Sort from the Compression Techniques menu. You can sort by date/time, name, extension, or size—and the sort can be ascending or descending. You can also opt for no sorting.

Print Report, the last selection in the Options menu, makes a report to the printer or to a disk file called COMPRESS.RPT. You must choose to make a report before starting the optimization. The report details how long the optimization took, the options you selected, and the number of used, unused, and bad clusters on the disk. If you want to write the report to a file, you must send it to a disk other than the one you are compressing.

RUNNING COMPRESS

Before running Compress, you can look at the amount and distribution of file fragmentation with the selections in the Analysis menu. To see a report on the disk, choose Disk Statistics and you will see a report like the one shown in Figure 8.2.

If the two copies of the FAT do not match, run DiskFix.

Figure 8.2 indicates that the two copies of the FAT agree, and that 12,093 clusters are in use by files 4,240 are available for use, and no clusters are marked as bad. There are 848 files on the disk, 80 of them are fragmented, which gives a fragmentation percentage of one percent. The number of non-contiguous free-space areas indicates how the unallocated free space on the disk is distributed. This number should be kept as small as possible so that the free space exists in a small number of large pieces, rather than a large number of small pieces.

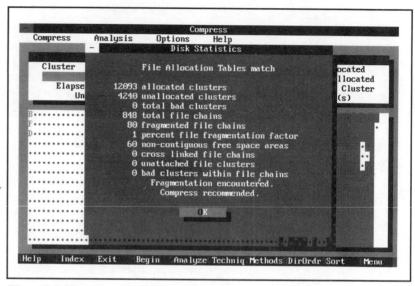

Figure 8.2: Compress Disk Statistics report for a hard disk

To look at the individual files on your disk in detail, choose File Fragmentation Analysis from the Analysis menu. Figure 8.3 shows a display for the PCTOOLS directory on a hard disk. The left side of the window shows all the directories on this hard disk and the right side of the window shows the files contained in the highlighted directory. Files are listed in the order in which they occur in the directory, along with the number of clusters in the file and the number of areas into which the file is divided. An unfragmented file shows a 1 in this column. A percentage-fragmented figure is also shown for each file. You can scroll through both directories and files in this window, use Tab and Shift-Tab to move between the windows, or click on the window you want to make active.

Each of the allocated block symbols in the main Compress window may represent more than one file; some may represent many files. Look at this level of detail by selecting Show Files in Each Map Block from the Analysis menu. A blinking cursor appears in the top-left corner of the disk-map display. Use the arrow keys or the mouse to position this blinking cursor on the area of interest on the disk map. Press Enter or click the mouse to open the Show Files in Each Map Block window as shown in Figure 8.4.

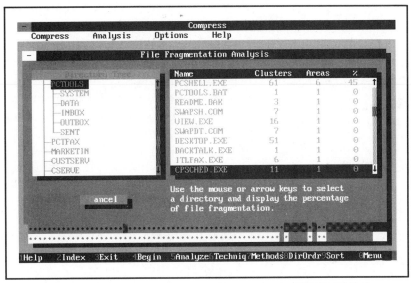

Figure 8.3: File Fragmentation Analysis display for the PCTOOLS directory
on a hard disk

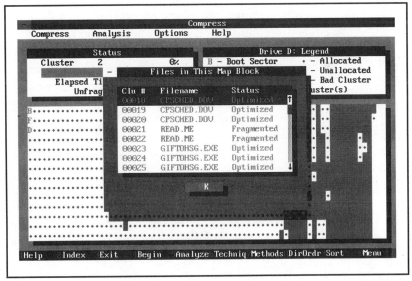

Figure 8.4: Examine your disk very closely with Show Files in Each Map Block

The cluster number is shown on the left of the window, the file name in the center, and on the right side of the window you see the status of the file described as **Fragmented** or **Optimized**. If you examine free space instead of an area occupied by files, the file name is replaced by the message **Not in use**, and if you look at an area containing bad clusters, you will see the message **∗∗ BAD ∗∗**.

Remove all disk-caching programs other than PC-Cache before you start the optimization process.

When you are ready to start the optimization, select Choose Drive from the Compress menu to confirm the drive you want to work with, then select Begin Compress (F4). A warning screen reminds you to disable all memory-resident programs and stop all disk activity. The warning screen also recommends that you make a complete backup before optimizing your disk. Press Escape or choose Cancel to return to the main Compress screen; choose OK to continue.

Optimization can take a long time, especially if you are unfragmenting an entire hard disk. Monitor the Percentage Complete and Elapsed Time displays to get an idea of how long it will take to complete the job. Press Escape if you want to stop the optimization; Compress will stop at the end of the current operation, but your disk may only be partially optimized.

As the compression proceeds, the disk map on the screen changes dynamically to reflect the new disk structure. At the end of the compression, the left side of the screen should be full of clusters-in-use characters and the right side should be full of free-space characters. If you selected the Optimize Directories, Unfragment Files, or File Sort option, there might be some areas of free space amongst your files.

A very small number of files may still be fragmented when the compression is finished, because they extend across a hidden or system file. Compress will not move either the hidden file or the regular file that spans it so as not to interfere with any copy-protection schemes.

Finally, before leaving Compress you should make a new Mirror file to record the new file and directory arrangement on your hard disk. Your old Mirror file is now completely out of date and the success of a future file or disk recovery depends on a current Mirror file. Compress reminds you that you need to make a new Mirror file, so do this now.

RUNNING COMPRESS AUTOMATICALLY

See Chapter 20 for a complete list of the optional parameters for all PC Tools programs.

You can run Compress by including it in a batch file and using several optional parameters to automate the operation. The general form for running Compress from the DOS prompt or in a batch file is

COMPRESS *drive parameter*

where *drive* is the letter of the drive you want to compress and *parameter* is an optional parameter to aid in automatic operation. If you don't enter a drive letter, Compress assumes that you want to use the current drive.

Specify your choice of compression selections with the following parameters:

/CC	Performs a full compression and clears all unused sectors
/CF	Performs a full compression
/CU	Unfragments your files but does not move the free space to the back of the disk
/CS	Collects all the free space together at the back of the disk, but does not unfragment files
/CD	Optimizes your directories but does not optimize files

Specify the physical file ordering from the DOS prompt or from a batch file with the following options:

/OD	Places the directory just before its files
/OO	Moves all directories to the front of the disk, followed by files arranged by directory
/OF	Locates files specified with Files to Place First at the front of the disk after directories, followed by all other files
/OS	Places directories at the start of the disk and files where they are most convenient for the program. This is the fastest ordering option, and is the one you will use most often

Select the type of sort from the DOS prompt or from a batch file with the following options:

/SE	Sorts by file extension
/SF	Sorts by file name
/SS	Sorts by file size
/ST	Sorts by file time

Finally, specify the sort order with one of the following:

/SA	Performs an ascending sort
/SD	Performs a descending sort

HANDLING COPY-PROTECTION SCHEMES

Some copy-protection methods that rely on hidden files insist that the hidden files stay in exactly the same place on the disk. If your copy-protection method uses hidden files and you move them to another location on the disk, your application program will often refuse to work—it thinks that you are using an illegal copy of the file. Compress recognizes and does not move these hidden files or files with the system attribute bit set, so as not to interfere with the copy-protection systems. Also, Compress does not move the DOS hidden files (IBMBIO.COM and IBMDOS.COM) that DOS places at the beginning of all bootable disks. If an application uses some other location-specific copy-protection scheme, the only way to be absolutely sure that Compress will not interfere with it is to remove the software package completely before running Compress and then reinstall it after Compress is done.

USING FILEFIND

FileFind is much more than a simple file-location utility; in fact, you can use it to perform the following complex tasks:

- Find files anywhere in your directory structure, on your local hard disk, or on a network

- Find duplicate files
- Locate specific occurrences of text inside those files
- Inspect and modify file attributes
- Delete, Rename, and Copy located files

LOCATING FILES

Sometimes you can remember the name of a file that you want to work with, but you can't remember where it is. Occasionally you can't even remember the complete name of the file. The DOS DIR command is of little use in this situation. However, you can use File-Find to locate lost or missing files.

To start FileFind, select it from the menu of System Tools in PC Tools, or type **FF** from the DOS command line. The FileFind opening screen is shown in Figure 8.5. The main menu selections are located at the top of the window, as usual in PC Tools, but there are also several command buttons arranged just below the menu line that you can use as well. However, you can use FileFind in its simplest mode—to locate one or more files on your disk—without using any of the menus or command buttons.

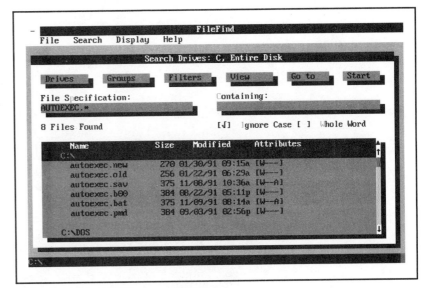

Figure 8.5: The FileFind opening screen

Determine the kinds of files you want to search using the File Specification box and specify the text to search for by entering it into the Containing box. For example, to find all the copies of the file AUTOEXEC on the current drive, type **AUTOEXEC.*** into the File Specification box. You can use the DOS wildcard characters ? and * when searching for a file, or you can merely enter as much of the file name as you can remember. Ignore the Containing box for the moment—I'll come back to that in a moment—and select the Start command button. FileFind displays a list of all the occurrences of AUTOEXEC.* in the lower part of the window, and a dialog box opens detailing the number of files found.

You cannot use wildcards in the Containing box, because FileFind will search your files for those specific characters.

If you want to search for a specific piece of text that you think is in one of your files, enter that text into the Containing box. FileFind now searches through your files, looking for the text you entered as the search string. My AUTOEXEC.BAT file contains the command @ECHO OFF to prevent commands from being displayed on the screen every time AUTOEXEC.BAT runs. To search for this in your AUTOEXEC files, type:

@ECHO OFF

into the Containing box and choose Start to begin the search. This time FileFind is looking for files called AUTOEXEC.* that also contain the string @ECHO OFF. The file names are listed in the lower box as they are located and a small window opens at the end of the search to tell you the total number of matches found. Click on OK to dismiss this dialog box. Click Stop if you want to halt the search.

To make the search as general as possible check the Ignore Case box. This makes the FileFind text search independent of upper- and lowercase letters. For example, *@ECHO OFF, @Echo Off* and *@echo off* will all match the search text *@ECHO OFF.* Alternatively, you can make the search more specific by turning Ignore Case off. To find whole words rather than disjointed pieces of matching text, turn on Whole Word.

CHANGING DRIVES AND DIRECTORIES

To change to a different drive, select the Drive command button or choose Selected Drives from the Search menu. The Selected

Drives/Directory window opens, listing all the drives on your computer. Click on a drive to include it in the search path, or click on it again to remove it. The Selected Drives box lists the drives currently included in the search path. There are three selections in this window you can use to refine the search, as follows:

- **Entire Drive** extends the search to the whole drive.

- **Current Directory and Below** starts the search in the current directory, extending thereafter to all subdirectories.

- **Current Directory Only** restricts the search to the current directory.

Select Change Directory if you want to change from the directory shown in the upper window. First place the highlight on the drive, then click on Change Directory to open the Change Directory window. Enter the directory you want to use and choose OK. This new directory is now listed in the main window opposite the drive you chose. To return to the original default search settings, choose Reset.

You can use the Go to Command button, or the Go to Directory selection in the File menu, to leave the FileFind program and change immediately to the directory containing the file you have just located with FileFind.

SEARCHING FOR GROUPS OF FILES

If you know that you will be searching for certain groups of files on a regular basis, you can collect them together in a group. You can name and save these groups for future use, and they can also be used in Undelete, as described in Chapter 7.

CREATING AND DELETING GROUPS To create a group, click the Groups command button or choose Groups from the Search menu, and then choose Edit to open the Edit Search Groups window. Existing groups are listed in the Search Group window. To create another group, choose New and enter a group name, then enter a file specification into the File Specification box. For example, if all your Lotus files are in a directory called 123 and the spreadsheet

files have a file-name extension of .WK1, you could call the group
"Lotus Files," and enter **C:\123*.WK1** into the File Specification
box. Choose Save to add this new group to the list in the Search
Group window.

To remove a group from the list, highlight the group and choose
Delete. Changing a group once it is defined is very similar to creating
a group. Highlight the group name, choose Edit, and change either
the group name or the file specification. Finally, select Save to make
your changes permanent.

DOING THE GROUP SEARCH To search the group of files,
select Groups, then click on the group you want to use. See that the
group file specification is loaded into the File Specification box. Type
your search text into the Containing box and choose Start to begin
the search. Files containing matches are listed in the main window
and a small dialog box opens to show the total number of matches
found. Choose OK to dismiss the dialog box.

PROTECTING FILES

There are many reasons why you might want to protect a file from
being changed or deleted; you might even want to hide a file so that
other people are not aware that it exists. If you are working on a local
area network, you may want to restrict access to files containing sensitive information, such as payroll data or personnel records. You
may also want to make important files *read-only* so that no one—
including yourself—can erase them accidentally.

You can provide some file protection by using the DOS ATTRIB
command, but FileFind offers a much more complete and powerful
set of capabilities.

FILE ATTRIBUTES IN DOS *File attributes* are characteristics that
DOS assigns to your files, as follows:

- A *read-only* file cannot be written to or erased by the normal
  DOS commands. However, you can print it or display it
  in listings made by DIR. Very few commercial software
  packages make use of the read-only bit.

- A *hidden* file does not appear in listings made by DIR and cannot be used with most DOS commands. However, you *can* copy it by using the DISKCOPY command, which makes a sector-by-sector duplicate of the original disk.

- A *system* file is a hidden, read-only file that DOS uses; it cannot be written to or erased.

- The *volume label* identifies the disk and is an entry in the root directory.

- A *subdirectory entry* has an attribute that differentiates it from files, indicating that its entry points to another directory.

- The *archive bit* indicates whether a file has been changed since it was last backed up. If the file has changed or has just been created, the archive bit is set. However, if you use the BACKUP command to copy the file, the archive bit is turned off; in this way, BACKUP keeps track of the files it has already copied and those it has not.

RESTORE, XCOPY, and some third-party backup programs also use the archive bit.

Bits are like toggles—they are either on (1) or off (0). You can also think of them as being *set* (1) or *reset* (0). (Another term for "reset" is *cleared*.)

A file's attributes are recorded in its *attribute byte*. The attribute byte is part of the file's directory entry, but unlike the other entries, the attribute-byte settings are not displayed in the usual DIR listing. Each attribute corresponds to a single bit in the attribute byte. An attribute is turned on, or set, if the value of its bit equals 1. Each bit in the byte can be set or reset individually without affecting the other bits. For example, a read-only file may also be archived.

FILE ATTRIBUTES ON A NOVELL NETWORK   As you might imagine, file attributes are a little more complex on a Novell network. In addition to the attributes described above for DOS files, there are attributes common to all versions of Novell NetWare, and some attributes specific to NetWare 386.

The following attributes are common to both NetWare 286 and NetWare 386:

- **Execute-Only** prevents the file from being copied. Once this attribute has been applied to a file, it cannot be removed, and it should only be applied after the file has been backed up; backup utilities will not back up these files.

- **Index**: NetWare automatically indexes files with more than 64 regular FAT entries to speed up file access.

- **Shareable** lets more than one user at a time read the file.

- **Transactional** indicates that the file is protected by the NetWare TTS (Transactional Tracking System).

The following file attributes are found only on networks running Novell NetWare 386:

- **Copy Inhibit** prevents the file from being copied.

- **Delete Inhibit** prevents the file from being deleted.

- **Purge** automatically purges the file after it has been deleted. A purged file cannot be salvaged.

- **Rename Inhibit** prevents users from renaming the file.

Some of these attributes are very powerful when combined with the rights and permissions security system on a network. For example, if a user has erase rights granted in a directory, but a specific file has the "delete inhibit" attribute set, the user cannot delete the file.

SPECIAL CONCERNS WITH HIDDEN AND READ-ONLY FILES
Some applications programs differ in their attitude to hidden files: some word processors load them, others do not. Certain commercial software packages use the hidden-file attribute as part of their copy-protection scheme. If you do not remove the software properly, these files will remain on your disk, occupying valuable space.

If you don't resist the temptation to make files hidden, the meaning of the saying "out of sight, out of mind" will become painfully evident. There is no point in hiding batch files or programs because you will soon forget their names, and when that happens, you will be unable to use them.

In addition, beware of making too many files read-only; many commercial software-installation programs configure files to match your system's hardware. These programs write the details of your hardware back into their own files. If you alter these files to read-only, then reconfigure the program with new information, the program will attempt to update its files, find that they are now read-only, and report an error. Some programs are well enough designed to issue a meaningful error message, but many are not. For example, if you use EDLIN on a read-only file, the program tells you File is READ-ONLY. dBASE, on the other hand, may display the more obscure message File not accessible.

SEARCHING WITH FILTERS

File attributes can refine the search criteria for FileFind. At the DOS command line, you can search for files using file size, date, attributes, and—if you are logged on to a Novell network—you can search using network attribute, dates, and owner information. Each search criterion you select is added to the others; in order to locate a file, it must match all the search conditions that you specify.

Click the Filters button, or choose Filters from the Search menu, and you will see the Search Filters window as shown in Figure 8.6. If you are on the network, you will see several additional file-attribute choices—including the owner of the file and the last modifier—and several time and date settings, including the modified date, last accessed date, last archived date, and creation date.

Turn on any attributes you want to include in the search filter; then you can refine the search even further with the next two settings:

- **Only These Attributes** finds files with exactly the attributes you selected.

- **Including These Attributes** finds files that have all of the attributes you selected, but may have other attributes, too.

You can also use the date, time, and file-size settings, as follows:

- **Modified** includes any files modified in the time period you enter here. The first box in each pair is for the date and the second box is for the time. The time entry is optional, and should be entered in the 24-hour format where 6:00 p.m. is entered as 18:00.

- **Size** specifies a size range in bytes (without delimiting commas) for the search.

If you are on the network, you can also use the following:

- **Owner** restricts the search to files owned by the user whose network identifier you enter here.
- **Last Modifier** restricts the search to files modified by the user whose network identifier you enter here.
- **Last Accessed** includes files that have been accessed during the range of dates you enter.
- **Last Archived** includes files that have been backed up within the range of dates you enter here.
- **Creation Date** includes files created in the date range you enter here.

When you have refined your filter, start the search with the Start command button in the main FileFind window. Each time you use a

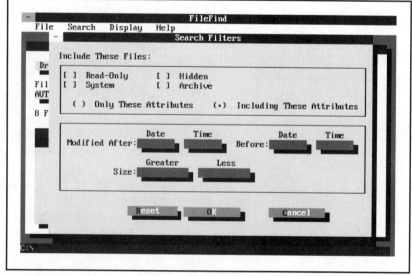

Figure 8.6: Setting the search criteria in the Search Filters window

filter, it stays active until you use the Reset button in the Search Filters window to remove it.

FINDING DUPLICATE FILES

If you think you may have several copies of the same file on your system, you can use FileFind to search for duplicate files. Choose Find Duplicates from the Search menu to open the Duplicate Search Status window shown in Figure 8.7. Find Duplicates is a toggle; it is either on or off, and a checkmark by the entry in the menu indicates its status. Set up your search criteria, including any groups or filters you want to use, then select Start.

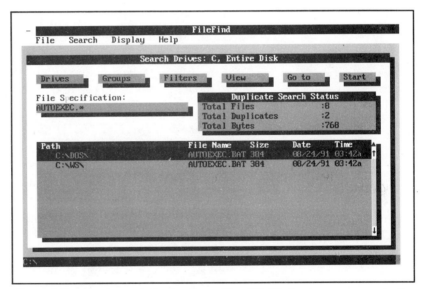

Figure 8.7: As you search for duplicate files, FileFind reports progress in the Duplicate Search Status window

When the search starts, the Duplicate Search Status window informs you of progress made, and when the search is complete, the statistics are as follows:

- **Total Files** is the number of files that FileFind has checked.

- **Total Duplicates** is the number of duplicate files found.

- **Total Bytes** is the combined size of all the duplicates found in the search.

The names, file sizes, dates, and times are shown in the main window. Files are sorted by name in ascending order. Once you use File-Find to confirm that you do have duplicate files, you can choose to delete some of them to save disk space.

MANAGING FILES WITH FILEFIND

If you are on the network, you must have the appropriate rights to perform these operations.

Once you have used FileFind to locate specific files, there are several powerful options in the File menu you can use to manage those files.

SELECTING FILES Select the files you want to work with by clicking on them in the main FileFind window. You can also use the arrow keys to move the highlight and press Enter to confirm your selection. If you want to work with all the files located by FileFind, use Select All from the File menu. You can also cancel this with Deselect All.

CHANGING FILE ATTRIBUTES To look at and change file attributes, highlight the file you want to work with in the main window, then choose Set Attributes from the File menu. If you are working in DOS, you will see the Set Attributes window open.

The attributes already set on the file are shown in the checkboxes at the top of the window. To change these attributes, click on the appropriate checkbox and then use Set. To change all the attributes, use Set All. You can also change the file date and time using the Modified boxes to the right of the window. Choose Next to look at the attributes on the next file if more than one file has been selected, and use Cancel to return to the main FileFind window.

On a Novell Network, the Set Attributes window is divided into two or three columns, depending on the version number of the network software you are using. The column on the left of the window lists the DOS attributes and the column in the center shows the NetWare 286 file attributes. If you are using NetWare 386, you will see a third column of attributes on the right side of the window that apply specifically to NetWare 386. Use Set, Set All, and Next to manipulate them.

COPYING AND MOVING FILES Choose Copy from the File menu if you want to duplicate the selected file(s). A dialog box opens showing details for the selected file(s), and asking for the destination path name(s). Choose Copy to copy one file, or choose Copy All to duplicate all the selected files.

To move one or more files, select them first, then choose Move from the File menu. Enter the destination path name, and choose Move to move the first file. Use Next to work with the next file from the list of selected files.

RENAMING AND DELETING FILES Renaming and Deleting files is very similar to the copying and moving operations; select the files first, then choose the appropriate menu selection from the File menu, and follow the dialog box on the screen.

PRINTING FILES Use the Print List selection from the File menu to print a list of all the files found using the current search criteria. You can print directly to your printer, or to a file called FILE-LIST.TXT for later printing.

CHANGING THE LIST FORMAT There are two selections in the Display menu that you can use to change how files are listed in the main FileFind window, as follows:

- **List Format** specifies the information that is displayed for each file shown in the main FileFind window. If you are working in DOS, you can show the file size, attributes, and the modified date and time. If you are logged on to the network, you can also display the owner, last modifier, creation date, last accessed date, and last archived date.

All of these searches can be in ascending or descending order.

- **Sort By** determines the order that files are listed in the main window. In DOS you can sort by file name, file extension, size, date and time, or you can leave the list unsorted. On the network, you can sort by several additional criteria, including owner, last modifier, creation date, last accessed date, and last archived date.

USING FILEFIND FROM THE DOS COMMAND LINE

This method works well only if you can type with few errors.

If you are in a hurry, you can use FileFind directly from the DOS command line, rather than in full screen-mode. The general form for using FileFind from the command line is as follows:

FF *filename search string switch*

For a complete list of all the command-line options for FileFind, see Chapter 20.

FINDING FILES   To find all of your AUTOEXEC files using FileFind from the command line, type:

FF C: AUTOEXEC.*

Each directory is searched in turn, and the files located are listed on the screen, along with their size, last modification time and date, and attributes. The total number of files found is given at the end of the search.

FINDING TEXT

If the search text includes spaces, enclose the whole search text in quotation marks.

To look for specific text inside the file, type

FF C: AUTOEXEC.* "@echo off"

and to make the search case sensitive, type

FF C: AUTOEXEC.* "@ECHO OFF" /CS

WORKING WITH FILE ATTRIBUTES   There are five switches you can use with FileFind when you enter file attributes at the command line:

- /CLEAR removes all the attributes from the files you specify.

- /A sets or resets the archive bit.

- /H sets or resets the hidden bit.
- /R sets or resets the read-only bit.
- /S sets or resets the system bit.

Specify a + after the switch letter to set the attribute; specify a − after the switch letter to reset the attribute.

CHANGING A FILE'S TIME AND DATE   FileFind lets you set or clear the date or time for an individual file or a group of files. For example, to reset the date for the MYFILE.TXT file in the current directory, type

Both the date and the time formats are determined by the COUNTRY code in your CONFIG.SYS file. The formats listed here are the defaults.

>   **FF MYFILE.TXT /D***mm-dd-yy*

in which *mm-dd-yy* represents the date format. To set the time for the previous example file, type

>   **FF MYFILE.TXT /T***hh:mm*

in which *hh:mm* represents the time format. To set the time and date to the current time and date, use

>   **FF MYFILE.TXT /CURRENT**

USING SYSTEM INFORMATION

PC Tools provides several methods by which you can examine and quantify your computer system's performance. System Information lets you inspect a great deal of internal computer information that you normally do not see; it also compares the performance of your computer with three industry-standard computers.

The System Information program provides a wealth of information about your computer's hardware, including disk specifications, and memory layout and usage. It calculates performance indices and can even print a detailed report of its findings. If your job entails installing, demonstrating, or troubleshooting hardware or software products on unfamiliar computers, this is the program for you. System Information can also save the average computer user much time and frustration. Many applications programs require users to supply hardware information during installation; however, most people do not know the details of their computer's hardware, particularly if they did not actually install it themselves. Also, some hardware can be used in different modes, which can further confuse the issue. Running System Information is a quick, efficient way to gather this information. You can run System Information from the DOS prompt or by selecting System Information from within the System Tools menu in PC Shell. To run System Information from the DOS prompt, type **SI**.

I will describe all of the options in System Information in the sequence that they occur in the menus, starting with the System Summary screen.

SYSTEM SUMMARY

The System Summary screen, shown in Figure 8.8, opens when you start System Information. It details the basic configuration of your computer, including information about your disks, memory, and other hardware systems. Several of the other display screens in System Information expand on the basic information shown in this screen.

This screen contains important information that is useful to all computer users; therefore, I will describe each of the elements in detail. On the left of the window is a short summary of the main elements present in your system:

- **System Type:** System Information retrieves the name of the computer from the system's read-only memory (ROM). For many IBM compatibles, System Information displays only a copyright notice or a general computer type rather than the actual computer name.

- **Operating System:** this is the version of DOS being run on the computer.

- **Video Adapter:** this is the name of the current video display adapter.

- **I/O Ports:** this entry reports the number of installed parallel and serial interface ports.

- **Keyboard/Mouse:** Keyboard lists either a standard 84-key or an extended 101-key keyboard. Mouse is the type of mouse (if one is in use) that is connected to your computer, either serial or bus. In Figure 8.8, the example system includes a serial mouse.

- **CMOS:** this entry indicates whether or not your computer stores certain system parameters in a special battery backed-up area of memory known as CMOS. This information is described in more detail under "CMOS Information" later in this section.

- **Network:** this entry lists the name of the network you are logged on to.

- **Drive Summary:** here you will see a short summary of the drives you have on your system.

You can click on any of the entries shown in this window to see more information on each topic, or you can access these same screens

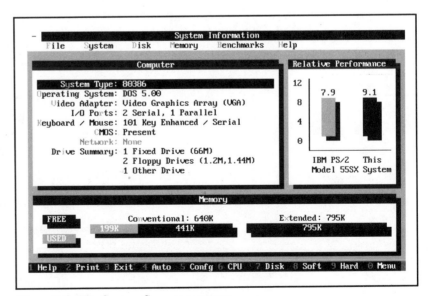

Figure 8.8: The System Summary screen

from the menus at the top of the window. You can also press the function keys on the message line at the bottom of the window to access many of these information screens.

At the upper right of the System Information window you see a diagram indicating the relative performance of your computer compared with another industry-standard computer. The IBM PC XT is assigned a performance index of 1 and all other computers are evaluated against this index. A Relative Performance index of 2 indicates that a computer that is twice as fast as the XT. This is discussed in more detail under the heading "CPU Speed Test" later in this section. This window is not selectable.

In the lower part of the System Information window is a simple diagram showing how the memory in your system is being used. The diagram shows conventional memory as well as expanded and extended memory, if present. You can click on the elements in this window to see more information on the types of memory and their usage in your system, or you can use the selections in the Memory menu to see the same information.

SYSTEM TYPE

The first selection in the System menu is System Type, which opens the General Information dialog box:

- **CPU Type:** this is the name of the microprocessor used in your computer. The microprocessor is the computer's engine: it translates information from RAM, ROM, or the files on a disk into instructions that it can execute, and it executes them very quickly. The IBM PC, IBM PC/XT, and most compatibles use the Intel 8086 or 8088 microprocessor, or the NEC V20 or V30. The PC/AT computer and compatibles use the Intel 80286 chip. More recent machines use the Intel 80386 or 80486 chip.

- **Co-Processor:** the Intel microprocessors used in PCs are designed so that other chips can be linked to them, thus increasing their power. One such additional chip is a math, or *floating point,* coprocessor, and the IBM PC and most

The Intel 80486 has an on-chip floating point unit as part of its circuitry. Software written for the 80387 math coprocessor runs on the 80486 on-chip floating-point unit without any modifications. The 486SX does not have the on-board floating point circuitry.

These coprocessors are not the same as the add-in accelerator boards that occupy a slot in the computer chassis and actually take over the original microprocessor's work by replacing it with a faster processor.

compatibles include a socket on the main motherboard for it. Each Intel chip has a matching math coprocessor.

For example, the 8087 is used with the 8086, the 80287 is used with the 80286, and the 80387 is used with the 80386. These '87s perform some of the number-crunching operations that the main microprocessor normally executes; in doing so, the coprocessors greatly increase the speed and accuracy of numeric calculations. In addition to simple add/subtract/multiply/divide operations, math coprocessors can do trigonometric calculations such as sine, cosine, and tangent. CAD applications and scientific or statistical programs usually benefit from the use of a coprocessor, whereas word processors generally do not.

The speed gained by using a math coprocessor varies widely from application to application, but generally a math coprocessor performs calculations five to fifty times faster than a regular processor.

- **Bus Size:** this is the size of the data bus in your computer expressed in terms of bits. A computer with an 8-bit data bus transfers data eight bits at a time, one with a 16-bit bus transfers 16 bits at a time, and a computer with a 32-bit bus transfers data 32 bits at a time.

- **Bus Type:** this describes the type of data bus that your computer uses. ISA (Industry Standard Architecture) is found in PC/XT and PC/AT computers; EISA (Extended Industry Standard Architecture) is a newer type of bus that supports 32-bit operations but retains compatibility with the original ISA; and MCA (Micro Channel Architecture) is IBM's proprietary bus for PS/2 computers.

- **Date of BIOS:** this is the creation date of the read-only memory basic input/output system (ROM BIOS). The BIOS is a layer of software that loads from ROM and lets DOS communicate with the computer's hardware. The BIOS handles the basic input and output functions in the computer. Certain early versions of the BIOS are incompatible with later hardware—$3^1/_2$-inch floppy disks, for example—and so a BIOS upgrade may be needed.

- **ID Bytes:** these two bytes represent the identification code for this version of the BIOS.

OPERATING SYSTEM

Choose Operating System from the System menu and you will see a screen that identifies the version of DOS you used to boot your system, as well as the original equipment manufacturer, or OEM. System Information can identify PC-DOS, MS-DOS, and Zenith DOS. Other versions of DOS may be identified as PC-DOS.

VIDEO ADAPTER

Choose Video Adapter from the System menu to see the window shown in Figure 8.9. This window describes the video board in use in your system. Four types of video-adapter boards are available: the monochrome display adapter (MDA); the color graphics adapter (CGA); the enhanced graphics adapter (EGA); and the video graphics array (VGA), which was introduced with the IBM PS/2 computer in 1987. (IBM introduced the professional graphics adapter (PGA) at the same time as it introduced the EGA. However, the PGA needed a high-resolution monitor that was incompatible with existing standards, so it was discontinued.)

Most video systems can be programmed with different parameters. This enables you to select from several different video modes. Each video mode is characterized by the *resolution* (the number of pixels displayed horizontally and vertically) and by the number of different colors that can be displayed at the same time. CGA video modes include 80-column-by-25-line mode and 40-column-by-25-line mode. The EGA can support as many as 43 lines of text; the VGA can support as many as 50 lines of text. The amount of video memory needed to support these different display adapters varies in each case, and certain applications programs may require a specific minimum amount of video memory to be able to display certain types of graphic images.

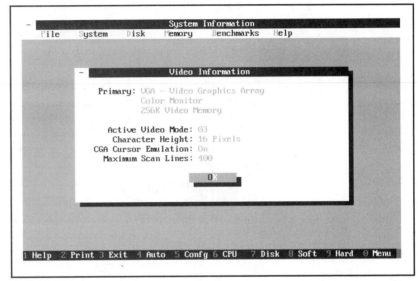

Figure 8.9: The Video Information window gives details about your video system

INPUT/OUTPUT PORTS

Choose I/O Ports from the System menu to see a list of the serial and parallel ports found on your system. The port name is given on the left side of the window and the base port address in hexadecimal is listed on the right. DOS 3.2 and earlier versions supported only two serial ports, but beginning with DOS 3.3, the number increased to four. These ports are named COM1, COM2, COM3, and COM4. The parallel port is normally used to connect the system printer; hence it is called LPT1. A second parallel port, if present, would be LPT2.

As their names imply, the serial port handles data serially—one bit at a time—and the parallel port handles several data bits at once—in this case, eight. Consequently, the data-transfer rate of a parallel port is usually higher than that of a serial port. The serial port, however, is more flexible and can be configured to work with a variety of devices, including a modem, mouse, serial printer, or digitizer.

KEYBOARD/MOUSE

Select Keyboard/Mouse from the System menu to see a brief description of your mouse and keyboard, as shown in Figure 8.10. The keyboard is usually described as an 83-key or a 101-key (sometimes called *enhanced*) keyboard. The 286 and 386-based computers have the ability to vary the *typematic rate,* the rate that keystrokes are sent to the computer and the speed with which a key repeats when it is held down.

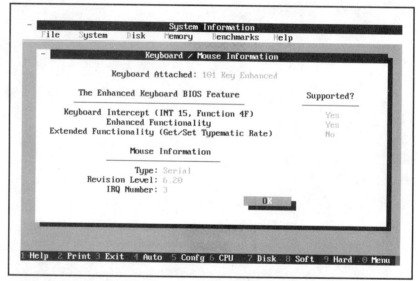

Figure 8.10: Keyboard configuration is listed above Mouse information in the Keyboard/Mouse window

The mouse is identified according to the revision level of the Microsoft device driver. For example, if you have a Logitech mouse and you are using Version 4 of the device driver, Keyboard/Mouse identifies the revision level as 6.02, because this is the number of the Microsoft device driver that corresponds to Logitech version 4. Keyboard/Mouse can identify several different kinds of mice, including serial, bus, and PS/2 mice, and mice from Hewlett-Packard and Inport.

IRQ Number stands for "interrupt request number," and this information is often needed when you are configuring or installing a new peripheral device like a mouse or a modem. If two peripherals try to use the same interrupt request at the same time, one or both the peripherals will not work. See the description under "Hardware Interrupts" later in this section for more details.

CMOS INFORMATION

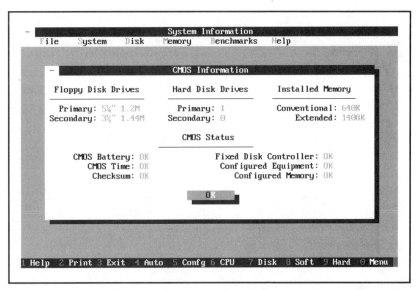

Remember to print out the CMOS values; then, if your computer battery fails and loses the current settings, you can simply reenter the values.

Computers made after the PC/AT use a portion of Complementary Metal-Oxide Semiconductor memory, abbreviated as CMOS and pronounced "sea-moss," to hold basic configuration information. This CMOS memory requires such low-power levels that it can be maintained by a small battery; therefore, this information is not lost when you turn off the power at the end of your session. Figure 8.11 shows a typical example from an 80386 computer, made by choosing CMOS Information from the System menu. If your computer does not contain CMOS, this menu entry is grayed out and you will not be able to select it.

Figure 8.11: The CMOS Information window lists details of the configuration information stored in CMOS

The PC Tools installation disk lets you make a Recovery Disk that you can use to restore CMOS data if it is ever corrupted or lost.

One of the most crucial pieces of information on this screen is the hard-disk–type number shown in the Hard Disk Drives column in the center of the screen. In Figure 8.11 the disk-type number for the first, or primary, hard-disk drive is 17. The BIOS in your computer can read many different types of hard disks from different manufacturers; this type number is the code that tells the BIOS how many heads and cylinders your specific disk drive has. If your computer's battery loses power, the contents of CMOS memory will be lost, and you will not be able to boot up your computer from the hard disk until you replace the battery and reset this number. With some computers you must use the ''setup'' disk that came with your computer to reset the number; other computers have the setup routines built into the ROM BIOS itself.

The rest of this screen displays details about your floppy disk types and installed memory, and includes additional information contained in CMOS.

NETWORK

If you are already logged on to a network, select Network from the System menu to see a list of file server names, as well as login information like current user, login time, and login date.

You must have at least console operator's privileges to use Disk Space.

There are several other selection buttons available from the Network Information window:

- **User List**. Choose this to see a list of all the users currently logged on to the network. There are two more selections available from this screen:

  Message sends a message of up to 50 characters to another user logged on to your network. The message does not identify the sender, so you should include this information in your message.

  Disk Space reviews all the directories and files that a user owns.

- **Vol Info.** This choice lists volume information, including volume names, and how much total and free space is available on each volume.

- **Group List.** Use this selection to see the names of groups currently on the file server.

- **File Info.** This choice is only available on networks running Novell NetWare 286. You also need console operator's privileges to access this information. File Info details file usage on a server, as well as certain file-usage statistics collected since the server was brought up.

- **Details.** This choice shows complex network configuration information, mostly of interest to system managers and administrators.

SOFTWARE INTERRUPTS

Before I discuss the information in the next two screens, Software Interrupts and Hardware Interrupts, let's briefly examine what interrupts are and how they work.

Often, after you have given the computer a task to perform, you will need it to respond quickly to a new request: for example, to begin a new task at the press of a key or the click of a mouse. The mechanism that accomplishes this is known as an *interrupt*. An interrupt is an "event" that causes the processor to suspend its current activity, save its place, and look up an *interrupt vector* in the *interrupt vector table*. The interrupt vector tells the processor the address of the *interrupt handler*, or service routine, to which it should branch. After the service routine performs its task, control is returned to the suspended process. DOS interrupts are often divided into three types: internal hardware, external hardware, and software interrupts. The Intel 80x86 family of processors supports 256 prioritized interrupts, of which the first 64 are reserved for use by the system hardware or by DOS itself.

In the IBM PC, the main processor does not accept interrupts from hardware devices directly; interrupts are routed instead to an Intel 8259A Programmable Interrupt Controller (PIC) chip. This chip responds to each hardware interrupt, assigns a priority, and forwards it to the main processor. Each hardware device is hardwired, or "jumpered," into inputs known as IRQs or *interrupt requests*; this is why you see an IRQ assigned to an interrupt.

All interrupts on the PC are channeled through the interrupt vector table, regardless of whether the interrupt is generated as an external or an internal hardware interrupt, or as a software interrupt. The entry into this table for hardware devices is directly related to the IRQ number. To find the address of the interrupt-handling routine for a hardware interrupt in the interrupt vector table, add eight to the IRQ number.

Select Software Interrupts from the System menu to see a list of all the entries in the interrupt vector table on your computer. Figure 8.12 shows a sample display for an 80386 computer.

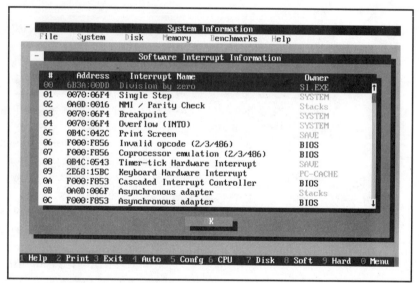

Figure 8.12: The Software Interrupts screen lists the entries in the interrupt vector table

Many of the software interrupts perform more than one service. For example, interrupt 21H is the main entry point for DOS services and offers the programmer more than 100 different *function calls,* including character input and output, file creation, file reading and writing, and file deletion.

HARDWARE INTERRUPTS

A hardware interrupt is generated by a device such as the keyboard, the computer clock, or one of the parallel or serial ports on the computer. To see a list of the IRQs on your computer, select Hardware Interrupts from the System menu. Your display will look similar to Figure 8.13.

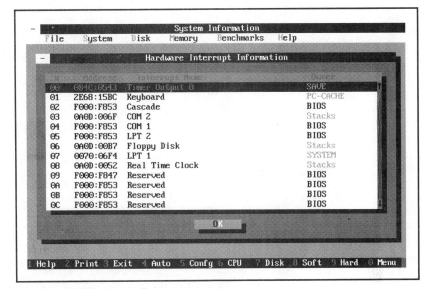

Figure 8.13: Hardware Interrupts screen

At the left of the screen is the list of IRQs, followed by their hex addresses. The hardware devices that need the most attention have lower IRQs, so the system timer has IRQ 0, the keyboard has IRQ 01, and so on up the list. The name and address of each interrupt is displayed at the center of the screen and the name of the owner of the interrupt is displayed at the right.

If you have an IBM PC or PC/XT (or clone) computer, you have one 8259A chip; you will see eight IRQs in the display, numbered from zero to seven.

If you have a PC/AT (or clone) or a Micro Channel PS/2 computer, you have two programmable interrupt controllers tied together. That is, interrupt number two on one of the interrupt controllers accepts its input from the other 8259A chip. This generates a total of 15 interrupts, with interrupt two usually described as the *cascade*.

The Model 25 and 30, like the PC and the PC/XT, have a total of eight interrupts, but they are shared. Interrupt one, assigned to the keyboard in PC-type computers, is shared by the keyboard, the mouse, and the time-of-day clock on the Model 25 and 30.

DRIVE SUMMARY

Select Drive Summary from the Disk menu to see a single-screen listing of all the disks on your computer. In Figure 8.14, drive A is a 5 1/4-inch floppy disk and drive B is a 3 1/2-inch floppy disk. Drives C, D, and E are three partitions on a 65MB drive. Drive F is a RAM disk of 128K; notice that it is described as a Driver in the Type column. The remaining drive letters are available. The current default directory is shown at the right side of the window for each disk.

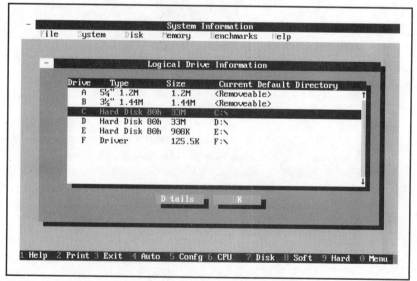

Figure 8.14: The Drive Summary screen lists the disks on your computer

DISK DETAILS

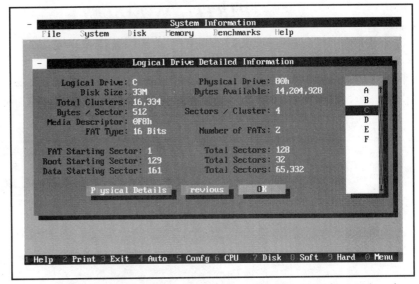 See Chapter 6 for detailed information about the disk structure.

Choose Details from this window or select Disk Details from the Disk menu to see more detailed information about the disk drives on your computer. Figure 8.15 shows the Disk Details screen for the same system depicted in the previous figure.

Figure 8.15: Disk Details screen gives more detailed disk information than Drive Summary

Use the selection bar at the right side of the screen to choose the drive you want to examine. Figure 8.15 shows information for drive C, a 33MB partition on a 65MB hard disk. The window is labeled Logical Drive Detailed Information, because all the elements shown on the screen are built up from groups of sectors. The window contains information about the layout of the disk from the DOS viewpoint, including the number of bytes per sector, the number of sectors per cluster, the total number of clusters, the number and type of the FAT, and the media descriptor byte. It also includes details of the starting location and size of the FAT, root directory, and the data area. If you are using a RAM disk, notice that it contains only one copy of the FAT. To see details of the physical information for this drive, click on the Physical Details button at the lower left of the window.

The Physical Details window provides details about the actual disk hardware, including the number of disk sides and tracks, and the number of sectors per track.

PARTITION TABLES

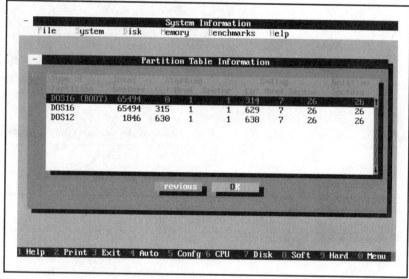

You can use the Recovery Disk made by the Install program to repair damaged partition tables.

Select Partition from this window to display the partition table information for your hard disk, as shown in Figure 8.16.

Figure 8.16: The Partition Tables display screen gives details of all three partitions on this 65MB hard disk

Because floppy disks cannot be shared between different operating systems, they do not have a partition table.

Figure 8.16 provides details about all three partitions on the sample 65MB hard disk, including starting and ending cylinder, head, and sector numbers. Note that partition number 1 is the partition from which the disk boots up. In this example, the first partition is located on hard disk number 1, which has 8 sides, or heads, and 639 tracks configured with 26 sectors per track.

If you reconfigure your system after a hard-disk repair or replacement, you can use the values from this screen to rebuild your disk system.

CONVENTIONAL MEMORY

To see a one-screen graph of the 640K of conventional memory used in your computer, select Conventional Memory from the Memory menu. You can also get to this information if you click on Conventional at the bottom of the opening System Information window. Your display will be similar to the one shown in Figure 8.17.

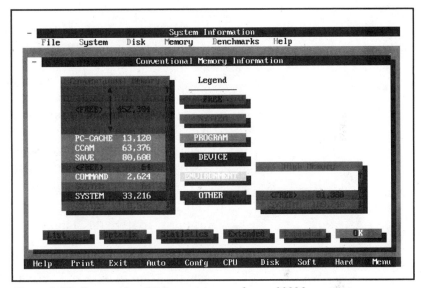

Figure 8.17: Conventional Memory screen for an 80386 computer

Conventional Memory reports on the amount of memory being used by DOS and any terminate-and-stay-resident (TSR) programs you have loaded, and the remaining free memory available for use by your applications program(s). Use the Summary/Details toggle to expand or contract the level of details shown in the List and Graph displays.

In the Graph window, the memory in your PC is divided into the following categories:

- **FREE.** This is the free space available for applications programs.

- **SYSTEM.** This is the area of memory occupied by DOS and COMMAND.COM.

- **PROGRAM.** This space is occupied by applications programs.

- **DEVICE.** This memory is occupied by device drivers. A *device driver* is a special program that manipulates one specific piece of hardware. DOS uses device drivers as extensions to the operating system. Some device drivers are actually part of DOS; these are called *built-in device drivers*. Others exist as separate files and are called *loadable device drivers*. These drivers free DOS from having to include code for every single piece of hardware that can be attached to a computer. As long as there is a device driver supplied with hardware, you can use it on your computer. When you want to use a new piece of hardware, merely connect it to your system, copy the device driver into a directory on your boot disk, and add a statement to your CONFIG.SYS or AUTOEXEC.BAT file to load the device driver at boot-up time. Loadable device drivers also reduce memory requirements; you only have to load the device drivers that you need for your specific hardware configuration.

- **ENVIRON.** The *environment* is a section of memory used primarily to store the settings of the variables for the DOS PATH, SET and PROMPT commands. When DOS loads a program, it gives the program a copy of the environment. The program may modify its copy of the environment, but this will not affect the original settings maintained by the command processor. Any program that remains resident in memory retains its copy of the environment; however, this copy is not updated by any subsequent commands that alter DOS's copy of the environment.

There are several selections you can make from this window, as follows:

List   This selection shows the memory blocks allocated for use by device drivers and terminate-and-stay-resident (TSR) programs. One of the main limitations of DOS is that it cannot support more than one program running at one time. DOS is a single-user, single-tasking operating system. The TSR program is an ingenious method that partially overcomes this limitation.

After you load a TSR program into memory, it returns control to DOS, but waits in the background. When you press a certain key combination (the *hotkey*), the TSR interrupts the application program you were running and executes its own services. When you finish using the TSR program and exit, control returns to your application program again.

Other memory-resident programs work in a slightly different way: they attach themselves to the operating system and remain in memory, working constantly in the background. The DOS PRINT utility is an example of this; indeed, PRINT is often called the first real memory-resident program. The PC-Cache program also falls into this category.

Because DOS interrupts are always channeled through the same interrupt vector table, it is relatively easy for a TSR program to alter these vectors to change the way the interrupts work. For example, virtually all programs read the keyboard through interrupt 16H, which normally points to a service routine in the BIOS. It is a simple matter for a program to change the response of the system to keyboard-read requests by rerouting this vector through an alternative procedure. These replaced vectors are called *hooked* vectors. You can see several of these hooked vectors listed in Figure 8.18.

In Figure 8.18, note that the PC-Cache program is using several interrupt vectors. At the left of the screen is a list of hex addresses used by the programs. The size in bytes is given next and is followed by the name of the owner—which could be, for example, PC-CACHE, Free Memory, or an Unknown Owner. The full path name of the owner is given in case you have several different versions of the same program on your system. With the full path name supplied, you can tell exactly which one is running.

As you move the highlight up and down the list of TSR programs, System Information displays additional information below the main window if it is available, including the command-line arguments used to load the program, the vectors used by the program, and the number of memory-allocation blocks that the program uses.

You can use these different displays to evaluate the effects of loading additional TSR programs on your system. The amount of memory in your computer is fixed, so as you add TSR programs, the

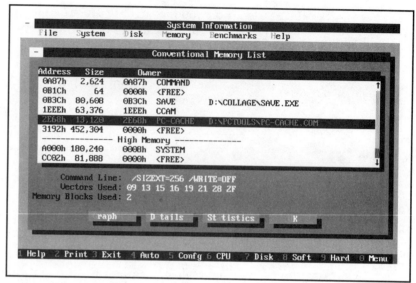

Figure 8.18: Conventional Memory List window displays program names
and hooked vectors

amount of free memory space available for your applications programs decreases. At some point you may find that you cannot open a
large database or use a large applications program because there is no
longer sufficient room. You must then decide whether the utility of
your TSRs is worth the memory space that they occupy; try to strike
the right balance for the way you work.

Statistics   Choose Statistics to see a brief description of conventional
memory usage. The Conventional Memory Statistics window lists
the total amount of conventional memory, how much of that memory is free for use by applications programs, and the size of the largest
single contiguous piece of memory. If you use a 386 or 486 computer
with DOS 5, you will also see information on upper memory
blocks (UMBs).

Extended   Click on Extended to see a similar display for extended
memory in your system, as shown in Figure 8.19. Extended memory
is the most common way of adding additional memory to the PC. As

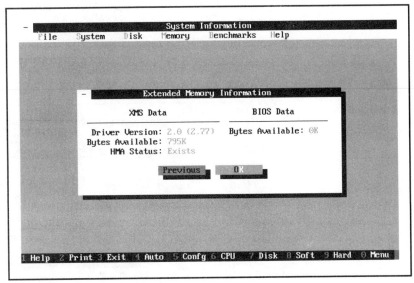

Figure 8.19: The Extended Memory Information window for a 386 computer

you can see in Figure 8.19, this window also displays the extended-memory driver-version number, as well as the amount of memory available.

Expanded Choose Expanded to see the same information for your expanded memory, if you have expanded memory in your system. This window also displays the kind of expanded memory you have: EMS 3.2 or EMS 4.0.

CPU SPEED TEST

Select CPU Speed Test from the Benchmarks menu to display a screen similar to the one shown in Figure 8.20. The CPU Performance Index is a measure of your computer's CPU or disk-independent computing power. A basic IBM PC/XT running an 8088 at 4.77 MHz has a computing index equal to 1, an IBM PC/AT running an 80286 at 6 MHz has a computing index of 2.2, and an IBM PS/2 model 55SX a computing index of 7.9. In other words, the PS/2 model 55SX runs the System Information computing index tests 7.9 times faster than the original IBM PC/XT. If your computer has a "turbo" button, press it and rerun the CPU Speed Test to see what effect changing the speed has on your computing index.

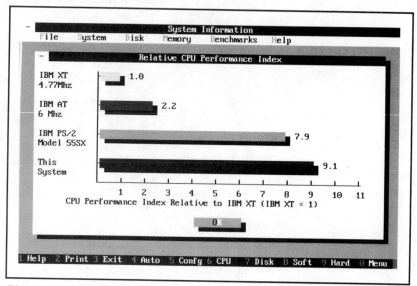

Figure 8.20: The Relative CPU Performance Index window compares the performance of your computer with that of three industry standard computers

DISK SPEED TEST

To evaluate the speed of your hard disk against other industry standards, select Disk Speed Test from the Benchmarks menu. The Relative Disk Performance Index is the second System Information calculated index, intended this time to let you rate your hard disk's performance against the same three industry-standard computers used in the previous test. Figure 8.21 shows the screen that reports the results of the Disk Index tests. If you have more than one hard disk installed in your computer, a window opens asking if you want to test the first drive or the second drive. Under the bar graphs shown in Figure 8.21, you will see several statistics for your hard disk, including the Average Seek time and the Track-to-Track access time (both in milliseconds), and the Data Transfer Rate (in kilobytes per second).

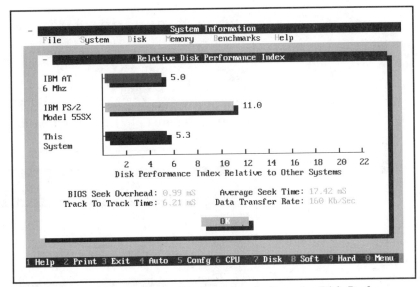

Figure 8.21: The Disk Speed Benchmark calculates the Disk Performance Index

The *BIOS seek overhead* is the additional amount of time imposed by the BIOS in your system. *Track-to-track time* is the length of time the disk takes to move from one track to the adjacent track. This measurement is determined by hard-disk design and construction, specifically in the type of head used and the number of platters in the disk. This is not the complete story of disk speed, however. The disk does not work in isolation; it also must work with the disk controller and the software controlling the drive.

A more complete measurement of system performance is the *Data transfer rate*—the rate at which data are read from the disk and passes through the disk controller card to the computer itself. This measurement encompasses raw disk speed, the effectiveness of the disk interface, and the computer data bus speed. After all, the performance of a fast disk might be bogged down by a slow controller or data bus. The *average seek time* is the average length of time the disk takes to access a random piece of data, based on a large number of disk accesses. Actual access times range from less than 5 milliseconds to as long as 150 milliseconds.

OVERALL PERFORMANCE INDEX

Choose Overall Performance from the Benchmarks menu to calculate your computer's Overall Performance Index, as shown in Figure 8.22. The Overall Performance Index is the integration of the CPU Speed Test and the Disk Speed Test into a single value. This lets you compare different systems easily.

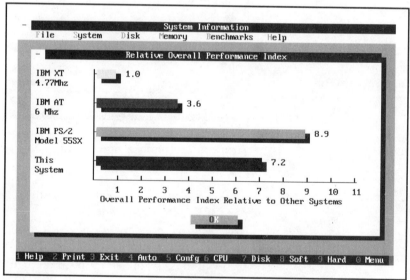

Figure 8.22: The Overall Performance Index benchmark display

NETWORK PERFORMANCE

The Network Performance selection from the Benchmarks menu tests the speed of the network in terms of disk reads and disk writes. You must be logged on to the network before you can use this selection, otherwise it will be grayed out and unavailable. The Network

Drive Benchmark screen depicts the relative speed of reads and writes for the system as a bar graph that indicates the average throughput in kilobytes per second.

DISPLAYING YOUR SYSTEM FILES

To see a listing of your AUTOEXEC.BAT file choose View AUTOEXEC.BAT from the File menu. The contents of the file are displayed on the screen. Use the cursor-control keys to scroll the listing or click on the scroll bars with the mouse.

To see a listing of your CONFIG.SYS file, choose View CONFIG.SYS from the File menu. Again, the contents of the file are displayed on the screen. Use the cursor-control keys to scroll through the listing or click on the scroll bars with the mouse.

USING PRINT REPORT

The report made by System Information can be very long if you select all of the print options; the report is not divided into pages. Send the output to a disk file first, then use a Desktop notepad to edit and arrange the information in the file so that the output is neat and orderly.

Choosing Print Report from the File menu brings up the screen shown in Figure 8.23. This screen lets you configure the System Information report to your requirements. Press Tab or the arrow keys to move through the items on the display. To turn an option on or off, press the highlighted key or the spacebar, or click on the option with the mouse.

After you have completed your choice of the report options, choose Print. Finally, select the device you want to print the report to from the Printing Options dialog box.

Choose LPT1 to send the report to your parallel printer or choose Disk File to send the report to a file. The default file name is SI.RPT.

MANAGING THE DIRECTORY STRUCTURE OF YOUR DISKS

One of the toughest problems in managing your hard disk is deciding how to organize your files into directories. You want to implement a system that allows you and others to find files easily. You can use Directory Maintenance to make or change directories, rearrange or delete directories, and make new volume labels—and use all these

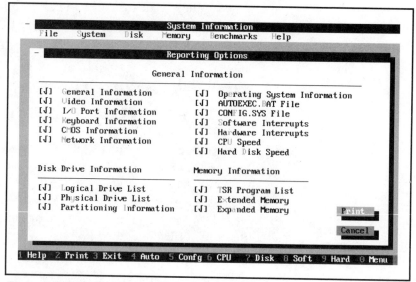

Figure 8.23: The Reporting Options screen

capabilities in full-screen mode or from the DOS command line. First, however, you should know something of how the file system in DOS works.

The most useful feature of DOS's file system is its ability to organize directories hierarchically. What this means is that directories can contain subdirectories as well as files.

The concept of the root and ordered hierarchical directories originated in UNIX (another computer operating system). All disks start with the root directory, so called because—like the roots of a tree—it is the lowest level of the hierarchy from which all others branch.

Because there is a limit to the number of entries that the root directory can hold, be careful to install as few files as possible in the root directory: AUTOEXEC.BAT, CONFIG.SYS, and COMMAND-.COM are enough. Other files should be put in directories. For example, one directory might contain your word processor, another your spreadsheet, another the DOS files, another your batch files, another PC Tools, and so on. This will enable you to find your way around the disk easily and quickly, and DOS will run more efficiently.

ORGANIZING YOUR HARD DISK

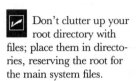
Don't clutter up your root directory with files; place them in directories, reserving the root for the main system files.

The key to successful hard-disk management is organization. You should always group related programs and their files together in their own directories and subdirectories, rather than putting everything into one directory. Placing all your files in the same directory defeats the purpose of DOS's hierarchical file system, which enables you to find files quickly.

Each software package that you install on your system (the program files, device drivers, help files, and so on) should go into the same directory. For example, if you are a Lotus 1-2-3 user, create a directory called 123 in the root directory and install Lotus 1-2-3 into it. If necessary, you can create additional subdirectories inside the 123 directory. Suppose you want to separate your quarterly budget files from the rest of your files. You could place them in a subdirectory of 123 called BUDGETS.

Note, however, that you don't want to create too many directories or levels of subdirectories. Otherwise, your files will quickly become so spread out that you will forget where they are. I recommend that you limit yourself to three levels (root, subdirectories, and sub-subdirectories); with any more levels you will find it too time-consuming to move through your directory structure.

When you want to use a file or directory, you tell DOS where it is in the hierarchy. In other words, you give DOS the file or directory's *path*. For example, to move from the root to your newly created BUDGETS directory, you would type

CD\123\BUDGETS

at the DOS prompt.

As you organize your directory structure, make sure you use the PATH command in your AUTOEXEC.BAT file to tell DOS where to look for the files that you've stored in subdirectories. For example, your PATH statement might contain the following entry:

PATH = C:\;C:\DOS;C:\123

This PATH statement tells DOS to look for a file in the root directory first, and, if it doesn't find the file there, to look in the DOS directory, then look in the 123 directory.

USING DIRECTORY MAINTENANCE

The PC Tools Directory Maintenance program includes all the DOS commands that manage directories, and even some commands that DOS doesn't have. Directory Maintenance allows you to change to a directory without specifying the complete path. You can even use Directory Maintenance on a network drive, no matter how complicated the directory structure on the file server becomes.

As with many of the utilities in the PC Tools package, there are several ways of starting Directory Maintenance:

- from inside PC Tools if you select Directory Maint. from the System Tools menu

- by choosing Directory Maintenance from the Disk menu in PC Shell

- by typing **DM** on the DOS command line

To follow the examples given in this section, start Directory Maintenance by typing **DM** at the DOS prompt without using any command-line switches.

The first time you start Directory Maintenance there is a short pause as the program reads details of the directories on the disk and records this information into a small file called TREELIST.*drive*. The file-name extension of this file reflects the drive letter; for example TREELIST.C represents drive C. Next, the Directory Maintenance window opens as shown in Figure 8.24, except of course with your own directories.

At the top of the window your disk drives are represented by small disk icons. Below these icons in the main part of the window is a list of the directories on the current disk. The directory structure is shown in graphical form, lines linking directories and subdirectories together. The current directory is highlighted. To the left of this list is a set of horizontal bar graphs; each bar represents a directory and the size of each bar indicates the size of the directory compared to the largest directory on the disk. An empty directory has no graph.

Below the main part of the window, the path name of the highlighted directory is shown, and below this is the Speed Search box.

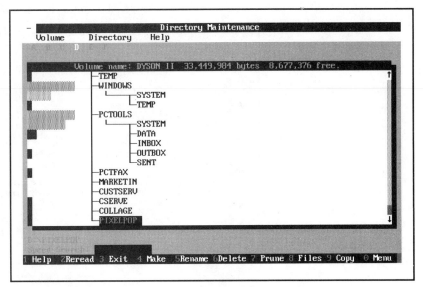

Figure 8.24: The Directory Maintenance window

CHANGING AND LISTING DIRECTORIES

To change to another directory, highlight it and press Enter, or double-click it with the mouse. Directory Maintenance will make it the current directory, end the program, and return you to the DOS prompt or to the program you used to start Directory Maintenance. Alternatively, you can use the Speed Search box at the bottom of the window to specify the directory you want. As soon as you type enough letters to identify the directory uniquely, Directory Maintenance moves the highlight to that directory. Press Enter to confirm your choice and return to DOS. If you have several directories with similar names, such as SYSTEM, for example, Speed Search will move to the first one as you start typing. To move to the next match, press →. To move to the previous match, press ←.

To see a list of the files in any directory, select Show Files (F8) from the Directory menu. Another window opens on the right of the directory list, as shown in Figure 8.25. The list of file names is a scrollable list, so you can use the mouse or the arrow keys to look through the contents of the directory.

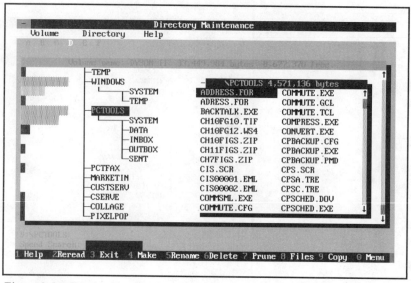

Figure 8.25: Display the files in a directory with Show Files

If the directory structure shown in the main window is not up-to-date because you have used the DOS commands to add or remove directories, select Reread Tree (F2) from the Volume menu to make Directory Maintenance reread the directories on the disk.

You can use the Change Drive option from the Volume menu, or click on one of the disk icons to change to another drive. It is much faster to click on the drive ions because you select the new drive directly. If you use Change Drive, the Drive Selection dialog box opens so you can choose a new drive to work with.

RENAMING, CREATING, AND DELETING DIRECTORIES

To rename a directory, place the highlight on it and choose Rename Directory (F5) from the Directory menu. The Rename Directory dialog box opens for you to enter the new name. Choose OK when you have entered the new name, or Cancel to return to the main Directory Maintenance window.

To create a new directory, move the highlight to the directory that will be the parent of the new directory and select Make Directory (F4) from the Directory menu. A dialog box opens for you to enter the name of the new directory, and as soon as you choose OK, the new directory is added to the diagram on the screen.

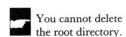 You cannot delete the root directory.

If you want to delete a directory, place the highlight over the directory you want to remove and choose Delete Directory (F6) from the Directory menu. A dialog box opens for you to confirm the delete operation before the directory is deleted. This gives you a chance to change your mind. Delete Directory can also remove all the files and subdirectories in a directory. If the directory you are trying to delete contains files or more directories, Directory Maintenance opens the dialog box shown in Figure 8.26 as a caution. Proceed very carefully.

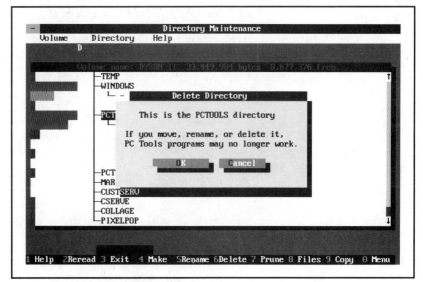

Figure 8.26: The Delete Directory dialog box opens if you try to remove a directory containing files

MOVING DIRECTORIES

You can use Prune and Graft (F7) from the Directory menu to move directories or groups of directories along with all their files and subdirectories to a new location on your disk. To move a directory, follow these steps:

1. Highlight the directory you want to move.

2. Select Prune and Graft (F7) from the Directory menu.

3. If you want to move the directory to a different disk, choose a drive by clicking on an icon, or by using Change Drive from the Volume menu.

4. Move the directory to the new location by dragging it with the mouse, or by using the arrow keys.

5. Press F7, or double-click with the mouse to confirm the new location.

CHANGING DIRECTORY ATTRIBUTES

You cannot change
network directory
attributes.

Use Modify Attributes to look at and perhaps change your directory attributes. Directory attributes are similar to the file attributes, and can be any combination of Read-Only, Hidden, System, or Archive:

- Read-Only protects the files from being modified, deleted or renamed.

- Hidden makes the directory invisible to the normal DOS commands. Directory Maintenance can still see hidden directories.

- System also makes the directory invisible. This attribute is not normally used.

- Archive is more appropriate for files and is not normally used with directories.

The root directory does not have any attributes.

PRINTING A DIRECTORY STRUCTURE

You can use Print Tree (F9) from the Volume menu to make a printout of your directory structure. The Print Tree dialog box contains the usual device options, but also contains three radio buttons to define the printout format, as follows:

- **Graphics Characters** uses real graphics characters on the printout, but not all printers can print them.

- **Non-graphics Characters** uses hyphens and plus signs instead of graphics characters. Most printers can print this style printout.

- **List Only** just prints a list of all the directory names.

Choose the format most applicable to your system.

IDENTIFYING YOUR DISKS WITH VOLUME LABELS

Each disk has a special entry in the root directory called the *volume label*. The DOS DIR and CHKDSK commands display the volume label at the start of every listing, and the label is often used as a title that describes the contents of the entire disk. For example, you might label a floppy disk containing word processing files ''MEMOS,'' or a disk containing Lotus 1-2-3 data files ''BUDGETS.''

The volume label on a disk can be up to 11 characters in length; it is displayed at the top of the directory window in the main Directory Maintenance screen.

Select Rename Volume from the Volume menu in Directory Maintenance to look at or change your disk's volume label. The Rename Volume Dialog box opens, showing the existing volume label. To change it, enter the new volume label and choose OK. Use Cancel if you change your mind.

USING DIRECTORY MAINTENANCE ON A NETWORK

Directory Maintenance can maintain directories on a network drive using Novell NetWare 286 Version 2.10, or later.

If you are logged on to a Novell network, you can use the functions I have already described for making and changing directories, as well as several network-specific functions. Select Network Rights from the Directory menu to look at your access rights. These rights are set up by the network supervisor; they determine what you can and cannot do with files and directories on the network. For example, everyone on the network may have "read access" to files, but only you have "write permission." This means that other users can access the data, but only you can change them.

You can change the look of the directory tree display with the Tree Data Display command from the Volume menu. There are five selections, as follows:

The network rights are slightly different between Novell NetWare 286 and NetWare 386.

- **Bar Graph** makes a horizontal bar to indicate the size of the current directory compared with the largest directory on the current disk.

- **Size** indicates the total size of all files in the directory in kilobytes or megabytes; subdirectories are totaled separately.

- **Creation Date** shows the date that each directory was originally made.

- **Owner** lists the name of the creator of each directory.

- **Rights** lists the rights or permissions you have for each directory.

All these selections can be used on a network, but only the first two, Bar Graph and Size, can be used with local DOS directories.

USING DIRECTORY MAINTENANCE FROM THE DOS COMMAND LINE

You need not load Directory Maintenance every time you want to perform some basic directory manipulation. You can also use Directory Maintenance at the DOS prompt.

CHANGING DIRECTORIES   You can change from any directory to another on the disk without having to type in the new directory's path. For example, suppose you are in the root directory and you want to change to C:\PCTOOLS\DATA. Just type

DM DATA

Directory Maintenance searches the disk's structure, finds the requested directory, and changes to it. In fact, you need only type the first few letters of the name—enough letters so that Directory Maintenance can locate the correct directory. If your disk contained directories with similar names, such as TEST and TEXT, for example, you would have to type more characters to make the entry unique.

UPDATING TREELIST The first time you run Directory Maintenance, it reads the complete directory structure from your disk and stores it in a small file called TREELIST.*drive,* where *drive* corresponds to the drive being read. The next time you run Directory Maintenance, the program will read the data from this file rather than read the directory structure again. This lets Directory Maintenance work very quickly. However, if you make changes to your directory structure using the DOS commands, Directory Maintenance will not know about the changes. You can make Directory Maintenance read the structure and update TREELIST if you type

DM /R

from the DOS command line.

MAKING AND REMOVING DIRECTORIES To practice making and removing directories with Directory Maintenance, we will work with a new directory called 123 as an example. To create this new directory, type

DM MD \123

from the root directory. You can also create subdirectories in another directory with Directory Maintenance—just specify the new directory's full path name when you create it. For example, if you want to create a BUDGETS subdirectory below the 123 directory, you must type:

DM MD \123\BUDGETS

To remove the BUDGETS subdirectory, type

DM DD \123\BUDGETS

from any directory. Remember that this command deletes all the files in this directory, as well as any subdirectories inside it.

USING VIEW TO LOOK AT FILES

View lets you look at the contents of files made by many applications programs without starting the application itself—and even without knowing which application created the file. View can display files made by over 30 different applications programs. If the file is a Lotus spreadsheet file, View automatically loads the 123 Viewer and displays the file in spreadsheet format; if the file is a dBASE file, View loads the dBASE viewer and displays the file in a database format. View can display spreadsheet, database, word processor, text, graphics, binary program, and archive utility files, all in an appropriate format. Table 8.1 lists all the file types that View can display.

You must have a CGA, EGA, or VGA to view PC Paintbrush .PCX files. If the file was originally created with a high-resolution display, you must have a similar display to view the file.

Table 8.1: File Types that View Displays

APPLICATION TYPE	APPLICATION NAME
Database Viewers	dBASE
	Desktop Database
	Microsoft Works
	Paradox
	R:BASE
Spreadsheet Viewers	Quattro Pro
	Lotus 1-2-3
	Lotus Symphony
	Microsoft Excel
	Microsoft Works
	Mosaic Twin

Table 8.1: File Types that View Displays (continued)

APPLICATION TYPE	APPLICATION NAME
Word-Processor Viewers	MultiPlan
	VP Planner Plus
	ASCII
	DCA
	Desktop Notepads
	DisplayWrite
	MultiMate
	Microsoft Windows Write
	Microsoft Word
	Microsoft Works
	Text
	WordPerfect
	WordStar
	XyWrite
Miscellaneous Viewers	ARC
	Binary
	LHARC
	PAK
	PCX
	ZIP
	ZOO

You can start View from the DOS command line, or you can call View from inside any of the following PC Tools programs:

- CP Backup
- FileFind

- File Fix
- PC Shell
- Undelete

If you start View from inside PC Shell, you can launch the application program that created the file without leaving PC Shell, and load the selected file as the data file.

To start View from the DOS command line, type

VIEW

if you want to work with files in the current directory, or type

VIEW *filespec*

to work with a specific file or directory. You can use the DOS wildcard characters ? or * with View to select more than one file. If you specified a single file on the command line when you started View, that file is displayed in the View window when the program starts, otherwise you will see a list of files on the screen—either those you specified or those contained in the current directory.

To view a file from this list, move the highlight to the file you want to view and double-click or press Enter. The View window opens with the type of viewer identified in the top line of the window, followed by the name of the file you are working with. If View cannot recognize the file type, it looks for text in the file and then loads the Text viewer. If this is not successful, View loads the Binary viewer.

There are several function keys available from the message line in this window, in addition to the usual F1 (Help), and F3 (Exit) keys, as follows:

- **Info** (F2) opens the Viewer/File Info window to display information about the current file, including the file name, length, number of rows and columns.

- **Files** (F4) opens the File selection window again, allowing you to choose another file to view. At the end of the list of files is a list of the drives on your system. This allows you to change to another drive without leaving View. This option is only available in View if you started the program from the DOS command line.

- **Go To** (F5) opens a small window to let you enter the row and cell number you want to go to next.

- **Viewer** (F6) opens a window listing all the viewers that View uses, with the current view shown highlighted. If you double-click to open a different viewer for the current file, you will probably see an error message saying that the viewer you selected cannot display the contents of the current file, and View will open the binary viewer instead.

- **Search** (F7) allows you to search for text of up to 30 characters in length. You can determine whether the search is case-sensitive or not, and you can look for whole words or parts of words. View highlights the found text. Press Shift-F7 (Again) to repeat the search.

- **Zoom/Unzoom** (F8) enlarges or shrinks the active window.

- **Previous** (F9) displays the contents of the previously selected file.

- **Next** (F10) displays the contents of the next file in the list.

If you are viewing a .PCX graphics image, F8 is the function key you use to switch from text mode to graphics mode.

VIEWING SPREADSHEET FILES

Figure 8.27 shows a Lotus spreadsheet file displayed in the Lotus viewer. Use the keys shown in Table 8.2 to navigate through the spreadsheet. To move horizontally using the mouse, hold down the right mouse button and drag the mouse to the left or to the right. To move vertically, hold down the right mouse button and move the mouse up or down.

VIEWING DATABASE FILES

If the file you choose is a dBASE (or dBASE-compatible) file, View loads the dBASE viewer, as shown in Figure 8.28. The file name is shown at the top of the window, next to the name of the

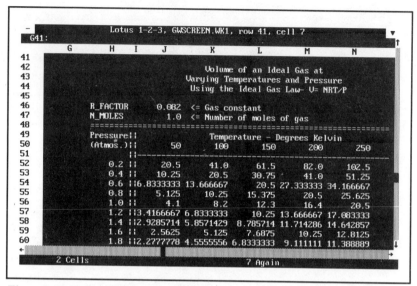

Figure 8.27: A Lotus spreadsheet file shown in the Lotus viewer

Table 8.2: Keys for Moving through Your Spreadsheet

KEY	FUNCTION
→	Moves right one cell
←	Moves left one cell
↑	Moves up one row
↓	Moves down one row
Ctrl-→	Moves right one window
Ctrl-←	Moves left one window
PgUp	Moves up one window
PgDn	Moves down one window
Home	Moves to the first cell in the spreadsheet
End	Moves to the last cell in the spreadsheet
/	Alternates between the top and the bottom of the file
Shift-F2	Opens a window listing the name, type, and length of the cells in the spreadsheet

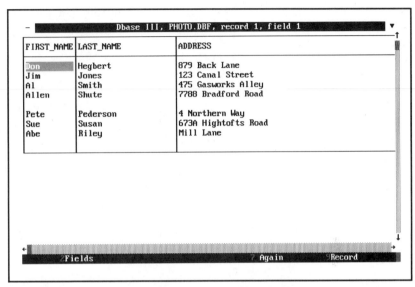

Figure 8.28: A dBASE file displayed in the dBASE file viewer

viewer in use. The record number and field number are shown on the same line. In addition to the normal function keys, two shifted function keys are dedicated to the database viewer:

> If you are viewing an R:BASE file, Shift-F4 lets you view and select from a list of tables.

- Shift-F2 (Fields) displays a list of all the fields in the database. This window shows field name on the left, field type in the center, and field size on the right.

- Shift-F9 (Browse/Record) toggles the main database viewing window between the browse mode display and the record mode display.

Use the keystrokes listed in Table 8.3 to move through the records in the database file.

VIEWING GRAPHICS FILES

If the file you want to view is a .PCX graphics file, View loads the PCX Viewer, as Figure 8.29 shows.

Table 8.3: Keys for Moving through Your Database

KEY	FUNCTION
Record Mode	
→	Displays the next record
←	Displays the previous record
↑	Moves up one field
↓	Moves down one field
PgUp	Moves up one window
PgDn	Moves down one window
Ctrl-PgUp	Moves to top of file
Ctrl-PgDn	Moves to end of file
Home	Goes to the beginning of the record
End	Goes to the end of the record
/	Toggles between the first and last record
Browse Mode	
→	Moves right one field
←	Moves left one field
↑	Moves up one record
↓	Moves down one record
PgUp	Moves up one window
PgDn	Moves down one window
Ctrl-PgUp	Moves to top of file
Ctrl-PgDn	Moves to end of file
Home	Goes to the beginning of the database
End	Goes to the end of the database
/	Toggles between the first and the last record

Figure 8.29: A graphics file displayed in the PCX viewer

Special keys available in the PCX viewer are as follows:

- Shift-F3 (Modes) opens a window listing the other video modes, with the recommended mode indicated with a checkmark.

- F8 (Graphics) toggles between the graphical display and the text portion of the PCX viewer.

VIEWING TEXT AND ASCII FILES

If the file you are working with is a text file, View loads the Text Viewer as shown in Figure 8.30. If your word processor is in the list shown in Table 8.1, View loads a special file viewer dedicated to it. These special viewers are very similar in operation to the Text Viewer. There is one special function key associated with the Text Viewer:

- Shift F3 (Wrap/No Wrap) toggles the text in and out of wrap mode. When the text is in wrap mode, it fits inside the View

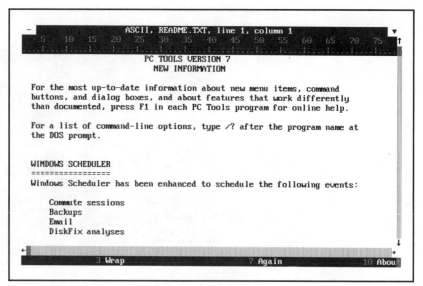

Figure 8.30: A text file displayed in the Text Viewer

window. When the text is no wrap, text flows out of the right side of the window, and you will have to use the mouse or the cursor keys to look at that text.

Use the keystrokes listed in Table 8.4 to move through your text file.

Table 8.4: Keys for Moving through Your Text or Binary Files

KEY	FUNCTION
→	Moves right one character
←	Moves left one character
↑	Moves up one line
↓	Moves down one line
Ctrl-→	Moves right 10 characters
Ctrl-←	Moves left 10 characters
PgUp	Moves up one window
PgDn	Moves down one window
Ctrl-PgUp	Moves to top of file

Table 8.4: Keys for Moving through Your Text or Binary Files (continued)

KEY	FUNCTION
Ctrl-PgDn	Moves to end of file
Home	Goes to the beginning of the file
End	Goes to the end of the file
/	Alternates between the beginning and end of the file

VIEWING BINARY OR PROGRAM FILES

If you select a binary or program file, View loads the Binary Viewer, as Figure 8.31 shows. The Binary Viewer looks a little different from the other viewers, and the data on the screen is divided into columns. The leftmost column of figures in the window shows the location of the data in terms of a hexadecimal byte count offset from the beginning of the file. The central area of the window shows the data in the file as two-digit hex numbers. Each line in the window displays 16 bytes of information. On the right side of the window are two more columns, the first of which shows an ASCII representation of the data using the extended ASCII character set, while the second column shows printable characters only. Use the mouse and the scroll bars or the arrow keys to move around in the display. The only shifted function key in this viewer is Again (Shift-F7), to repeat searches instigated using Search (F7).

If the file you are working with was made by one of the popular file-compression utility programs like ARC, LHARC, or PKZIP, you will see another file viewer, as Figure 8.32 shows. The Zip Archive Viewer lists data for each of the original files inside the ZIP file, including the file name, size in bytes, the compression method, the date and time, and the CRC (Cyclical Redundancy Check)—a kind of checksum. The other archive viewers show very similar information.

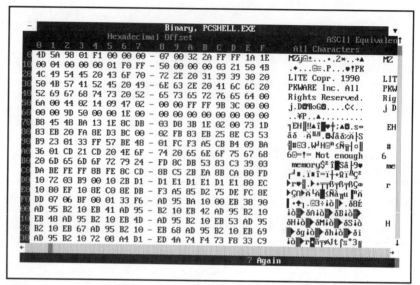

Figure 8.31: A binary file displayed in the Binary Viewer

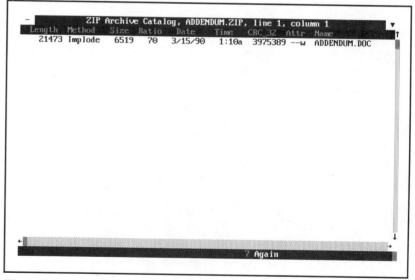

Figure 8.32: A PKZIP file displayed in the Zip Archive Viewer

USING PC-CACHE TO INCREASE DISK PERFORMANCE

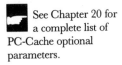 Just use one disk-cache program at a time; unpredictable results may occur if you use more than one. For example, if you are a Windows user, do not install PC-Cache and SMARTDRV.SYS on the same system.

When your application program needs data from the disk, it asks DOS to find it. DOS reads the data and passes it back to the application program. If you are updating your database, for example, this can mean that the same data are requested and read many times during the update. A *disk-cache* program mediates between the application and DOS. When the application program requests data that is on the disk, the cache program first checks to see if the data are already in the cache memory. If they are, then the disk-cache program reads the data from the cache memory rather than from the disk. If the data are not in memory, then the cache program reads the data from the disk, copies them into the cache memory for future reference, and then passes the data to the application program. Figure 8.33 shows how a disk-cache program works.

LOADING PC-CACHE

PC-Cache can use conventional, expanded, or extended memory, and can support several hard disks at the same time. You use PC-Cache from the DOS prompt since it does not have a full-screen option.

You must install PC-Cache after Mirror but before any other memory-resident programs. See Chapter 19 for more details on memory-resident programs and loading order.

If you used PC Setup to install PC Tools, PC-Cache will be installed in the correct sequence. If you do the installation yourself, make sure to place PC-Cache after the Mirror program and before any other memory-resident programs such as PC Shell, Desktop, and so on.

To see a list of the PC-Cache parameters, type (from the DOS prompt)

PC-Cache /?

To run PC-Cache from the DOS prompt, type

PC-CACHE *parameters*

See Chapter 20 for a complete list of PC-Cache optional parameters.

where *parameters* come from the list in Table 8.5.

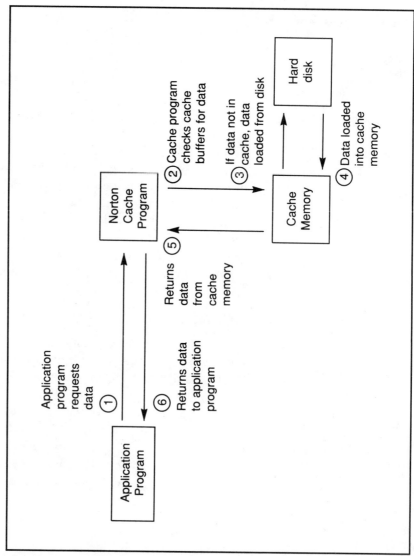

Figure 8.33: PC-Cache mediates between your application program and the hard disk

Table 8.5: PC-Cache Parameters

PARAMETER	MEANING
/EXTSTART = *n*K	Specifies the start of the cache buffer in extended memory; EXTSTART must be larger than 1MB—that is, 1,024K. PC-Cache is compatible with VDISK.SYS
/FLUSH	Empties the cache and writes cache contents to disk
/I*drive*	Specifies the drive or drives that should not be cached, where *drive* is a letter or number
/ON	Turns the cache on
/OFF	Turns the cache off
/PAUSE	Used under special circumstances if you are having problems with PC-Cache. Follow the directions on the screen
/QUIET	Turns off the PC-Cache startup information, so that PC-Cache can be used in batch files
/STATUS	Displays information showing the current status of the cache
/UNLOAD	Removes the cache as long as the cache was the last TSR loaded
/WIN	Resizes the cache when Windows is started
/WRITE = ON	Turns on disk-write caching
/WRITE = OFF	Turns off disk-write caching
/?	Displays a help screen showing all PC-Cache's parameters. Use this to confirm the version number of the PC-Cache you are using

PC-Cache supports standard memory (up to 640K), expanded memory (memory that conforms to the Lotus/Intel/Microsoft expanded memory specification), or extended memory (AT-style memory above 640K). When a cache is created in expanded or extended memory, a small amount of standard memory must also be used. You may use only one /SIZE parameter; you cannot mix standard, expanded, and extended memory. You can specify the size of the cache with one of the parameters listed in Table 8.6.

Table 8.6: PC-Cache /SIZE Parameters

PARAMETER	MEANING
/SIZE = nK	Specifies the amount of standard memory for the cache; if no size is given, the default is 64K
/SIZEXP = nK	Specifies the amount of expanded memory for the cache; the smallest size is 10K and the default is 256K
/SIZEXT = nK	Specifies the amount of extended memory for the cache. This parameter can only be used on computers using Intel's 80286 and 80386 processors; the default is 256K
/SIZEXT* = nK	Allows PC-Cache to decide the best method for accessing extended memory

For example, to install a cache of 128K in standard memory, add the following line to your AUTOEXEC.BAT file:

```
PC-CACHE  /SIZE = 128K
```

You should use as little of your conventional memory as possible for the cache; use expanded or extended memory if you have it available. To install a cache of 256K in expanded memory, include the line

```
PC-CACHE  /SIZEXP = 256K
```

To make a cache of 256K in extended memory, use the line

PC-CACHE /SIZEXT = 256K

Reboot your computer after you have changed AUTOEXEC.BAT so that the new cache is installed. Remember, you can only use one /SIZE statement in the cache specification.

As well as caching disk reads, PC-Cache can also cache disk-write operations. The default setting for delaying disk writes is ON, and you can change this specification if you use the parameter

Some versions of MS-DOS 3.1 do not work properly if delayed disk writes are used.

PC-CACHE /WRITE = OFF

in your AUTOEXEC.BAT file if you want to make sure all writes are completed without caching. When disk-write caching is on, all disk-write operations are saved until DOS is idle—then they are completed.

UNDERSTANDING THE PC-CACHE STATUS DISPLAY

The PC-Cache Version 6 parameters of /MEASURES, /PARAMS, /PARAMS*, and /INFO have all been replaced by /STATUS. If you use one of these older parameters, PC-Cache responds with the /STATUS display.

To see how well your cache is performing after you have been using it for a while, use the /STATUS parameter from the DOS prompt, as follows:

PC-CACHE /STATUS

or

PC-CACHE /S

This version of PC-Cache does not cache floppy disks or Bernoulli boxes.

The results are shown in Figure 8.34.

The status display is divided into three windows: Settings, Memory, and Disk Statistics. On the left, the Settings window details the cache parameters being used, either as default settings or because you specified their use. Defaults are shown enclosed in parentheses. On the right, the Memory window details memory usage in terms of conventional, extended, or expanded memory. For each type of memory, PC-Cache shows a bar graph indicating how much is used

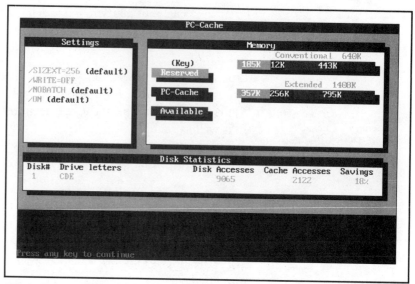

Figure 8.34: PC-Cache display using the /STATUS parameter

by DOS, by PC-Cache, and the amount of free memory left. In the Disk Statistics window, PC-Cache lists the following performance indicators for each drive:

- **Disk Accesses** is the number of data transfers that have occurred between the disk and the cache.

- **Cache Accesses** is the number of data transfers that have occurred between the cache and the current application.

- **Savings** is the number of physical transfers saved by using PC-Cache expressed as a percentage.

OPTIMIZING PC-CACHE

If your computer is an PC/XT or a laptop with no extended or expanded memory, you will have to balance the speed increase gained through using the cache against the conventional memory space lost to the cache program and the cache buffers themselves. Usually, the bigger the cache, the faster your system appears to run—up to a point. You have to determine where that point is, given your own particular hardware circumstances.

Different applications programs use memory in different ways. If you use the /WIN option, PC-Cache automatically reduces the amount of memory it takes when you run Windows 3.0 or later, making that space available for Windows to use instead. Lotus 1-2-3 uses memory in a different way, so a cache does not make much difference to performance. If you use Lotus frequently, use a small cache so that most of the memory is available to Lotus. Word processors and databases access their files frequently, especially index files, so be sure that the cache is big enough to handle the average index file.

PC FORMAT— A SAFE FORMATTING PROGRAM

A Bernoulli box (developed by Iomega Corporation) uses a high-density, removable cartridge containing flexible disks for data and program storage. They can contain up to 44MB and are capable of up to 22 millisecond access times.

PC Format provides a faster, easier-to-use alternative to the DOS FORMAT command. It can format floppy disks, hard disks, and Bernoulli boxes, but you cannot use it on a networked disk or file server. PC Format adds many useful safety features, including the ability to preserve the original contents of the disk you are formatting so that you can recover the original data on the disk.

You have already learned what happens when you run the DOS FORMAT command on a hard disk. The FAT and root directory entries are destroyed. On a floppy disk, FORMAT writes a character into every location on the disk, completely destroying the disk's original data.

Using PC Format with a floppy disk allows Rebuild to recover the original contents of the disk, including the first letter of all the file names.

If you use PC Format on a floppy disk, the program first tries to read the disk. If it cannot find any data or if tracks 0 and 1 are empty, PC Format overwrites every track on the disk. If PC Format finds any data on the disk, it leaves the data intact but clears the FAT and the first character of all the file names in the root directory. It stores the first character of the file names in a special area in the root directory.

Similarly, if you use PC Format on your hard disk, the program does not destroy the original data on the disk. It clears the FAT and the first character of the file names in the root directory and saves this information in a special place in the directory. You cannot use PC Format to perform low-level formatting of your hard disk.

RUNNING PC FORMAT IN FULL-SCREEN MODE

If you used the PC Setup install program to load PC Tools onto your hard disk, the installation program renames the DOS FORMAT command to FORMAT!. So now when you type **FORMAT** PC Format loads, rather than DOS FORMAT. You can also start PC Format from the list of system tools in PC Shell. The opening window allows you to choose the floppy or hard disk you want to format, then the next screen lets you choose the formatting options you want to use, as Figure 8.35 shows.

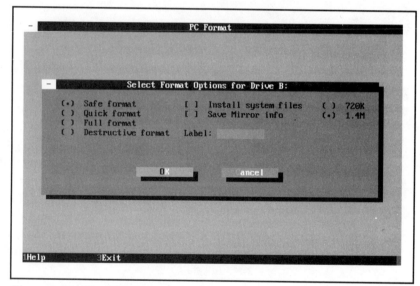

Figure 8.35: The PC Format window allows you to choose from several different formatting options

If you use 3½-inch disks, do not format high-density disks as 720K disks, and do not format 720K disks as 1.44MB disks; you will lose data if you do.

Next, select the formatting method you want to use:

- **Safe Format** formats the disk so that you can recover the contents using Unformat if necessary.

- **Quick Format** can be used on Bernoulli boxes as well as on floppy disks. This selection erases the root directory and FAT, but does not erase any data.

- **Full Format** reads and formats each track, rewriting the data. It clears the root directory and the FAT. This option is not available on hard disks; use Safe Format instead.

- **Destructive Format** formats the disk by erasing all traces of the original data. Use this option if you want to obliterate confidential data from the disk. This option is not available on hard disks either.

The next three selections help you customize the format further:

- **Install System Files** allows you to install the appropriate DOS files to make a bootable disk.

- **Save Mirror Information**. Use this selection if you used Mirror on the disk in the past and you want to preserve that information.

- **Write Volume Label** lets you add a volume label of up to 11 characters to the disk.

Finally, select the disk size you want to use. If you are using $3^1/_2$-inch disks, be careful to choose the correct format. The labeling on disk cartons can vary tremendously: a disk suitable for formatting to 1.44MB can be labeled as ''2.00MB,'' ''High Density,'' or ''MF-2HD.''

There is no such easily visible difference for $5^1/_4$-inch disks. The label must suffice.

The rule is as follows (see Figure 8.36) if the disk has a square hole cut into the case at the opposite end to the sliding metal shutter (other than the write-protect hole), you should only format the disk as a 1.44MB disk. If there is only the write-protect slide, format the disk as 720K only. If you format these disks incorrectly, you will eventually loose all the data on the disk.

If PC Format finds any files on the disk, a window opens listing the files, and asks whether you want to continue with the formatting. This is a good safety measure, as it prevents you from inadvertently formatting the wrong disk. Select OK to continue with the format or Cancel to return to the disk-selection screen.

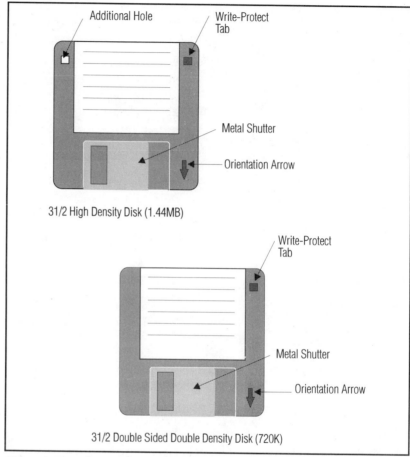

Figure 8.36: Distinguishing between high-density and double-sided, double-density disks

RUNNING PC FORMAT FROM THE DOS COMMAND LINE

To run PC Format from the DOS command line to format the floppy disk in drive B, enter

FORMAT B:

Figure 8.37 shows the resulting screen.

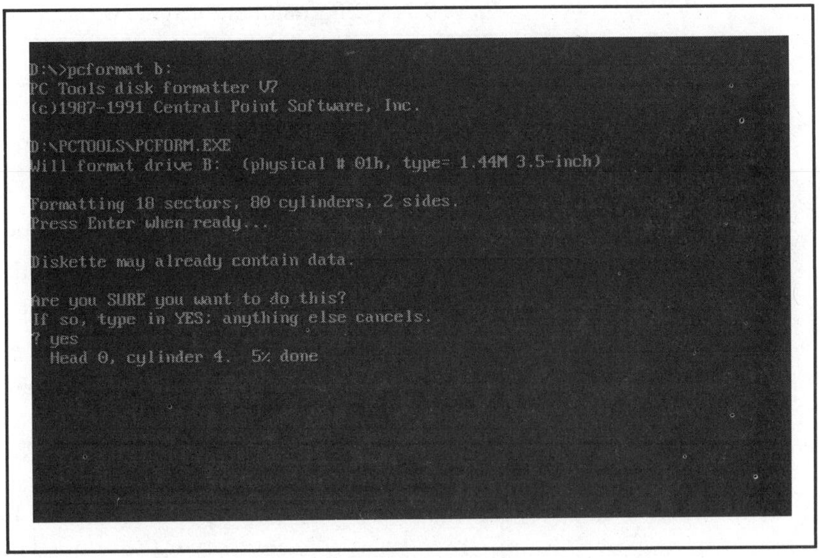

```
D:\>pcformat b:
PC Tools disk formatter V7
(c)1987-1991 Central Point Software, Inc.

D:\PCTOOLS\PCFORM.EXE
Will format drive B:  (physical # 01h, type= 1.44M 3.5-inch)

Formatting 18 sectors, 80 cylinders, 2 sides.
Press Enter when ready...

Diskette may already contain data.

Are you SURE you want to do this?
If so, type in YES; anything else cancels.
? yes
   Head 0, cylinder 4.  5% done
```

Figure 8.37: PC Format formatting a floppy disk in drive B

PC Format identifies the type of drive—in this case a 3½-inch 1.44MB floppy—and selects the correct format mode. PC Format checks the disk for existing data by reading tracks 0 and 1 before writing anything onto the disk. If they are empty, PC Format overwrites every track. In this case, since the disk already contained data, PC Format asks

Are you SURE you want to do this?

If you answer yes, the formatting starts. A small display of disk head number, cylinder number, and percentage completed shows the progress of the format.

You can use PC Format with several optional parameters directly from the DOS command prompt to perform specific functions. Table 8.7 lists the optional PC Format parameters for floppy disks and Table 8.8 lists those for hard disks.

Table 8.7: PC Format Parameters for Use with Floppy Disks

PARAMETER	USE
drive	Specifies the drive for formatting
/1	Selects single-sided format
/4	Formats a 360K floppy disk in a 1.2MB drive
/8	Formats the disk with eight sectors per track
/DESTROY	Formats the disk and erases all data using a destructive format
/F	Specifies a full format. PC Format reads the data on each track, formats the track, and rewrites the data. This may be slower than the other modes, but it can clean up poor disks. The FAT is cleared, but Rebuild can still recover the original data on the disk
/F:*n*	Formats the disk to the specified size: 160, 180, 320, 360, 720, 1,200, or 1,400K
/N:*x*	Specifies the number of sectors to format. Must be used with the /T parameter
/P	Prints the information on the screen to LPT1
/Q	Quickly reformats an already-formatted disk and erases the FAT and root directory
/R	Revitalizes the floppy disk by reformatting and rewriting each track. The FAT, root directory, and data all stay intact. This has the same effect as using Revitalize a Disk in DiskFix
/S	Copies the DOS system files after formatting to make the disk bootable
/TEST	Simulates a format without writing to the disk
/T:*x*	Specifies the number of tracks to format. Must be used with the /N parameter
/V	Adds a volume label; PC Format asks for the label when the format is complete

Table 8.8: PC Format Parameters for Use with Hard Disks

PARAMETER	USE
drive	Specifies the drive for formatting
/P	Prints the information on the screen to LPT1
/Q	Quickly reformats an already-formatted disk
/S	Copies the DOS system files to the disk after formatting to make the disk bootable. Before using /S, boot the computer with a floppy disk containing the version of DOS you want transferred to the hard disk
/TEST	Simulates a format without writing to the disk
/V	Adds a volume label; PC Format prompts you for the label when the format is complete

If you use PC Format to format a floppy disk, you can probably use Rebuild to recover the original data. The only data lost is the FAT, which Rebuild can reconstruct as long as the disk did not contain any fragmented files.

PC Format is a considerable advance over the DOS FORMAT command, and adds many useful safety features, including the ability to recover the original data on the disk if necessary.

CHAPTER

9

Protecting Files with the Security Tools

In this chapter I describe the security tools provided by PC Tools, including PC Secure (a file-encryption program), Data Monitor (a multi-function protection program), Wipe (a file-obliteration program), and VDefend (a virus detector).

USING PC SECURE

DOS has virtually no built-in security features. If you keep confidential files such as payroll records or personnel files on your computer, you may want to encrypt them for increased security. Or you may want to employ a data-compression technique called *block-adaptive Lempel-Ziv-Welch compression* to shrink your files and use your disk space more effectively.

THE DATA-ENCRYPTION STANDARD

If you want to know more about DES, see the U.S. Department of Commerce/National Bureau of Standards, Data-Encryption Standard, Federal Information Processing Standard Publication 46, 1977, which contains full details of the algorithm.

Since the DES algorithm cannot be shipped outside the U.S., PC Secure is shipped overseas with the encrypt/decrypt option removed. File compression/expansion is still active, however, and can give some security, although that is certainly not its prime purpose and the result is not as secure as a file encrypted with DES.

PC Secure uses the DES (data-encryption standard) to encrypt and decrypt files. The DES is a block cipher that works by a combination of transposition and substitution. It works on blocks of eight bytes (64 bits each), encrypting or decrypting them using a 56-bit user-supplied key. With a 54-bit key, there are about $7.2 \times 1,016$ possible keys. Due to the algorithm's complexity and length, it is not reproduced here.

DES was developed after years of work at IBM, rigorously tested by the National Security Agency, and finally accepted as being free of any statistical or mathematical weaknesses. This suggests that it is impossible to break the system using statistical frequency tables or to work the algorithm backwards using mathematical methods. DES is used by federal departments and most banks and money-transfer systems to protect all sensitive computer data.

DES has the following features:

- It has remained unbroken despite years of use.
- It completely randomizes the data in the file.
- Even if you know some of the original text, you cannot use it to determine the encryption key.

- After DES encryption, it is virtually impossible to decrypt the file without the key.

COMPRESSING FILES

Do not confuse references in this section to "file compression" (which actually makes a file smaller) with the Compress program in PC Tools (which unfragments and rearranges files on your disks).

Using DES encryption increases security by scrambling the contents of a file. However, one of the other selections in PC Secure allows you to compress your files—that is, to make them actually smaller so that they occupy less space on your disk. You will see the biggest change in size with text files; there is little, if any, change with program or other binary files. PC Secure uses the block-adaptive Lempel-Ziv-Welch (LZW) compression method. This method can be done in one pass across the file, unlike Huffman coding (another common data-compression technique, often used by fax machines), and does not require that a translation table be stored or transmitted with the compressed file. You can transmit a compressed file by modem or back up a compressed file to a floppy disk much faster than you can process the larger original.

ENCRYPTING YOUR FILES

You can load PC Secure through the menu in PC Shell or run it from the DOS prompt by typing **PCSECURE**.

If you lose the key or password used to encrypt a file, you will never be able to decrypt the file again, so be very careful.

CREATING A KEY   The first time you run PC Secure, you are asked to create a master key. The key can be either a combination of hexadecimal numbers or alphanumeric characters. If you enter alphanumeric characters, the key must be from five to 32 alphabetic or numeric characters long. The key is case-sensitive, so "computer," "Computer," and "COMPUTER" are three different keys. Keys must be longer than five characters, since it is too easy to guess keys of fewer than five characters.

As you type in your alphanumeric key, for security reasons PC Secure displays a * instead of the character you enter. You are asked to confirm your key by typing it a second time.

Press F9 if you would rather enter your key directly in hexadecimal. If you choose this option, the key must be exactly 16 characters long. In hexadecimal entry, you only type your key once; you are not asked to confirm it. Also, the characters are displayed as you enter them.

Consider the following when choosing your keys:

- Do not choose keys that others might easily guess.

- Do not lose your keys.

- Do not tell other people what your keys are.

The worst keys are the obvious ones: initials, place names or people's names, phone numbers, birth dates, or complete English words (there is only a limited number of words in the English language and a computer can try them all very quickly). The best keys are longer rather than shorter, and usually contain a combination of letters and numbers. Your key should be easy for you to remember but meaningless to anyone else.

The key is stored in the PCSECURE.EXE file for safekeeping, and it will be used to encrypt any file except those encrypted in expert mode.

You can use PC Secure to encrypt and compress all sorts of files. You cannot, however, use it on files that are already compressed by utilities like ARC or other encryption schemes (if you run PC Secure on these files, they will probably grow slightly larger). You can compress Lotus spreadsheet files by up to 60 or 70 percent, and word-processing files by 50 to 60 percent. The results you get will depend on the type of file you work with.

Since encrypted or compressed files are binary files, you cannot use ASCII file-transfer methods to send the file over a modem. Use XMODEM instead.

Do not encrypt or compress applications that use some sort of copy-protection scheme. PC Secure will compress and encrypt the file, but the application will not run if certain information is not accessible. You can use PC Shell File and Disk commands as well as the DOS equivalents to copy, delete, back up, and restore encrypted files. You can even run the hard-disk optimizing program called Compress on PC Secure files. Remember that the compressed or encrypted files are binary files, so be careful to select the appropriate file-transfer method if you want to transfer the file to another computer over a modem. You cannot use ASCII-transfer methods on a binary file; use XMODEM if it is available.

PC Secure is also compatible with standard DOS networks, but you should be careful not to place a decrypted file on the network-server disk where others may find it. Copy the encrypted file to your local station and decrypt the file there to maintain security.

CHOOSING ENCRYPTION OPTIONS Before proceeding, you should choose the encryption selections you need from the Options menu shown in Figure 9.1.

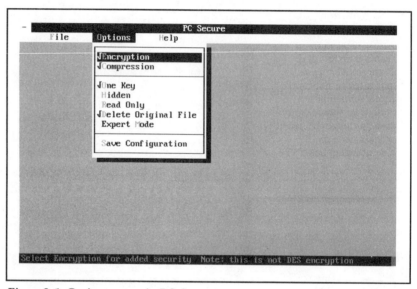

Figure 9.1: Options menu in PC Secure

To perform compression only on your file, turn off both the Full DES Encryption and the Quick Encryption options.

Your selections are indicated by a check mark to the left of the item in the menu. If there is no mark, the option will not be used when you start file encryption:

- **Full DES Encryption** gives the file the full 16 encryption rounds as defined in the standard.

- **Quick Encryption** enacts only two encryption rounds, which saves time but is much less secure.

- You can choose **Compression** with or without encryption. PC Secure uses LZW compression, a more advanced method than Huffman coding or Adaptive Huffman coding. Also, LZW compresses the file in one pass and does not require that a translation table be stored with the file. PC Secure compresses most files from 20 to 70 percent.

- With the **One Key** selection on, PC Secure only asks you to enter the key the first time you work on a file, and continues to use the same key for all following files. With this option off, PC Secure asks you for the key for every file you work with.

- **Hidden** sets the hidden bit of the file's attribute, making it invisible to the normal DOS commands.

- **Read Only** makes the file read-only so that the DOS commands DELETE and ERASE cannot access it. If you try to delete a read-only file, DOS responds with the message

  Access Denied.

- With the **Delete Original File** selection on, PC Secure copies your original file, encrypts the copy, and then destroys the original. There must be enough room on the disk for both files at the same time. This selection provides high security, but remember, you cannot undelete a file that PC Secure has destroyed.

  If this option is off, a copy of your original file is encrypted and the extension .SEC is added. The original file is not affected. Again, you must have enough room on the disk for both files at the same time.

- If you encrypt a file with **Expert Mode** off and you forget the key used for encryption, you can use the master key that you entered when you started PC Secure for the first time.

  If you encrypt a file with Expert Mode on and you lose the key, your master key cannot decrypt the file. In fact, there is no way to decrypt the file. You would have to break DES to do it, and no one has ever done that.

- **Save Configuration** saves your current settings into a file as the default settings for PC Secure.

COMPLETING THE ENCRYPTION   When you have made your choices from the Options menu, open the File menu and choose Encrypt File, or press F4 to start the encryption process.

This brings up the File Selection dialog box, which contains a list of the files in the current directory. Select a file from the list box or type a new name into the file-name box. Choose Encrypt to proceed. A dialog box opens requesting the key. Enter the key; you are asked to type it again for verification. If you make a mistake entering your key, another dialog box responds with the message

The keys are not equivalent.

PC Secure starts work on the file according to the selections you made from the Options menu. Figure 9.2 shows the Encryption Progress screen.

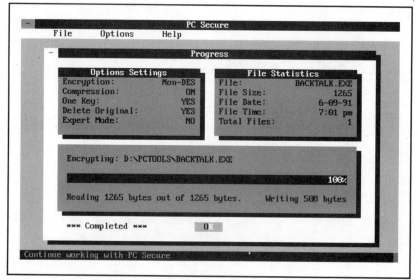

Figure 9.2: The Encryption Progress screen

The horizontal bar moves from left to right as the file is encrypted to show the amount of progress made.

To encrypt a whole directory in one pass, select the directory from the File Selection dialog box. This time choose the Directory button. A message box warns you that this option will affect more than one file, and asks for your permission to continue. There is a check box if you want to include all subdirectories in the encryption process. After making your choices, you are prompted for your key as before, and the encryption begins.

DECRYPTING YOUR FILES

When you decrypt a file, you restore it to its original condition. Choose Decrypt (F5) from the File menu to display the File Selection dialog box.

Choose the file for decryption and click the Decrypt button. If the One Key choice in the Options menu is on and there is a check mark by the entry, you will not be asked for a key here. Otherwise, enter the key you used to encrypt the file. A second dialog box asks for confirmation of the key. If the keys don't match, a dialog box responds with the message

The keys are not equivalent.

Enter the correct key. If you type the wrong key, you'll see a dialog box with the message

Bad password, try again?

If you try to decrypt a file that is not encrypted, you will see the message

This is not a PC Secure file.

As PC Secure decrypts the file, its progress is shown on the horizontal bar graph.

To decrypt an entire directory, select Decrypt (F5). Then select the directory you wish to decrypt from the File Selection dialog box.

Enter your keys and proceed with the decryption.
If you see the message

File already exists. Replace?

when you are decrypting a file, proceed with care. If you encrypted
the file with Delete Original File set to off, the original file remains
on the disk. When you come to decrypt the file, PC Secure attempts
to restore the file to its original name, but finds that the file already
exists. If the file has not changed since you encrypted it, you can
decrypt the file on top of the original. Once you have two versions of
the file—the older one encrypted and the newer one not—be very
careful not to destroy the newer file. Copy the newer file to another
directory, or better yet, rename the file before proceeding with the
decryption.

You should also be careful if you encrypt files with the same file name
but different extensions. For example, if you encrypt the files
PCTOOLS.EXE and PCTOOLS.HLP with the Delete Original
File option set to off, the first file will be called PCTOOLS.SEC
after encryption, and so will the second one. PC Secure sends you the
message

> If you set the Delete
Original File option
to off and then encrypt
files with the same name
but different extensions,
files may be overwritten
and lost.

File already exits. Replace?

as it processes the second file. If you answer yes to replace the file, the
first file is overwritten by the second. If you had encrypted the first
file with the Delete Original File option set to on, you could be left
without a copy of the file. To avoid this, either rename or move one of
the files.

To exit from PC Secure and return to the DOS prompt, choose
Exit (F3) from the File menu.

PROTECTING DELETED FILES FURTHER

If you start PC Secure by typing

PCSECURE /G

For a list of the other optional parameters you can use with PC Secure, see Chapter 20.

For more information on cleaning deleted files, see the description of Wipe later in this chapter.

you invoke the Department of Defense (DOD) standards for file deletion. This parameter is used in conjunction with the Delete Original File selection in PC Secure.

If you use the /G parameter, and Delete Original File is set to on and the original copy of your file is removed according to DOD standards. The deleted file is overwritten seven times and then verified to be sure it can never be recovered. Use this option if you need complete security. This process obviously takes longer than the normal procedures in PC Secure.

PROTECTING YOUR SYSTEM WITH DATA MONITOR

Data Monitor provides several kinds of protection for your system: Delete Protection improves the chances of recovering accidentally deleted files, Screen Blanker clears your computer screen, Directory Lock lets you keep your data files in a password-protected encrypted directory, Write Protection allows you to protect different parts of your hard disk, and Disk Light indicates all disk accesses on your screen.

DATA MONITOR'S COMPATIBILITY WITH WINDOWS OR NETWORKS

Not all the options in Data Monitor are compatible with all operating environments, especially graphics programs that write directly to the screen. Table 9.1 lists the options that are compatible with Microsoft Windows and Novell NetWare. If either Screen Blanker or Disk Light is turned on in Data Monitor and you start Windows, it will be turned off until you leave your Windows session, when it is turned back on again.

If you want to use Delete Sentry, Directory Lock, Disk Light, or Write Protect on a Novell network, you must remember to load Data Monitor after you have loaded the network device drivers.

Table 9.1: Data Monitor Network and Windows Compatabilities

NETWORK COMPATIBLE	WINDOWS COMPATIBLE
Delete Sentry	Delete Sentry
Directory Lock	Delete Tracker
Disk Light	Directory Lock
Screen Blanker	Write Protection
Write Protection	

STARTING AND RUNNING DATA MONITOR

If you plan to use any of the Data Monitor features regularly, you should load Data Monitor as a memory-resident program. Add the following command to your AUTOEXEC.BAT file:

DATAMON */option +*

where *option* + is one or more of the following:

- DATALOCK, which turns on Directory Lock
- LIGHT, which turns on Disk Light
- WRITE, which turns on Write Protection
- SCREEN, which turns on the Screen Blanker
- TRACKER, which turns on Delete Protection Delete Tracking
- SENTRY, which turns on Delete Protection Delete Sentry

You can only use one of these two Delete Protection options at a time, as they are mutually exclusive.

See Chapter 20 for a complete list of all the Data Monitor optional switches.

If you only use Data Monitor occasionally, just type

DATAMON

at the DOS prompt and you will see the screen shown in Figure 9.3. The main selections inside Data Monitor are listed on the left side of the window and a brief description of each is shown on the right. Use the arrow keys or the mouse to make selections from this screen.

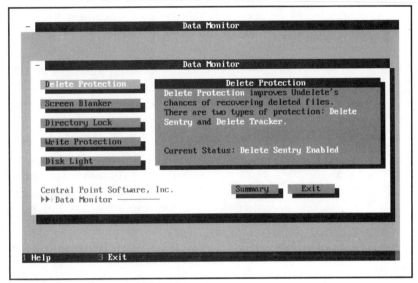

Figure 9.3: The Data Monitor opening screen

CONFIGURING DELETE PROTECTION

When you choose Delete Protection from the opening Data Monitor window, you are presented with three options:

- **Delete Sentry** copies files into a directory called /SENTRY as they are deleted. This gives Undelete the best chance of successfully recovering accidentally deleted files. Delete Sentry can be used on your local disks or on the network.

- **Delete Tracker** keeps track of where on the disk your deleted files were originally located. This gives Undelete a good chance of being able to recover deleted files.

- Choose **None** if you don't want to use any kind of protection. If your files are not fragmented and consist of large contiguous numbers of clusters, Undelete may well be able to recover them even without delete protection.

CONFIGURING DELETE SENTRY   When you choose Delete Sentry, a window opens as Figure 9.4 shows, so that you can tell the program which files you want to save. Select All Files to protect all the files on your disk, or choose Only Specified Files. With this option you can use the Include and Exclude boxes to specify your file choices in more detail. These settings are applied across all your disk drives. To exclude a file or group of files, enter a minus sign before the file name; for example, to extend Delete Sentry protection to all files except WordStar backup files, enter *.* in the Include box, and –*.BAK in the Exclude box.

If you are a Windows user, you probably have designated a directory where Windows programs can store their temporary files. These temporary files, along with the swap files Windows uses to simulate memory, are constantly being created and deleted as you use Windows. There is no need to protect these files using Delete Sentry, so add the following file types into the Exclude box: *.SPL (print spooler files), *.SWP, and *.WOA (swap files).

If the Do Not Save Archived Files box is not checked, all files are protected. You can specify the number of days after which the files preserved in the SENTRY directory will be removed, or purged from your disk. Or you can specify the percentage of disk space the SENTRY directory can occupy, so that once the directory grows to this upper limit, files are automatically purged—beginning with the oldest files. Click the Drives button to extend Delete Sentry protection to other disks on your computer or to the disk on the network.

> Data Monitor initially devotes 20 percent of your disk space to the SENTRY directory. If you delete a file bigger than this from a floppy disk, Delete Sentry cannot preserve the file.

CONFIGURING DELETE TRACKER   Delete Tracker is easy to set up; just choose the drives you want to protect in the Drive Selection window. Delete Tracker updates a hidden file called PCTRACKR.DEL located in the root directory of the protected drive. This file contains the names of deleted files and a list of the cluster numbers they occupied. This information is used by Undelete to recover accidentally deleted files. The PCTRACKR.DEL file is invisible to the DOS DIR command, but you can see the file if you use PC Shell or Directory Maintenance.

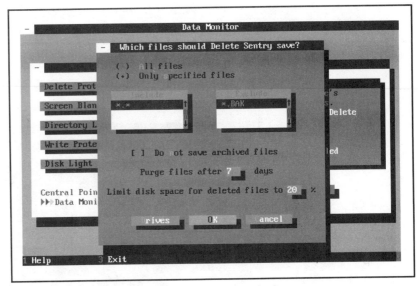

Figure 9.4: Choose the files that you want Delete Sentry to save

USING DELETE SENTRY ON A NETWORK If you want to use Delete Sentry on the network, your network supervisor should use Data Monitor to create the SENTRY directory. What happens next depends on the version of Novell NetWare that you are using; if you have NetWare 286, your supervisor should assign all rights except Parental to the SENTRY directory; if you use NetWare 386, your supervisor should grant all rights except Access Control and Supervisory.

SCREEN BLANKER

You will often see ghost images on ATM screens.

If you display the same image on your computer screen for a long enough time, it is possible to burn that image onto the screen permanently. This is especially true with older monitors; when you finally change the display, a faint ''ghost'' of the original image remains. Also, if you work with confidential information, it could be very useful to be able to blank the whole screen to hide that information if someone came into your office, rather than have to close the application program and start again after they left. Screen Blanker helps with both these situations.

Choose Screen Blanker from the Data Monitor main window and
you will see a display like the one shown in Figure 9.5. Check the Load
Screen Blanker box so that Screen Blanker is loaded when you exit Data
Monitor, then specify the period of time that Screen Blanker should wait
after your last operation before it clears the screen.

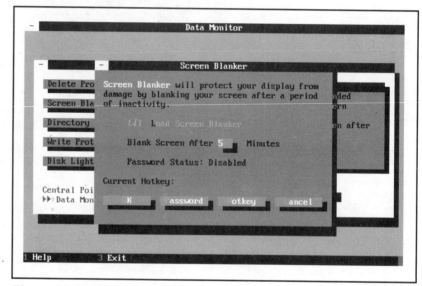

Figure 9.5: Configure Screen Blanker to clear your screen after a specified
period of time

If you want to protect your system further, you can configure
Screen Blanker so that you have to enter a password before the screen
display is restored. Click the Password button from the Screen
Blanker display and a dialog box opens requesting the password.
After you have entered the password, a second dialog box opens ask-
ing you to type in your password again for confirmation. Now, when
Screen Blanker clears your computer screen, you must key in the
password before you can resume operations.

To clear the screen on command, click the Hotkey button from the
Screen Blanker window. Choose a key combination with the Ctrl key
or the Alt key. The keys you choose are shown in a dialog box; press
the Enter key to confirm your choice. When you return to the Screen

Blanker window, click OK and select Exit in the Data Monitor window. Be sure to save your changes as you exit. Now, when you use the hotkey combination, the screen is blanked immediately.

DIRECTORY LOCK

Directory Lock · must be configured using Data Monitor; you cannot turn it on from the Install program.

Directory Lock does not use full DES encryption methods; if you need DES protection, use PC Secure instead.

Directory Lock creates a new encrypted directory on your hard disk; any files you copy into this directory are automatically encrypted. The directory is also password-protected, so you must know the password to be able to access the directory; people without the password cannot access your data.

Select Directory Lock from the Data Monitor window and you will see a screen like the one shown in Figure 9.6. Check the Load Directory Lock box, so that the program is started when you exit Data

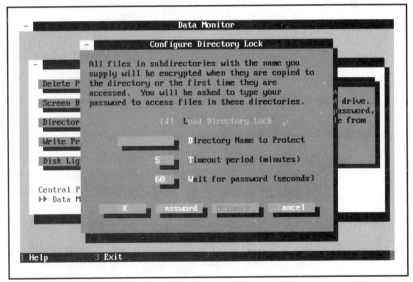

Figure 9.6: Set up the Directory Lock options using the Configure Directory Lock window

Monitor. Enter the name of the directory you want to lock into the Directory Name to Protect box. All directories with this name will be protected on all your hard and floppy disks. The Timeout Period controls the length of idle time before you are asked to input the password again. Set this value to zero or leave it blank so that you are asked for the password only once during a session. This Timeout Period is disabled while you are using Windows. The Wait for Password setting specifies the number of seconds that Directory Lock will wait for you to enter the password. If you do not enter the password inside this time period, the program stops running.

Click the Password button in the Configure Directory Lock window to specify your password. This is the password you must enter before you are allowed to read files from the protected directory.

Click the Network button to specify a network directory for protection. Do not include a drive letter in this specification; it is not needed because Directory Lock protects all the network drives that you are logged on to. Choose OK when you have made your selections and remember to save your changes as you exit Data Monitor.

WRITE PROTECTION

Write Protection prevents files from being erased, overwritten or damaged on your hard and floppy disks. Select Write Protection from the opening Data Monitor window, and you will see the display shown in Figure 9.7.

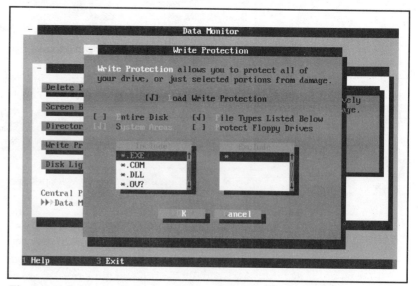

Figure 9.7: Select the files you want to protect in the Write protection window

Check the Load Write Protection box, so that the program is loaded when you exit from Data Monitor. The other options in this window allow you to configure Write Protection to your own individual needs. You have four options, as follows:

- **Entire Disk** allows you to write-protect your entire disk, including the system area, the FATs, the directories, and the unused free space on your disk. This selection stops all writes to all disks, including RAM disks, unless you manually allow each write yourself.

- **System Areas** protects the hard-disk partition table, the boot record, and FATs.

- **File Types Listed Below** allows you to use the Include and Exclude boxes to specify individual files for protection. You can use the DOS wildcards to extend protection to groups of files.

- **Protect Floppy Drives** extends protection to your floppy disks too. If you select this option, you can still format floppy disks while maintaining all other levels of protection.

When Write Protection is on, you are warned whenever a write is attempted on one of the protected areas of your disk. A window opens and informs you that a write operation was attempted on a protected area of your disk; Data Monitor gives you the choice of choosing Cancel to stop the write operation, Continue to allow the write to take place, or Disable to turn Write Protection off. If you are using Microsoft Windows when the write operation is attempted, your choices are slightly different. Data Monitor opens the warning window, then gives you the option of choosing OK to allow the write, or Cancel to stop the write operation. Because each write can be monitored at several different levels, you may have to answer Data Monitor several times for the same write operation.

DISK LIGHT

Disk Light displays a small indicator at the top right of your screen whenever you access your disks. This may be useful if you use a hardcard or work on a network, or if your computer is in a tower configuration on the floor under your desk, so the disk light is hard to see.

Check the Load Disk Light box, then select OK. Remember to save your changes when you exit Data Monitor.

Now if you access drive C, you will see Cr while data are being read from the disk, and Cw when data are being written to the disk. The indicator is not shown when you use graphics-based programs like Microsoft Windows.

CHANGING YOUR DATA MONITOR CONFIGURATION

If you decide that you want to change the way you have configured Data Monitor, you must first unload Data Monitor by typing the following command from the DOS command line:

DATAMON /UNLOAD

This removes Data Monitor from memory. Now run Data Monitor to change the options you want to use.

To find out how Data Monitor is set up in your computer now, type

DATAMON /STATUS

from the DOS command line and you will see a short summary showing which options are turned on and which ones are off.

USING DATA MONITOR FROM THE DOS COMMAND LINE

See Chapter 20 for a complete list of all the Data Monitor command-line options.

You don't have to use the full-screen version of Data Monitor; you can select individual options with special command-line switches. To turn Disk Light off from the command line, type

DATAMON /LIGHT–

To turn on Delete Tracking, type

DATAMON /TRACKER+

OBLITERATING FILES WITH WIPE

If your job involves demonstrating a software package on a client's computer, you will need to install the package on the hard disk to demonstrate the speed and efficiency of the program. However, if the client does not want to buy the package, simply deleting the files using DOS commands will only remove the entries from the FAT. With a good utilities package, your client could probably unerase the files quite easily. This is, of course, illegal.

Here's another example: Let's say you have just finished working on the documentation for a confidential project. You keep backup copies of your files in a safe place, but you want to remove all traces of the original files from your hard disk.

In both cases, your solution is the PC Tools Wipe program. Using this utility ensures that the deleted files are removed permanently. Not even the PC Tools Undelete program can recover files that have been overwritten by Wipe. Wipe writes new data into each sector of the file on your disk, overwriting any data that were already there.

USING WIPE IN PC SECURE

To practice using the Wipe program, first make a small test file on a blank floppy disk in drive A by typing

    COPY CON A:MYFILE.TXT
    This is a short test

Wipe is a powerful and irreversible process, so proceed slowly and carefully.

at the DOS command line. Press F6 to end the file and then press Enter to return to the DOS prompt. This small file now exists on the floppy in drive A. Assuming that the disk is a newly formatted 360K floppy, sector 0 is the boot sector, sectors 1 to 4 contain the FAT, sectors 5 to 11 contain the root directory, and MYFILE.TXT should start in sector 12.

Now use Wipe to clear the disk's contents. To do this, choose Wipe from the menu in the PC Tools program. Select the lowest of the three buttons on the left side of the screen to open the Configuration window, as shown in Figure 9.8.

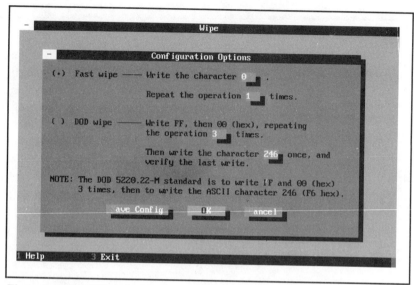

Figure 9.8: The Wipe Configuration Options window offers two choices

- **Fast Wipe** writes the value you specify into each sector that the file occupies. The default value is zero; to change this value, enter the ASCII-decimal equivalent of the character you want to use. For example, to write an *E*, enter **69** in decimal. Specify the number of times you want to repeat the Fast Wipe; the default is 1.

- **DOD Wipe** is much slower than Fast Wipe, but it meets the latest Department of Defense 5220.22-M 116b(2) standards for media protection. This specifies that a 0/FFH pattern must be repeated three times, followed by a write of the characters F6H, followed by a verification of the last write.

Choose Save Configuration so that Wipe uses your chosen selections every time you run the program. The settings are saved in the WIPE.CFG file. To use these settings only for the current Wipe session, choose OK; otherwise, choose Cancel.

Next, choose File from the main Wipe screen to display the window shown in Figure 9.9. The current directory is shown in the File Specification box; use the backspace key if you want to change or edit this entry. You can include details of the drive, path, and file name, and you can also use the DOS wildcard characters.

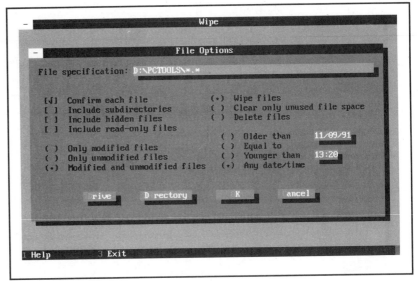

Figure 9.9: Choose the file you want to wipe in this window

The top section of the screen displays the following four checkboxes:

- **Confirm Each File** forces the program to ask for permission before wiping a file. Use it if you are not sure of what is on the disk. This is the default setting.

- **Include Subdirectories** removes all the subdirectories on the disk.

- **Include Hidden Files** removes hidden files. The default setting leaves hidden files intact.

- **Include Read-Only Files** removes files with the read-only bit set in the attribute byte. Again, the default setting leaves these files untouched.

Next, choose the wiping method that the program will use:

- **Wipe Files** deletes files and then writes the specified pattern into every location on the disk occupied by those files. This is the default.

- **Clear Only Unused File Space** wipes the unused slack area at the end of the file.

- **Delete Files** deletes the specified files but does not wipe the space that they occupied. This is the same as using the DOS DEL or ERASE command, except that you can use it to remove complete directory trees from your hard disk if you check the Include Subdirectories box.

Now choose which files to wipe:

- **Only Modified Files** wipes only those files with the archive bit set, that is, files that have been changed since they were last backed up.

- **Only Unmodified Files** wipes only those files whose archive bit is not set.

- **Modified and Unmodified Files** ignores the status of the archive bit.

Finally, select the date criteria to use:

- **Older Than** wipes files whose date and time are earlier or the same as those entered here. Enter a new date in MM/DD/YY format.

- **Equal To** wipes the files whose date and time information exactly match the data entered here.

- **Younger Than** wipes files whose date and time are the same as or later than those specified here.

- **Any Date/Time** ignores the date and time settings.

You can click the Directory button at the bottom of the screen to change to another directory, or the Drive button if you don't want to work with the current drive.

When you are ready to test Wipe, be sure the current drive is drive A and that MYFILE.TXT is shown as the File Specification entry. Check the Confirm Each File box, select Wipe Files, Modified and Unmodified Files, and Any Date/Time. A warning window opens, as Figure 9.10 shows, to remind you that you are about to wipe MYFILE.TXT and that the file will be lost forever if you proceed. Choose the Wipe box to continue. There are three options in this window:

- **Skip** lets you cancel the operation for the file shown in the window. The next file that matches the file specification you entered is listed on the screen.

- **Wipe** (or **Delete**). The title of this box varies according to whether you selected Delete Files or Wipe Files in the File Options window. When you choose Wipe, the highlighted file or the slack unused area at the end of the file is wiped.

- **Cancel** aborts the current operation.

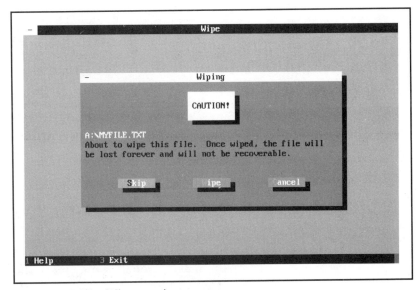

Figure 9.10: The Wipe warning message

You can also run Wipe to wipe only the erased or unused portion of a disk if you choose Disk from the opening window; in fact, this is probably one of its most frequent uses of the utility. The top part of the window shows you the current default drive and the lower portion lets you choose one of the two following wiping methods:

- **Wipe Disk** obliterates everything on the drive, including the system area and any files. If you chose the DOD Wipe method you will have to reformat the disk if you want to use it again.

- **Clear Only Unused Disk Space** wipes the unused area of the disk, including the space occupied by any deleted files.

Click the Change Drive button to change to another drive.

Wiping an entire disk can be a lengthy procedure, depending on the options you choose. For example, performing a DOD Wipe on a large hard disk could take all day.

USING WIPE FROM THE DOS COMMAND LINE

You don't have to use the full-screen method with Wipe; you can run it from the DOS command line. The general form of the command is:

WIPE *filespec file-switches common-switches*

For example, to remove all the *.BAK files from the floppy disk in drive A, type

WIPE A:*.BAK /SUB

This command wipes all .BAK files in all directories on drive A; the /S switch tells Wipe to include all subdirectories in the search for files matching the file specification.

As a final cautionary word, remember that Wipe actually writes over files and destroys the original data. After this treatment, the original files cannot be recovered by utility programs, not even by programs like PC Tools Undelete.

THE VDEFEND VIRUS-PROTECTION PROGRAM

VDefend is a small memory-resident program that can protect your computer system from attack by over 400 different viruses. Before I describe how to use VDefend, lets take a moment to look at the different types of viruses and how they might get onto your computer system in the first place.

WHAT IS A VIRUS?

The term *virus* is a generic name for any program that alters something about the way your system runs without your knowledge or permission. In the DOS world, there are actually three main kinds of intruders:

- A *virus* is a program that attaches itself to your executable or program files and then spreads to all your other programs, infecting them all. Not all viruses are harmful; some are harmless and just plain annoying. The most famous virus of all is probably the Israeli or Jerusalem virus, also known as Friday the 13th, discovered on a computer at the University of Jerusalem in July of 1987. This virus slows down your system and draws black boxes on the lower-left part of the screen. If the virus is in memory on Friday the 13th, every program executed is erased from the disk.

- A *worm* is a tiny program that reproduces itself many times over; it is not usually designed to be harmful. Eventually, your computer memory or disk will fill up completely.

- A *Trojan horse* is an apparently useful program that suddenly turns malicious. For example, it might attempt to low-level format your hard disk.

There are several precautions you can take against infection by a virus, including:

- Don't use pirated copies of software. Not only is this illegal, but the programs may be infected, allowing a virus to install itself on your system undetected.

- If you download files from bulletin boards, make sure that the sysop (system operator) checks for viruses before the programs are posted on the bulletin board.

- Backup your system regularly so that you can reinstall the original uninfected copies of your programs.

- Check for viruses on a routine basis.

USING VDEFEND

Installing VDefend on your system is a fundamental step in virus protection, because the program checks for viruses in two ways:

- VDefend prevents unauthorized attempts to format your hard disk.

- VDefend examines program files for evidence of infection when the program is run or copied.

To load VDefend into memory every time you start your computer, add the line:

    VDEFEND

to your AUTOEXEC.BAT file. When you next start your computer, you will see a small message on the screen indicating that VDefend has been loaded successfully.

If VDefend finds a virus, a dialog box opens identifying the virus. If this happens, you should delete the infected file and reinstall the program from your original backup disks. You can also run one of the virus-removal programs, like Central Point Anti-Virus (available as a separate product) to disinfect your system.

When VDefend detects that an attempt is being made to low-level format your hard disk, the program opens a dialog box to confirm that you want to proceed with the format. Low-level formatting of a hard disk is usually destructive, and it is how several of the more common viruses work. But because there is a chance that *you* could have originated the format using the PC Tools DiskFix program rather than the virus, VDefend gives you the following choices in this dialog box:

- **Continue.** Choose Continue if you initiated the low-level format yourself. The program performing the format will proceed as normal.

- **Stop.** Select Stop if you did not start the format. VDefend will pass a ''Format Failed'' message back to the program doing the formatting and the program should stop.

- **Boot.** If the program does not stop, and you see this dialog box again, select Boot to make VDefend reboot your computer and stop the format. After the reboot, be very careful how you start your system up again because you will not want to restart the virus as well.

If you are on a network and you want to load a network device driver after you load VDefend, be sure to include the following switch in your AUTOEXEC.BAT file:

VDEFEND /N

KEEPING VDEFEND UP-TO-DATE

Modem Communications contains the number of the Central Point Software bulletin Board. The number is (503)690-6650.

VDefend protects your system against over 400 known viruses by keeping information on the known viruses in a signature file called SIGNATUR.CPS. Because virus makers keep changing the way that viruses work, it is important that you keep this file as up-to-date as possible. As new viruses are detected, new versions of SIGNATUR.CPS are made available from Central Point Software. You can use the Modem Communications in Desktop to download a copy of this file from the Central Point Software bulletin board, or from the Central Point Forum on CompuServe. When you have downloaded the file, copy it into the directory on your system that contains VDefend to update SIGNATUR.CPS.

CHAPTER

10

Backing Up Your System

Throughout this book, I remind you to back up your entire system before performing certain operations. For example, before running the file-unfragmentation program for the first time, I suggest that you back up your system. A *backup* is an up-to-date copy of all your files that you can use to reload your system in case of an accident. Backups are insurance against anything happening to the hundreds or possibly thousands of files you might have on your hard disk. If the unthinkable did occur—you lost all of your system's data and didn't have backup copies—it could take you weeks or even months to recreate all those data, if indeed they could be recreated.

WHEN SHOULD YOU MAKE A BACKUP?

You should get into the habit of backing up your system regularly so that you never have to do any extra work as a result of damaged or missing files. How often you should make a backup depends on how much work you do on your computer. For example, computer programmers do a lot of new work during a week; because they stand to lose a lot of work in the event of an accident, they should back up their files on a daily basis—even sometimes twice a day. People running what-if financial analyses might back up their work every two or three days because that is as much as they could afford to lose. If you write only an occasional memo, however, you can probably get away with backing up your system once a week.

Plan your backup strategy and, most important, stick to it. With no backup plan, you'll accumulate disk haphazardly, and you will waste disks, tapes, and most importantly, hours looking for that elusive file.

Use 3½-inch disks if you can, rather than 5¼-inch disks, because the smaller disks are much more robust and less prone to damage. Don't try to save money by using generic disks for your backup; this will turn out to be a false economy. Use the best quality disks you can afford. If you have more than 20 or 30MB of files to back up on a regular basis, consider buying an internal tape drive. A good tape drive can back up your entire system while you are out to lunch.

As a rule, most people make a full backup at the end of the work week and smaller daily backups of the files that have changed during the day. This ensures that you have all your files on a backup disk somewhere. For example, if your hard disk crashed during the day on Thursday, you could restore last Friday's full backup, as well as the partial backups for Monday, Tuesday, and Wednesday; all you would have lost is Thursday's work.

Keep one full backup of your system in storage somewhere for at least six months; a year is even better. The file that you most want to recover may be the file you deleted three months ago, and your most recent backups won't show a trace of it.

There are several other occasions when you should back up your entire system. If you are going to move your computer, you should make a complete backup of the hard disk. Even if you are only moving next door, your hard disk may not survive the trip. Similarly, if you are sending your computer in for any kind of service work, especially work on the disk drives, you should have a complete system backup first.

Whenever you need to remove directories and files because you are running out of space on your hard disk, you should back up your hard disk completely (dating the backup) before making the deletions. You may need these files again sometime. Similarly, if someone leaves your company, a complete backup is a good way to preserve his or her work, allowing a new employee to start work without any anxieties about handling old files on the computer.

You can also use a backup as a way of moving files from one computer to another. Make the backup using the method that does not change the archive bit on the files concerned, and you can still include them in your next regular backup.

If you are going to run a program such as a file-unfragmenting program like Compress, which optimizes your hard-disk file layout by rewriting all your files, be sure to have a new complete backup of your hard disk before you start running the program; your hard disk and the optimizing program may be incompatible. Also, power outages and brownouts can occur at any time, even during the optimization itself.

RUNNING CP BACKUP IN DOS OR WINDOWS

PC Tools contains two versions of the backup program called CP Backup: one runs in plain DOS, the other in Microsoft Windows. Because the way you use both programs is so similar, the following discussion can be applied equally well to either version. Figure 10.1 shows the opening screen of the DOS version of CP Backup and Figure 10.2 shows the same screen for the Windows version; you can see how alike they are. The Windows version of CP Backup has a row of command buttons at the top of the window; all these options are also available from the regular menus, and by keyboard shortcuts.

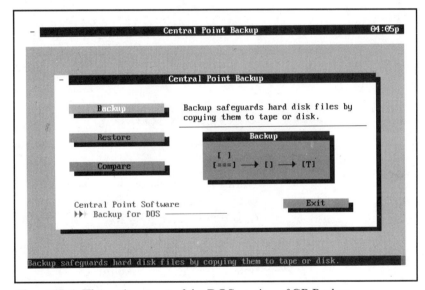

Figure 10.1: The main screen of the DOS version of CP Backup

Throughout the discussion that follows, I describe the DOS version of the CP Backup program, so all figures will be taken from this version.

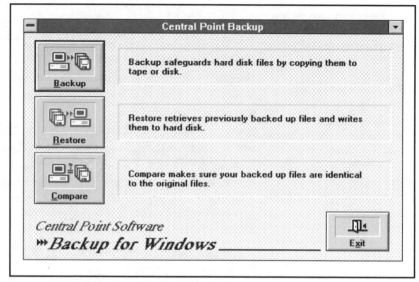

Figure 10.2: The main screen of the Windows version of CP Backup

CONFIGURING CP BACKUP FOR THE FIRST TIME

The first time you run CP Backup, you must configure the program so that it takes advantage of the hardware you have installed on your system. This configuration process defines the types of floppy disk drives you have on your computer, as well as the type of floppy disk you plan to use to store the backup. CP Backup also performs a backup confidence test to prove that your chosen configuration works properly. All this information is then stored in a file called CPBACKUP.CFG if you are using DOS, or WNBACKUP.INI if you are using Microsoft Windows. The next time you run CP Backup, this file will automatically load your default settings.

It is not difficult to complete this configuration process; just follow the instructions given in each of the opening windows.

To start CP Backup from the DOS prompt, type **CPBACKUP**. Notice that there are no spaces in the program name; DOS does not allow them. You can also start CP Backup from the PC Tools program menu.

If you are using Windows, double-click on the CP Backup icon in the PC Tools group in the Program Manager, or on the CP-BACKUP file name in the File Manager. You can also choose CP Backup from the Central Point Launcher, if it is installed on your system.

DEFINING YOUR HARDWARE

The opening screen contains a message informing you that the next few dialog boxes are for you to configure the CP Backup program to your hardware. Select Continue and the next dialog box asks whether you have a tape drive connected. CP Backup supports over 25 models of tape drives from 11 major manufacturers. If you answer Yes to this question, another dialog box opens containing two choices, Search and Configure:

- Choose **Search** if your tape drive is connected to your floppy-disk controller. CP Backup will go out and look for the tape drive. CP Backup automatically detects many tape drives from Colorado Memory Systems, Irwin Magnetic Systems, Mountain Network Solutions, and Tecmar.

- Select **Configure** if your tape drive is connected to a secondary tape-controller card in your computer. In this case, another dialog box opens, asking you to enter the following information about the tape controller card:

    Address is the 3- or 4-byte hex address of the card.

    IRQ is the number of the interrupt request line used with the tape controller.

    DMA is the number of the Direct Memory Access channel used with the controller card.

    Data Rate. Enter the desired data rate. If you are unsure which setting to choose, select Default and then consult your tape controller manual for more information. If you know the maximum data rate that your tape drive can handle, choose from

250 Kbps (kilobits per second), 500 Kbps, or
1,000 Kbps.

Commonly used values for several tape drives from different manufacturers are listed in Table 10.1.

Table 10.1: Tape Controller Cards, Addresses, IRQs, and DMA Channels

TAPE DRIVE	ADDRESS	IRQ	DMA CHANNEL
Alloy FTFA Controller	340	3	2
Alloy Retriever 60e	340	3	2
Colorado FC10	180	3	2
Irwin 4100	370	3	1
Tecmar QT	300	3	1
Tecmar QT-40e	300	3	1
Mountain MACH2	3E7	6	2
Wangtek Lightning	300	3	1

The next window, the Define Equipment window, is shown in
Figure 10.3. This window lists all the disk and tape hardware it can
find on your system. Figure 10.3 shows drive A is a 5¼-inch 1.2MB
floppy, drive B is a 3½-inch 1.44MB floppy, and a tape drive is also
present. If you do not have a tape drive in your system, CP Backup
will not show the tape-drive icon in this window. Select OK to move
on to the Choose Drive and Media window shown in Figure 10.4.

Choose one of the radio-button selections in this window as your
default backup choice. If drives A and B are of the same type, you can
elect to make a One Drive Backup or a Two Drive Backup. Select the
Two Drive Backup option to minimize any waiting time as you
change disks. If you select Fixed Drive and Path, or Removable
Drive and Path, you are prompted to enter a path name, and your
configuration is complete.

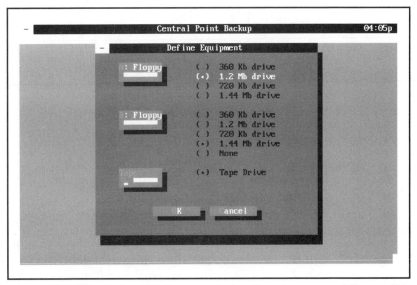

Figure 10.3: The Define Equipment window lists the tape and floppy disk drives available on your system

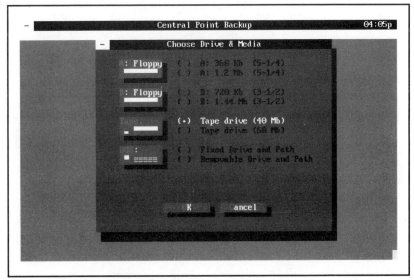

Figure 10.4: The Choose Drive and Media window helps you select the drive and disk type to use for the backup

CH. 10

Next, CP Backup tests your computer and determines the best speed to use for the backup.

RUNNING THE BACKUP CONFIDENCE TEST

The backup confidence tests actually performs a short backup to your chosen backup device, thus eliminating any doubt about CP Backup's effectiveness or compatibility. Be sure and run this test on your computer before you make any backups:

1. Select Continue in the Backup Confidence Test window to start the test.

2. Insert a blank formatted floppy disk into the drive you selected. If the disk has files on it, a window opens telling you that the disk contains data. These files will be lost if you continue with the confidence test.

3. Choose OK to start the test.

Test progress is shown on a horizontal bargraph, and the test usually only takes a few moments. A window opens at the end of the test, as Figure 10.5 shows. Select OK and the next screen you see is the main CP Backup window. The configuration is complete and you are now ready to back up your system.

BACKING UP YOUR HARD DISK WITH CP BACKUP

PC Tools offers a fast and easy-to-use alternative to the DOS commands for disk backup. The opening screen, shown in Figure 10.6, has three main options:

- **Backup** selects the files and directories to backup and selects the backup options to use.

- **Restore** selects the files and directories to restore from the backup.

Run another backup confidence test if you change any of the hardware in your computer, particularly hard disks or expansion boards. These additions can have subtle effects on the way DMA works, and you should know about them before you realize you cannot restore lost files.

Turn off your fax card before starting a backup. If a fax arrives in the middle of a backup, you may get unpredictable results.

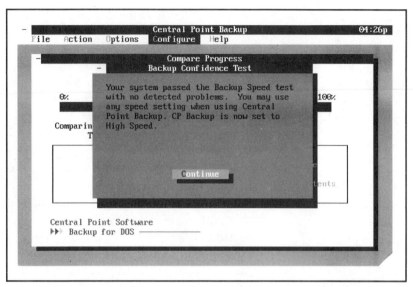

Figure 10.5: When the confidence test is complete, this window opens indicating that you may use any speed setting with CP Backup

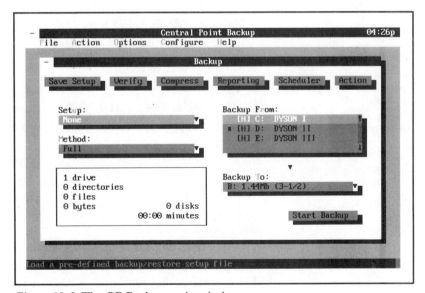

Figure 10.6: The CP Backup main window

• **Compare** compares your backup against the original files on your hard disk to ensure that they are identical.

Using the CP Backup program you can back up your hard disk—in whole or in part, and at one of three different speeds—to any floppy disk, hard disk, or tape drive attached to your computer. If you change any of the drives attached to your computer, or you want to backup to a different backup media, use the selections from the Configure menu to change your configuration.

If you change any of the hardware associated with making backups, choose Define Equipment (F8) from the Configure menu. This selection puts you back into the configuration part of the CP Backup program, which starts with the question, **Do you have a tape drive connected to this PC?** To change to another media type, select Choose Drive and Media (F7). The dialog boxes for both these menu selections are exactly the same as I described above in the sections called "Defining Your Hardware" and "Running the Backup Confidence Test," so I will not describe them here.

CHOOSING THE BACKUP SPEED

CP Backup can backup your files at different rates, depending on your equipment selections.

Some PC-compatibles may not support DMA due to hardware limitations. If you are unsure of your system, run a test backup and try comparing the files to ensure that they are identical. If they are not, try one of the slower-speed methods.

HIGH-SPEED DMA BACKUPS   To lighten the load on your computer's microprocessor, some parts of your system can transfer data to and from memory without going through the microprocessor or central processing unit (CPU). This operation is known as *direct memory access,* or DMA, and is handled by a chip known as the DMA controller. DMA speeds performance considerably, because transfers can take place at the full speed of the bus and memory; they are not slowed down by the CPU.

DMA backups are much faster than DOS-compatible backups. However, you can only make them to floppy disks and certain tape drives, not another hard disk. The backup files are recorded in a special format that DOS cannot read. PC Tools provides a program called CPBDIR that enables you to read disks made by a DMA backup. CPBDIR is described in full later in this chapter.

If you have a Copy PC II Deluxe Option Board installed in your system, CP Backup can use it to increase the speed with which it formats new disks during a DMA backup. The degree of improvement depends on your CPU, disk speed, and other factors, but can be as much as 20 to 30 percent.

MEDIUM-SPEED DMA BACKUPS   If you have problems using the high-speed DMA method, try the medium-speed method. This still uses DMA, but in a non-overlap mode: reads and writes are not done simultaneously, but one after the other in serial form. This format can be used on both floppy disks and tape systems.

LOW-SPEED DOS-COMPATIBLE BACKUPS   The DOS-compatible selection makes backups to any DOS-supported device, including floppy disks, another hard disk, or a tape drive. In fact, if you want to use anything other than floppy disks or tape drives, you *must* use this method to make your backup.

RESTORING BACKUP FILES   The files in a backup are stored in a special way to reduce the amount of space they occupy, so you must restore the files before you can use them.

Backups made with high- or medium-speed methods must be restored using similar methods, and backups made using the low-speed DOS-compatible method must be restored using the low-speed method. You cannot restore backups made with a high-speed method using a slow-speed restore, and vice versa.

CHANGING YOUR USER LEVEL

In CP Backup you can choose from three different user levels to customize your work environment to your own requirements. Select the User Level option from the Configure menu and you will see the screen shown in Figure 10.7.

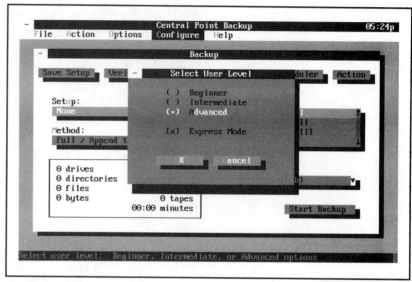

Figure 10.7: The Select User Level screen from the Configure menu

The three user levels are as follows:

- Beginner
- Intermediate
- Advanced

Make your selection from this list, and select the OK button. The advanced level is active by default. Use the Cancel button if you don't want to change your user level.

The other option in the Select User Level window, Express Mode, is on in CP Backup by default. In Express Mode, you see a row of command buttons across the top of the main window, just below the menu line. If you turn Express Mode off, these command buttons are replaced by three other small windows across the top of the screen: Settings on the left, Statistics in the center, and Estimates on the right. The lower portion of the screen shows a directory tree on the left and a file list on the right. Also, a row of function keys appears at the bottom of the screen.

The user level determines the entries shown in the CP Backup Options menu and which of the six command buttons across the top

As you become more familiar with the selections available in the options menu, you will want to increase your user level.

of the screen are available. To keep the selections under Options to a minimum, choose the beginner level. Some of the command buttons at the top of the screen will be grayed out, indicating that the default (and safest) selections are being used and cannot be changed. For a larger selection of commands, giving more complex options, choose the intermediate level, and for the complete set of menu items choose the advanced level. Table 10.2 lists the Options menu selections by user level. All the figures in this chapter are made at the advanced user level, with Express Mode turned on.

Table 10.2: The Options Menu Selections by User Level

BEGINNER	INTERMEDIATE	ADVANCED
Reporting	Reporting	Reporting
	Backup Method	Backup Method
	Selection Options	Compress
	Display Options	Verify
		Format Always
		Error Correction
		Media Format
		Virus Detection
		Save History
		Time Display
		Overwrite Warning
		Selection Options
		Display Options

MAKING A COMPLETE BACKUP

To back up your whole disk, follow these steps:

1. Click on the drive you want to back up in the Backup From box. This selection is available as Backup From Entry in the Action menu.

2. Select the appropriate Backup To drive from the selection shown in the drop-down box. This selection is available as the Choose Drive and Media command in the Configure menu.

3. Select Start Backup (F5) from the Action menu.

4. If you are backing up to tape, insert a tape cartridge into the tape drive. Any backups already on the tape are listed; you can choose to erase the tape, replace it with another, or select OK to continue.

5. Enter a descriptive name for the backup, up to 30 characters long. If you use a unique name for each backup, perhaps based on the date and the disk you are backing up, it becomes easier to tell one backup from another.

6. Enter a password if you want to protect your backup. If you use a password, you will have to enter that same password when you come to restore the backup, so don't forget it. This password is unique to each backup.

7. If you are backing up to a floppy disk, insert a disk. You may notice that the floppy-disk drive light stays on for long periods of time during the backup if you use one of the high-speed modes. This is normal and is nothing to worry about.

The name of the directory and file being backed up, as well as the track number, all appear on the main display, so you can watch the progress of the backup. The lower portion of the screen indicates the progress by counting down as each file and directory is completed. The time elapsed since you started the backup and the time remaining to complete the backup, as well as the percentage compression achieved, are also shown. CP Backup prompts you to insert each disk or tape in turn.

To stop the backup, press the Escape key and a window opens with the following options:

- **Resume** continues the backup without any loss of data.

- **End** completes the current file and then stops.

- **Quit** cancels the backup immediately.

When the backup is complete, a directory for the entire backup set is written to the last disk. You should carefully number each of the disks in your backup, since the Restore selection will want you to load the backup disks in the same order.

At the end of the backup, you'll see a dialog box that contains statistics for the backup. This dialog box includes the total number of directories, files, and kilobytes backed up, the total number of disks used, the time the backup took to complete, the average transfer rate in kilobytes per minute, and the total compression achieved during the backup, as shown in Figure 10.8.

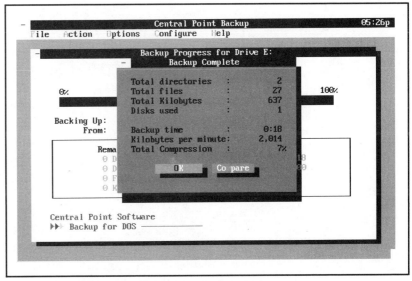

Figure 10.8: CP Backup screen of backup statistics

Choose OK to return to the main CP Backup window, or choose Compare to make CP Backup run a comparison between the files it has just backed up and the original files on your hard disk. Compare is discussed in detail later in this section.

MAKING A PARTIAL BACKUP

You may not always want to back up your whole disk. Often you will want to back up only files that have changed, or files that changed after a certain date, or even only a certain type of file. CP Backup lets you use two different methods to select the files that you want to backup: if Express Mode is on, use the Selection Options from the Options menu to backup groups of files; if Express Mode is off, select the files individually from the Tree display—a time-consuming process if you have more than just a few files. Once you have made your selections, you can save that setup in a file to save time on future, similar backups.

Many of the selections described in this section are only available at the advanced user level.

SUBDIRECTORY INCLUSION   Subdirectory Inclusion adds all of a selected directory's subdirectories to the backup if it is on, or excludes them if it is off. The default is on. A check mark appears to the left of its name in the Options menu to indicate that Subdirectory Inclusion is on. Selecting it again turns it off. Make this selection before using Include/Exclude Files.

INCLUDE/EXCLUDE FILES   Include/Exclude Files allows you to choose individual files for a backup. The default is Include All Files. This is shown in the Include/Exclude editor by the DOS wild-card designation *.*.

The screen allows up to 16 lines of files to include or exclude, and the list is always processed from top to bottom. To exclude a file or group of files, place a minus sign in the left-hand column of the screen. Table 10.3 shows examples of Include/Exclude options.

The Check Path for Existence and Log Drives selection is not saved, and is always off when you start CP Backup. Turn it on if you want CP Backup to validate that the path entries represent existing directories.

If you change the Subdirectory Inclusion setting after making Include/Exclude choices, you must reenter the Include/Exclude

Table 10.3: Sample Include/Exclude Options Using DOS Wildcard Characters

OPTION	RESULT
.	Includes everything on the disk, all files and subdirectories (setting Subdirectory Inclusion has no effect on this selection)
-*.*	Unselects everything on the disk
.	Selects all files in the root directory
\WORDPROC*.*	Selects all files in the WORDPROC directory. If Subdirectory Inclusion is on, also selects all files in all subdirectories below WORDPROC
\LOTUS*.WK1	Selects all files in the LOTUS directory with the extension .WK1, all Lotus worksheets, and—if Subdirectory Inclusion is on—all files in all subdirectories below LOTUS with the .WK1 extension
-\WORDPROC*.BAK	Excludes all files with the extension .BAK in the WORDPROC directory and—if Subdirectory Inclusion is on—excludes all files in all directories below WORDPROC with the .BAK extension

screen and choose OK again to make this change affect the previously chosen files.

ATTRIBUTE EXCLUSIONS Attribute Exclusions modifies any of the file-selection techniques in use in CP Backup. You can exclude hidden files, system, or read-only files:

- **Hidden Files** excludes all hidden files from the backup. Hidden files are sometimes used on copy-protection schemes where they are usually location-specific. They do not like to be moved and will often refuse to work if you change their position.

- **System Files** excludes all system files from the backup. The DOS files are system files, as well as location-specific, and you should exclude them from the backup.

- **Read Only Files** excludes all read-only files from the backup.

The default setting for all three attribute exclusions is off; this means they will be backed up.

DATE RANGE SELECTION   Date Range Selection allows you to back up files before, after, or between certain dates. Date Range Selection works with Include/Exclude Files. If Include/Exclude Files is off, Date Range Selection does nothing. If Include/Exclude Files is on and you make a date-range selection, only those files meeting both criteria are backed up. Specify the date as *MM/DD/YY,* entering both digits for each number.

SELECTING FILES FROM THE TREE   If you work extensively with PC Shell and want to think in terms of the directory tree and the file list when choosing files for a backup, you can pop up a directory tree from inside the main CP Backup screen, or you can turn Express Mode off. To display the directory tree, double-click the appropriate drive icon in the Backup From list box and you will see a display like the one shown in Figure 10.9. When you first enter this window, all directories and files are selected for the backup. Click on the root directory; if Subdirectory Inclusion is on, this will deselect everything. Now you can select just the directories you want to back up.

You can also view any file in any directory, just as you would in PC Shell. Use NextDrive (F4) to display details of the next drive

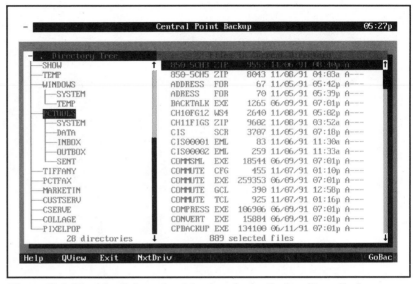

Figure 10.9: Double-click on the drive icon in the Backup From list box to see a directory tree for that drive

in sequence, and use GoBack (F10) when you are ready to return to the main CP Backup window.

BACKUP FROM DIRECTORY You can specify a particular path for the backup, or allow several drives to be backed one after another in CP Backup. First, turn off Express Mode in the User Level selection from the Configure menu, then choose Backup From to see the window shown in Figure 10.10. Click on a drive icon to select that drive for the backup. When a single drive is selected, you can enter a specific path that you want to have backed up. To toggle between single and multiple drive backups, click on the Allow Single Drive Backups button to change it to Allow Multiple Drive Backups. If you select Allow Multiple Drive Backups, the path box disappears and you can select more than one drive for the backup.

CHOOSE DIRECTORIES This is another selection that works when Express Mode is turned off. Select Choose Directories from the Action menu and choose the directories and files you want to backup with the arrow keys or by clicking on them with the mouse.

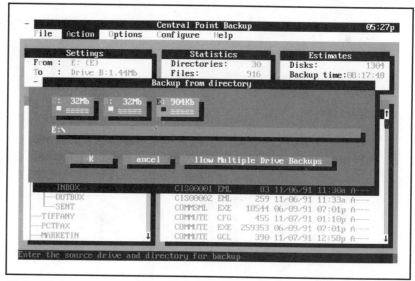

Figure 10.10: The Backup From Directory window lets you toggle between single drive backups and multiple drive backups

To choose all the files in your word-processing directory, move the highlight to the WORD directory and press Enter or click the mouse. All files are now selected. Press Tab or click in the file-list window to select that window, then start to select individual files.

When you have chosen all the directories and files you want to include in the partial backup, click on Start Backup, or choose Start Backup from the Action menu. You are asked to name the backup set and assign a password if you wish. Then the backup starts and CP Backup guides you through the process, asking you to change disks or tapes at the appropriate times.

ADVANCED SETTINGS

There are many other settings available from the Options menu that you can use to customize your backups. The Options menu is shown in Figure 10.11. The current settings of several of these choices are shown (in parentheses) to the right of the menu items; other selections show a check mark to the left of the menu item, indicating the selection is on or is active. Using the selections from the

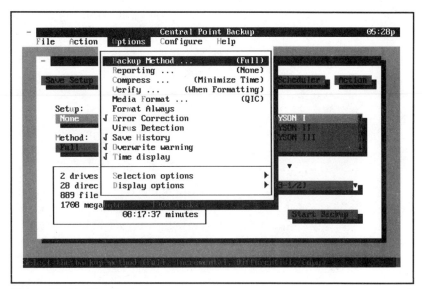

Figure 10.11: The Options menu

Options menu, you can make CP Backup perform any number of different kinds of backup operations. In the next few sections I will explain what these options are and suggest ways you can use them to your best advantage.

BACKUP METHODS   Depending on the settings you chose for drive, media type, and backup speed, you can select one of the following backup methods either by opening the Method menu in the main CP Backup screen or by choosing Backup Method in the Options menu: Full, Full Copy, Full/Erase Tape, Full/Append to Tape, Incremental, Separate Incremental, Differential, or Virus Scan Only.

The two tape options are only available if you selected a tape drive as the backup media. The default setting is for a full backup, and this setting cannot be changed at the beginner user level. Any settings you make will affect which files are backed up:

If you backup to tape, buy preformatted tapes to save time. CP Backup will format the tape for you if you wish, but this operation can take from 30 minutes to three hours, depending on the length of the tape and the format you choose.

- **Full** backs up all the files in all the directories you selected, regardless of the status of the archive bit in the file's attribute byte. When the backup is complete, the archive bit is reset. This mode is CP Backup's default mode.

- **Full Copy** backs up all the files in all the selected directories, but does not reset the archive bit.

- **Full/Erase Tape** is a variation on the Full method when you use tape as the backup media. This setting starts the backup at the beginning of the tape, erasing anything previously written on the tape.

- **Full/Append to Tape** does not start the backup at the beginning of the tape, but adds it at the end of any existing backups already on the tape.

- **Incremental** backs up files that have been created or modified since the last backup and appends them to the end of the previous backup set. The archive bit is reset at the end of the backup. The Incremental setting is not available if you select Fixed Drive or Removable Drive as the backup media, Low Speed as the backup speed, or you use QIC format for a tape backup.

- **Separate Incremental** creates a new backup set and resets the archive bit when the backup is complete.

- **Differential** creates a new backup set but does not reset the archive bit for all the files. This selection is not available for low-speed backups, or for backups made to a fixed or a removable drive.

- **Virus Scan Only** checks all the selected files for a virus. If it finds one, it opens a window containing the name of the affected file, giving you the chance to rename the file. If you rename the file, it will not be backed up during the current CP Backup session, but will be backed up during future sessions. This selection does not back up any files. The default setting for Virus Scan Only is off, and this can only be changed at the advanced user level.

REPORTING   If you select Reporting before you start your backup, you can have CP Backup print a report when the backup is complete. You can choose whether to send the report to a disk file or the printer; the default is off:

- **None** generates no report.
- **Report to Printer** sends the report to the printer.
- **Report to File** sends the report to a disk file in the directory from which CP Backup runs.

> If Reporting is on, CP Backup also generates a report after you use Compare (discussed later in this chapter under "Comparing Files").

A sample report of a full backup is shown in Figure 10.12. The file name becomes AYYMMDDN.RPT, where:

- *A* is the drive letter of the backed up drive.
- *YY* are the last two digits of the year.
- *MM* is the number of the current month.
- *DD* is the current day.
- *N* is a letter indicating the *n*th backup of the day, where *A* is the first and *Z* is the 26th.
- *RPT* is the extension used for all report files.

COMPRESS You can set Compress to minimize the time the backup takes or to minimize the number of disks used for the backup. The default setting is Minimize Time:

> CP Backup will not try to compress files with the following extensions, because these files are already compressed: .ZIP, .PAK, .SEC, .SQZ, and .ARC.

- **None** gives you no compression.
- **Minimize Space** minimizes the number of disks or tapes used during a backup. Files are compressed as they are backed up to reduce the number of disks needed for the backup. Compression results depend on the type of files being compressed. Program files do not change very much; data files, word-processing files, and spreadsheet files compress much more. This option works for both DOS-compatible and high-speed DMA backups.
- **Minimize Time** does as much compression as it can in the time allowed without slowing down the operation. The faster your disk and CPU speed, the more compression will be accomplished.

```
Central Point Backup V7 Directory Report
(c) Copyright 1991 Central Point Software, Inc. All Rights Reserved.
Backup Performed on 11/08/1991 at 05:01p

Backup Method: High-Speed DMA
Media Type: 1.44 MB
Verify When Formatting was ON.
Compression was ON - Minimize Time.
DOS Format.
Error Correction was On.


Include/Exclude Selections:
    *.*

Total Directories:    2
Total Files:         27
Number of Disks:      1

         Name            Size        Date       Time    Atrib Vol


Directory: E:\
    IMAGE.IDX               29   07/27/1990    03:47a   -SHR   1

Directory: E:\AVIRUS\
    CHKLIST.CPS            351   04/17/1991    01:00p   ----   1
    WNGRPHIC.DLL       21,488   04/17/1991    01:00p   ----   1
    BOOTSAFE.EXE       24,881   04/17/1991    01:00p   ----   1
    WNTSRMAN.EXE       12,128   04/17/1991    01:00p   ----   1
    CPSCOLOR.DAT        5,492   04/17/1991    01:00p   ----   1
    CPAV.PIF              545   04/17/1991    01:00p   ----   1
    CPAV.GRP            2,531   04/17/1991    01:00p   ----   1
    WNTSR.386           4,713   04/17/1991    01:00p   ----   1
    WNTSR.DLL           7,552   04/17/1991    01:00p   ----   1
    CPSHELP.OVL        26,049   04/17/1991    01:00p   ----   1
    VIRLIST.DOC         1,385   04/17/1991    01:00p   ----   1
    README.TXT         12,063   04/17/1991    01:00p   ----   1
    CPAV.EXE          158,321   04/17/1991    01:00p   ----   1
    CPAV.ICO              766   04/17/1991    01:00p   ----   1
    AVINST.HLP         60,190   04/17/1991    01:00p   ----   1
    ISCPSTSR.EXE        4,401   04/17/1991    01:00p   ----   1
    CPAV.HLP           39,569   04/17/1991    01:00p   ----   1
    EXCEPT.CPS            300   04/17/1991    01:00p   ----   1
    VWATCH.SYS         14,185   04/17/1991    01:00p   ----   1
    VWATCH.COM         13,195   04/17/1991    01:00p   ----   1
    CPSMAIN.FNT        14,753   04/17/1991    01:00p   ----   1
    VSAFE.COM          32,556   04/17/1991    01:00p   ----   1
    VSAFE.SYS          31,713   04/17/1991    01:00p   ----   1
    INSTALL.EXE       162,577   04/17/1991    01:00p   ----   1
    CPAV.INI              341   08/23/1991    04:34a   ----   1
    ACTIVITY.CPS          315   08/27/1991    02:34a   ----   1

Total Bytes:   652,389

Total Compression  :     7
```

Figure 10.12: A sample CP Backup report

VERIFY   CP Backup will verify the data on your backup disks; the
default setting is Verify When Formatting:

- **None** gives you no verification.

- **When Formatting** causes CP Backup to verify a disk as it is formatted. This is the most-likely time to find a disk error.

- **Always** verifies the disk every time something is written to it. This selection slows down the backup process, but you should choose it to be absolutely certain of a good quality backup. This setting also performs an automatic Compare after a tape backup—an excellent insurance policy, because it confirms that the files recorded on tape actually are the files you think they should be.

This option can only be changed at the advanced user level.

MEDIA FORMAT   This selection lets you choose the format to use with floppy disks and tape drives, as follows:

- **CPS Floppy Format** is a special proprietary format that crams more data onto a disk. DOS cannot read disks formatted using this method.

- **DOS Standard Format** is the normal DOS format. This is the default setting.

- **CPS Tape Format** is a special proprietary format that allows you to stop and start the backup, and also allows data compression. This is the default setting.

- **QIC Tape Format** is the standard QIC (quarter-inch compatibility) tape format, one of the first standards developed specifically for the PC. QIC-40 and QIC-80 format standards indicate the file format on the tape; hence using this selection allows you to interchange tapes made with different backup software. (A Reed-Solomon error-correction algorithm is also part of the QIC standard.)

FORMAT ALWAYS   When Format Always is off, the backup medium is only formatted when it has to be; if you turn Format Always on, the backup disk or tape is formatted every time it is used. This is not usually necessary, and with tape can waste a lot of time. The default for this command is off, and it can only be changed at the advanced user level.

Always back up your files with error correction selected, especially if you use tape as the backup medium.

ERROR CORRECTION With Error Correction turned on, CP Backup can recover from a multitude of errors on a damaged disk. To be able to do this, CP Backup stores additional information along with the backed-up files on each backup disk. This process takes slightly longer than a standard backup, but is much safer.

If you turn error correction off, you will see a warning window open when you start the next backup. You can turn error correction back on again from this message window.

VIRUS DETECTION When Virus Detection is turned on, a scan is made of all files and directories before the backup starts. If an infected file is found, a window opens giving you three choices:

- **Continue** resumes the backup and backs up the infected file.

- **Rename** lets you change the name of the file to one using an extension of Vn where n is a number between 0 and 99.

- **Cancel** stops the backup and returns to the main CP Backup window.

SAVE HISTORY A file that contains information on the files backed up, the time of the backup, and the type of backup performed is added to the last disk of each backup you make. If Save History is turned on, this file is also written to your hard disk. When you restore or compare files from your backup, the process goes much quicker if CP Backup can read the file from your hard disk, rather than ask you to insert the last floppy disk so that it can search for the history file.

Save History does not apply to low-speed backups where the history file is always stored on the last floppy disk of the backup, or in the directory used in the Choose Drive and Media configuration window, regardless of the Save History setting.

OVERWRITE WARNING The overwrite warning warns you that the disk in use has already been used in a backup, and that existing files will be overwritten. If you are doing a restore, Overwrite Warning alerts you to the act that existing files on your hard disk may be overwritten by files from the backup. The default is on. During a restore, the Overwrite Warning box contains the following options:

- **Overwrite** replaces the existing file with the file from the backup.

- **Overwrite With Newer File Only** replaces the file on the hard disk only if the file from the backup is more recent than the file on the disk. This ensures that the files on a disk after a restore are the most recent version.

- **Skip This File** does not overwrite this file.

- **Repeat For All Later Files** works in conjunction with one of the earlier settings.

TIME DISPLAY   You can choose whether or not to display the elapsed backup time. This may be a problem on some PC compatibles, or if you are working on a network. (Networks are notoriously bad at keeping good time and can sometimes reset the workstation time.) The default is on.

DISPLAY OPTIONS   Display Options, the last selection available in the Options menu, has two commands that let you specify how files are displayed on the screen in the tree list:

- **Sort Options** lets you sort the files by name, extension, date, or size; the sort can be in ascending or descending order.

- **Long Format** shows file name, extension, size, date, time, and attributes when it is selected. When it is deselected, only the file name and extension are displayed.

CHANGING AND SAVING CP BACKUP CONFIGURATIONS

Once you have made your choices from the complex list available from the Options menu, you can save your selections using the File menu. The next time you want to use those same settings, simply load the file rather than redo all the settings.

SAVING THE SETUP   After selecting from the many available options, save them in a file for use in another CP Backup session. When choosing a file name for the configuration file, choose one that you can remember easily. For example, you might save the configuration for backing up your word processing files in a file called WORDBACK, or you might save your daily backup format in a file called DAILY and your weekly backup settings in a file called WEEKLY. CP Backup adds the extension .SET.

The following list shows all the CP Backup options saved in the configuration file:

- Backup From Entry: drives and directories

- Backup Device: drive type and tape or disk media

- User Level and Express Mode settings

- Backup Speed: DMA or DOS format

- Backup Method: Full, Full Copy, Incremental, Separate Incremental, or Differential

- Attribute Exclusions

- Compression Type: Minimize Disks or Minimize Time

- Date range selections

- Formatting Options: Always, DOS, Central Point, or QIC

- Include/Exclude Files

- Overwrite Warning

- Subdirectory Inclusion: on or off

- Reporting: on, off, and report destination

- Time Display

- Verification Type

- Manual Directory and File selections

- Display Options: sorting or long format

- Error Correction: on or off

- Save History: on or off

- Virus Detection: on or off

Save Setup saves these changed items into the default CP Backup configuration file. To write the settings to another file, choose Save Setup As also in the File menu. If there is no setup file currently loaded, this selection is grayed out. Save Setup is not available at the beginner user level.

LOADING THE SETUP   Once you have saved a configuration in a file, you can reload it into CP Backup with the Load Setup selection in the File menu. This means that you can make several different types of backups without having to reconfigure the program. You just load the appropriate file and start the backup.

USING CP BACKUP IN A BATCH FILE

You can load the configuration file into CP Backup if you are using a batch file or running CP Backup from the DOS command prompt. To make a backup that saves all your Lotus worksheet files, for instance, use the Options selection to choose the backup method and use the Save Setup As option to keep this configuration information in a file called LOTUSBCK. Include the line

```
CP Backup LOTUSBCK
```

in your batch file and CP Backup will prompt you to insert the backup disks in sequence. When the backup is complete, control is passed back to the batch file and execution continues at the next line.

BACKING UP A NETWORK DRIVE

You or your network supervisor can install CP Backup in a write-protected directory on a Novell NetWare or IBM LAN network file server. Then the program can be run from any station that has access to files on the network and has the CP Backup directory in its path.

Also, your network supervisor should add an environment variable to your AUTOEXEC.BAT file specifying where the CP Backup user-specific configuration files should be saved. The command might look like this:

```
SET CPBACKUP = E:\HOME
```

On a Novell network station, directories are displayed on the tree only when the user has read privileges for that directory. If you try to restore a backup without the correct write privileges, you will see a warning message on the screen.

When you are setting up CP Backup on the network, make the directory path available to all users and use a system login script to define the CPBACKUP environment variable for all users. The command might look like this:

```
SET CPBACKUP = "E:\\HOME\\%LOGIN_NAME"
```

where the directory below HOME has the same name as the user's login name and the user has full write privileges. Include the quotation marks and the double backslashes, and capitalize LOGIN-_NAME, or you may see an error message.

If you are running CP Backup from the file server, but you want to backup your local disk, start CP Backup by specifying the local disk-drive letter on the command line:

CPBACKUP D:

When the program is started without a drive letter on the command line, it assumes that you want to back up the drive that the program was launched from. The network file server may be a huge disk, containing many thousands of files, and it will take CP Backup a very long time to build the tree list. By starting CP Backup from the local drive, only the tree structure of the local disk is built, which will be much faster.

CP Backup does not back up Novell bindery files or any files that are open during the backup. The *bindery* is a kind of database maintained by the network operating system that keeps track of users, groups, servers, and so on. The backup should be performed during a time when the majority of the users are logged off the system.

SCHEDULING AN AUTOMATIC BACKUP

The PC Tools program CPSCHED schedules unattended automatic backups to tape or to another hard disk. This means you can backup your hard disk at a time when you are not using your computer; in fact if you back up to tape, you don't even have to be present. You can back up your system after work or—better still—during lunchtime or a regularly scheduled meeting. If you are still using your computer when the backup is scheduled to start, CP Backup gives a 15 second warning; if there is no response to the dialog box, CP Backup interrupts the current application and starts the backup. When the backup is complete, CP Backup returns to the interrupted application. The DOS version of CP Backup cannot interrupt Microsoft Windows or any program that runs in 386-protected mode. In such a case, use the Windows version of CP Backup instead.

If you plan on using this automatic feature often, add this line to your AUTOEXEC.BAT file:

CPSCHED

If you used the Install program to configure CPSCHED, this step is not necessary.

You can remove CPSCHED from memory with Kill if you need to recover that memory space for a different application.

You can also use the Appointment Scheduler in the memory-resident Desktop to schedule automatic backups, in which case CPSCHED is not necessary.

You must use CP Backup setup files to load the backup configuration for unattended backups. To create a setup file for a weekly backup, follow these steps:

1. Change to the advanced user level in the Configure menu.

2. Choose Full/Erase Tape as the Backup Method using the Options menu or the Method drop-down list.

3. Choose the Minimize Time Compression method.

4. Make sure that Error Correction is turned on.

5. Select Report to File from the Report options.

6. Choose Save Setup As from the File menu, enter **WEEKLY**, and click on OK.

Next, without changing any of the other settings, create a setup file for a daily backup:

1. Choose the incremental or separate-incremental backup method.

2. Choose Save Setup As from the File menu, enter **DAILY**, and choose OK to complete the process.

Now select the Scheduler command button, or Schedule Backups from the Action menu, and you will see the display shown in Figure 10.13.

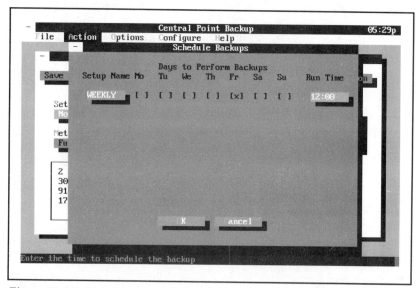

Figure 10.13: Use the Schedule Backups window to configure unattended backups

Use the Schedule Backups window to configure your unattended backups. Enter the name of the setup file you want to use, WEEKLY (press F4 to see a list of all your setup files), select the day you want to make your weekly backup, Friday, and the time you want the backup to start—in this example, 12:00 noon. Click on OK and you will see that the command buttons at the bottom of this window now include more choices:

- **Add** lets you specify another setup file.
- **Modify** allows you to change the highlighted entry.
- **Delete** lets you delete the highlighted entry. Be careful: as soon as you click on Delete, the entry is removed from the list (although not from the disk).
- **Save** stores your list and returns to the main CP Backup window.
- **Cancel** returns to the main CP Backup without saving any of your changes.

Enter the name of the next setup file, DAILY, select the days you want this backup to run, Monday through Thursday, and the time, again 12:00 p.m. You have now configured CP Backup to run unattended daily backups every weekday at lunchtime, except on Friday when CP Backup will run the larger weekly backup.

Make sure your computer is turned on, has the correct system time and date, and has the right tape cartridge loaded before you leave for lunch. Every day, while you are out at lunch, your computer will back up all the files that have changed since the previous day's backup; on Friday, your entire system will be backed up.

The DOS version of CP Backup saves this scheduling information in a file called CPBACKUP.TM; the Windows version of CP Backup uses a file called WNBACKUP.TM.

COMPARING FILES

After making a backup, you should compare the files contained in the backup against the original files on your hard disk. In this way, you can be sure that the files you backed up match the files on your hard disk and can be restored successfully. If you add new expansion boards to your computer, remember to use the Compare command

If you back up to tape and set the Verify option to Verify Always, a compare is generated automatically when the backup is complete.

to be sure that the new board has not affected your backup in some subtle way.

When you choose Compare from the opening CP Backup screen, or select Compare in the Action menu, the Compare screen opens, as Figure 10.14 shows. All the command buttons across the top of the Compare window are available as menu selections from the Actions menu; this means you can still use Compare even when Express Mode is turned off.

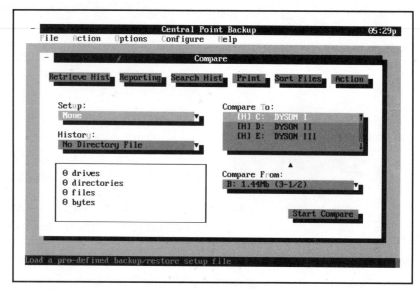

Figure 10.14: The main Compare screen

To compare a backup set, follow these steps:

1. Select Compare from the Action menu.

2. Choose History and select the History file for the backup set you are working with.

3. Select the Compare From drive from the drop-down list if the history file is not available. CP Backup asks you to insert the last tape or disk of the backup set you want to compare. You can use the Retrieve History command button for this, too.

4. Select the Compare To drive from the lists of drives. This is the hard disk you originally backed up.

5. Select the Start Compare command button or use Start Compare (F9) from the Action menu. Enter the password if you are using one.

6. Insert the first tape or disk of the backup set, and the compare begins.

Progress of the compare is shown on the horizontal bar. At the end of the compare, a window opens to show you the results. If some of your files did not compare, double-click the history file you just used to show the directory tree of the selected history file. A special symbol next to the file name indicates which file(s) compared with the original file(s); these special symbols are listed in Table 10.4.

Table 10.4: Compare Symbols Describing the Comparison

SYMBOL	MEANING
=	The backup file and the hard disk file are identical
<	The backup file is older than the hard disk file and the files are not identical
>	The backup file is newer than the hard disk file and the files are not identical
s	The date and time of the backup was different from the hard disk file, but the files were the same
–	The backup file is not present on the hard disk
x	The backup file is different from the hard disk file, even though the dates and times are identical

If an *x,* indicating that a problem exists with the backup, appears next to any of your files, check that there are no TSR programs running that might change a file during the backup. You can also try making the backup at a slower speed, but remember to make another compare to make sure that the backup is good.

RESTORING FILES FROM YOUR BACKUP

You must use the same speed for the restore that you used for the original backup.

Restore either reloads files onto the hard disk after a hardware problem or moves files from one machine to another. If you are reloading your system after disk-related problems, note that Restore assumes that you have already formatted the hard disk and loaded all the DOS files and the PC Tools files into their respective directories.

MAKING A COMPLETE RESTORE

If you used a setup file during the backup, use the same file during the restore.

Select Restore from the opening CP Backup screen and you will see a screen like the one shown in Figure 10.15.

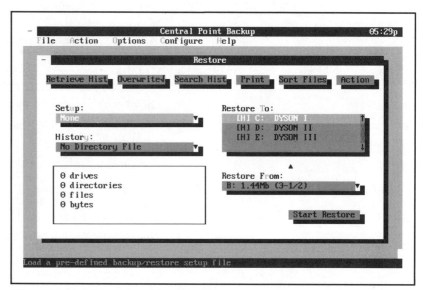

Figure 10.15: The main Restore window

To make a complete restore, follow these steps:

1. Select the right backup media in the Restore From drop-down list.

2. Select the correct hard disk drive in the Restore To drop-down list.

3. Choose Retrieve History and insert the last disk or tape of the backup you are about to restore to read the history file off the disk into memory.

4. Select Start Restore and insert the first disk or tape of the backup set.

The progress of the restore is shown on the screen. Continue to insert tapes or disks as prompted, until the restoration is complete.

RESTORING SPECIFIC FILES OR DIRECTORIES

Often a partial restoration may be all you need. For instance, you might want to recover just one file or just one directory from your backup.

To find and restore a specific file, turn Express Mode off in the Configure menu and follow these steps:

1. Select Search History Files and enter the file name(s) you want to locate. You can use the DOS wildcard characters ? and * if you wish; separate each entry from the last by a space.

2. Enter a date range for the original file if you wish.

3. Select the history file to search or choose Select All to search all of them.

4. Choose Search and all the selected history files on your hard disk are searched for the file(s) you are looking for.

5. Select Load to retrieve the history file for the restore, or select Search if you want to make another history search.

The directory tree lists the directories in the history file and the other side of the window shows the files in the current directory. CP Backup assumes you want to restore every file, so all files and directories are highlighted. If you only want to restore a part of the backup, move the highlight onto the root directory and press Enter or click the mouse. This deselects all files and directories. Now you can choose which files to restore using the same mechanisms you used to make the backup. You can use the following options from the Options menu:

- Subdirectory Inclusion
- Include/Exclude Files
- Attribute Exclusions
- Date Range Selection

These commands work with Restore just as they did with Backup, but the conditions apply to the files you are restoring rather than to the files you are backing up.

Click on the Start Restore command. You are prompted to insert the appropriate disks. When the restore is complete, the message

Restore Completed!

appears in a dialog box on the screen. The tree and file-list windows are updated to show the information from your backup disks.

If you lose a backup disk, continue with the restore operation anyhow. Restore will tell you that the disk is out of sequence and will then continue to restore all the complete files. If a file crosses a disk boundary—with one part of the file on one disk and another part on another disk—and the disk is lost, the file cannot be restored.

Also, if you lose the last disk in the backup, Restore can rebuild the directory information it contained from the other disks in the set, so you can still make the restore.

Restore senses that the directory information for the backup set is missing and asks whether you want to rebuild it. Rebuild reads all the disks in the set and makes a new directory. It then opens a dialog box and asks whether you want to continue with the restore operation or write out the directory information to floppy disk. Save the directory information to a new disk so that you don't overwrite any of your backup files.

If you use the Central Point tape format and lose the last tape of a multi-tape set—and there is no history file on your hard disk—you cannot restore your data. Also, if you use a QIC format tape and you lose the first tape in a multi-tape set, you cannot restore the backup.

LOOKING AT CP BACKUP FILES

The Install program locates CPBDIR in the SYSTEM directory below the main PCTOOLS directory.

When CP Backup makes a high-speed DMA backup, it does so in a form that DOS cannot read. For this reason, PC Tools includes a program called CPBDIR that lets you look at these backup disks. CPBDIR does more than just list the disks, however. If you forgot to label your backup disks, it can help you put them in the right sequence.

To run CPBDIR on a high-speed DMA backup disk in drive B, type

CPBDIR B: /X

You will see the information shown in Figure 10.16. CPBDIR shows the date and time the backup was made, the number of the disk, and other information about how CP Backup was configured.

CONVERTING FOREIGN BACKUP SETUP FILES

You can also use the Install program to find and convert the files for you.

If you have used Norton Backup (by Symantec) or Fastback Plus (by Fifth Generation Systems) backup programs, PC Tools includes a small utility program that converts setup files made by these two programs into setup files that CP Backup can understand and use.

To start the conversion program from the DOS prompt, type

CONVERT *drive switch*

where *switch* can include the following:

- /CPBACKUP looks for setup files made by CP Backup.
- /DEST = specifies the destination directory for converted files.
- /FASTBACK searches for and converts FastBack setup files.
- /NORTON searches for and converts setup files made by the Norton Backup program.

For a complete list of all the command-line options, see Chapter 20.

```
D:\PCTOOLS\SYSTEM>CPBDIR B: /X
Central Point Backup Directory Report U7
Copyright (c) 1990,1991 by Central Point Software. All Rights Reserved.


Disk is number 1 of a CP Backup set, backed up at 05:25p on 11/08/1991.
Disk was created with release 6.0 or 7.0 of CP Backup
The directory starts on track 37 (25h) of this disk.
This disk is recorded in DOS standard format.
Advanced Error Correction was ON for this backup.
Backup device was a 1.44MB drive, Media selected was 1.44MB.
Disk is formatted with 80 tracks of 18 sectors per side.
The compression setting for this backup is Minimize Time.
This disk was formatted by CP Backup.  The backup speed used was High.


What floppy drive contains the backup disk (default B:), Q to quit?Q
```

Figure 10.16: CPBDIR information on a high-speed DMA backup disk in drive B

CHAPTER

11

*Operating a
Remote Computer
with Commute*

The Central Point Software License agreement allows you to use one copy of Commute to make what it calls "a single unique connection between two computers even if multiple computers must be traversed to make the connection."

Commute is a communications program you can use to take over a remote computer, using a direct connection, a modem, or a Local Area Network (LAN). Once you have control of the remote computer you can transfer files, run programs, provide hands-on training and technical support, even work on your office computer from home or from your motel room when you are out visiting clients.

First, make sure that both computers have Commute loaded. You can use Install to load and configure Commute, or you can do it yourself. If *you* transfer the files, you will find COMMUTE.EXE (or COMMSML.EXE, the small version) in the PCTOOLS directory, several configuration files in the PCTOOLS\DATA directory, and several more files, including device drivers, in the PCTOOLS\ SYSTEM directory. You need them all. If you plan to use Commute automatically, you also need the scheduler on both systems; make sure you have the CPSCHED.EXE file, too.

CONFIGURING COMMUTE

Before you start Commute, you must first decide how the two computers will communicate by choosing the connection type:

- **Connect by Modem.** Make sure both computers are attached to their modems, and that the modems are turned on and connected to the phone lines before starting Commute.

- **Connect by LAN.** Log on to the Novell NetWare network from both computers before starting Commute.

- **Direct Connection.** Connect the two computers using a null-modem adapter with a regular serial cable, or use a specially adapted null-modem cable.

You can also run a version of Commute that uses less conventional memory if you type **COMMSML** at the DOS prompt.

To start Commute from the DOS command line, type **COMMUTE**. The first time you start Commute, you may be asked for configuration information. In that case, the Commute User's Name dialog box opens, asking you to enter your user name. Commute uses this name to identify you to other Commute users. If you are logged on to the network, your login name is shown as the default; you may use it or change it to another name, if you wish. Next, the

Connection Type dialog box opens, as shown in Figure 11.1, asking you to select the type of connection you will use most often. Select one method from the list and choose OK; you can always change your mind later. If you chose Connect by LAN, your configuration is now complete and you will see the Call Manager window on your screen.

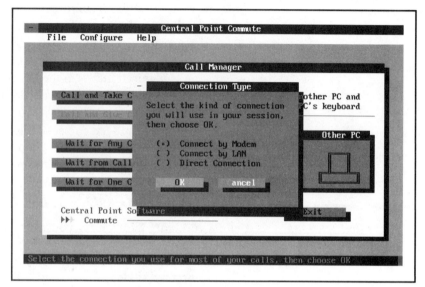

Figure 11.1: Select the communications method you will use most often in the Connection Type window

If you chose Connect by Modem, you will see the Modem List window next, as Figure 11.2 shows. Find and choose the kind of modem you use; if the brand of modem you use is not shown on the list, select the Hayes option with the same speed as your modem. Choose OK to move on to the next window.

If you chose Direct Connection or Connect by Modem, the last configuration screen is the COM Port screen. Select the COM port that your modem or null-modem cable is connected to, then choose OK.

If you have a non-PS/2 computer and you want to use COM3 or COM4, you must click the Edit button to supply the IRQ (interrupt request number) and address for the COM port you want to use.

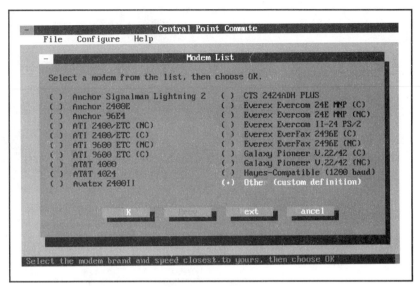

Figure 11.2: Choose your modem from the selections shown in the Modem List window

Commute uses the following default settings:

COM 1   IRQ = 4   Address = 3F8h

COM 2   IRQ = 3   Address = 2F8h

COM 3   IRQ = 4   Address = 3E8h

COM 4   IRQ = 3   Address = 2E8h

To use a different setting, edit these default settings as required. Configuration is now complete, and you will see the Call Manager window on your screen.

USING THE CALL MANAGER

The Call Manager window is shown in Figure 11.3. Five Call Manager command button selections are shown down the left side of the window and a small diagram on the right side of the window illustrates each of these selections.

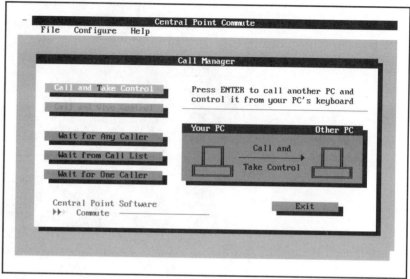

Figure 11.3: The Call Manager window

When you use Commute to *take control* of another computer, your screen shows whatever is on the remote computer's screen. This can be somewhat disconcerting at first, but you will get used to it quite quickly. When you use Commute to *give control* to another computer, the remote user controls your computer just as if he or she were sitting at your keyboard. The Call Manager screen decides which of the two computers will be in control, as well as which calls the remote computer will accept. The Call Manager screen shows the following options:

- **Call and Take Control** lets you call another computer and take control of the keyboard and disk drives. Anything that appears on the remote computer's screen appears on your screen.

- **Call and Give Control** lets you call another computer and give control to the remote computer.

- **Wait for Any Caller** lets you set Commute up in memory-resident mode to wait for any caller.

- **Wait from Call List** lets you set up Commute in memory-resident mode, to wait for a call from a user on your Call List.

- **Wait for One Caller** lets you set Commute up to wait for a specific caller, and ignore all others.

An example will illustrate these concepts much better. For our purposes, imagine that you want to take control of a remote computer. To establish this as a Commute session, follow these steps on the remote computer:

1. Set up the remote PC to wait for a call. Load and configure Commute, then choose Wait for Any Caller in the Call Manager window.

2. The Connection Type dialog box opens; select the appropriate kind of connection: Connect by Modem, Connect by LAN, or Direct Connection.

3. Choose OK and Commute goes into memory-resident mode to wait for the call. This means that the person using the remote computer can continue working as usual—with a word processor, spreadsheet, or whatever—and Commute will run in the background, waiting for the call.

Now that the remote computer is waiting for your call, you can call it and take control from your PC:

1. Load and configure Commute, then select Call and Take Control from the Call Manager window.

2. The Private Call list appears with information on frequently called computers, just like a phone list.

3. If you are using a LAN connection choose the LAN User List. The LAN Server List dialog box opens, showing you all the LAN servers that are available. Choose a server, then choose a user from the LAN User List.

4. If you are using a modem connection, choose Manual Call and enter the phone number of the modem on the remote

computer into the Dial box. If you must dial 9 for an outside line, separate it from the rest of the number with a comma. Hyphens and parentheses are ignored by Commute, so you can use them in the number for visual clarity, if you wish. Select Modem, then choose OK.

5. If you are using a direct connection, choose Manual Call and select Direct.

Commute makes the call and a dialog box opens indicating the status of the connection. Status boxes on the remote screen inform the user that a Commute call is being processed. Depending on how the remote computer is configured, you may be asked to enter your Commute user name and the password for the computer you are taking over. If your name or password is not accepted after three tries, your call is rejected.

After making a successful connection, your computer shows whatever is on the remote PC's screen: your keystrokes or mouse clicks control its disk drives, programs, and printer. In this mode you can work with the other computer just as though you were sitting at the keyboard.

USING THE SESSION MANAGER

You can use the Session Manager to send messages to the other computer user, to transfer files, and to end the session. After you have linked up with and are in control of the remote computer, type the Commute hotkey, Alt–Right-Shift—i.e., hold down the Alt key and press the right-hand Shift key. The Session Manager screen opens, as shown in Figure 11.4.

You have the following options in the Session Manager:

- **End the Session** breaks the connection between the two computers and ends the Commute program. You return to whatever you were doing before the Commute session started. Commute also resets the modem, if you were using Connect by Modem.

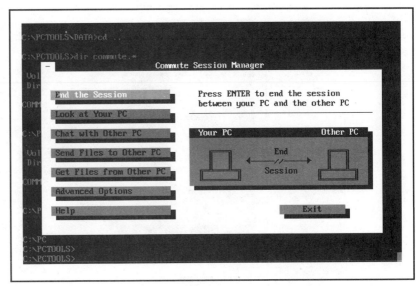

Figure 11.4: The Session Manager window

- **Look at Your PC** lets you return to DOS so you can check a
  file name, delete files to make room for files you are about
  to transfer, or perform other DOS tasks on your local computer. Type **EXIT** at the DOS prompt when you are ready
  to return to the Session Manager.

- **Chat with Other PC** lets you keep in touch with the user of
  the remote computer. The Chat window opens and everything you type appears in the Chat window on both computers. If you are using the remote computer, pressing the
  hotkey opens the Chat window, so either computer can
  start a chat session. Press F10 in the Chat window to ring
  the bell if you need to get someone's attention quickly.
  When you have finished your chat, press F3 to return to
  the Session Manager.

- **Send Files to Other PC** lets you copy a file or group of files
  from your computer to the remote computer. The Send
  Files to Other PC dialog box is shown in Figure 11.5. (The
  file-transfer options shown in the lower half of the screen

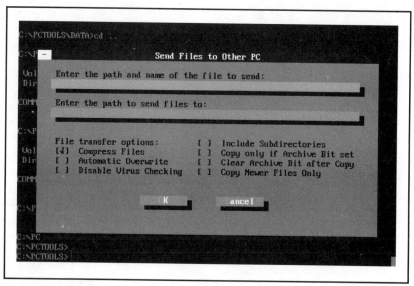

Figure 11.5: The Send Files to Other PC dialog box

are described later.) You can use the two DOS wildcard
characters to extend the copy to multiple files, and a minus
sign to exclude files. For example, to copy all the files from
your word-processing directory, except files with the .BAK
extension, enter **C:\WP*.* –*.BAK**. You must also enter
the path of the destination directory on the remote computer, the directory where you want to locate the copied
files. A dialog box opens to show the progress of the file
transfer. This dialog box shows the percentage of the current file transferred, percentage of the total number of files
transferred, elapsed time, time remaining, and the names
of all the files that have been transferred successfully.

- **Get Files from Other PC** works very like Send Files to Other
  PC, uses a very similar dialog box with the same file transfer options.

- **Advanced Options** contains several features you can use
  during your Commute session:

    Reboot Other PC. Use this selection to reboot
    the remote PC. This option may be unavailable,

depending on the security settings in effect on the remote computer. You can also press Ctrl, Alt and Del keys all at the same time on your own keyboard to reboot the remote computer; your own computer remains unaffected.

Lock Other Keyboard. When you are in control of the remote computer, Commute continues to accept commands from both keyboards or mice. You can disable the keyboard and mouse on the remote computer with this option and prevent unauthorized users from accessing the computer. Once you select Lock Other keyboard this command changes into Unlock Other Keyboard, so that you can unlock the keyboard again if you wish. The hotkey combination is still effective when the keyboard is locked, however. Again, the security settings on the remote computer may disallow this option.

Print Direction. This selection lets you use your local printer, the remote printer, both your local and the remote printer, or neither printer during your Commute session. If you print to your own printer during your session, make sure that it is compatible with the software that you are controlling.

Redraw Your Screen. This command refreshes or redraws your screen.

Save Current Screen. Use this command to take a snapshot of the correct screen. The snapshot is saved into a text file; Commute cannot capture graphics screens.

Screen Options. This selection lets you choose different screen configurations that can help to speed up a Commute session. The Screen options dialog box is shown in Figure 11.6. The Maximum Received Resolution refers to the level of video information your computer is receiving from the remote PC. This should be set to the lowest common denominator; if you have a VGA and the

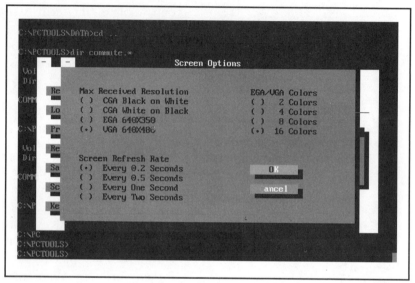

Figure 11.6: The Screen Options dialog box

remote computer has a CGA, the best resolution
you can receive is CGA resolution. EGA/VGA
Colors determines the amount of color information
sent in graphics mode. Using fewer colors speeds
up Commute. Screen Refresh Rate determines how
often Commute updates the screen during a session. Use a fast update rate in a text-based program
like a word processor, but use a slower rate in a
graphics program or a paint program.

Keyboard Level. If your keyboard does not work
as you expect during a Commute session, use this
option.

- **Help** is available during Commute.

- **Exit** closes the Session Manager and returns you to the
  Commute session. You can achieve the same result if you
  press F3 or Escape.

There are seven file-transfer options shown in the lower half of the
Send Files to Another PC dialog box (see Figure 11.5) that you can

use to speed up the file transfer:

- **Compress Files.** Commute compresses each file in memory at the start of the transfer and decompresses it again before writing the file out to disk. If your modems perform their own data compression, do not use this option.

- **Automatic Overwrite.** This option is only available when you try to transfer a file into a directory where a file of the same name already exists. When you select Automatic Overwrite, Commute replaces the existing file with the new file. With this option off, the Overwrite dialog box opens each time, so that you can decide how to proceed. The Overwrite dialog box gives details of both files, including size in bytes, date and time; you have the option of overwriting or skipping the file. You can also choose to repeat your selection here (overwrite or skip the file) on all later existing files during this transfer. Cancel stops the transfer immediately.

- **Disable Virus Checking.** You can check the transferred files for the presence of a virus with this option. If Commute finds evidence of a virus, a warning window opens, showing the name of the infected files. Commute asks if you still want to send the file or not. Here you also have the option of repeating your selection on all other infected files found later on during the transfer.

- **Include Subdirectories.** If you used the DOS wildcard characters to specify a group of files, you can use this selection to include all subdirectories in the transfer. If you do not use Include Subdirectories, only the files in the original directory are transferred.

- **Copy Only if Archive Bit Set.** This selection copies all files that have their archive bit set, indicating that they have changed since they were last backed up. If you use Commute to back up files from one computer to another, use this option along with the one right below.

- **Clear Archive Bit after Copy.** This selection clears the archive bit after the file has been transferred to indicate that it has been backed up.

- **Copy Newer Files Only.** Use this option to replace older files that already exist on the remote computer with newer files from your PC. When you select this option, the Automatic Overwrite setting is ignored.

CHANGING COMMUTE'S CONFIGURATION

Making two computers communicate over any kind of link is often a complex task; there are many subtle problems to overcome. The items in the Configure menu, shown in Figure 11.7, are designed to make this process as easy as possible. You set up some of the Commute communication parameters when you started Commute for the first time; if you ever want to change them, use the Configuration menu.

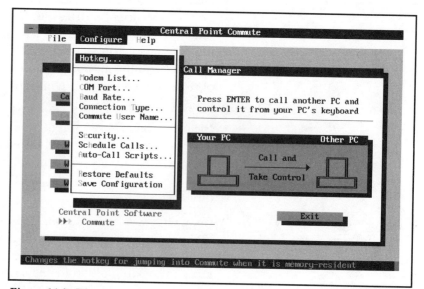

Figure 11.7: The Configure menu lets you make the appropriate choices for Commute

The Configuration menu presents you with the following choices:

- **Hotkey.** Normally you activate Commute by pressing Alt–Right-Shift. Use this selection if you want to change this hotkey to another key combination. The Hotkey window opens; hold down either the Ctrl or the Alt keys and press another key to create a new hotkey combination. Commute distinguishes between the right and left shift keys. Press Enter when you have made your choice.

- **Modem List.** If you have changed your modem, use this selection to choose your new modem. There are four pages of modems; press Next and Previous to move from page to page. Modems use a set of characters called a *string* for different kinds of configurations. The Custom Definition option in the Modem List window lets you configure your own modem-initialization string, as well as the dial string, the answer string, and the hangup string if you have a modem that is not on the Commute list.

- **COM Port.** Choose the COM port you want to use for the Commute session.

- **Baud Rate.** Commute automatically adjusts the baud rate on both computers in a session to be as fast as it can be; you will not have to change this setting very often.

- **Connection Type.** Choose one of the connection types from Connect by Modem, Connect by LAN, or Direct Connection.

- **Commute User Name.** Use this selection if you want to change your user name.

- **Security.** Choose this option to open the Security Settings window, shown in Figure 11.8.

You have the following choices in the Security Settings window:

- **Auto-Login From List** lets Commute callers supply their user name and password automatically from the caller's Private Call List.

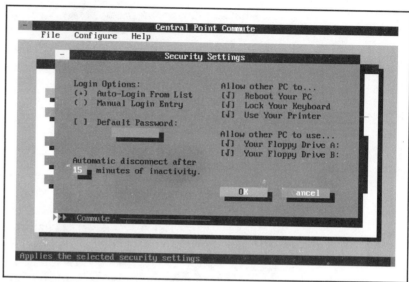

Figure 11.8: The Security Settings window

- **Manual Login Entry** requires Commute callers to enter their name and password manually each time they call your computer. If you choose this setting, they cannot use an Auto-Call script to take control of your computer.

- **Default Password** requires callers to know the default password. If you have a specific password for a caller in your Give Control list, he or she must use this password instead of the default password.

- **Automatic Disconnect** terminates a connection after a period of inactivity. Enter the number of minutes to wait, up to a maximum of 60 minutes, or enter a value of zero if you don't want Commute to disconnect automatically.

- **Reboot Your PC.** When this selection is checked, the controlling PC can reboot your computer.

- **Lock Your Keyboard.** When this selection is checked, the controlling computer can lock the keyboard to prevent unauthorized use.

If you deselect Reboot Your PC, Lock Your Keyboard, or Use Your Printer, the corresponding commands in the Advanced Options dialog box on the other computer are disabled during a Commute session.

- **Use Your Printer.** If you select this option, the controlling computer can use your printer during a Commute session.

- **Floppy Drive A and B.** Specify which floppy disk drives the controlling computer can use on the remote PC. If you select drive A only, and the controlling computer tries to access drive B, the controlling computer will see the Invalid Drive Specification error.

- **Restore Defaults** reloads the original Commute settings from the file COMMUTE.CFG.

- **Save Configuration.** Use Save Configuration after you have completed all your changes; you will also have the opportunity to save your configuration when you exit from Commute.

There are also several important configuration entries in the File menu:

- **Record Activity** saves information about a Commute session in a file called COMMUTE.LOG. This includes whom you called, how long the session lasted, and which files were transferred. If Record Activity is turned on, you will see a check mark next to it in the File menu.

- **Print Activity Log.** Once you have recorded Commute activity, you can print the information as either a Detailed Report or as a Brief Report. You can send the report to your printer or to a file for later printing.

- **Ignore All Calls.** This command is only available if you have loaded Commute into memory and hotkeyed back into the program again. If you are in the middle of a task and you don't want to be interrupted, use Ignore All Calls. A check mark appears next to the selection in the File menu. Choose the command a second time to turn calls on again.

- **Unload From Memory.** If you have loaded Commute memory-resident to wait for a call and you find that you now need the memory space back, you can hotkey into

Commute and use this command to unload Commute from memory, along with any other memory-resident programs that were loaded after it.

- **DOS Shell** returns to DOS for a moment so you can check a file name or a directory name. When you are ready to return to Commute, type **EXIT** at the DOS prompt.

- **Exit** quits Commute and returns to DOS or the program from which you started Commute. You have the opportunity to save any configuration changes you made during your Commute session.

USING THE PRIVATE CALL LIST

If you find that you call the same people over and over, add them to your Private Call List so you won't have to type their name, phone number, and password each time you call.

Choose Private Call List in the File menu. When the Private Call List window opens, click on the maximize button or press F8 to show the whole window, including the names and phone numbers or LAN user name. The first two entries in this list are always Manual Call and LAN User List. To add a name to this list click the New command button; to edit an existing entry, highlight the entry and choose Edit. Either way, the Edit Call List window opens, as in Figure 11.9.

The options in this window are as follows:

- **Private Name.** Enter the name of the remote computer you will be taking over. This name is for your reference only; you do not have to match any other name.

As this phone number is sent directly to your modem, you can include modem control characters in the number if you wish.

- **Connect By Modem.** Select this connection type if you usually connect to this computer by modem. When you choose this selection, you also have to enter a phone number and a password into the boxes in the lower portion of the window. If you have to dial 9 for an outside line, separate the 9 from the rest of the number with a comma. You can include hyphens and parentheses in the number if you want to; they are ignored by Commute.

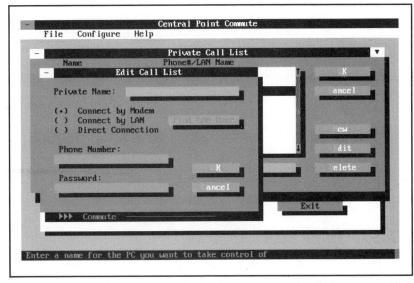

Figure 11.9: The Edit Call List window lets you enter details for a new caller

- **Connect By LAN.** Choose this selection if you normally connect to this person over a LAN. When you choose Connect By LAN, the phone-number box at the bottom of the window changes to Commute User Name. Enter the Commute user name of the computer you want to call on the LAN. You can also click the Find LAN User command button to locate the PC you want to take control of. First the LAN Server List window opens showing a list of all the servers currently available to you. To see more information about each server, press F8 or click on the maximize button. Select the server you want to access and choose OK. The next window is the LAN User List window, which shows all the Commute users currently logged on to the LAN who are waiting for a call. This window displays Commute user names. Select Show All LAN Users if you want to see a list of all the users who have accounts on this server. Select a Commute user, then choose OK, and the Edit Call List window reappears showing the new entry. Click OK to close the Edit Call List window and click OK again to return to the main Commute window.

- **Direct Connection.** Select this option if you usually take
over the remote computer using a null-modem cable, rather
than a LAN or a modem. There are no additional options
when you choose Direct Connection.

These entries are saved in a file called COMMUTE.PCL. If you
want to delete an entry in the Private Call List, highlight the entry
and click the Delete command button.

USING THE GIVE CONTROL LIST

If you often give control of your computer to another Commute
user, there is an option in the File menu to automate this process.
Choose Give Control List in the File menu and you will see the window shown in Figure 11.10. The Give Control List works just like the
Private Call List: you can add names to the list by using New, change
entries with Edit, or remove entries with Delete. When you use New
to add a new entry, the window shown in Figure 11.11 opens.

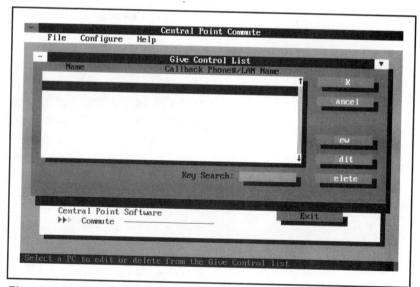

Figure 11.10: The Give Control window

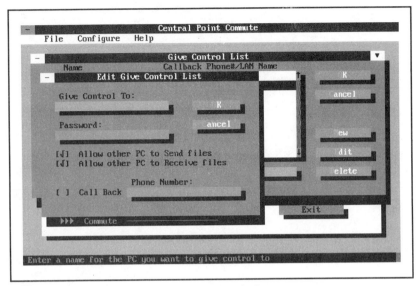

Figure 11.11: The Edit Give Control List window

You can make the following entries in this window:

- **Give Control To.** Enter the Commute user name of the person you will be giving control of your computer.

- **Password.** If you want to force the other user to type a password before gaining access to your computer, enter the password here.

- **Allow Other PC to Send Files.** When this option is selected, the controlling computer can send files to your PC during a Commute session.

- **Allow Other PC to Receive Files.** When this option is chosen, the controlling PC can receive files from your computer during a session.

- **Call Back.** Select Call Back if you want to pay for the call. After contact is made, Commute hangs up the modem and reinitializes the session by calling this number immediately.

- **Phone Number.** Enter the phone number for the Call Back.

All the entries in the Give Control List are saved in a file called COMMUTE.GCL.

AUTOMATING A COMMUTE SESSION

There are two selections in the Configure menu that you can use to help automate your Commute sessions: Auto-Call Scripts and Schedule Calls. If you repeat a sequence of commands in your Commute sessions, such as transferring files or using specific DOS commands, use the Commute Auto-Call feature to include these operations in a script file. Once you have created the script file, you can use Schedule Calls to run the script file while both computers are unattended, if you wish.

Select Auto-Call Scripts from the Configure menu and a window opens that lists all the available script files. Use New to create a new script; Commute opens a dialog box asking you to enter a name for the script file. Enter a name and choose OK to advance to the Script File Editor, as shown in Figure 11.12. The Script File Editor has a row of command buttons across the top of the window that you can click to assemble a script. When you open a new script, only the Call

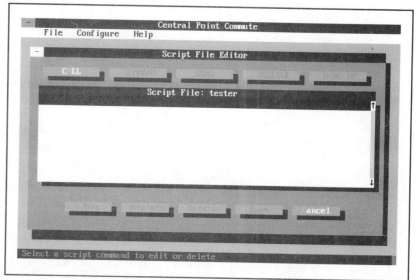

Figure 11.12: The Script File Editor window

button is active, as all scripts must begin with a Call command. Select Call and the Private Call List appears over the top of the Script File Editor. Place the highlight over the person you want to call and choose OK. The main window in the Script Editor now contains a Call command followed by the name you just selected.

Now the bottom row of command buttons is active. Choose New to insert a new line in your script, Replace to edit an entry in an existing script, Delete to remove an entry from a script, or Cancel to leave the Script Editor. Use Save when you have completed your changes and Commute stores your script in a file with the extension .CSF. Because all scripts must begin with a Call statement, you cannot delete or replace this statement.

When you choose Replace or Delete, the rest of the command buttons across the top of the window become active:

- **Call** inserts a Call command into your script. All scripts must begin with Call.

- **Command** adds a DOS command into your script. When you choose Command, the DOS Command dialog box opens so that you can type in a DOS command to run on the remote computer during your Commute session. You can run a program, run a batch file, list files, or any other DOS command. Make sure that the remote computer is at the DOS prompt and not running a program when you issue the DOS command. These DOS commands just run during a session, not before and not after.

- **Send** transfers files to the remote computer. When you choose Send, the Send Files to Other PC dialog box opens. Specify the files you want to transfer and choose the file-transfer option as you would for a regular transfer. Do not change the settings for Automatic Overwrite or Disable Virus Checking, because you do not want an unattended transfer interrupted by an unwanted dialog box.

- **Receive** receives files sent from the remote computer. When you select Receive, the Get Files from Other PC dialog box opens. Again, select the files as you would normally, and do not change the settings of Automatic Overwrite and Disable Virus Detection.

- **Hang Up.** Add a Hang Up command to the end of each script file that you want to run automatically. Commute disconnects the two computers and the Commute session ends.

After you have created a script that contains all the commands you want to use in a Commute session, you can add the name of the script file at the command line. If your script file is called BORIS, type **COMMUTE BORIS** at the DOS prompt. The Commute program starts, makes the call, and establishes the connection; then the script file takes over.

To run an Auto-Call script at a particular time, use the scheduling program called CPSCHED. Add CPSCHED to your AUTOEX-EC.BAT file so that the program is loaded automatically into your computer.

If you use Desktop in memory-resident mode, you don't need to use CPSCHED, because Desktop can do it for you.

Choose Schedule Calls from the Configure menu to open the Schedule Calls dialog box. Choose New to add an item to the list on the screen. After you enter the script file name (without the extension), choose the day and time that you want the script to run. Choose Save to return to the main Commute window. Commute saves this scheduling information in a file called COMMUTE.TM.

USING COMMUTE IN WINDOWS

Commute can run Windows on the remote computer, and there are several things you can do to optimize your Commute session with Windows. A LAN connection is by far the fastest way of running Windows, with a direct connection next; a modem connection is definitely the slowest. Because Windows works entirely in graphics mode, each Windows screen contains much more information than a regular text screen does, so each screen takes longer to transmit to the other PC. If the remote computer is running Windows, you don't have to wait for the full screen to be redrawn every time, because your keystrokes are buffered. This means you can type ahead of what you see on the screen and your keystrokes will not be lost.

If the screen redraws are just taking too long, you can adjust them in the Session Manager. Start by using a video refresh rate of one second and increase or decrease the rate depending on what kind of Windows application you are using.

If Commute doesn't answer a call when you are in Windows, make sure you have installed the PC Tools Windows TSR Manager. This is how Commute talks to you when you are using Windows.

To use Windows while you are waiting for a call:

1. Start Commute as you normally would, either from the DOS command line or from your AUTOEXEC.BAT file. Commute loads and returns you to DOS.

2. Start Windows and your Windows application.

When another computer calls, a dialog box opens informing you of the call.

USING COMMUTE WITH A NULL-MODEM CABLE

RS-232C cables should usually be limited to runs of less than 50 feet. However, it is possible to extend this limitation with a high-quality cable.

You can use Commute with a direct physical connection as well as with modem and LAN connections. PCs use an industry standard for communications over serial lines known as RS-232C. This standard defines the voltages and signal characteristics for serial communication. The cable you use to connect two computers together for a Commute direct link is a special serial cable called a *null-modem cable*. This cable has sending and receiving wires crossed over, so that the wires used for sending by one computer are used for receiving by the other computer, and vice versa. You can make your own null-modem cable if you modify your serial cable as shown in Figure 11.13. Figure 11.13 gives detailed connections for both a 25-pin connector and a 9-pin connector; the other wires in the 25-wire standard can be ignored.

Alternatively, you can use a normal serial cable with a null-modem adapter. Your local computer store will be able to supply all these items. However, not all null-modem cables are identical; for Commute, you need one with the connections shown in Figure 11.13.

DeskConnect also uses a null-modem cable for a direct computer-to-computer link, but is somewhat less exacting in its requirements of the cable. DeskConnect will work properly with a cable that Commute uses, but the reverse is not necessarily true. In addition to the data lines (lines 2, 3, 4, and 5) being crossed, Commute also requires that some of the control lines in the cable (lines 6, 8, and 20) be configured correctly.

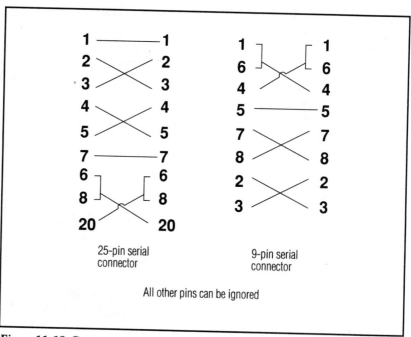

Figure 11.13: Commute serial cable connections for 25- and 9-pin connectors

CHAPTER

12

Using the
Windows-Only Tools

Not only can many of the DOS-based programs in PC Tools be run under Microsoft Windows 3.0, but PC Tools includes several programs specifically designed to run under Windows. The Install program automatically configures a program group for these utilities, and if you select the group, you will see their graphical icons on the screen.

This chapter covers the PC Tools programs that are only available as Microsoft Windows applications, they are:

- the Program Launcher
- the TSR Manager
- the Scheduler

THE PROGRAM LAUNCHER

The Launcher lets you run any DOS or Windows program from any Windows application using the Launcher's custom cascading menu system, without having to return to the Program Manager. You can tell when the Launcher is installed on your system by looking at the control box at the top left of the Windows title bar. It's supposed to look like a little filing-cabinet drawer with a handle on it, because it has to do with controlling files. If you can see a red handle on the filing cabinet, you know that the Launcher is installed; if the handle is its usual gray color, the Launcher is not installed.

If the Launcher is not installed on your system and you would like to try it out, just double-click on the Launcher icon in the PC Tools group to install the Launcher automatically. This is a temporary installation only, however. To install the Launcher permanently on your system, run the PC Tools Install program again, or modify your WIN.INI file to include WNLAUNCH.EXE.

To use the Launcher, click on the control box in any Windows application and you will see a new selection at the bottom of the menu, CP Launcher. Click on this selection to display a cascading menu, as Figure 12.1 shows. Depending on the choices you made when you installed PC Tools, you may see other PC Tools programs in this custom menu.

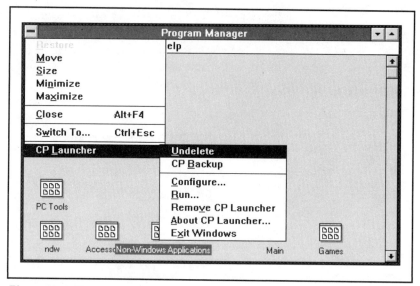

Figure 12.1: The Launcher cascading menu

You can run any of these programs by choosing it from the menu; press the underlined letter in the menu or click on the program name with the mouse.

The CP Launcher menu contains the following five commands:

- **Configure** lets you add or remove programs from the Launcher menu system.

- **Run** lets you run a program not on the Launcher cascading menu system.

- **Remove CP Launcher** unloads the Launcher from the control box in all Windows applications.

- **About CP Launcher** displays program information.

- **Exit Windows** lets you shut down all applications programs and exit Windows.

ADDING A NEW PROGRAM WITH CONFIGURE

To add a new program to the Launcher menu system, choose Configure and you will see the window shown in Figure 12.2. Enter a file name into the Launch Command box, either by typing the name directly or by using Browse if you are not sure of the path of the item you want to add. Browse opens the window shown in Figure 12.3. Use the Directory and File lists to select the file, then choose OK; the program name, initial directory, and a suggested menu item name appears in the appropriate text boxes in the Configure window.

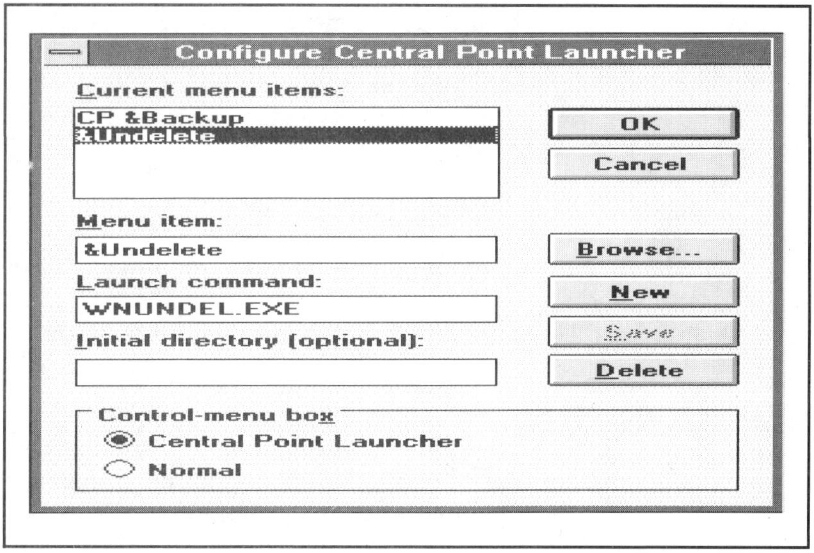

Figure 12.2: The Configure window lets you add new programs to the Launcher menu system

Windows automatically associates most documents with its own applications programs, and you can take advantage of this if you add a document name to the Launcher menu. When you select the document from the Launcher menu, Windows automatically starts the associated application and loads the document. For example, if you use a particular Lotus Ami Pro form letter, add the menu item ''Form Letter'' to the Launcher menu. When you choose this selection, Windows loads both Ami Pro and the form letter automatically.

Next, to add this new entry to the Launcher menu, move to the Menu Item box and accept the name that Browse places there, or type

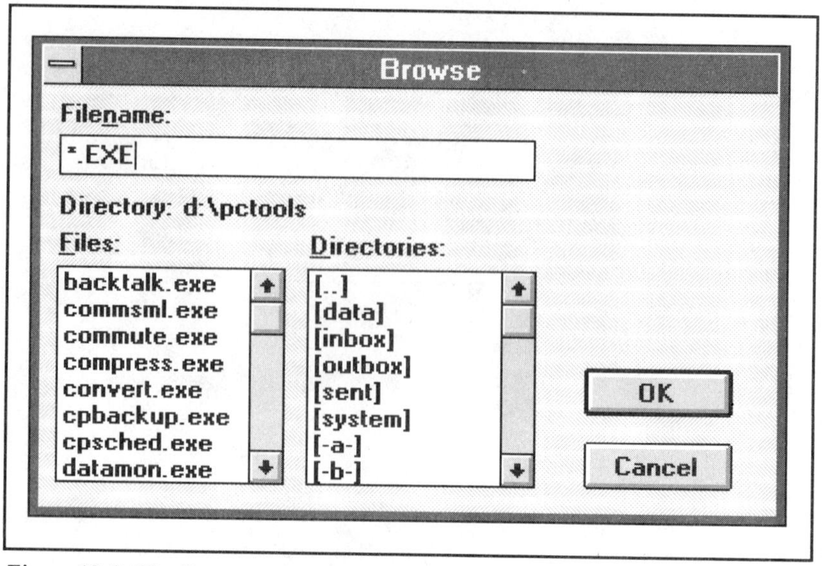

Figure 12.3: The Browse window lets you choose the file name to add from the list of directories and files

in your own name. This way you can make the name more descriptive than the terse eight-character DOS file name. If you want to be able to start this program by pressing a single key from the keyboard, indicated by an underlined letter in the Launcher menu, type an & immediately before the letter you want underlined on the screen. Choose Save to add this new entry to the list of items in the Current Menu Items list, then choose OK to close the Configure window.

The next time you open the CP Launcher menu, you will see this new item in the menu.

USING THE RUN COMMAND

You can also start an application that is not on the custom menu by choosing Run from the Launcher menu. The Run window opens, as in Figure 12.4. Choose an entry from the Directories and Files lists, and choose OK to run your selection. When your chosen program completes, you return directly to Windows.

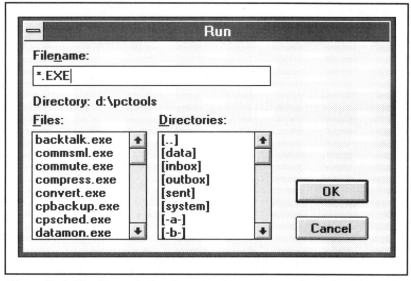

Figure 12.4: The Run window lets you choose a name from the Directories and Files lists

THE TSR MANAGER

The TSR Manager is a PC Tools Windows application that lets the PC Tools DOS TSR programs communicate to Windows users via a dialog box. If you select the TSR Manager from the PC Tools group, you can configure the following utilities:

- VDefend
- Data Monitor Directory Lock and Write Protection
- Commute

THE SCHEDULER

You can use the Scheduler to perform automatic operations of several PC Tools programs:

- Backup, to run unattended backups
- Commute, to start remote communications sessions

- Desktop Telecommunications E-mail, to schedule the transfer of electronic mail

- DiskFix, to check periodically for common disk problems

If one of the DOS-based programs schedules an event, you will be notified as long as the Windows Scheduler is running. If you run Windows in real or standard mode, a scheduled event interrupts the current application, performs its task, and then returns control to the originally interrupted program. If you run Windows in 386 enhanced mode, an icon appears on the desktop to indicate that the scheduled event is running on your system. A dialog box will prompt for any needed information.

When you click on the Scheduler icon in the PC Tools group, a window opens containing four command buttons, one for each of the application programs Backup, Commute, Desktop E-mail, and DiskFix. Click the appropriate command button to configure the application program you are working with.

The Options menu contains four selections:

- **Show Icon** displays an icon when the Scheduler runs. To edit or change any of the Scheduler settings, double-click on the Scheduler icon in the Program Manager.

- **Prompt Before Event** displays a dialog box giving a 30-second warning before an event occurs. You can choose to cancel or postpone the event. If you give no response, the event occurs at the scheduled time.

- **Enable Desktop Events** allows Desktop events to occur when you are using Windows. The Scheduler must be running (it can be running minimized and hidden) and you don't need CPSCHED, the DOS scheduling program, in memory. When an appointment occurs, for example, a reminder is displayed in a dialog box. DOS applications run in full-screen mode, so your Windows session will be interrupted until the DOS application completes its tasks.

- **Exit** lets you quit the Scheduler to stop any further monitoring of events, or minimize the Scheduler so that it can continue. When you select Minimize, you will see the minimized Scheduler icon at the bottom of the Windows window.

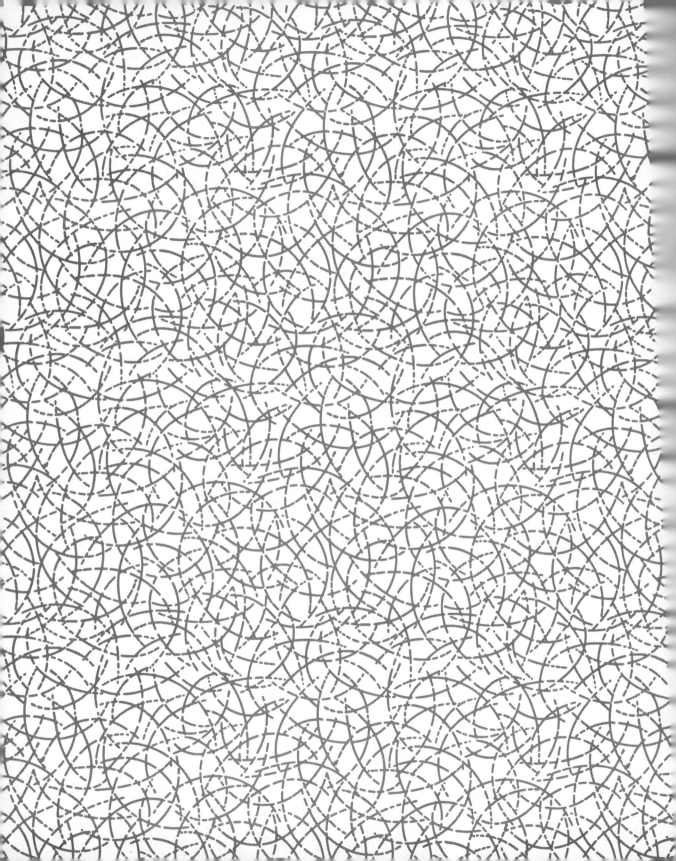

PART IV

Desktop Tools

CHAPTER

13

*Working with Notepads,
Outlines, the Clipboard,
and the Macro Editor*

This first chapter on PC Tools Desktop describes how you can use Desktop with words and ideas. It describes Notepads, Outlines, the Clipboard, and the Macro Editor. Once you use Notepads to enter and edit text, using Outlines, the Clipboard, and the Macro Editor will be easy, since they all share the same user interface.

USING NOTEPADS

PC Tools Desktop contains a word processor called Notepads. If you run Desktop in memory-resident mode, you can use Notepads from inside your foreground application. With Notepads, you can cut and paste text to the Clipboard, search for and replace text strings, print your work with headers and footers, and even check your spelling. You can work with ASCII text files (such as AUTOEXEC.BAT and CONFIG.SYS) or with PC Tools-format files. You can also work with multiple files; in fact, you can have as many as 15 different Notepads files open simultaneously. This is very useful if you are working on several documents at once.

Notepads works with files no larger than 64K, equivalent to a file of approximately 64,000 characters or about 10,000 words (20 single-spaced or 40 double-spaced pages). If you try to load a file larger than 64K into a *notepad* (a Notepads window), you will see the warning message

File too big for Notepad, it will be cut off to fit

and you have the option to cancel or continue. If you choose to continue, the first 64K of the file will be loaded but the remainder of the file will be discarded. It's possible to edit this file, but first you must delete some of the original text to make room for any new text.

When you first select Notepads from the Desktop main menu, you must choose one of these selections:

- load an existing file
- make a new document

Remember to press the Alt key before the letter of the pulldown menu you want to use. This tells Desktop that you want to select a menu rather than type the letter into the notepad.

- cancel this operation

- delete a file

Select New to make a new document and open the Notepads window in the middle of the screen. To make the window as large as possible, click on the maximize box at the far right of the window title bar. This expands the Notepads window, as shown in Figure 13.1.

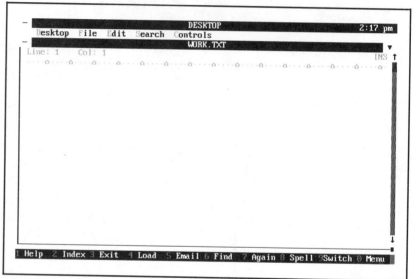

Figure 13.1: The Notepads screen

The Notepads window is similar to the window in other PC Tools programs. The main menu selections are shown along the top line and a scroll bar is located on the right side of the window. The current computer time appears at the upper-right of the window, and several function-key shortcuts appear on the message line. In the upper-left corner of the window, under the menu bar, the line and column counters keep track of where you are in your document, and in the center of the window is the name of the file you are working on (in this case, the temporary file WORK.TXT—the name PC Tools gives a new file). INS indicates that Notepads is in insert rather than typeover mode. A ruler line is also shown.

ENTERING TEXT

There are three ways to enter text into Notepads:

- by typing in new text
- by loading or inserting a file you previously prepared elsewhere
- by cutting and pasting using the Clipboard facilities

This section deals with typing in new text and loading a file. Using the Clipboard to cut and paste is described later in this chapter.

To start entering your text, just start typing. You can use the Backspace or Delete keys to edit any mistakes, and the Enter key to end a paragraph (but *not* a line, as words wrap around automatically). Press the arrow keys to move around the screen, and the PgUp and PgDn keys to move the window up and down. Table 13.1 lists the keystrokes you can use in a notepad. You can do all the major word-processing operations you need with the key sequences from this list.

Table 13.1: Control Keys Available in a Notepad

KEY	FUNCTION
Delete	Deletes character above the cursor
Backspace	Deletes character to left of cursor
Enter	Ends a paragraph
Spacebar	Inserts a space at the cursor
Tab	Inserts a tab at the cursor
Alt-*number*	Inserts a character from the extended ASCII character set. Press and hold down the Alt key, then enter the decimal code for the ASCII character you want
←	Moves cursor left one character
→	Moves cursor right one character
Ctrl-←	Moves cursor left one word

Table 13.1: Control Keys Available in a Notepad (continued)

KEY	FUNCTION
Ctrl-→	Moves cursor right one word
↑	Moves cursor up one line
↓	Moves cursor down one line
Home	Moves to the beginning of the line
End	Moves to the end of the line
PgUp	Moves text up one window
PgDn	Moves text down one window
Ctrl-PgUp	Scrolls display up one line without moving cursor
Ctrl-PgDn	Scrolls display down one line without moving cursor
Home Home	Moves to the beginning of the window
End End	Moves to the end of the window
Ctrl-Home	Moves to the beginning of the file
Ctrl-End	Moves to the end of the file

To load a file as you load Notepads, start Desktop from inside the PCTOOLS directory and select Notepads; you will see the File Load dialog box. For this example, the README.TXT file is used to illustrate the features of Notepads. Either enter the file name READ-ME.TXT directly, or choose it from the list of files and then choose Load to load the file. The contents of the file will be displayed on the screen, as shown in Figure 13.2.

You can also load a file after Notepads is loaded with the Load selection in the File menu. Be careful when you do this, however. If a file is already open and you select Load, it will be closed—but you will lose any changes you made since you last saved the file. This does not affect any files you might have open in other notepads.

The tab ruler is shown across the top of the text in the Note-pads window. Each small triangle indicates a tab. Select Tab Ruler

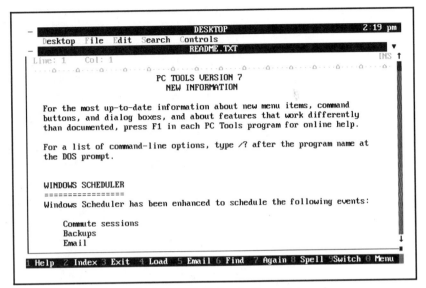

Figure 13.2: The README.TXT file loaded into Notepads

Display from the Controls menu; if there is a check mark by this item, the tab ruler display is on. Toggle it off by selecting it again.

You can add to or replace the original tab settings. Choose Tab Ruler Edit from the Controls menu to edit them. Press ← or → to move the cursor to where you want a new tab, or to an existing tab that you want to erase. Press the Insert key to insert a new tab stop or the Delete key to remove an old tab stop.

To enter a set of evenly spaced tabs very quickly, choose Tab Ruler Edit and type in the number of spaces you want between tab stops. The numbers you type do not appear anywhere on the screen, but the tab marks will align themselves according to the new interval you have chosen. Press Escape when you are finished with adjusting tabs.

Another important item in the Controls menu is the Overtype Mode setting. Usually, you will want to be in Insert mode. In Insert mode, the abbreviation INS appears in the upper-right corner of the Notepads window. As you type in your text, it is inserted at the cursor, while all the existing text is moved to the right. In Overtype mode, your new text overwrites and replaces the old text. Select

Overtype Mode from the Controls menu to set Overtype on; select it again to toggle it off. A check mark beside the menu entry indicates that it is on.

In Notepads, you can look at the control characters (usually spaces, tabs, and carriage-return characters) embedded in your file to see their exact positioning. Turn this feature on with Control Character Display from the Controls menu. When this setting is turned on, spaces are indicated by dots between words, tabs by small arrows, and carriage-return characters by small return symbols (←). A check mark beside the menu entry indicates that this setting is on.

As menioned earlier, you should not press Enter at the end of a line of text, since Notepads automatically moves to the beginning of the next available line when you reach the right margin. This feature is known as *word wrapping*. Toggle it on or off from the Controls menu. Again, a check mark by the menu entry indicates that the setting is on.

You can also control the auto-indent feature from the Controls menu. Turn auto-indent on to line up all your text vertically with the first character of the previous line. This is useful for lists or tables. A check mark by the menu entry indicates that the setting is on.

EDITING TEXT

Moving around inside your document is easy. Press ↑ and ↓ to scroll one line at a time, and PgUp and PgDn to move one window at a time—or use the scroll bar to scroll through your document. You can also go directly to a line of text, search for and replace text, and check your spelling.

The Goto selection helps you find a particular line in your file. This is particularly useful if you work with large files. When you choose Goto from the Edit menu, a dialog box asks you which line number you want to go to. (The line and column numbers are shown in the upper-left corner of the Notepads window.) Enter the line number and select OK to position the cursor at the first character on that line.

At some point, you may want to merge a second file into the body of a file you are working on in a notepad. You can do this with Insert File from the Edit menu. Position the cursor at the correct location in the file using Goto and then choose Insert File. Type the name of the file into the dialog box and select Load. The file is merged with the current file at the cursor location as long as the combined size of the two files is less than 64K. If the combined file size is more than 64K, you will see the File too big for Notepad warning message mentioned earlier in this chapter. If this happens, you will probably want to choose Cancel to abort the merge.

If your editing is not going as planned, you can start over again with the Delete Text selection from the Edit menu. This command empties the notepad but keeps the file on the disk open to it (i.e., the file is open but empty). This is a potentially dangerous operation, so Notepads asks you to confirm that you want to erase the document. From the dialog box, select OK to erase the document or Cancel to return to the notepad and leave its contents intact.

SEARCHING AND REPLACING TEXT As you work with a document in a notepad, you can use the options in the Search menu to search for and replace specific strings of text in your file. Choose the Find selection from the Search menu to display the screen shown in Figure 13.3. You can enter a search string of up to 48 characters (including spaces), and you can narrow down the search in two ways:

- **Case Sensitive** makes the search sensitive to the case of the text. In this mode, Find considers *Mother* and *mother* to be two different words. With this option off, case is ignored.

- **Whole Words Only** finds complete words rather than parts of words. For example, if you search for the word *moth* with this selection on, Notepads will find *moth* but not *mother*.

The search starts at the cursor location and continues until a match is found. When Notepads finds a match, it positions the cursor at the beginning of the string. Use F7 or Find Again from the Search menu

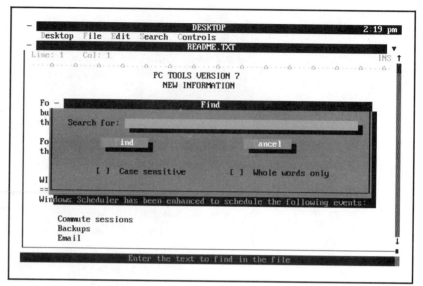

Figure 13.3: The Find selection from the Search menu

to look for more occurrences of the search string. When there are no more matches, Desktop beeps to indicate that it has finished.

If the text file README.TXT is still loaded in your notepad, take a moment to experiment here. Enter the text **PCTOOLS** (in upper-case) as the search string, turn on the Case Sensitive and Whole Words Only options, and start the search. Each time the search string is found, the search stops and the match is displayed. Choose Find Again to search for the next occurrence of the string.

When working with text, you often want to do more than just find all occurrences of a particular string. You probably want to replace one or more occurrences of the text. Choose Replace from the Search menu or press F6 to display the screen shown in Figure 13.4.

The Find and Replace window opens on the Search For box. Enter the string for which you want to search. Then move down to the Replace With box and enter the new text you want to use in its place. The search string can be up to 44 characters, case sensitive or

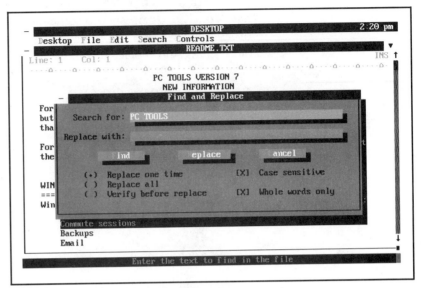

Figure 13.4: The Find and Replace options

not, and you can search for whole or partial words. You also have the following options:

- **Replace One Time** finds and replaces only the next occurrence of the search string.

- **Replace All** automatically finds and replaces all occurrences of the search string from the current cursor location to the end of your file.

- **Verify Before Replace** finds the search string and stops for you to verify that you want to replace this particular occurrence of the search string. Press Enter to replace the found text. The search continues to the next occurrence of the search string.

You can use Find and Replace in many ways. For instance, if you change your section numbers in a document, you can easily find all references to Section V and replace them with Section VI. If you have consistently misspelled someone's name (your spelling checker probably won't find this error), you can search the document for the old spelling and replace it with the new.

CHECKING YOUR SPELLING   You can check the spelling in your document over three different ranges:

- a single word
- all the words displayed in the current Notepads window
- all the words in your file

As Notepads checks your spelling, the message

Spell checking in progress. Please wait

is displayed just above the ruler line. Once the spelling checker finds a word that it doesn't understand, you have the following options:

- **Ignore** overlooks this word now and for all future occurrences in the document. Use this option to ignore file-name extensions, proper names, and other items that the dictionary does not know but are spelled correctly.

- **Correct** displays the Word Correction dialog box, shows the misspelled word, and waits for you to enter the correction. You can also choose one of the replacement words supplied in the Suggestions box to replace the misspelled word.

- **Add** accepts the unknown word and then adds it to the Notepads dictionary for future use. Be careful with your spelling, though, because once you add a word to the dictionary you cannot remove it again.

- **Quit** leaves the word as it is, closes the dialog box, and exits the spelling checker.

Run the spelling checker on the example file README.TXT and notice the kinds of words it flags as misspelled. They are special names (the dictionary does not recognize *Microsoft*, for instance), file-name extensions, program names, and command-line parameters.

FORMATTING PRINTER OUTPUT

Before you print your document, you must make several important decisions about page layout and headers and footers. From the Controls menu, choose Page Layout to see the display shown in Figure 13.5—the default settings for printing a Notepads document. The Page Layout dialog box displays a small diagram of the printer page: as you select different page layout options, they are shown on the diagram.

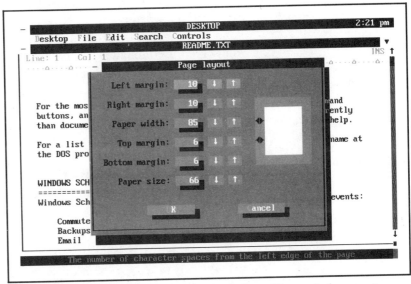

Figure 13.5: Page Layout selections for printing a Notepads document

If you want to change these settings, select the option to change and enter your new value:

- **Left Margin** is the number of spaces in from the left edge of the paper to where text begins.

- **Top Margin** is the number of lines down from the top of the page to where text begins.

If you have a laser printer, set the top and bottom margins to 2 and the page length to 60 for proper printing.

- **Right Margin** is the number of spaces in from the left edge to where text ends.

- **Bottom Margin** is the number of lines up from the bottom of the page to where text stops.

- **Paper Size** is the number of lines per page you are printing on. Normal 8½″-by-11″ paper takes 66 lines and legal-sized paper (8½″-by-14″) takes 84 lines. These lines-per-page numbers assume that your printer is set up for 6 lines per inch.

You can also add headers or footers to your printed document. A header is text that is printed at the top of every page of your document, and a footer is text that is printed at the bottom of every page. In Notepads, the headers and footers are restricted to a single line of up to 50 characters, which are centered when they are printed. Choose Header/Footer from the Controls menu. Figure 13.6 shows the screen used to enter the text for headers and footers.

The # (pound) symbol at the start of the footer text represents automatic page numbering, starting by default at page 1. Page numbering is controlled by information entered in the Page Layout screen. Delete this character if you do not want your pages numbered at the

You can save all your selections from the Controls and Window menus by using Save Setup in the Controls menu. This way, the next time you open Notepads, you will have the settings you want.

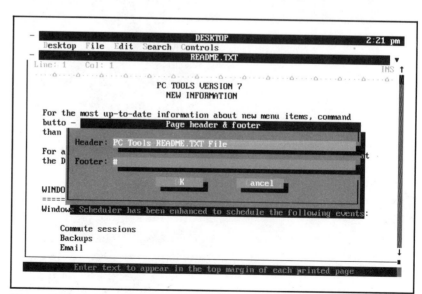

Figure 13.6: The Page Header & Footer screen

bottom. Insert the # symbol at the start of the header line if you want page numbers at the top of each page.

If you plan to have several versions of a document, it will be useful to add the file name and today's time and date as headers or footers. That way, you'll know which version of the document someone is referring to.

Now you are ready to print your Notepad document. Choose Print from the File menu. You can print to one of several devices:

- **LPT 1, 2,** or **3** selects which parallel printer to send your file to. Printer 1 is the default printer.

- **COM 1, 2, 3,** or **4** selects which serial printer port to send your file to.

- **Disk File** formats your file for printing as specified in Page Layout, but writes it to a file so that you can print it later. The file has the same name as the original Notepads file, but has the .PRT extension.

- **Number of Copies** determines the number of copies of your document to print.

- **Line Spacing** selects single, double, or triple spacing for your document.

- **Starting Page #** selects the first page for printing.

Make your selections from these menus and start printing READ-ME.TXT. The file is divided into neat pages, and is formatted according to your selections. The whole file takes up several pages.

You can use advanced formatting commands in your Notepads documents by inserting printer-control macros into your text. PC Tools contains macro files suitable for the Epson FX-80, the IBM Proprinter, the HP LaserJet, and Panasonic printers. See the section "Making Keyboard Macros" later in this chapter for more details on how to use these macros.

SAVING YOUR WORK

When you click on the close box or press Escape to leave a notepad, your work is always saved automatically. Additionally, you can save a file any time by selecting Save in the File menu. There are several Save options. You can save the file as a PC Tools-format file or as an ASCII file:

- **PC Tools Format** is the default setting. It saves your text as well as all the page-layout commands, headers and footers, tab-stop settings, screen colors, and window sizes in the file along with your text.

- **ASCII Format** saves your work as an ASCII file without any formatting information of any kind (just the text with a carriage-return character at the end of each line). Use the ASCII format if you want to load this file into another word processor, since the ASCII format gives you the most flexibility. (Also, remember to use this format if you are modifying your AUTOEXEC.BAT or CONFIG.SYS files.)

You can also make a backup copy of your file when you save it, if you check the Make Backup File box. The backup file has the same file name as your work file, but the extension .BAK. This means that you must make your file names unique, without using an extension. For example, don't call separate proposal files SECTION.1, SECTION.2, and so on, because at the end of the day, you will only have one backup file called SECTION.BAK—a backup file for the last section you worked on; all the other backup files will have been overwritten. Instead, name your files SECTION1.TXT, SECTION2.TXT, and so forth. The backup files will then be called SECTION1.BAK, SECTION2.BAK, and so forth.

Select the Autosave option from the File menu to save your file automatically at specified time intervals. This can be a life-saver if your area is prone to brownouts or power outages. When you select Autosave, a dialog box allows you to set the time interval in minutes. Autosave is a global feature of Desktop; it is used in Notepads, Outlines, the Appointment Scheduler, and the Macro Editor. When you turn Autosave on in any of these applications, you turn it on for all of them. Likewise, if you turn it off, you turn it off for all applications.

Finally, you can leave a notepad without saving your work by selecting Exit Without Saving from the File menu.

STRUCTURING YOUR IDEAS WITH OUTLINES

Outlines is a tool to help organize your thoughts into a structured list. Each line in an outline represents one point or idea, and its position relative to the other items in the list determines its position in the outline's hierarchy. Use Outlines whenever you want to make a structured list of items: a meeting agenda, a book proposal, the outline for a class you are going to teach, the outline of a magazine article you plan to write, etc. You can use it to prepare an outline that you later flesh out in a notepad. An Outlines file can hold up to 60K, which is equivalent to approximately 650 lines of text.

The advantage of using an outliner rather than a word processor is that each level of indentation in the outline represents a different level in the document's hierarchy. Main headings are flush left, secondary headings are indented one tab, tertiary headings two tabs, quaternary headings three tabs, and so on. You can promote or demote headings to different levels as your outline evolves, or you can collapse a portion of the outline to show just the major headings, so you can work on another part of the outline without distractions. If you run Desktop in memory-resident mode, you can open up to 15 different outlines at a time without leaving your main foreground application.

CREATING AN OUTLINE

The main screen in the outliner is similar to the Notepads main screen. Indeed, the File, Edit, Search, and Controls menus are identical and so are not discussed in detail here. (To learn more about these menus, refer back to the Notepads section.) Just remember that editing text, searching and replacing specific text strings, cutting, and copying and pasting to and from the Clipboard are all possible in Outlines.

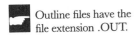 Outline files have the file extension .OUT.

To make a new outline, select Outlines from the Desktop main menu and create a new file called TEST.OUT. To have your screen look like the examples in this chapter, maximize the outline window so that it occupies the whole screen. This is convenient when you are dealing with large outlines.

To start working on your outline, just start typing. The first line you type becomes the first entry in the outline. Press the Tab key to indent lower levels in the list. For example, if you were preparing a meeting agenda, you might enter the main headings first and add the lower-level detail later. The first level headings for a meeting agenda are shown in Figure 13.7.

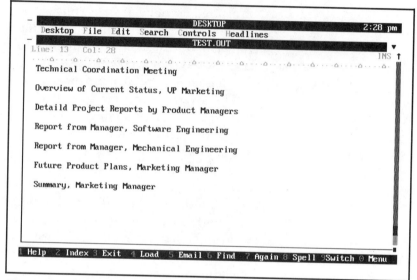

Figure 13.7: First-level headings in an outline

Just type in the text for an item and press Enter at the end of the item. The cursor stays the same number of tab spaces from the margin, so you can enter the next heading at the same level. Once you have established a level, you can edit the text of the entry in the normal way.

Under each of these main headings, you can add detail as you wish. To add an item at a lower level, press Tab to indent the right amount. To return to the previous level, press the Backspace key. To insert a new entry, position the cursor at the end of the previous line and press Enter. The cursor moves to the beginning of the next line at the same level as the entry above it. After you add second- and third-level headings, the meeting agenda might now look like Figure 13.8.

Since tabs are used to indicate hierarchy in the structure of the outline, you cannot use them in the body of the text.

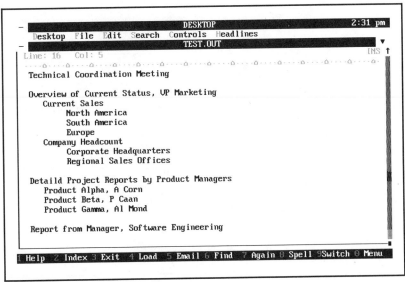

Figure 13.8: Meeting agenda with second- and third-level headings

You can add detail to the outline until you have the whole meeting sketched out with presentation topics, the names of the presenters, time limits for each presentation, and so on.

EXPANDING AND COLLAPSING THE OUTLINE

The menus in Outlines are similar to those in Notepads. However, there is one new menu item, Headlines, which contains options that allow you to manipulate your outline entries, as shown in Figure 13.9.

As you work on your outline, you may want to hide all but the highest level of entries so that you can get a better picture of the whole. Select Collapse Current or Main Headline Only from the Headings menu to accomplish this:

- **Collapse Current** collapses the lines below the current line and displays a small symbol in the left margin next to the main heading to show that there is hidden text below this item.

- **Main Headline Only** hides everything except for the first level headings.

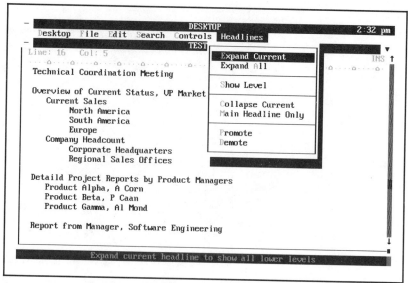

Figure 13.9: The Headlines menu

Only *visible* entries can be copied or cut to the Clipboard. If any entries in your outline are hidden, they will not be moved. So use Expand Current or Expand All to bring back those levels that you want to transfer to the Clipboard.

When you want to see more detail of an outline, you can select Expand Current or Expand All:

- **Expand Current** expands all the subentries below the current line, assuming that there are entries to expand.

- **Expand All** expands the *whole* outline to show all the previously hidden text.

Since you will inevitably change your mind as you develop your outline, you need to be able to change the level of an entry. This is the feature that really separates an outliner from an ordinary word processor. You can quickly change a heading level with Promote and Demote:

- **Promote** moves a heading up to the next highest level. All the subheadings in the group below this level are also moved.

- **Demote** is the reverse of Promote, moving headings to a lower level.

When your outline is complete, you can print it. Often you will want to print a simplified version first, to circulate to your colleagues for comment, for example, or to give your supervisor the gist of your proposal. To do this, select Show Level from the Headlines menu. Show Level hides all entries below a certain level. For example, if you position the cursor on a first-level heading, all first- and second-level headings will remain visible, but any third- and lower-level headings will be hidden. (Entries are not deleted from an outline, they are just hidden.) To bring back the detail in the current group, select Expand Current. To bring back all headings in the entire document, select Expand All.

PRINTING YOUR OUTLINE

Now you are ready to print your outline. As in Notepads, the Controls menu contains the entries Page Layout and Header/Footer. Use Page Layout to establish the margin settings and page length you need. Use Header/Footer to enter header or footer text. Enter the date, time, and file name as headers or footers to help keep track of the evolution of your document.

Select Print from the File menu to print the outline. Your options here are the same as in Notepads: You can print to one of the serial or parallel printers, or to a disk file for printing later if you prefer. You can also specify the number of copies to print, the line spacing, and the starting page number.

CUTTING AND PASTING WITH THE CLIPBOARD

The Clipboard only handles text, it cannot handle graphics such as clip art or scanned images.

You can leave pieces of text up to 4K (between 80 and 90 lines of text) on the Clipboard, a kind of temporary storage area, until you are ready to use them. You can also use the Clipboard as a channel between applications: cutting and pasting among Outlines, Notepads, the Macro Editor, and your main foreground application if you have Desktop configured as a memory-resident program.

Once you have text on the Clipboard, you can use the Clipboard's editing capabilities to make changes before pasting the text into another application.

If you reboot your computer, the contents of your Clipboard will be lost.

OPENING THE CLIPBOARD

Select Clipboard from the main Desktop menu, and maximize it to make the window as large as possible. The opening Clipboard screen is shown in Figure 13.10. The first portion of the meeting agenda prepared with the outliner is shown on the Clipboard.

CUTTING TO THE CLIPBOARD

To take full advantage of features of the Clipboard, you must run Desktop in memory-resident mode. That way, you can cut and paste text to the Clipboard using the normal full-screen display, or cut and paste without opening the Clipboard by using a special hotkey sequence.

To cut and paste using the menus, install Desktop without the /CS parameter. See Chapter 20 for more information.

To cut and paste using the normal Desktop display and the Clipboard menus (i.e., in non–memory-resident mode), position the cursor in approximately the right place in your application and follow this sequence:

1. Hotkey into Desktop by pressing Ctrl-spacebar.

2. Select Clipboard from the main Desktop menu.

3. Choose the Copy to Clipboard selection from the Cut/Paste menu. The Clipboard screen disappears and the previous screen, your original application, reappears.

4. Move the cursor to the beginning of the text you want to copy to the Clipboard and press Enter.

5. Highlight the block of text and press Enter to copy the text to the Clipboard. The Clipboard display reappears, showing the copied text. Since the Clipboard is open, you can edit the text if you want.

If you are using a mouse, just follow these even easier steps:

1. Hotkey into Desktop by pressing Ctrl-spacebar.

2. Select Clipboard from the main Desktop menu.

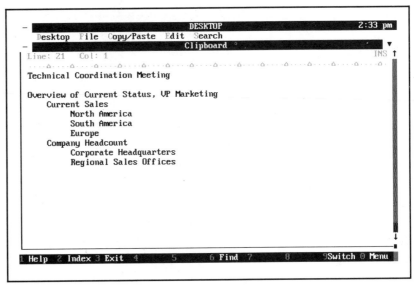

Figure 13.10: The Clipboard opening screen

3. Choose the Copy to Clipboard selection from the Cut/Paste menu. The Clipboard screen disappears and the previous screen, your original application, reappears.

4. Move the mouse to the beginning of the text you want to copy to the Clipboard. Press the left mouse button and hold it down.

5. Drag the mouse until the text you want to copy is highlighted, then release the mouse button. The highlighted text is copied to the Clipboard, and you can edit it if you want.

If you have Desktop loaded in memory-resident mode, you can use a different hotkey sequence to copy text to the Clipboard without actually opening Desktop or the Clipboard. This is the fastest way to copy text from your main foreground application onto the Clipboard:

⊙ If there is already text on the Clipboard and you cut or copy more text, the original text is destroyed.

1. Press Ctrl-Delete from inside your main application to start the process. A large cursor appears on the screen.

2. Position the cursor at the beginning of the text you want to copy and press Enter.

3. Mark the block of text you want to copy to the Clipboard and press Enter to copy the text to the Clipboard.

If you want to view or edit the text, hotkey into Desktop and select the Clipboard in the usual way from the main Desktop menu.

If you are using a mouse:

1. Press Ctrl-Delete from inside your main application to start the process. A large cursor appears on the screen.

2. Move the cursor to the beginning of the text you want to copy to the Clipboard. Press and hold down the (left) mouse button.

3. Drag the mouse until the text you want to copy is highlighted; then release the mouse button. The highlighted text is copied to the Clipboard.

Hotkey into Desktop and open the Clipboard in the usual way if you want to edit the text.

PASTING FROM THE CLIPBOARD

Moving text from the Clipboard to your foreground application is known as *pasting*. Position the cursor where you want the pasted text to appear and follow these steps:

1. Hotkey into Desktop by pressing Ctrl-spacebar.

2. Select Clipboard from the main Desktop menu.

3. Choose the Paste from Clipboard selection from the Cut/Paste menu.

4. Your original foreground application reappears and the Clipboard text is inserted at the cursor position.

There is a special hotkey that you can use to paste the Clipboard text directly into your foreground application without opening the Clipboard. Position the cursor in your foreground application where

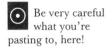
Be very careful what you're pasting to, here!

you want the pasted text to appear and press Ctrl-Insert. The Clipboard text will be pasted into your application at the cursor location.

If you do not have a foreground application running when you paste the Clipboard text, the text will be copied to the DOS command line, which can have unpredictable and sometimes undesirable results. For example, suppose you make a directory listing of your root directory with the DOS DIR command, and copy it to the Clipboard. When you paste that text back to the DOS command line, it is as though you were typing in all those lines by hand. If your root directory contains a file called AUTOEXEC.BAT, which of course it should, pasting the text AUTOEXEC.BAT to the DOS command line actually causes DOS to execute all the commands in the batch file. In other words, proceed with caution when pasting text directly with the Ctrl-Insert key.

SETTING THE PLAYBACK DELAY

If you paste text from the Clipboard into another application program and your computer beeps, or not all of the characters are transferred, it may be because the characters are being sent too fast for it to handle. The Set Playback Delay command in the Copy/Paste menu allows you to insert a short delay between each character to slow down the transfer slightly. By default, characters are sent every $1/18$ of a second; the number you enter specifies the additional $1/18$ second between characters ($2 = 2/18$ second, $3 = 3/18$ second, etc.):

- **Delay** (clock ticks) is the number of $1/18$-second time periods you want to insert between each character.

- **On** turns on the playback delay.

- **Off** turns off the playback delay.

EDITING TEXT IN THE CLIPBOARD

Once you have copied text to the Clipboard, you can use the editing commands to change the text. These editing commands are the same as those in Outlines and Notepads, so I will only discuss them briefly here. Refer to the discussion on Notepads for more detail.

Besides the normal text-editing keystrokes such as Delete, Insert, and Backspace, the Edit menu provides several important options:

- **Erase Block** deletes a marked block of text from the Clipboard.

- **Mark Block** marks a block of text for deletion.

- **Unmark Block** removes the block marks.

- **Delete All Text** erases all the text from the Clipboard in preparation to receive new text, leaving your original work file open.

- **Insert File** inserts the contents of a text file at the cursor location. If inserting the entire file would cause the Clipboard to overflow, a message will indicate that the file will be truncated. Choose Cancel to stop the insertion, or OK to proceed. Only the portion of the file that fits will be loaded into the Clipboard.

- **Goto** allows you to go directly to a line in the Clipboard that you specify by line number.

You can also find or find-and-replace a specific text string with selections from the Search menu.

Finally, if you want to print the text on the Clipboard, choose the Print option from the File menu. You have the same options that you had in Notepads and Outlines: printing to one of the serial or parallel printers, or to a disk file for later printing if you prefer. You can also specify the number of copies to print.

MAKING KEYBOARD MACROS

A *macro* is a series of commands that is activated by a single keystroke. In other words, you can program the keys on your keyboard to perform specific functions. Use a macro as shorthand for long sets of keystrokes that you use frequently, or to simplify complex and repetitive jobs.

DOS itself provides keys on the keyboard with certain editing capabilities. In fact, you can use the PROMPT command to produce the same effect as that with the Macro Editor. However, you

If you run the Desktop in memory-resident mode and you have other applications in your path, select your macros carefully. Any applications using the same key combinations will be interfered with.

can only use the DOS commands at the DOS prompt. In contrast, if you run Desktop in memory-resident mode, the Macro Editor makes your macros available everywhere, even inside other applications. You should avoid key conflicts between macros and foreground applications, however. Otherwise, you may get unexpected results when you invoke your macro. This section first describes the DOS editing keys and then shows you how to redefine your keyboard with PROMPT. Finally, it explains why the Desktop Macro Editor is more powerful and flexible than these other methods.

When you execute a command at the DOS prompt, it is copied into a special buffer. You can edit this buffer and reissue it if you want to. This is handy, for example, if you have to deal with many files with similar names. For example, pressing F1 retypes the last command you entered, one character at a time. Pressing F3 types, all at once, the rest of the line you typed. Using these two keys in combination with the Insert and Delete keys, you can edit simple commands quite effectively. Several of the function keys have a special function, as listed in Table 13.2. F1 and F3 are by far the most useful of these special editing keys.

Table 13.2: Function Keys with Special Functions in DOS

KEY NAME	FUNCTION
F1	Retypes one character at a time from the previous command
F2	Retypes all the characters from the previous command up to the one identical to your next keystroke
F3	Retypes all the remaining characters from the last command
F4	Retypes all the characters in the last command starting with the first character you typed
F5	Allows direct editing of all the characters in the last command
F6	Puts a special end-of-file code at the end of the currently open file, sometimes referred to as Ctrl-Z

If you include the ANSI.SYS driver in your CONFIG.SYS file, you can use the PROMPT command to program virtually any of the keys on your keyboard to type DOS commands. Assigning new meanings to keys requires a special command called an *escape sequence*. In this case, the sequence starts with $e[and continues with the ASCII value of the key you wish to use (if the key is a regular letter or number key), followed by a *p*. The *p* terminates the key-assignment sequence. If you want to assign a command to one of the function keys, you must use a zero followed by a special code to indicate the key. These special function-key redefinition codes are listed in Table 13.3.

Suppose you want to assign the DOS FORMAT command to a function key, since you use the command frequently. To make the F5 function key automatically type the command **FORMAT A:**, you should add the line

> A semicolon separates each statement in the PROMPT command.

        PROMPT $e[0;63;"FORMAT A:";13p

to your AUTOEXEC.BAT file, or modify your current PROMPT command to include this new statement.

The **$e[** alerts DOS that an ANSI escape sequence is starting, and 0 indicates that the key to be redefined is on the extended keyboard. Code 63 stands for F5 and "**FORMAT A:**" is the command to be assigned to the F5 key. Code 13 represents a carriage-return character, and *p* is the terminating character for the whole sequence. Remember that after changing your AUTOEXEC.BAT file you must reboot your computer to load the new commands.

Now when you want to format a disk, just press F5 to invoke the FORMAT command and then press Enter.

CREATING DESKTOP MACRO FILES

The macros you can assign using DOS and the PROMPT command are limited, since they are only available from the DOS prompt. If you run Desktop in memory-resident mode, however, you can use your Desktop macros from inside Desktop *and* inside your foreground application. (If you do not run Desktop in memory-resident mode, your Desktop macros are only available inside Desktop.)

Table 13.3: Function-Key Redefinition Codes

FUNCTION KEY	REDEFINITION CODE	FUNCTION KEY	REDEFINITION CODE
F1	59	Shift-F1	84
F2	60	Shift-F2	85
F3	61	Shift-F3	86
F4	62	Shift-F4	87
F5	63	Shift-F5	88
F6	64	Shift-F6	89
F7	65	Shift-F7	90
F8	66	Shift-F8	91
F9	67	Shift-F9	92
F10	68	Shift-F10	93
Ctrl-F1	94	Alt-F1	104
Ctrl-F2	95	Alt-F2	105
Ctrl-F3	96	Alt-F3	106
Ctrl-F4	97	Alt-F4	107
Ctrl-F5	98	Alt-F5	108
Ctrl-F6	99	Alt-F6	109
Ctrl-F7	100	Alt-F7	110
Ctrl-F8	101	Alt-F8	111
Ctrl-F9	102	Alt-F9	112
Ctrl-F10	103	Alt-F10	113

You can use macros to start up PC Tools programs, such as CP Backup or Compress, that use command-line switches.

Among other things, you can design Desktop macros to print text files with custom features, load often-used applications programs, or override other keyboard functions.

Desktop macros are usually compatible with macros made with ProKey version 4 or higher (a common macro-making program), with only a few exceptions:

- Some key combinations are not supported by the Desktop Macro Editor (see Table 13.4).

- The Desktop Macro Editor does not include support for guarding macros or unique macro names.

- Since the Desktop Macro Editor recognizes the standard IBM BIOS keyboard scan codes, it does not support redefinition of the entire keyboard.

Table 13.4 lists the key combinations *not* supported by the Desktop Macro Editor.

Macros, which are like small programs, have a particular structure that you must observe. Creating a macro involves

- writing the macro
- activating the macro
- testing the macro

Before starting to write a macro, decide what you want it to do. Then be careful to follow the rules for macro creation, which I will explain in a moment.

Once you have written your macro, you have to activate it and specify where it should be active. You can make your macro active only inside Desktop, only outside Desktop, or everywhere. You can also turn your macro off if you don't want to use it anymore. All active macros are saved in a special area of memory and are ready to go to work when you press the correct keystrokes.

Once you have written and activated your macro, take the time to test it to make sure it does what you think it should. How you test it really depends on what the macro does. Some can be tested from the DOS prompt; others require you to be inside another application program. If the macro misbehaves, press Escape to stop it from running any further.

Finally, remember to give your macro a descriptive name to help you to remember what it is for. You can also write comments inside your macros as additional reminders.

Table 13.4: Key Combinations Not Supported by the Desktop Macro Editor

CTRL	ALT	SHIFT
Ctrl-c		
Ctrl-q		
Ctrl-s		
Ctrl-1		
Ctrl-2		
Ctrl-3		
Ctrl-4		
Ctrl-5		
Ctrl-6		
Ctrl-7		
Ctrl-8		
Ctrl-9		
Ctrl-0		
Ctrl- –	Alt- –	
Ctrl- =	Alt- =	
Ctrl-[	Alt-[	
Ctrl-]	Alt-]	
Ctrl-;	Alt-;	
Ctrl-'	Alt-'	
Ctrl-\	Alt-\	
Ctrl-,	Alt-,	
Ctrl- .	Alt- .	
Ctrl-/	Alt-/	
Ctrl-Escape	Alt-Escape	Shift-Escape
Ctrl-Tab	Alt-Tab	
	Alt-Backspace	Shift-Backspace

Table 13.4: Key Combinations Not Supported by the Desktop Macro Editor (continued)

CTRL	ALT	SHIFT
	Alt-Enter	Shift-Enter
	Alt-Print	Shift-Print
	Alt-Home	Shift-Home
	Alt-PgUp	Shift-PgUp
	Alt-End	Shift-End
	Alt-PgDn	Shift-PgDn
Ctrl-↑	Alt-↑	Shift-↑
	Alt-←	Shift-←
	Alt-→	Shift-→
Ctrl-↓	Alt-↓	Shift-↓
Ctrl-Insert	Alt-Insert	Shift-Insert
Ctrl-Delete	Alt-Delete	Shift-Delete
Ctrl-keypad 0	Alt-keypad 0	Shift-keypad 0
Ctrl-keypad 1	Alt-keypad 1	Shift-keypad 1
Ctrl-keypad 2	Alt-keypad 2	Shift-keypad 2
Ctrl-keypad 3	Alt-keypad 3	Shift-keypad 3
Ctrl-keypad 4	Alt-keypad 4	Shift-keypad 4
Ctrl-keypad 5	Alt-keypad 5	Shift-keypad 5
Ctrl-keypad 6	Alt-keypad 6	Shift-keypad 6
Ctrl-keypad 7	Alt-keypad 7	Shift-keypad 7
Ctrl-keypad 8	Alt-keypad 8	Shift-keypad 8
Ctrl-keypad 9	Alt-keypad 9	Shift-keypad 9
Ctrl-keypad .	Alt-keypad .	Shift-keypad .
Ctrl-keypad +	Alt-keypad +	Shift-keypad +
Ctrl-keypad −	Alt-keypad −	Shift-keypad −

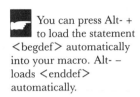
You can press Alt- + to load the statement <begdef> automatically into your macro. Alt- − loads <enddef> automatically.

The Macro Editor ignores anything that is not between the <begdef> and <enddef>.

In PC Tools, the general form of a macro is as follows:

<begdef> *keystrokes script* <enddef>

where <begdef> stands for "begin definition" and <enddef> stands for "end definition" (the angle brackets are necessary). The body (or script) of your macro, the part that actually does the work, must be contained between these two statements. These commands are not enclosed in angle brackets unless they are special command words.

As mentioned above, you can add comments to a macro. In fact, it is an excellent idea always to add explanatory comments to your macros to help you and others remember what the macro is for and how it works. Place your comments before the <begdef> statement.

As an example, look at the following macro:

```
<begdef>
     <ctrlf> FORMAT A: <enter>
<enddef>
```

The <begdef> statement starts the macro and <ctrlf> indicates that you must press Ctrl-f to invoke the macro. *FORMAT A:* is the command you want to execute and <enter> is equivalent to pressing the Enter key. The <enddef> statement ends the macro. Now when you want to format a floppy disk in drive A, you just press Ctrl-f.

Macros can be a lot more complex than this simple example, of course. You can use a macro to call your favorite Desktop application. You can also add time delays to your macros, accept fixed-length or variable-length input to a macro, and even add the date and time to a macro. Table 13.5 shows reserved words that have special meanings in the Macro Editor. Some of them have shortcut keystrokes, which are also shown in the table.

To create a new macro from scratch to automate a complex task, you should jot down all the keystrokes you use when you perform the job manually. That way when you use the Macro Editor, you can construct the macro using your notes. Alternatively, you can use the Learn Mode selection from the Macro Editor, which automatically records all your keystrokes.

Table 13.5: Reserved Words with Special Meanings for the Macro Editor

RESERVED WORD	SHORTCUT	MEANING
begdef	Alt- +	Statement that always begins a macro definition
cmd		Indicates that the following entries must be treated as commands instead of key entries
d*n*		Time delay, where *d* indicates that the number that follows (represented by *n*) is to be treated as the time delay.
date		Includes the date in a macro
desk		Shorthand name for Desktop, for use in macros only
enddef	Alt- –	Statement that always ends a macro definition
enter		Terminates a delay sequence, or is used to generate carriage return/line feed
esc		Escape sequence for printer macros
ffld	Ctrl-]	Indicates a fixed field label
time		Includes the time in a macro
vfld	Ctrl- –	Indicates a variable field label

EDITING MACRO FILES

Select the Macro Editor from the Desktop menu and then select
SAMPLE.PRO from the Macro Files screen to see the opening
screen, as shown in Figure 13.11.

The Macro Editor works much like the other text-handling programs in Desktop—Notepads, Outlines, and the Clipboard. However, the Macro Editor has several unique commands, which are
covered here. The other commands are discussed only briefly; see the
section on Notepads for more details.

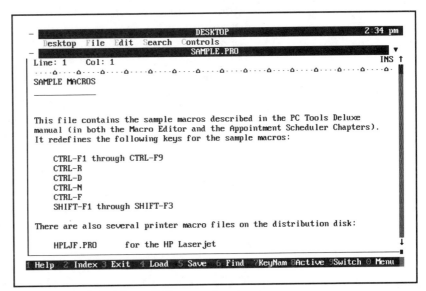

Figure 13.11: The Macro Editor opening screen

In the Macro Editor, besides the normal text-editing commands,
the Edit menu contains the following specialized selections:

- **Cut to Clipboard** moves a portion of text from the Macro
  Editor to the Clipboard.

- **Copy to Clipboard** copies a portion of text to the Clipboard.

- **Paste from Clipboard** moves a portion of text from the Clipboard to the Macro Editor.

- **Mark Block** marks a block of text for deletion.

- **Unmark Block** removes the block marks.

- **Delete All Text** erases all the text from the Macro Editor in preparation to receive new text.

- **Insert File** inserts the contents of a text file at the cursor. If inserting the file would cause the Macro Editor to overflow, a message will indicate that the file will be truncated.

- **Goto** allows you to go directly to a line in the Macro Editor that you specify by line number.

You can also find or find-and-replace a specific text string with selections from the Search menu in the Macro Editor.

The File menu contains the following selections:

- **Load** loads another file into the Macro Editor, replacing the current contents.

- **Save** saves the contents of the Macro Editor to a file. The file can be in ASCII or in PC Tools format, and you can opt to make a backup file at the same time.

- **Autosave** automatically saves your work periodically at an interval that you set.

The last option in the File menu, Macro Activation, requires more explanation. With this selection you can choose which macros are active and where in your system they are active. Choose Macro Activation to display the screen shown in Figure 13.12.

In Macro Activation, you have the following options:

- **Not active.** None of the macros in the current file are active.

- **Active when in PCTOOLS Desktop.** The macros in the current file are active only when you are in Desktop. This is particularly useful for printer macros, which cannot be used outside Desktop.

- **Active when not in PCTOOLS Desktop.** The macros in the current file can be used anywhere in DOS or in your other applications programs, but not inside Desktop.

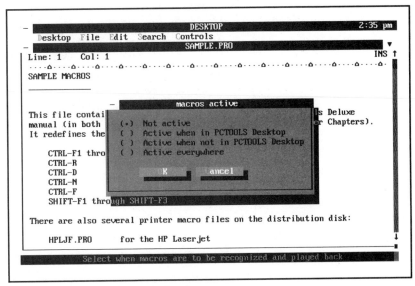

Figure 13.12: The Macro Activation screen

> • **Active everywhere.** The macros in the current file can be used anywhere on your system, including inside Desktop.

All your active macro files are kept in a special buffer, ready for you to invoke with the appropriate key sequence. When you edit a macro file, the system updates existing active macros, so you do not have to reactivate them.

The Controls menu, shown in Figure 13.13, contains four special commands for use with macros:

> • **Erase All Macros** erases your macros from the special buffer where they are kept once you have activated them. This command does not erase macro files from your disk, nor does it affect the contents of the Macro Editor.
>
> • **Playback Delay** introduces short wait periods between each character in the macro. If you use multiple keystrokes in your macros, the system may feed them into your application faster than it can process them. You specify this playback delay period in terms of the PC system clock, which

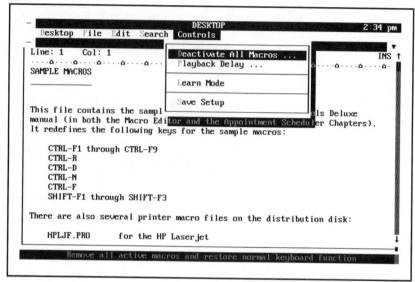

Figure 13.13: The Controls menu in the Macro Editor

ticks at a rate of 18 ticks per second. Enter the number of $1/18$-second time periods you want to wait between keystrokes. A value of zero sends a character every $1/18$ second. The default setting for Playback Delay is off, so you must turn it on if you want to use it.

- **Learn Mode** records all your keystrokes in a special buffer. This is an easy way to create strong, accurate macros. When you restart the Macro Editor, your macro is saved into a special file called LEARN.PRO. Remember that Learn Mode stays on until you turn if off again.

- **Save Setup** saves the current Macro Editor Controls settings.

You must run Desktop in memory-resident mode for the Learn Mode command to work.

To use Learn Mode, turn it on inside the Macro Editor and hotkey out of Desktop. When you are ready to record your keystrokes, press Alt- +. This starts the macro and indicates that all subsequent keystrokes will be copied into the Macro Editor. A large square cursor appears. Next, press the keystroke combination you want to use to invoke this macro, and then create the script for the macro by typing the keys in your application as you would normally. When you have finished, close the macro by pressing Alt- – . Your keystrokes are entered in one long line (with no formatting) in a file called LEARN.PRO, which is created the next time you hotkey into the Macro Editor. You can use the Macro Editor to view or modify the keystrokes in this file.

This is a fast and easy way to make a macro. Be especially careful, however, if you make a mistake when you are typing the keys that form the macro script. If you mistype a key and press Backspace to remove the offending letter, the Backspace keystroke is also copied into the macro script. For instance, if you mistyped CPBACKUP as CPBBACKUP, your macro might look like this:

```
<begdef><ctrla>CD\PCTOOLS<enter>CPBB<bks>
ACKUP/BW<enddef>
```

Use the editing features of the Macro Editor to remove the extra *B* as well as the unwanted <bks>. This is a good reason for reading your macros carefully before turning them on for activation.

USING YOUR MACROS

You can use a macro to start Desktop by using the reserved word <desk>. You must run Desktop in memory-resident mode for this to work. The following macro opens Desktop at the main startup menu when you press Shift-Tab:

```
<begdef>
    <shifttab><desk>
<enddef>
```

But you can be more specific than this: if you use one of the Desktop calculators very often, you can open it directly with the following macro:

```
<begdef>
    <shifttab><desk>CS
<enddef>
```

This macro opens the Scientific calculator immediately. In fact, you can use any of the letters that Desktop uses for menu selections inside your macros. The example above opens Desktop with the reserved word <desk> and then uses *C* to access Calculators from the main Desktop menu and *S* to select the Scientific calculator. You can set up a macro to open a notepad and load a specific text file or to start Database up in a certain way.

Table 13.6 lists some of the codes you can use to open your Desktop applications via macros.

Table 13.6: Two-Letter Codes for Opening Specific Desktop Functions

CODE	FUNCTION
<desk>	Opens Desktop
<desk>N	Opens Notepads
<desk>O	Opens Outlines
<desk>D	Opens the Database
<desk>A	Opens the Appointment Scheduler
<desk>T	Opens Telecommunications
<desk>M	Opens the Macro Editor
<desk>b	Opens the Clipboard
<desk>CA	Opens the Algebraic calculator
<desk>CF	Opens the Financial calculator
<desk>CP	Opens the Programmer's calculator
<desk>CS	Opens the Scientific calculator
<desk>U	Opens the Utilities
<desk>P	Opens PC Shell

You can invoke other applications programs from macros. The following macro changes to the Lotus directory called \123 and loads Lotus 1-2-3 when you press Shift-Tab:

```
<begdef>
    <shifttab>CD\123<enter>123<enter>
<enddef>
```

The next macro changes to the \PCTOOLS directory and loads CPBACKUP:

```
<begdef>
    <shifttab>CD\PCTOOLS<enter>CPBACKUP<enter>
<enddef>
```

By introducing a delay into your macro, you can make an event happen at a specific time. For example, you can dial a remote database when rates are lowest. The delay can be from $1/10$ of a second to 256 hours. Delays have the following form in a macro:

```
<begdef>
    <cmd> dn <enter>
<enddef>
```

where <cmd> indicates that what follows should be interpreted by the Macro Editor as commands rather than keystrokes. The *d* indicates that a delay follows and *n* defines the length of the delay in the format *hours:minutes:seconds.tenths*. For example, 15:0:0 is a 15-hour delay, 15:0 is a 15-minute delay, and 15 is a 15-second delay.

If you want to use the date and time in a macro, the Macro Editor provides two more reserved words that you can use for this purpose:

The spacing between the reserved words <date> and <time> in the macro determines the final spacing of the date display on the screen.

```
<begdef>
    <ctrld><date>, <time>
<enddef>
```

Now if you press Ctrl-d, you will see the date and time displayed as follows:

04-10-91, 5:00

You can also make macros that wait for you to enter information from the keyboard, entries that can be fixed or variable in length. For example, you can write a macro that makes a directory listing of a disk after asking you for the drive letter. The drive letter always has a fixed length of one character—*A, B,* or *C*—so you can use what the Macro Editor calls a *fixed field label,* <ffld>. Pressing Ctrl-] in the Macro

Editor generates <ffld>. The final macro looks like this:

```
<begdef>
    <ctrld>DIR <ffld>#<ffld>:<enter>
<enddef>
```

DIR is the DOS directory-listing command and it is followed by a space that separates the command from the drive letter you enter when the macro is running. The first <ffld> indicates the start of the fixed-length label; you can press Ctrl-] from the Macro Editor to display it. The # character indicates the length of the label. You can use any character you like; you don't have to use #. Just remember that # means that you enter one character, ## means that you enter two characters, and so on. The second <ffld> terminates the fixed-length label.

To run this macro, escape from Desktop back to the DOS prompt and press Ctrl-d. The macro generates DIR, leaves a space, and waits for you to enter the drive letter. After you enter a drive letter, the macro adds the colon and DOS generates a listing for the appropriate drive.

If the input to your macro is not always the same length or the same number of characters, you must use a variable field label <vfld> instead of a fixed field label <ffld>. In this case, the Macro Editor always requires two placeholder characters between the <vfld> statements in the macro (for example, <vfld>##<vfld>) to hold the variable-length input. Using this technique, you can enter file names and other variable-length input into your macros.

You can only use printer macros inside Notepads, Outlines, and Database forms. You cannot use them outside Desktop.

The final type of macro described in this section is the *printer macro*. These are commands that you insert into the body of your text. When you print the file, they create special formatting effects such as italics or superscripts. These commands never appear in the printed text; instead, they are sent to the printer to make it do something specific. Since printers from different manufacturers observe different conventions, you need a special file for each different type of printer. PC Tools is shipped with files tailored to common printers like the Epson FX-80, the HP LaserJet, the IBM Proprinter, and Panasonic printers.

An example printer macro that turns on near–letter-quality mode looks like this:

```
<begdef>
    <ctrlf1>¦NLQON¦<esc>x1
<enddef>
```

The <begdef> statement starts the macro, which you invoke by typing Ctrl-F1. The ¦NLQON¦ statement appears in the body of your document to show where in the text the macro takes effect. The <esc>x1 statement turns on near–letter-quality mode for Epson printers, and is the sequence that is actually sent to your printer by the macro. The <enddef> ends the macro. To turn the mode off again, write another macro such as:

```
<begdef>
    <ctrlf2>¦NLQOFF¦<esc>x0
<enddef>
```

This time, the label ¦NLQOFF¦ appears in your text file where you turn the mode off.

You can use macros like these to turn boldface on or off, turn subscript or superscript on or off, or change anything that is controllable by a character sequence. See the appendices of your printer manual for specific details on which features you can control on your printer.

Use Macro Activation from the File menu in the Macro Editor and turn your printer macro on by choosing the Active option in PC Tools.

CHAPTER

14

Figuring with the
Four Calculators

How often do you use your pocket calculator for figures in a report that you are writing with a word processor, even though you could perform the calculations with your computer? With PC Tools, those days are gone.

PC Tools Desktop includes four different calculators: the Algebraic Calculator, the Financial Calculator, the Programmer's Calculator, and the Scientific Calculator. If you are running Desktop in memory-resident mode, you can use any of these calculators from within your foreground application.

THE ALGEBRAIC CALCULATOR

Before you use the numbers on your ten-key pad, make sure the NumLock key is toggled on.

Using the Algebraic Calculator is like using an adding machine with a paper-tape printout. To enter numbers, use the keys on the ten-key pad or the keys along the top of your keyboard. Press the keyboard keys to represent addition (+), subtraction (−), multiplication (*), and division (/); with the mouse, you can click on the screen keys instead. As you make calculations, the numbers, the operations, and the results are recorded on the "tape". The current operation is shown in the single display line at the bottom of the tape window. Figure 14.1 shows the main screen for the Algebraic Calculator.

This calculator uses infix notation—the kind of notation you're probably most used to. For example, to add 50 to 75, type

50 + 75

Press Enter or type the equal sign to see the result, 125. To subtract 39 from 1,989, type **1989 − 39 =** to see the result of 1,950. Similarly, to multiply 12 by 20, type **12*20 =** ; the result is 240. Finally, to divide 160 by 8, type **160/8 =** ; the answer is 20.

You probably think of percentages in terms of whole numbers rather than decimal fractions—"6 percent" rather than "0.06," for instance. You can use whole numbers in the calculator if you follow them with the % symbol. To work out a 15-percent tip on a $50 restaurant bill, multiply 50 by 15 percent by typing

50*15% =

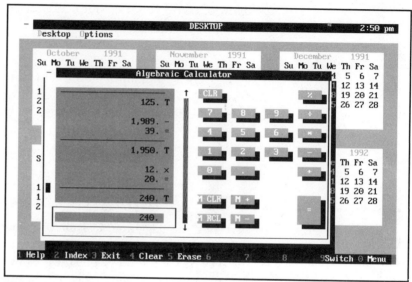

Figure 14.1: The main screen for the Algebraic Calculator

The result is 7.5, or a tip of $7.50. You can even add or subtract a percentage of a number. To work out the sales tax on a $200 item, type

   200 + 6.5% =

The answer is 213, or a total of $213.

EDITING CALCULATIONS

The calculator tape can hold up to 1,000 lines, the last 12 of which you can see in the calculator window. You can scroll through the tape to check your earlier entries with the arrow keys, or with the scroll bar. If you find any mistakes, you can correct them easily. Press the arrow keys to move the number to be corrected into the calculator display and enter the correct number, then press the End key to rerun the calculation. The new values appear on the tape and in the display. Calculated results themselves are not editable; you may edit only the inputted data.

If you fill the tape, the entries at the top will be removed to make room for the new ones at the bottom.

Numbers are displayed with a comma between each group of three digits and a period as the decimal point. Toggle the comma on and off by pressing the comma key.

You can set the number of decimal places by typing **D** followed by the desired number of decimal places. If you set the number of decimals in the display to zero and you calculate with fractions, however, the display may not look right.

Table 14.1 summarizes the functions of the Algebraic calculator.

Table 14.1: Algebraic Calculator Functions

FUNCTION	KEYBOARD	MOUSE
Add	+	+
Subtract	–	–
Multiply	*	*
Divide	/	/
Total	Enter *or* =	=
Clear	C	CLR
Calculate percentage	%	%
Add to memory register	M *and* +	M +
Subtract from memory register	M *and* –	M –
Erase memory register	M *and* C	M CLR
Recall memory register	M *and* R	M RCL
Toggle the separator character	,	,
Set number of decimals (0–9)	D	D

USING MEMORY REGISTERS

The Algebraic Calculator has one memory register, which you can use to collect the totals from a series of calculations when you only care about the combined total. If you use the memory register, an *M* in the lower-left corner of the tape reminds you that the memory register is nonzero. There are four memory functions:

- add a number to the total in memory
- subtract a number from the total

- clear the memory register
- recall a number from memory

USING OTHER FEATURES

The Options menu contains two entries to help you use the calculator: Clear Display and Erase Tape. These are duplicated in the message line with the function keys F4 for Clear Display and F5 for Erase Tape. Clear Display removes the current total from the total box and Erase Tape clears the whole tape window.

If you want to move calculations into a document that you are working on, select Copy to Clipboard from the Options menu to copy the last 160 lines (approximately 4,000 characters) of the tape into a file called CALC.TMP. You can even open a Clipboard window on top of the calculator if you want to edit the data.

To print the results of your calculations, choose Print Tape from the Options menu. You can send the output directly to your printer or to a disk file so that you can work on it later. The disk file is called CALC.PRT and is saved in the current directory.

Wide Display toggles the wide and narrow displays; your current choice is indicated by a checkmark to the left of the selection. The wide display includes the mouse keys, while the narrow display shows only the width of the tape.

THE FINANCIAL CALCULATOR

The Financial Calculator is based on Hewlett-Packard's HP-12C calculator. You can use it to perform simple or compound-interest calculations, to solve five-key problems and mortgage calculations, discounted cash-flow analyses, depreciation and appreciation problems, and statistical calculations. As with most advanced HP calculators (including the Scientific Calculator modeled after the HP-11C and the Programmer's Calculator modeled after the HP-16C, which are both described later in this chapter), the Financial Calculator uses reverse Polish notation (RPN) to enter numbers and operations.

If you are familiar with the HP-12C calculator, the Financial Calculator will be easy to use. If you have not used the HP-12C, don't worry; RPN is quite straightforward. In a two-number calculation, enter the numbers for the calculation first and the operator last. For example, to add 50 to 75, type **50**, press Enter, type **75**, and hit the + key. You will see 125 in the calculator's display.

When making a one-number operation like finding the square root of a number, enter the number followed by the square-root operator. For example, to find the square root of 81, type **81** and press Enter. Press F8 followed by the $\sqrt{x}$ key and you will see the result, 9, in the calculator's display.

Your calculations can obviously get much more complex than this, especially when you consider that most of the keys on the calculator keyboard can have several functions. The keyboard layout is shown in Figure 14.2.

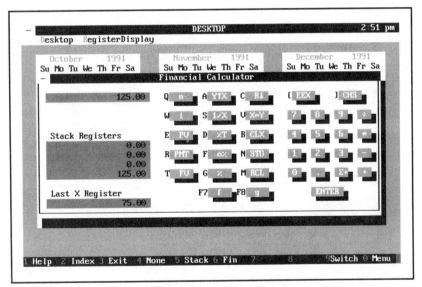

Figure 14.2: Keyboard layout of the Financial Calculator

Press the spacebar to get the primary functions back.

The main function of each key on the calculator is indicated in white on the key. If the key has secondary functions, you can see them by clicking the f or g prefix key. To use these secondary functions, click f or g—or press F7 or F8, respectively. Finally, if you are using your keyboard rather than a mouse, a letter you can type to access the function is shown to the left of some of the keys on the calculator.

For example, the key at the top left of the calculator is the n key used in five-key problems to represent the number of identical time periods in an analysis. To use it, click on the key with the mouse or press Q on your keyboard. A secondary function of this key is AMORT, used in calculating amortization schedules. To use it with a mouse, click on the f prefix key and then click on the n key (now labeled AMORT). To do the same thing from the keyboard, press F7 followed by Q. The other secondary function for this key is the annualizer, 12X. To access this with a mouse, click on the g prefix key and then click on the key now labeled 12X. Or press F8 followed by Q.

Table 14.2 lists the financial, mathematical, and statistical functions available on the Financial Calculator.

Table 14.2: Financial Calculator's Financial and Mathematical Functions

KEY	FUNCTION
Financial Functions	
n	Number of identical sequential time periods
i	Interest rate accruing over each n period
PV	Present value
PMT	Payment, or the once per period cash flow
FV	Future value
AMORT	Computes amortization schedule over a given number of periods
NPV	Computes net present value
PRICE	Computes a bond's PRICE for a desired YTM
YTM	Computes a bond's yield to maturity given the PRICE
SL	Computes straight line depreciation

Table 14.2: Financial Calculator's Financial and Mathematical Functions (continued)

KEY	FUNCTION
Financial Functions	
SOYD	Computes sum-of-the-year's-digits depreciation
DB	Computes declining balance depreciation
DAT	Computes the new date by adding a number of days to an old date
ΔDY	Computes the number of days between two dates
DMY	Sets calendar date entry mode to Day.Month Year format and displays d.my in the calculator's display
MDY	Resets calendar date entry mode to Month.Day Year format; nothing is shown in the display
BEG	Payment is due at the beginning of the payment period
END	Payment is due at the end of the payment period
IRR	Computes internal rate of return
12x	Multiply by 12 to calculate an annualized total
12÷	Divide by 12 to calculate a monthly total
Mathematical Functions	
CFo	Amount of cash flow in the first group
CFj	Subsequent cash flow amounts
Nj	Number of periods CFo or CFj amounts apply to
INT	Computes partial interest over a short period
Y↑X	Exponent; raises Y to the X power
$\sqrt{x}$	Computes the square root of the number in the display
1/X	Computes the reciprocal, or multiplicative inverse, of the number in the display

Table 14.2: Financial Calculator's Financial and Mathematical Functions (continued)

KEY	FUNCTION
Mathematical Functions	
LN	Computes the natural logarithm, the logarithm to the base *e*
FRC	Returns the fractional part of a number
INT	Returns the integer portion of a number
RND	Rounds the internal 12-digit mantissa of the value in the display to match the number of digits specified by the current fixed or scientific specification
CHS	Changes the sign of the number in the display, or the sign of the exponent of 10 in the display
%T	Computes the percentage of the total
Δ%	Computes the percentage difference
%	Computes percentage
Statistical Functions	
Σ+	Accumulates a series of data points into the statistical storage registers for statistical analysis
Σ−	Removes a data point from the statistical storage registers to correct an error in data entry
x,r	Computes a linear projection for *x*, based on the rate of change of *y*
y,r	Computes a linear projection for *y*, based on the rate of change of *x*
x	Computes the arithmetic mean from the data points in the statistical storage registers
s	Computes standard deviation
xw	Computes a weighted mean from data entered into the statistical storage registers

USING STORAGE REGISTERS

The Financial Calculator uses several different sets of registers to store the results of different types of calculations:

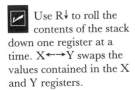 To perform five-key calculations properly, observe the sign conventions carefully.

- The five *financial registers* are used by the Financial Calculator to solve five-key problems relating to different kinds of mortgages, interest rates, and so on. You can use the data in any four of the registers to solve for the unknown fifth. The registers are:

n	number of identical sequential time periods
i	interest rate accruing over each of these n periods; i and n always apply to the same period of time
PV	present value
PMT	payment
FV	future value

You can look at the contents of the financial registers by selecting Financial Registers (F6) from the Register Display menu.

Use R↓ to roll the contents of the stack down one register at a time. X←→Y swaps the values contained in the X and Y registers.

- *Stack registers* store the intermediate results of your calculations. The number in the calculator display is stored in the X register. When you enter another number or perform an operation, the numbers already on the stack are moved up or down one place.

  You can look at the contents of all the stack registers by selecting the Stack Registers option in the Register Display menu, or by choosing F5 from the main calculator window.

- *Data registers* are 20 general-purpose registers named R0 to R9 and R.0 to R.9. Use STO and RCL to store or recall numbers, respectively, from these registers. STO copies the number in the X register into the data register that you designate by number. RCL performs the reverse operation, copying a number from a data register into the X register. To clear all data-storage registers, click on f (or press F7) followed by REG. (This also clears the statistical storage registers, described below.)

You can look at the contents of all the data registers by choosing the Data Registers option in the Register Display menu.

- *Statistical storage registers* store the results of statistical calculations. These special registers, R1 to R5, are handled automatically by the calculator. They cannot be inspected from the Register Display menu. You can clear these registers by clicking on f (or pressing F7), followed by Σ. (This also clears all stack registers.)

Keys on the calculator devoted to keystroke and internal-register management are listed in Table 14.3.

If you calculate an extremely large number that cannot fit into the display, the calculator automatically changes from fixed to scientific notation.

Table 14.3: Financial Calculator's Key and Register Management Functions

KEY	FUNCTION
Key Manipulation	
f	When selected before a function key, performs the function above the key
g	When selected before a function key, performs the function below the key
EEX	Indicates that the next numbers entered are to be used as the exponent of a number
Register Management	
FIN	Clears the financial registers
REG	Sets all the storage registers to zero; to clear an individual register, store zero into the register
R↓	Rolls down the contents of the stack

Table 14.3: Financial Calculator's Key and Register Management Functions (continued)

KEY	FUNCTION
Register Management	
X⟷Y	Swaps the contents of the X and Y registers
CLX	Sets to zero the value of the displayed X register
STO	Stores a number into the R.0 to R.9 and R0 to R9 data registers, or into the financial registers
RCL	Recalls a stored number. Follow the RCL key with the register number to recall

The calculator normally uses a fixed notation to display the results of your calculations. You can change the number of decimal places shown in the display by clicking on f (or pressing F7), followed by the desired new number of decimal places. You can select from 0 to 9 decimal places for the display, but internal calculations are still performed to the full 12 digits.

Alternatively, you can select scientific notation by pressing F7, followed by a period. Now if you enter **45,678** in fixed format with six places of decimals and then select scientific notation, the number will be displayed as

4.567800 E + 4

This number is equivalent to 4.5678 times 10 raised to the fourth power (the *E* stands for exponent). If you select two decimal places, the number looks like this:

4.57 E + 4

There are three calculator settings that affect the way calculations are performed:

- You can calculate compound interest in two ways: straight line or continuous. Both give the same result at the end of the period, but different results during the period. Select STO followed by EEX to turn continuous compounding on. A c appears below the display to confirm your setting. Press STO and EEX again to return to straight line. Notice that the c disappears.

- The calculator defaults to calculations based on payment at the end of the payment period. To indicate that payment is at the beginning of the period, click on g (or press F8) followed by the BEG key. The abbreviation beg appears below the display, and all loan and annuity calculations are performed with the assumption that payment is made at the beginning of the period.

- Normal entry of dates is in the format *Month.DayYear.* To enter dates in the *Day.MonthYear* format, click on g (or press F8) followed by the DMY key. The characters d.my appear below the display as a reminder. To revert to the normal method of entry, click on g, followed by the MDY key.

ERROR MESSAGES

Finally, the Financial Calculator can display four error messages:

- **ERROR 0:** you attempted an impossible operation, such as division by zero.

- **ERROR 1:** you tried to enter too many values into the storage registers.

- **ERROR 2:** you tried to enter an improper statistical operation, such as performing a linear regression before entering any data points.

- **ERROR:** you pressed two unsuitable keys in sequence.

Press any key on the keyboard or click the mouse to clear any one of these errors.

THE PROGRAMMER'S CALCULATOR

The Programmer's Calculator is based on Hewlett-Packard's HP-16C calculator (though it is not programmable). You can use it to convert values into different numbering schemes, perform arithmetic in 1's or 2's complement or in unsigned mode (described later), and look at the results of using the logical operators and the shift-left and shift-right operators.

NUMBERING SYSTEMS

Before describing how to use the calculator, I would like to describe the different numbering schemes used when working with computers. Understanding these systems will make it easier to work with your computer—you'll have a better grasp of what is happening and why. The main thing to remember about these different systems is that they are all methods of representing the *same thing*.

DECIMAL   The *decimal* system is the system people are most familiar with. It counts in base 10, using the ten digits from 0–9 to represent all numbers. The position of each digit determines the value of the number: the rightmost position is the ones place, the second position (moving to the left) is the tens place, the third is the hundreds place, and so on.

BINARY   The *binary* system uses only two digits, 0 and 1, which represent the only possible states of a bit—off or on. Counting in binary is relatively straightforward, although it is rather different from the traditional decimal-numbering scheme. In the binary system, the rightmost position is the ones place, the second position is the twos place, the third is the fours place, and so on.

The binary system may represent the exact state of the bits in a byte well, but it is inconvenient when all you want to know is the value of the byte and don't care about the status of its individual bits. In cases like this, it is often easier to work with the hexadecimal system, described next.

HEXADECIMAL   The third major numbering scheme used when working with computers is the *hexadecimal* system. This is often abbreviated to hex or the single letter *H*. Sometimes even the *H* is omitted, and you have to guess from the context that the number is expressed in hexadecimal.

The hexadecimal system counts in base 16, using the digits 0–9 and the letters *A–F* in the sequence 0, 1, 2, 3, 4, 5, 6, 7, 8, 9, A, B, C, D, E, and F. In a hexadecimal number, each digit's value is 16 times greater than the digit immediately to its right. So the rightmost position is the ones place, the second position is the sixteens place, the third is the two-hundred-and-fifty-sixes place, and so on.

Hexadecimal notation is a convenient way to express byte values because a single hexadecimal digit is equivalent to four binary digits. Since there are eight binary digits in a byte, the value of a byte can be expressed as two hex digits.

The hexadecimal digits A–F are written in uppercase.

OCTAL   The *octal* numbering system works in base 8. This system has only eight digits, 0 to 7; there are no eights or nines. Octal is more commonly found in minicomputers and mainframes rather than in the world of personal computers, where the hexadecimal system is used almost universally.

CONVERTING NUMBERS

The Programmer's Calculator works with words from 1 to 64 bits in size, but the default word size is 16 bits. This means you can enter up to 64 bits in binary or up to 1,844,674,407,370,955,161 bits in decimal. The current word-size setting is shown on the right side of the calculator display. To change the word size, enter a number between 1 and 64 and press the F7 function key followed by the WSZ key.

Use the mouse or ↑ and ↓ to select the numbering scheme you want to use. Choose HEX to calculate in hexadecimal, OCTAL to calculate in octal, BINARY to calculate in binary, or DECIMAL to calculate in decimal. When the calculation is complete, the result is shown in all four numbering systems.

To convert a number from one system to another, just select the starting numbering scheme and key in the number. The calculator automatically converts the number into the other numbering systems and displays the result.

For example, to convert FB in hexadecimal notation into all the other systems, select the HEX system for entry, and type **FB**. The results—373 in octal, 251 in decimal and 11111011 in binary—are shown in the display. Figure 14.3 shows this calculation.

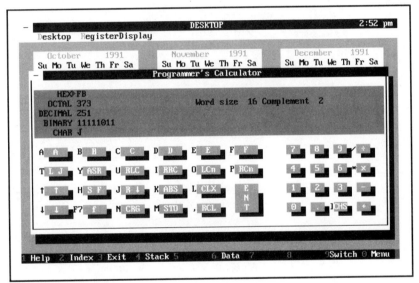

Figure 14.3: Sample operations using the Programmer's Calculator

The CHAR display shows the ASCII character corresponding to the low-order hex byte, which in this case is the $\sqrt{}$ character. If the number is less than 32 in decimal, the normal abbreviation for the ASCII control character is displayed. If the decimal number is 32, the word SPACE is shown in the CHAR display. If the decimal number is greater than 32, the normal ASCII character is displayed.

PERFORMING CALCULATIONS

The main function of each key on the calculator is shown in white on the key. Most of the keys have secondary functions, and these are

The real HP-16C has both f and g prefix keys; only the f prefix key is used on the Programmer's Calculator.

See the section "The Financial Calculator" for a description of how to use reverse Polish notation for data entry.

accessed with the f prefix key. The character you can type from the keyboard to access a function is shown to the left of some of the keys on the calculator. As an example, the key at the top left of the calculator keyboard is the A key. To use it click on the key with the mouse or press A from your computer keyboard. The secondary function of this key is S L (shift left), which moves all the bits in a word one place to the left and replaces the empty one on the right with a zero. To access S L with the mouse, first click the f prefix key, then the S L key. To do the same thing from the keyboard, press F7 followed by A.

To perform calculations with the Programmer's Calculator, you must use reverse Polish notation. For instance, to perform the calculation

$$F + 3$$

type **F** and press Enter, then type **3** and press the + key. The solution—12 in hex, 22 in octal, 18 in decimal, and 10010 in binary—is shown in the display. The CHAR line in the display shows the ASCII control-character equivalent, DC2.

Table 14.4 lists the arithmetic, logical, and register-manipulation functions of the Programmer's Calculator.

Table 14.4: Functions Included in the Programmer's Calculator

KEY	FUNCTION
Math Functions	
$\sqrt{x}$	Computes the square root of the number in the X register
1/X	Computes the reciprocal, or multiplicative inverse, of the number in the display
CHS	Changes the sign of the number in the display
ABS	Computes the absolute value of the number in the display
RMD	Remainder from a division

Table 14.4: Functions Included in the Programmer's Calculator (continued)

KEY	FUNCTION
Math Functions	
f	When selected before a function key, performs the function above the key; the display shows f
ENT	Enter key
LST	Recalls the number displayed before the last function was executed
BSP	Backspaces one character
S F	Sets a flag when followed by the flag number
C F	Clears a flag when followed by the flag number
CPX	Clears a prefix (f, C, G, or P)
ZER	Allows the display of leading zeros
Calculator Register Manipulation	
STO	Stores a value into the R0 to R9 and R.0 to R.9 data registers
RCL	Recalls a stored number when followed with the register number to recall
X'Y	Swaps the contents of the X and Y stack registers
R ↓	Rolls down the contents of the stack
R ↑	Rolls up the contents of the stack
CLX	Sets the value of the displayed X register to zero
CRG	Clears a register when followed by the register number
Mode Selection	
↑	Select numbering scheme
↓	Select numbering scheme

Table 14.4: Functions Included in the Programmer's Calculator (continued)

KEY	FUNCTION
Mode Selection	
PRC	Sets precision for floating-point operations
WSZ	Sets word size
RST	Restores the calculator's start-up state
1 s	Selects 1's complement mode
2 s	Selects 2's complement mode
UNS	Selects unsigned mode
Logical Operators	
AND	Compares bits in two words and returns a 1 at that location if both bits are ones
OR	Compares bits in two words and returns a 0 at that location if both bits are zeros
NOT	Inverts the value of all the bits in the X register
XOR	Compares bits in two words and returns a 1 at that position if the two bits are different
Masking Operations	
MKL	Masks left
MKR	Masks right
Bit Operations	
# B	Counts the number of bits in the X register
C B	Clear bit
S B	Set bit
L J	Left justify

Table 14.4: Functions Included in the Programmer's Calculator (continued)

KEY	FUNCTION
Bit Operations	
S L	Shift left
S R	Shift right
R L	Rotate left
R R	Rotate right
RLC	Rotate left through carry
RRC	Rotate right through carry
RLn	Rotate left n bits
RRn	Rotate right n bits
LCn	Rotate left through carry n bits
RCn	Rotate right through carry n bits
ASR	Arithmetic shift right
Double Functions	
DBX	Double multiply
DB÷	Double divide
DBR	Double remainder

COMPUTATION MODES

The Programmer's Calculator can represent numbers in three forms: 1's complement mode, 2's complement mode, and unsigned mode. These modes use different methods of representing negative binary numbers:

- 1's complement mode represents any negative number by alternating the bit configuration of all the bits in the numbers. For example, 100101 is the 1's complement of 011010.

- In 2's complement mode, a positive or negative number is changed to the opposite sign by changing all the ones to zeros and zeros to ones, then adding 1 to the result.

- In unsigned mode, the most significant bit is used as a data bit rather than a sign bit. For two-byte numbers this implies a number range from 0 to 64,436 rather than from −32,768 to 32,767.

The default mode is the 2's complement mode, the most common mode used today. The current mode is shown to the right of the wordsize in the calculator's display as Complement 1, Complement 2, or Complement U.

SYSTEM FLAGS

The Programmer's Calculator has three system flags to control leading zeros, number carry-over, and number overflow. It also has an indicator for further input:

- **Flag 3** manages the display of leading zeros, which are suppressed if this flag is not set. Z appears in the calculator display to indicate that this flag is set.

- **Flag 4** is set if an arithmetic operation results in a remainder. C appears in the calculator display to indicate that this flag is set.

- **Flag 5** is set whenever a result cannot be expressed in the current word size. G appears in the calculator display to indicate that this flag is set.

- **P** appears in the display to indicate that an operation is incomplete and requires more input. Operations like STO, RCL, SF, and CF all generate a P if incomplete.

You can set these flags by pressing the S F (Set Flag) key, followed by the number. To clear a flag, press the C F (Clear Flag) key followed by the number.

STORAGE REGISTERS

The Programmer's Calculator uses two sets of registers to store the results of different kinds of calculations:

You can use R↑ or R↓ to roll the contents of the stack up or down one register at a time, respectively. X⟷Y swaps the values contained in the X and Y registers.

- *Stack registers* store intermediate results from your calculations and are labeled T, Z, Y, X, and LSTX. The number in the calculator display is stored in the X register. If you enter another calculation, the values on the stack are moved one place.

  You can look at the contents of all the stack registers by selecting the Stack Registers option from the Register Display menu, or by pressing F4 from the calculator main screen.

- *Data registers* are 20 general-purpose registers called R0 to R9 and R.0 to R.9. Use STO and RCL to store numbers in or recall numbers from these registers.

  You can view the contents of the data registers with the Data Registers option from the Register Display menu, or by selecting F6 from the main calculator display.

If you enter a number containing a decimal, the Programmer's Calculator switches into floating-point mode automatically, and the default word size changes to 64 bits. Decimals are not shown in the hex, octal, or binary numbering schemes.

ERROR MESSAGES

The Programmer's Calculator can display several error messages:

- **Improper Mathematical Operation**: you divided a number by zero or tried to calculate the square root of a negative number.

- **Illegal digit for this number base**: you entered 8 or 9 as an octal number; A, B, C, D, E, or F as a decimal number; or anything other than 0 or 1 as a binary number.

- **Decimal Already Entered**: you entered the decimal point and tried to enter another.

- **Improper Flag Number**: you attempted to set or clear a flag using the wrong index number.

THE SCIENTIFIC CALCULATOR

See the section "The Financial Calculator" for a description of how to use reverse Polish notation for data entry.

To access the secondary function of a key, click on either the f or g prefix key, or press F7 or F8, respectively, before selecting the function key.

The Scientific Calculator is immensely powerful. You can use it to perform mathematical functions, probability and statistical functions, and the usual set of transcendental functions. Several sets of internal registers are available for use in complex calculations.

The Scientific Calculator emulates the functions of the HP-11C calculator, except that it is not programmable. As with other Hewlett-Packard calculators, it uses reverse Polish notation for the entry of numbers and operations, rather than the infix notation used by the Algebraic Calculator. The keyboard layout is shown in Figure 14.4.

The main function of each key on the calculator is indicated in white on the key. If the key has secondary functions, they are shown when you use the f or g prefix keys, as with the other calculators. You can also press the F7 or F8 function key in place of the f or g prefix

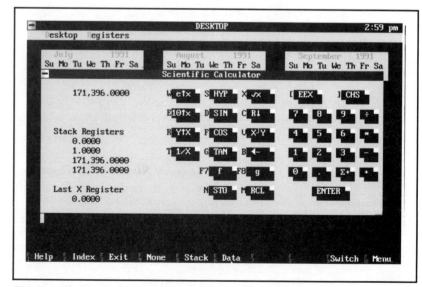

Figure 14.4: The Scientific Calculator keyboard layout

key, respectively. If you are using your keyboard rather than a mouse, the character you type to access the function is shown to the left of some of the keys on the calculator.

For example, the key at the top left of the calculator is the e↑x key, which raises *e* to the power of the number in the display. To use it, click on the key with the mouse or press W from your keyboard. A secondary function of this key is LN, which calculates the natural logarithm of the number in the display. To access LN with a mouse, first click on the g prefix key and then on e↑x (now LN). To do the same thing from the keyboard, press F8 followed by W.

COMPUTATION FUNCTIONS

Table 14.5 lists the math, transcendental, statistical, and probability functions available on the Scientific Calculator.

Table 14.5: Mathematical Functions Included in the Scientific Calculator

KEY	FUNCTION
Math Functions	
LN	Computes the natural logarithm, the logarithm to the base *e*
e↑x	Computes the natural antilogarithm. Raises *e* to the power of the number in the display
LOG	Computes the common logarithm (base 10) of a positive number
10↑x	Computes the common antilogarithm: raises 10 to the power of the number in the display
Y↑X	Exponent: raises the number in the Y register to the power of the value in the display
%	Computes X percent of the value in the Y register
1/X	Computes the reciprocal or multiplicative inverse of the number in the display
$\sqrt{x}$	Computes the square root of the number in the X register

Table 14.5: Mathematical Functions Included in the Scientific Calculator (continued)

KEY	FUNCTION
Math Functions	
x^2 or x^0	Computes the square of the number in the X register
x!	Computes the factorial of an integer. (To compute the gamma function, Γ, subtract 1 from the number and then calculate x!.)
$\Delta\%$	Computes the percent change between the number in the Y register and the number in the X register
π	The constant $\cong 3.141592654$
CHS	Changes the sign of the number or the sign of the exponent of 10 in the display
ABS	Computes the absolute value of the number in the display
INT	Returns the integer portion of a number
FRAC	Returns the fractional portion of a number
RND	Rounds the internal ten-digit mantissa of the value in the display to match the number of digits specified by the current FIX, SCI, or ENG specification
Trigonometric Functions	
SIN	Sine of x
COS	Cosine of x
TAN	Tangent of x
ASIN	Arcsine of x
ACOS	Arccosine of x
ATAN	Arctangent of x

Table 14.5: Mathematical Functions Included in the Scientific Calculator
(continued)

Key	Function
Hyperbolic Functions	
HYP	Hyperbolic sine (sinh), cosine (cosh), or tangent (tanh), using SIN, COS, or TAN of x
AHYP	Inverse hyperbolic sine ($sinh^{-1}$), cosine ($cosh^{-1}$), or tangent ($tanh^{-1}$), using SIN, COS, or TAN of x
Probability Functions	
Py x	Permutation: computes the number of permutations of y taken x at a time, without repetitions (must be a positive integer)
Cy x	Combination: computes the number of combinations of y taken x at a time, without repetitions or order (must be a positive integer)
Statistical Functions	
Σ +	Collects information from numbers in the X and Y registers into the statistics storage registers R0 through R5 as follows: R0: the number of data points collected R1: the sum of the x values, Σx R2: the sum of the squares of the x values, Σx^2 R3: the sum of the y values, Σy R4: the sum of the squares of the y values, Σy^2 R5: the sum of the products of the x and y values, Σxy

Table 14.5: Mathematical Functions Included in the Scientific Calculator (continued)

KEY	FUNCTION
Statistical Functions	
Σ –	Subtracts information from the statistics storage registers to correct data collection. Delete and reenter both x and y in the correct sequence, even if only one value is incorrect
Σ	Clears the statistics storage registers and the stack registers, but leaves the LAST X register intact, removing data from previous calculations
x̄	Computes the arithmetic mean of the x and y values in the R1 and R3 registers
s	Computes the standard deviation of the x and y values collected using Σ +. R0, R1, and R2 values are used to calculate the standard deviation of the x values, and R0, R3, and R4 values are used for the standard deviation of the y values
L.R	Computes linear regression using the linear equation $y = Ax + B$, placing the slope (A) in the Y register and the intercept (B) in the X register
y,r	Computes the linear estimate and correlation coefficient. Assuming that the x and y values approximate a straight line, the linear estimate is placed in the X register and the correlation coefficient in the Y register

DISPLAY AND UNIT CONVERSIONS

Table 14.6 lists all display and unit conversions available on the Scientific Calculator.

The Scientific Calculator can display information in fixed format, in scientific (or exponential) notation, and in engineering format:

- In *fixed format*, numbers in the display are always shown with the same number of digits after the decimal point.

Table 14.6: Display and Unit Conversions Available on the Scientific Calculator

KEY	FUNCTION
Display Conversions	
FIX	Fixes the number of decimal places for the display, between 0 and 9
SCI	Sets the display to scientific notation
ENG	Sets the display to engineering notation
DEG	Sets the display mode to degrees for trigonometric functions
RAD	Sets the display mode to radians for trigonometric functions
GRD	Sets the display mode to gradians for trigonometric functions
Units Conversions	
HMS	Converts decimal hours to hours, minutes, seconds, or decimal degrees to degrees, minutes, seconds
H	Converts hours, minutes, seconds to decimal hours, or degrees, minutes, seconds to decimal degrees
DG	Converts radians to degrees
RAD	Converts degrees to radians
Polar-Rectangular Coordinate Conversions	
←R	Converts the polar coordinates in the X and Y registers (magnitude r, angle ϕ) to rectangular coordinates (x,y)
←P	Converts the rectangular coordinates in the X and Y registers (x,y) to polar coordinates (magnitude r, angle ϕ)

You can set the number of decimal places from 0 to 9, by selecting f (or F7), the FIX key, and entering a number for the number of decimal places to show. The calculator initially starts with four decimal places.

- In *scientific notation,* you can display a very large or very small number easily with the minimum of digits. Numbers are shown as a multiple of 10 raised to a power. For example, 45,678 is displayed as **4.5678 04** (consider this 4.5678 times 10 raised to the fourth power), and −45,678 is displayed as **−4.5678 04**. To select the number of decimal places, select f, the SCI key, followed by the number of decimal places to display. If you chose SCI 3, the number 4.5678 will be shown as **4.568 04**.

- *Engineering notation* is similar to scientific notation, but the exponent (the power of 10) is always a multiple of 3, so any number in the display can be read easily in units of k (kilo, or 10^3), or m (milli, or 10^{-3}) commonly found in engineering. The digit following the selected number of places is automatically rounded off. Select f and the ENG key followed by the number of digits to display after first significant figure.

STORAGE REGISTERS

Managing the keystrokes and internal registers on the calculator can become quite complicated. Table 14.7 lists all calculator key and internal register-management functions available on the Scientific Calculator.

The Scientific Calculator uses several different sets of registers to store the results of different kinds of calculations:

When you start a new calculation, make sure that no old values remain in these registers. You can clear them by clicking on f (or pressing F7) followed by Σ.

- *Stack registers* store the intermediate results of your calculations, and are labeled T, Z, Y, X, and LSTX. The number in the calculator display is stored in the X register. If you enter another number or perform an operation, the numbers already on the stack are moved up or down one place.

   Use R↑ or R↓ to roll the contents of the stack up or down one register at a time. X⟷Y swaps the values contained in the X and Y registers. When you perform a calculation,

Table 14.7: Calculator Key and Internal Register Management Functions Available on the Scientific Calculator

KEY	FUNCTION
Key Manipulation	
f	When selected before a function key, performs the function above the key; the display shows f
g	When selected before a function key, performs the function below the key; the display shows g
PREFX	Cancels the f (F7) or g (F8) prefixes for partially entered functions
ENTER	Enters a copy of the number displayed into the Y register
EEX	Indicates that the next numbers entered are to be used as the exponent of a number
Calculator Register Manipulation	
STO	Stores a number in the R0 to R9 and R.0 to R.9 data registers˙
RCL	Recalls a stored number. Follow RCL with the register number to recall
X⟷Y	Swaps the contents of the X and Y stack registers
R↓	Rolls down the contents of the stack
R↑	Rolls up the contents of the stack
REG	Sets all the storage registers to zero. To clear an individual register, store zero into the register
CLX	Sets the value of the displayed X register to zero

the number that was in the X register before the calculation is moved into a special register called LAST X. You can recall this number into the X register with g LST or F8 Enter, so you don't have to reenter the number in the next calculation.

You can look at the contents of all stack registers with the Stack Registers option in the Register Display menu, or by pressing F5 from the main calculator screen.

To ensure that no results from previous calculations remain, clear the stack registers by clicking on f (or pressing F7) followed by S. This does not clear LAST X, however.

- *Data registers* are 20 general-purpose registers called R0 to R9 and R.0 to R.9. Use STO and RCL to store or recall numbers from these registers. STO copies the number in the X register into the data register you designate by number. RCL performs the reverse operation, copying a number from a data register into the X register. To clear all the data-storage registers, click on f (or press F7) followed by REG. (This also clears the statistical storage registers.)

   You can view the contents of all data registers with the Data Registers option in the Register Display menu, or by pressing F6 from the main calculator screen.

- *Statistical storage registers.* The results of statistical calculations are stored in another set of registers, R1 to R5. These are special registers, handled automatically by the calculator. They cannot be inspected from the Registers Display menu.

   These registers are used as follows:

R0	number of data points collected
R1	sum of the x values, Σx
R2	sum of the squares of the x values, Σx^2
R3	sum of the y values, Σy
R4	sum of the squares of the y values, Σy^2
R5	sum of the products of the x and y values, Σxy

ERROR MESSAGES

Finally, the Scientific Calculator can display three error messages:

- **ERROR 0**: you attempted an impossible operation, such as division by zero.

- **ERROR 1**: you tried to enter too many values into the storage registers.

- **ERROR 2**: you tried to enter an improper statistical operation, such as performing a linear regression before entering any data points.

Press any key from the keyboard or click the mouse to clear any one of these errors.

CHAPTER

15

*Increasing
Your Efficiency with
the Appointment Scheduler*

This chapter concentrates on the Desktop Appointment Scheduler. It shows how to use it to organize your time. You will learn how to make a to-do list, load your schedule automatically, and customize the Appointment Scheduler. You'll also learn how to print an appointment schedule and run a program at a time that you specify.

OVERVIEW OF THE APPOINTMENT SCHEDULER

Desktop's Appointment Scheduler consists of three separate parts for organizing your time: a monthly calendar, a time planner, and a to-do list. When you enter appointments into the time planner, you specify the time and duration of the appointment; you can also attach a note or reminder. You can set an alarm that sounds just before your next appointment. You can also search for a particular appointment or find the next block of free time. You can make a to-do list with different priorities attached to the items in the list. Finally, you can use macros to pop up notes before a meeting, run a program when you are away from your computer, or dial a phone number.

You are not restricted to making appointments or scheduling meetings with the Appointment Scheduler. You can use it to remind you of birthdays, anniversaries, or other special regularly occurring dates. You can also use it to track the time you spend working on different projects.

When you start the Appointment Scheduler from the Desktop main menu, the File Load dialog box lists any files with the .TM extension in the current directory. If several different people are using the computer, you can create individual Appointment Scheduler files, each with a different name.

The Appointment Scheduler creates files with a .TM extension.

You see the screen shown in Figure 15.1 after you start a new appointment file. Press Tab to move from the monthly calendar window to the time-planner window or the to-do list window, or click the mouse in the window you want to make active. The shortcut function keys are shown on the message line at the bottom of the screen.

A three-month calendar is shown in the upper half of the window, with today's date highlighted. This is a perpetual calendar: there is no end date. To select a new date using the keyboard, press the left or

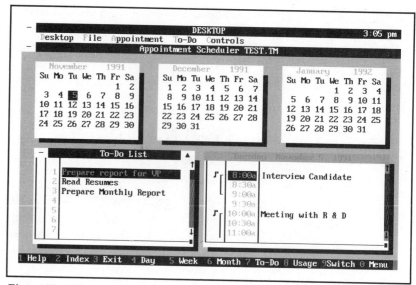

Figure 15.1: The Appointment Scheduler opening screen

right arrow keys. If you move past the beginning or end of the month, the calendar scrolls to show the previous or next month. Press Tab to activate/highlight Calendar and PgUp or PgDn to change to another month. Press the Ctrl key with PgUp or PgDn to change the year.

The time-planner display on the right side of the screen shows today's appointments listed by their scheduled time. The default business day runs from 8:00 a.m. to 5:00 p.m. and is divided into 15-minute intervals. However, you can change this interval using the Controls menu commands. The highlighted bar shows the current time. To select a time from the keyboard, press Tab to select the daily schedule and ↑ and ↓ to choose the time, or page through the list with PgUp or PgDn. With the mouse, just click on the time you want to select or use the scroll bar to move through the list.

Today's to-do list is displayed below the calendar in the lower part of the window, arranged in order of priority. You can move through the list one line at a time with the up or down arrow keys, or you can page through the list using PgUp or PgDn. Home selects the first entry in the list and End selects the last. You can enter as many as 80 items in this list, although the window cannot show them all at once.

The Appointment Scheduler uses your computer's internal clock. Always make sure that the clock is set correctly after you turn on your computer.

Maximize the to-do window to show the first 36 items. The to-do list is independent of the calendar and the list of appointments on the time planner.

MAKING APPOINTMENTS

All the selections you need to make, delete, or edit appointments are contained in the Appointment menu, shown in Figure 15.2.

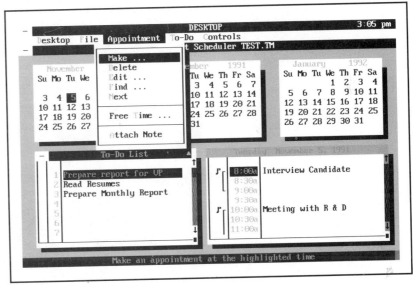

Figure 15.2: The Appointment menu

To make a new appointment, you can use several shortcuts as alternatives to this menu:

- Select the appropriate time on today's time planner display and either press the Enter key or click on it with the mouse.

- Select the appropriate month from the monthly calendar and then choose the correct day for the appointment. Now move to the time planner display and select the time for the appointment.

Whichever method you use, the Make Appointment screen appears, as shown in Figure 15.3.

The selections in the Make Appointment screen are as follows:

If you try to make an appointment for a date that has passed, or try to make a recurring appointment that has an end date prior to today's date, you will receive a warning message.

- **Description:** enter a message of up to 24 characters to remind you of the purpose of the appointment. This text is displayed opposite the appointment time in the time-planner display when you return to the main Appointment Scheduler display.

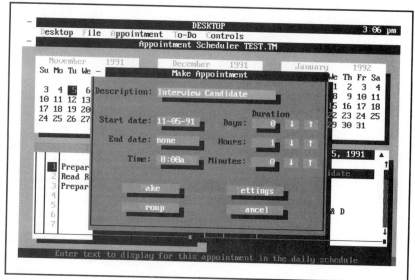

Figure 15.3: The Make Appointment screen

- **Start Date:** enter the start date for recurring appointments or the appointment date for single appointments.

- **End Date:** enter the end date for a series of recurring appointments or leave the field blank for a single appointment.

- **Time:** enter the appointment time.

- **Duration:** enter the length of time you expect the appointment to take in days, hours, or minutes. If this conflicts with an existing appointment, the Appointment Scheduler displays a message to this effect when you select Make to save the appointment.

Choose Settings to select the special appointment settings you need, as Figure 15.4 shows.

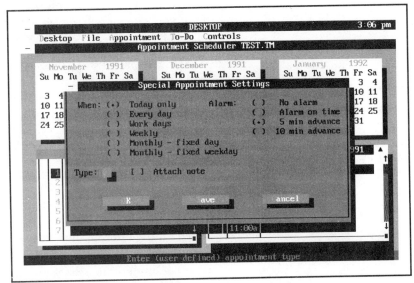

Figure 15.4: The Special Appointment Settings dialog box allows you to customize your appointments

Choose from the following:

- **When:** allows you to specify when an event takes place. Use Today Only for a one-time appointment and the other choices to schedule regular activities. You can schedule lunchtime each day by selecting Work Days. Schedule regular weekly meetings with Weekly. If you want an appointment to repeat each month on the same day, select Monthly—Fixed Day; if you want the appointment on the same day of the week each month, choose Monthly—Fixed Weekday.

- **Alarm:** sets an alarm to go off at the time of an appointment, or five or ten minutes beforehand. The Appointment Scheduler interrupts your foreground application program with a message and beeps when the alarm goes off. You can acknowledge the alarm or select the Snooze button, which reactivates the alarm after five minutes. You can also select No Alarm. Remember, alarms use the clock in your computer; if it is wrong, your alarms will not ring when you expect them to.

- **Type:** classifies your appointments. This is especially useful if you categorize your activities. Differentiate between clients by giving each client a unique code.

- **Attach note:** attaches a notepad to the appointment. Among other things, this is useful for meeting agenda or making notes for a presentation. If you choose Attach Note, a Notepads file opens on top of the Appointment Scheduler screen when you select the Make button to save the appointment. The top line of the notepad displays the appointment reminder note along with the date and time; the rest of the file is empty and ready for text. All the usual Notepads features are available. The file will have the same name as the current appointment file, but with a file-name extension based on the internal identification number of the selected appointment. The file is created in the same directory as the appointment file. Press Escape or click on the close box with the mouse to return to the Appointment Scheduler when you have finished your note.

Select OK and choose Make when you have entered all the information for the appointment. You will return to the main display, which now shows the appointment you have just entered. The duration of the appointment is shown as a vertical bar down the left side of the time-planner display. If appointments overlap, the overlapping times are indicated on the duration bar.

If you set an alarm, a musical note symbol is also shown opposite the appointment. A double musical note indicates a recurring appointment with alarm. If you attached a note to the appointment, the letter N appears to the left of the musical note.

DELETING APPOINTMENTS

If you want to delete an appointment, move the highlight to the appointment and press Enter. A dialog box opens with the following options:

- **Delete** deletes the appointment.

- **Edit** edits the appointment; this opens the Make Appointment box so you can enter your changes.

- **Alter Note** allows you to alter the information in the Notepads file.

- **Cancel** cancels the appointment deletion.

If the appointment you delete is a recurring appointment, the Appointment Scheduler will ask whether you want to delete this particular appointment for today only or delete all occurrences of the appointment.

SEARCHING FOR AN APPOINTMENT

Search for a particular appointment with the Find Appointment option from the Appointment menu. You can search by text (the text that you originally entered in the note box in the Make Appointment screen), appointment type, appointment time, or appointment date. Select Find Appointment or click on Find to start the search. Starting the search without a text entry finds all appointments after the current time and date.

Use Next Appointment from the Appointment menu to find the next appointment scheduled for today. If you are free for the rest of the day, the cursor moves to the current time.

To find your next available period of free time, select Free Time from the Appointment menu. You will see the screen shown in Figure 15.5.

Find Free Time can search up to a year ahead to find the block of time you need.

When searching for the next available period of free time, you can establish the following criteria:

- **Start Time.** Enter the time of day at which you want the search to start.

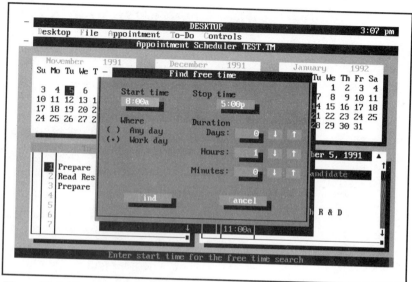

Figure 15.5: The Find Free Time screen

- **Stop Time.** Enter the time of day at which you want the search to stop.

- **Where.** Choose between Any Day or Work Day.

- **Duration.** Enter the length of the free period you are looking for in days, hours, and minutes.

Start the search by clicking the Find button. The Appointment Scheduler moves the cursor through the time planner as it searches for the first block of free time to match the search criteria.

For example, suppose you have to interview a candidate for a position and you want to hold the interview during normal business hours on a work day sometime this week. You estimate that the interview will last for 90 minutes. Using Find Free Time, set Start Time to 8:00 a.m. and Stop Time to 3:30 p.m. If you search any later than 3:30 p.m., you may not complete the interview inside normal business hours. Choose Work Day from the Where column and enter the Duration as 1 hour and 30 minutes. Click Find to start the search for the next free period that matches these criteria.

Press F5 (Week) to look at a complete week of appointments, as Figure 15.6 shows. A six-day week is shown, Monday through Saturday. Use the scroll bars at the right of each day to look at each day's activities. Click on the day you want to look at in detail, or press Tab to move from day to day.

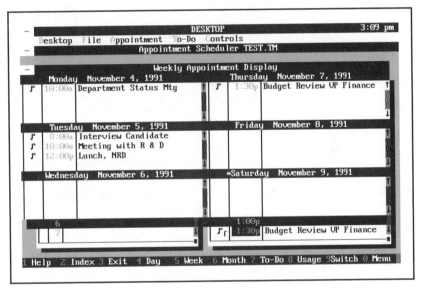

Figure 15.6: Look at a whole week of appointments

To see how you are using your time, press F8 to display a five-day schedule on the screen, as shown in Figure 15.7. The solid bars represent free time, the divided bars represent appointments, and the dots show scheduling conflicts. All days in the week are shown, not just work days. You can use the arrow keys or the mouse to move through the five-day window one day at a time, or press PgUp or PgDn to move five days at a time. Press the Home key to return to today's date.

An appointment must exist before you can attach a notepad to it.

You can attach a notepad to an appointment when you create it. If you decide to add a notepad after you have made the appointment, however, you must select Attach Note from the Appointment menu and enter the actual text as described earlier under ''Making Appointments.''

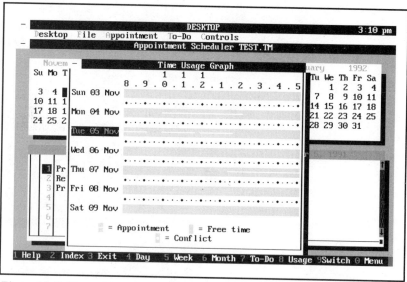

Figure 15.7: Show time usage display

MAKING GROUP APPOINTMENTS

To run PC Tools on your network, you must have a network license from Central Point Software.

The Appointment Scheduler also allows you to make appointments for groups of people who all work on the same network. The first step is to create the appropriate directories on the network, because each group must be associated with a specific directory. For example, if you are in the Marketing Department, ask your system administrator to create a directory called \MARKETING\ GROUP on the network file server. Your system administrator will also assign the correct read and write privileges for each user. To make group appointments, you must have write privileges; to read appointments, you just need read privileges. Once the directory is established, the next step is to use the Appointment Scheduler to create the groups.

Choose Groups from the File menu to open the Subscribe to a Group dialog box, as shown in Figure 15.8. Choose New and enter the name of the group to which you want to belong. Next, type in the name and full path of the directory on the network that is associated with your group. Each person who wants to join a group must follow these steps until everyone has joined. Once you are a member of a group, you can set and cancel appointments for the whole group.

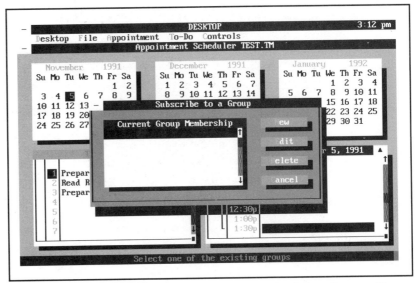

Figure 15.8: Set up the appropriate groups in the Subscribe to a Group dialog box

To see an appointment made by another member of your group, you must log onto the network before you start the Appointment Scheduler. When you open the Appointment Scheduler, you will be notified of the appointment.

You may belong to several different groups if you wish; you are not restricted to just one. For example, if you are a project manager, you can belong to the marketing group as well as the engineering group, and be notified of meetings held by both groups.

To make an appointment for a group, complete the entries in the Make Appointment dialog box, and select Group rather than Make. Choose the group for which you are making the appointment from the entries in the Select Group dialog box and select Make.

You can edit a group appointment just like any other appointment, except that a message box opens reminding you that if you edit the appointment, you will change it for all members of the group.

To edit group membership information, choose Groups from the File menu, select the group you want to work with from the list, choose Edit, and enter the new information into the group name or group directory text boxes. If you want to remove yourself from a group, select Groups from the File menu, choose the appropriate group from the list, and use Delete. Your name will be removed from the group list, and any subsequent appointments set for the group will not appear in your Appointment Scheduler.

MAKING A TO-DO LIST

The to-do list is completely independent of the time planner and the monthly calendar. You can enter up to 80 items in your to-do list, although only a few of them can be displayed on the screen at one time. You can attach a priority to each entry—from 1 for the highest priority to 10 for the lowest—and the list will be displayed in priority order. You can also attach a notepad to each item if you wish. The items in the to-do list are displayed only for as long as you specify when you create each item; then they are removed from the list.

There are several ways to create a new entry in the list:

- Position the cursor on a blank line in the to-do list, enter the name of the item, and press Enter.

- Position the cursor on a blank line in the to-do list and press Enter.

- Click the mouse on a blank line in the to-do list.

- Choose the New To-Do entry from the To-Do menu.

Any of these methods opens the New To-Do entry box on the screen, as shown in Figure 15.9.

Enter the information into the screen as follows:

- **Description.** Enter the name of the item in less than 24 characters. This is the text that appears in the to-do list shown on the main Appointment Scheduler screen.

- **Start Date.** This is normally filled automatically with today's date.

- **End Date.** Enter the last date you want this item to be active. If you do not specify an end date, the item stays on the list until you delete it manually.

- **Priority.** Assign a priority from 1 to 10. Items in the list are displayed in this priority order. Most people find a three- or four-level priority sufficient; more levels than this tend to confuse things. Try categorizing your to-do list into the four categories of vital, important, useful, and wasteful.

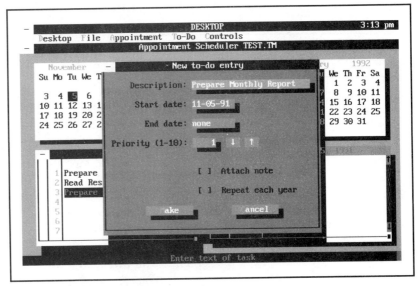

Figure 15.9: The New To-Do entry box

- **Attach Note.** Press Enter or click to mark this box if you want to attach a note to the entry. A notepad will open when you select the Make button to save the entry. The letter *N* beside the item in the to-do list indicates that a note is attached.

- **Repeat Each Year.** Mark this box to display the reminder note for the same time interval next year. This is especially useful for birthday or anniversary reminders.

Select the Make button to confirm your entry. If you selected Attach Note to add a note to your item, a notepad will open, ready to receive your text.

When you return to the main Appointment Scheduler screen, your entry is displayed in the to-do list according to the priority you selected.

If you want to delete an item from your to-do list, position the cursor over the item in the list and press the Enter key, or click on the item with the mouse. Alternatively, position the cursor over the entry and choose Delete To-Do Entry from the To-Do menu. In either case, you will see a dialog box containing the following options:

- **Delete** deletes the item from your to-do list.

- **Edit** opens the New To-Do entry box so you can edit your entry.

- Use **Alter Note** if you want to keep the to-do item intact but want to change or review the contents of the Notepad.

- **Cancel** cancels and closes the dialog box and returns you to the main Appointment Scheduler screen.

If you forgot to attach a notepad to your to-do list item when you created it, you can add one now by positioning the cursor on the item and selecting Attach Note from the To-Do menu. A Notepads window opens on top of the Appointment Scheduler. The top line of the notepad contains the text of the to-do item, the date and the time, and the priority you assigned to the item; the rest of the screen is blank for you to add your text. All the usual Notepads text-editing features are available. The Notepads file is created in the same directory as the Appointment Scheduler file with the same file name. The file-name extension is a number based on an internal Appointment Scheduler counter. Press the Escape key to return to the Appointment Scheduler.

AUTOMATICALLY LOADING YOUR SCHEDULE

If you run Desktop in memory-resident mode, you can add a parameter to your AUTOEXEC.BAT file to open the Appointment Scheduler and display the day's time planner and to-do list every time you boot up your system. Add the following line to your AUTOEXEC.BAT file to make the Appointment Scheduler open when you boot up your system:

DESKTOP /RA

☑ Make sure that the DESKTOP entry is the last entry in your AUTOEXEC.BAT file, because any commands that come after it will not be executed until after you leave Desktop.

The /R parameter loads Desktop in memory-resident mode, and the A parameter automatically opens the Appointment Scheduler. All the other parts of Desktop are also fully functional at this point.

If you do not have an active Appointment Scheduler file containing appointments, Desktop comes up in the main screen as if you had loaded it with the

DESKTOP /R

parameter in your AUTOEXEC.BAT file.

CUSTOMIZING THE APPOINTMENT SCHEDULER

You can move, resize, open, or close any of the Appointment Scheduler windows to arrange the display to fit your needs best, but there are also several options in the Controls menu that you can use to personalize the Appointment Scheduler. Figure 15.10 shows the Controls menu.

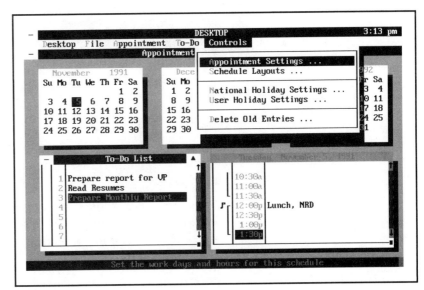

Figure 15.10: The Controls menu

To change the work days, method of date entry, or the start and stop time for your work day, select the Appointment Settings option from the Controls menu. A dialog box opens, as shown in Figure 15.11.

You can change any of the following settings:

- **Work Days.** Select which days of the week are your work days. If you free-lance or do consulting work, all the days may be work days.

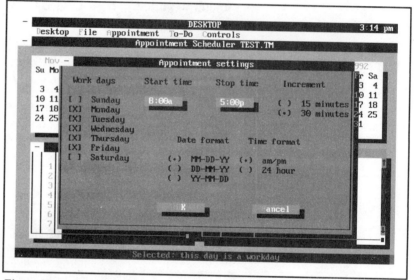

Figure 15.11: The Appointment Settings dialog box

- **Start Time.** Specify the time you want your work day to begin. This is normally 8:00 a.m., but if you do shift work—or have flextime—you can select a different start time.

- **Stop Time.** This is the time you want your work day to end, and is normally 5:00 p.m. If you do shift work, have flextime, or if you make evening appointments, change the stop time to suit your needs.

- **Increment.** Choose between a 15- or 30-minute increment for the time planner, depending on the degree of accuracy you require.

- **Date Format.** The Appointment Scheduler offers three different date formats. You can use MM-DD-YY if you work in the United States, DD-MM-YY if you work in Europe, or YY-MM-DD if you work for the military.

- **Time Format.** Similarly, you can choose between two different time formats: am/pm or 24-hour.

When you are satisfied with your choices, select the OK button to save them and return to the main Appointment Scheduler screen. Your new settings are now in effect.

To rearrange the size and arrangement of the three Appointment Scheduler windows, choose Schedule Layouts from the Controls menu. Figure 15.12 shows the Default Screen Layout dialog box. On the left of the dialog box is a list of the default settings labeled Style A through Style E. On the right side of this dialog box is a small diagram that represents the location of the three windows on your screen. Style A has a one-month calender at the top left of the screen,

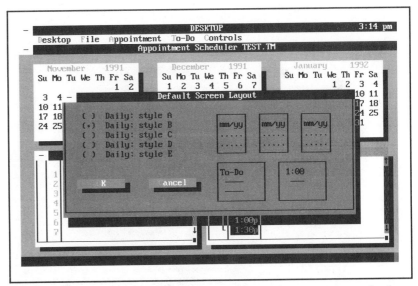

Figure 15.12: Use the Default Screen Layout dialog box to rearrange the three Appointment Scheduler windows

with the to-do list at the lower left and the list of appointments occupying the right half of the screen. Style B shows a three-month calendar across the top of the screen and contracts the appointment list to the lower right. Style C shows just a to-do list on the left and an appointment list on the right. Style D shows only a one-month calendar at the upper left and an appointment list across the bottom. Style E expands the calendar to three-months across the top of the screen and keeps the appointment list at the bottom. Select the style that most appeals to you and choose OK. The Appointment Scheduler changes to the new style as soon as you leave the dialog box.

Recurring appointments are not made on holidays.

To avoid scheduling appointments on holidays, designate which holidays you want to observe by using two selections in the Controls menu. Use the National Holidays dialog box as shown in Figure 15.13 to confirm the statutory holidays. If there is a mark in the box opposite the holiday, it is turned on. To change the setting, select the holiday and press Enter to toggle the setting on or off.

If you work outside the U.S.A., you can set additional holidays with the User Holiday Settings from the Controls menu, as Figure 15.14 shows. Any day designated as a holiday is shown on the

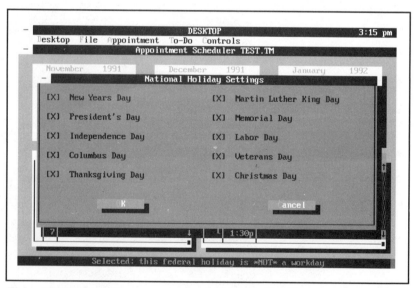

Figure 15.13: Confirm your statutory holidays in the National Holidays dialog box

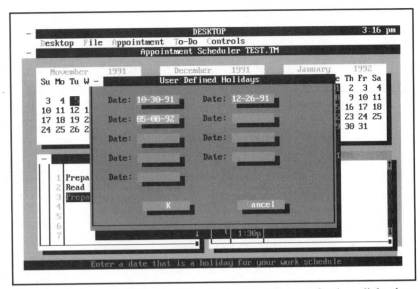

Figure 15.14: Set additional holidays in the User Holiday Settings dialog box

time planner screen with an asterisk beside it. Add new holidays by entering them into the Date boxes. Remember to use the format you chose in the Appointments Settings for the date entry here.

To prevent your appointments file from growing too large, delete old appointments from the file. Choose Delete Old Entries from the Controls menu. A dialog box opens, asking you for a cutoff date. All appointments with dates before this date are deleted when you choose the Delete button. Use the Cancel button if you do not want to delete old appointments.

LOADING AND SAVING APPOINTMENT SCHEDULER FILES

To load an existing Appointment Scheduler file, use the Load option in the File menu. The File Load dialog box opens, listing all the files in the current directory that have the .TM file-name extension. Select the desired file from the list and choose Load. When you load a file in this way, the Appointment Scheduler file you were working with is saved before the new file is loaded.

Files in the Appointment Scheduler are saved when you click on the close box with the mouse or when you exit the Appointment Scheduler. You can also save your file using Save from the File menu. If you want to save your appointments in a file with a different name, specify the new name in the Save File to Disk dialog box. You can also use Autosave to save your files at intervals that you specify. Remember, Autosave is global to the Appointment Scheduler, Notepads, Outlines, and the Macro Editor. That is, when you turn Autosave on in one of these applications, you turn it on in all of them. Likewise, if you turn it off in one of them you turn it off in all of them. To use Autosave, first turn it on and then specify the time interval in minutes.

PRINTING AN APPOINTMENT SCHEDULE

The Appointment Scheduler has several different printing options, shown in Figure 15.15.

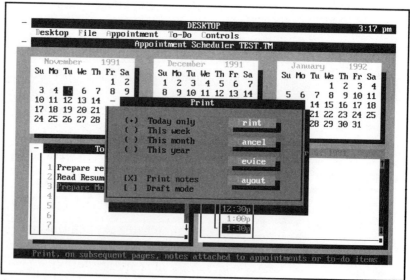

Figure 15.15: Appointment Scheduler printing options

You can choose from:

- Today only

- This week

- This month

- This year

Click the Print Notes checkbox if you want to print the notepads associated with an appointment or an item in the to-do list. The notepads will be printed at the end of your schedule. To print in the faster but lower-quality draft mode, check the Draft mode box. Not all printers support draft mode.

Choose Device to confirm or reselect your printer from the list; you can also choose the port to send the print to, or you can send the report to a disk file for later printing.

Layout lets you choose the format of your appointment report; you can specify the size of the report as well as the contents, as Figure 15.16 shows. You can choose from:

- US Legal

- US Letter

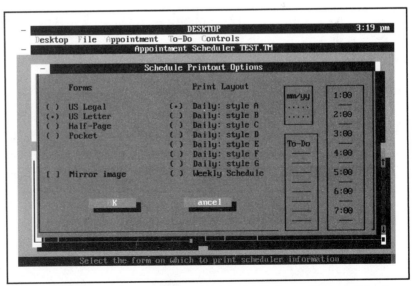

Figure 15.16: Select report options in the Schedule Printout Options dialog box

- Half-page

- Pocket

If you use the small day-planner books, choose Pocket and you can add your schedule directly into your book. If you use a Day-Timer or a Franklin Day Planner, you can buy blank forms that correspond to the form types in the Appointment Scheduler Layout dialog box. The printout style options are shown on the right side of this dialog box. They range from Style A through Style G, and Weekly, giving you eight different options. Select the Mirror Image checkbox if you want to invert the report.

Select OK when you have completed your selections in the Schedule Printout Options dialog box, then select Print to print the report. Press Cancel at any time if you change your mind and want to return to the Appointment Scheduler. An example of the Style A report is shown in Figure 15.17.

RUNNING A PROGRAM AT A SPECIFIC TIME

You can use the Appointment Scheduler to run a program at a specific time if you use a special character in the Note text box in the Make Appointment dialog box. The broken vertical bar (¦) character has a special meaning when you use it in this way. The general form of the entry is

> *note¦file name*

Do not use spaces around the ¦ character.

where *note* is any text you want to associate with the alarm and *file name* is the name of the file you want to run. For example, use this feature when you want to start programs that take a long time to load or programs that can run without any operator interaction, such as backup programs that back up to tape. You can schedule the program for lunchtime or after work.

If you want to load WordStar at 1:00 p.m., enter

Run WordStar¦WS.EXE

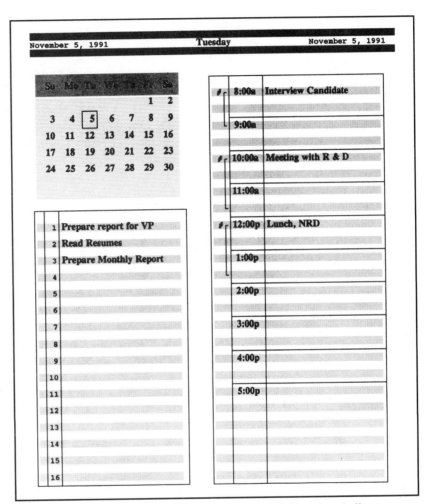

Figure 15.17: Example printout with today's schedule and to-do list

Include the file-name extension of .BAT, .COM, or .EXE when specifying program names. If the program you want to run is in a different directory, you must enter the whole path name unless it is already included in your path statement.

opposite the 1:00 p.m. time slot in the time-planner display, or enter it into the Note text box in the Make Appointment screen. At 1:00 p.m., a window will open, asking if you want to run the program. If you select the OK button, WordStar runs just as though you had entered the name from the DOS command line at that moment.

To make WordStar run without asking your permission, enter

¦WS.EXE

without any text in front of the file name. When the alarm goes off, DOS issues the program name and the program loads automatically.

If you want to load a program that needs a large number of command-line parameters, there may not be room for all of them in the small text-entry box. If so, create a batch file that contains the parameters in the correct sequence and enter the name of this batch file into the text box instead. The batch file runs at the specified time, loading the application program and passing all the parameters to it as though you had entered them from the DOS command line.

Similarly, you can load a Notepads file automatically. Enter

¦**STAFFMTG.TXT**

into the text box opposite 2:00 p.m. in the time planner, and select a ten-minute advance alarm in the Make Appointment screen. When the alarm goes off, the file STAFFMTG.TXT containing your notes from last week's meeting is loaded into a notepad. You now have ten minutes to review your notes before the meeting starts.

> Remember to select the Activate Everywhere option from Macro Activation in the File menu before using macros in your appointments.

Finally, you can use macros with appointments if you include the macro name in the Note box after the broken vertical bar symbol. The macro name must be enclosed in angle brackets. To run a macro called <CTRLF1> at a specific time, enter

¦**<CTRLF1>**

into the Note box in the Make Appointment screen. Macros are not just restricted to the Appointment Scheduler. You can use them from other places in DOS and you don't need to create many batch files to do the job.

CHAPTER

16

Using the Database

The database in desktop stands alone. You can use it for any database purpose, ranging from a patient address list to a catalog of your stock photography slides. You can prepare the text of a form letter in a notepad and then merge that letter with the addresses in your database to produce personalized letters. You can also use files originally made with dBASE by Ashton-Tate (or any program that makes a dBASE-compatible file) because the Desktop Database file format is compatible with dBASE. This compatibility lets you make ad hoc queries against a dBASE file from Desktop without having to load dBASE.

WHAT IS A DATABASE?

A database is any organized collection of information. Common examples are the patient record cards at your dentist or the personnel files at work. When this collection grows too large and cumbersome for a person to manage, the system is often computerized. A computerized database consists of two main parts:

- The database software. This is the program that organizes the data. It usually allows you to add, delete, sort, and update the information in the database. A large computerized database is often referred to as a database management system or DBMS.

- Data, the actual information contained in the database. A database can contain information on just about anything that is useful to you or your company. It usually consists of items that contain similar elements: for example, addresses that include street names and numbers, cities, and states. Databases often contain tax records, club membership lists, company financial records, personnel data, and so forth.

Here are some of the advantages of a computerized rather than a manual database system:

- Manual, paper-based systems occupy lots of space (a file cabinet). Computerized systems are much smaller (a few disks).

- Accurate, up-to-date information is available at all times in a computerized database.

- Speed is one of the primary advantages of a computerized database. The computer can search the database much faster than a human.

- Using a computer to maintain the data removes the need for a human to spend time updating all the paper records.

There are many different database models, but most systems developed recently tend to be *relational* or have a large component of the relational model. In such databases, the data appear to the user as a set of tables.

DESKTOP DATABASE FILES

Before you learn more about the Desktop Database, you need to understand the basic components of the Database system, including the different file types and some of the limitations on data storage:

- A database *file* is a group of records. A file may contain a list of the names, addresses, and telephone numbers of a number of people—say, photographers.

- A database *record* is a collection of fields. For example, one database record could contain all the details for one of the photographers.

- A database *field* is one of the pieces of information in the record, such as the photographer's first name, street address, or work phone number.

The Desktop Database has three different types of files associated with it: database files, record files, and form files.

> If you load a dBASE file with more than 10,000 records, you can only read it, not change it.

- *Database files* contain the actual data. They have the file-name extension .DBF and are compatible with dBASE files. If you try to load a dBASE file that contains more than 10,000 records, the file is truncated to fit.

- *Record files* have the file-name extension .REC and contain information on various Desktop Database settings like sort settings, display options, and so on. These files are specific to Desktop Database and have nothing to do with dBASE. For your database to work properly, your database files and your record files must have the same file name and either the .DBF or the .REC extension, respectively.

- *Form files* have the file-name extension .FOR. They are standard Notepads files that allow you to view data in a particular way. For example, one might contain the text of a letter you want to send to all the photographers in your database. You can make your own form files or, if you prefer, have Desktop Database make one for you with the same file name as the database and record files, but with the .FOR extension.

These limits only apply to files inside Desktop; they do not apply to dBASE files used in dBASE.

There are several limitations on the amount of data you can maintain in a Desktop Database:

- There is a maximum of 10,000 records per database, meaning you could expand your photographer's database to include up to 10,000 photographers.

- There is a maximum of 4,000 characters per record, meaning you can keep up to 4,000 characters of information on each of the photographers.

- There is a maximum of 128 fields per record, meaning you can keep up to 128 different pieces of information on each photographer as long as you stay below the limit of 4,000 characters per record.

- There is a maximum of 70 characters in each character field, meaning you can keep up to 70 characters in each character field for each photographer in the database.

- There is a maximum of 19 digits in each numeric field. The size of the entry is determined by the size of the field and the number of decimal places you specify.

Before you start working with your database, you must make several important decisions on record structure, field size and type, and field names. Desktop Database supports several different data types.

The memo field type is supported in dBASE but not in Desktop Database. If your dBASE file contains memo fields, they will be ignored in Desktop Database.

- Character data are any data consisting of letters or numbers that are not used in calculations in dBASE. For example, in addition to names and addresses, you could enter social security numbers, phone numbers, and zip codes as character data. If you enter zip codes as numeric data, the beginning zero (if there is one) will always be suppressed. You can have up to 70 characters in any field in Desktop Database (though dBASE supports up to 254). If you are working with dBASE files, remember that any fields with more than 70 characters will be truncated. The default field size for character data is one character.

- Numeric data are values used in calculations. Desktop Database does not perform any calculations on the data (though dBASE does).

- Logical data represent the condition of true or false. True is represented by *T, t, Y,* or *y,* and false by *F, f, N,* or *n*. You can use an entry in a logical field to divide your database into two parts. If you want to differentiate between people who have and have not renewed their subscription to your photography newsletter, for instance, use a logical field. The default for a logical field is *F* for false. Logical fields are always one character long.

- Date fields are eight-character fields that can only contain dates in the form *mm/dd/yy,* where *yy* is assumed to be in this century. The default date field contains 00/00/00. You can use dates for sorting data, but you cannot use them in dBASE formulas.

The other two criteria you must define are the field name and the field size. The *field name* is the name of an item in a database record. For example, for an address list you would need to enter the first name, last name, street address, city, state, and zip code. It makes sense to call the fields by very obvious names like FIRST NAME, LAST NAME, ADDRESS, CITY, STATE, and ZIP. For a horticultural database, you would need fields such as PLANT NAME, LATIN NAME, CLIMATE, SOIL TYPE, as well as logical fields for DECIDUOUS, EVERGREEN, SUN, SHADE, and so on. The field name must be no longer than ten characters and cannot begin with a number. All lowercase letters are converted into uppercase, and the Desktop database automatically replaces spaces between words by underscore characters (so PLANT NAME becomes PLANT_NAME). Blank names are not allowed.

> ◀ dBASE and other databases do not allow spaces in field names; you must type in underscores. In the Desktop Database, you must type in the underscores only when specifying fields that have already been named.

The *field size* is the size of the field, in characters. It reserves space in the database for future additions. To select the right field size, find the length of the longest item you anticipate including in your database and then add a few more characters for good measure. For example, if the longest city name you can think of is Sacramento at ten letters, make the field length 20 so that it can include Lake of the Woods (17 letters) in Minnesota. Seventy characters is the maximum size for any character field in a Desktop Database. If you need more space, consider breaking the entry into two sections. For example, if you need to include extensive comments in an entry, call the first field COMMENTS1 and the next COMMENTS2 to create enough space. A numeric field can be up to 19 characters. The decimal point counts as one character. The default is one digit with no decimals. Date fields are always limited to eight characters, and logical fields to one character.

Once you have entered a field type and field size into the Database, you cannot change them without creating another database. However, you can edit the field name if you have made a spelling mistake.

CREATING A DATABASE FROM SCRATCH

For the example database, you will make a mailing list for a photographic newsletter. The database will maintain accurate, up-to-date mailing addresses for the newsletter, make address labels for the mailing, record which subscribers have paid the yearly subscription, and send out renewal-reminder letters to subscribers in arrears. You can use many of the items in this example database as the basis for your own database.

DEFINING THE DATABASE STRUCTURE

Now that you know what the database is for, you can define its structure. Information on each subscriber should include first name, last name, address, city, state, zip code, and subscription-status information.

Select Databases from the Desktop main menu and enter a new file name into the Database Files Load dialog box. Call the file PHOTO.DBF. The next screen to appear is the Field Editor, shown in Figure 16.1, which is used to establish all the fields in the database.

To create the fields needed in the Photo database:

1. Enter the name of the first field into the Field Name box. You can use upper- or lowercase letters because all names

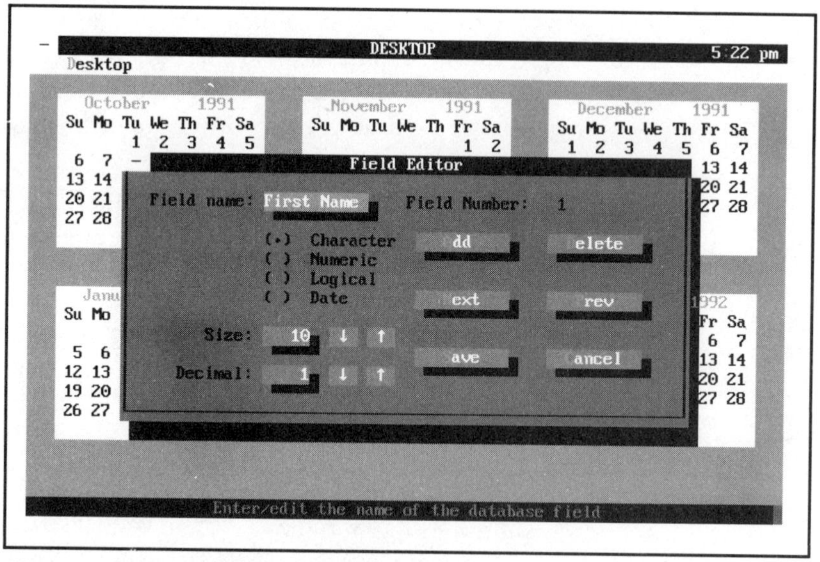

If you want to use the Autodialer to dial phone numbers from the database, *make sure* that you position the phone-number field before any other fields likely to contain groups of numbers. If you happen to put the zip code before the phone number, the Autodialer will try to dial the zip code!

Figure 16.1: The Field Editor screen

are automatically converted into uppercase, with the underscore character representing spaces. Since the field-name length is restricted to ten characters, the name of the last field, Subscription Status, must be abbreviated to SUB_STATUS.

2. Select the type of data the field will contain from Character, Numeric, Logical, or Date. All the fields in the Photo database except one are character data; SUB_STATUS is a logical field.

3. Select the size of the field in characters. This varies from field to field.

4. Select the number of decimal places for numeric data. This does not apply to the Photo database, since it does not contain any numeric data.

5. Click the Add button to add the field to the database. The field is created and the screen clears, ready to accept input of the next field. Each field is numbered automatically by Desktop Database.

When you have added all the fields needed for the Photo database, click the Save button to save all the entries in the PHOTO.DBF file. The field names, sizes, and types for the Photo database are summarized in Table 16.1.

Table 16.1: Field Names, Types, and Sizes for the Photo Database

FIELD NAME	FIELD TYPE	FIELD SIZE
FIRST_NAME	Character	10
LAST_NAME	Character	20
ADDRESS	Character	50
CITY	Character	25
STATE	Character	12
ZIP	Character	10
SUB_STATUS	Logical	1

After you save the fields, the dialog box is replaced by the form file, which displays an empty record. A line of dots corresponding to the size of the field is displayed opposite each field name in Browse mode. (If you're in Edit mode, the screen is divided into columns.) These are useful guides when you start entering the data for the database, since it shows the maximum length for each field. The default F (false) is shown opposite the logical field SUB_STATUS.

Other options on the Field Editor screen are as follows:

- **Next** selects the next field, if there is one.

- **Delete** deletes the selected field.

- **Prev** selects the previous field, if there is one.

- **Cancel** cancels the database creation and exits Desktop Database without saving the database.

Now you should be ready to enter the subscriber data into the database, one record at a time. These data are summarized in Table 16.2. To keep things simple, there are only seven subscribers in this example; a real photographic newsletter would have many more subscribers.

Table 16.2: Example Data from the Photo Database

FIRST NAME	LAST NAME	ADDRESS	CITY	STATE	ZIP	SUB_STATUS
Don	Hegbert	879 Back Lane	Todmorden	MA	07381	F
Jim	Jones	123 Canal Street	Rochdale	MN	09876	T
Al	Smith	475 Gasworks Alley	Cleckheaton	PA	13254	T
Allen	Shute	7788 Bradford Road	Macclesfield	IA	50312	F
Pete	Pedersen	4 Northern Way	Huddersfield	MA	71542	F
Sue	Susan	673A Hightofts Road	Giggleswick	CA	95819	T
Abe	Riley	Mill Lane	Golcar	CA	96678	T

Type in the data for the first field on Don Hegbert and press Enter. If you make a mistake, just use the Backspace key to remove it, then retype the information. Table 16.3 shows the other keys you can use to edit your entries. When you have entered all the information on Don, press F8 or choose the Add New Record option from the Edit menu to add the next new record. Continue adding records until you have entered the data for all seven subscribers.

Several shortcut function keys are available on the message line as you enter these data. Press F8 to add another record to the database. F6 loads and displays the next record in alphabetical order, if there is one, and F5 loads and displays the previous record. Use F4 to go from the first record to the last record. The F7 shortcut key provides direct access to the search facilities in Desktop Database (discussed in full later in this chapter).

EDITING EXISTING RECORDS

As subscribers to the newsletter change their addresses, or as you add and remove subscribers, you need to edit or update the information in the database. To edit an existing record, first locate and display the record on the screen using the shortcut function keys shown on the message line: F4 (First), F5 (Previous), or F6 (Next). Alternatively, you can use the Goto Record option from the Search menu to go directly to a record. The number of the record being displayed is always shown at the top of the main Desktop Database screen. With Goto Record, you access the record by number: once you have located the right record, move to the field you want to change and type in the new information.

By default, you edit the database in overstrike rather than insert mode—that is, the characters you type replace the existing entry. If you want to edit in insert mode, press the Insert key on your keyboard. This way, existing text will be pushed to the right as you insert text in front of it. When you finish editing the data, press the Enter key to add the new information to the field. The data are automatically updated and saved and the cursor moves to the next field.

To add a new subscriber, you must add a new record to the database. Open the Edit menu and choose Add New Record, or just press

Table 16.3: Editing Keys in Desktop Database

KEY	FUNCTION
Backspace	Deletes character to left of cursor
Enter	Ends a field entry
Tab	Moves to the next field
Shift-Tab	Moves to the previous field
Alt-*n*	Inserts a character from the extended ASCII character set. Press and hold the Alt key and then enter the decimal code for the ASCII character you want
←	Moves cursor left one character
→	Moves cursor right one character
Ctrl-←	Moves cursor left one word
Ctrl-→	Moves cursor right one word
Home	Moves to the beginning of the field, record, window, or file
End	Moves to the end of the field, record, window, or file
↑	Moves cursor up one line
↓	Moves cursor down one line
PgUp	Moves text up one window
PgDn	Moves text down one window
Ctrl-PgUp	Scrolls display up one line without moving cursor
Ctrl-PgDn	Scrolls display down one line without moving cursor
Home Home	Moves to the beginning of the window
End End	Moves to the end of the window
Ctrl-Home	Moves to the beginning of the form
Ctrl-End	Moves to the end of the form

F8. The screen shows an empty record, ready to accept your input. Enter the new subscriber information into each field, pressing Tab or Enter to go to the next field. The new record is added to the database when you press Enter after the last field. A new record may be added at any point in the database.

To delete a record from the database, open the Edit menu and choose Delete Record. Delete Record does not immediately erase the record; instead, the record is marked for deletion and is deleted the next time you pack the database, which permanently deletes marked records from the database. Until you pack the database, the records are still in the database and you can use the Undelete Records option in the Edit menu to bring them back into view.

At times, you may not want all the records in the database to be viewable. In such cases, you can hide records from view. A hidden record is still part of the database; it just won't be displayed or printed and cannot be deleted. To hide a record, choose Hide Current Record from the Edit menu. The record displayed on the screen is hidden and the next record is displayed.

To restore any hidden records, use the Select All Records option from the Edit menu. All previously hidden records will be restored to view.

If you want to look at all the fields in many records at the same time, select the Browse mode from the File menu. All the fields in each record in your database are displayed on the same line on your screen. A check mark appears next to Browse in the menu to show that it is selected. Choose Browse again to remove the check mark and return to the single-record display. All Database functions, including editing and printing, are available in Browse mode. Figure 16.2 shows the Photo database displayed in Browse mode.

With a large database, some fields will run off the right side of the screen. To see these fields, press the Tab key to move across the screen, and Shift-Tab to move back again. If you are using a mouse, just hold down the left button and move the mouse beyond the borders of the screen to move horizontally or vertically across the database.

If you print your database while you are in Browse mode, the field names will print across the top of each page followed by the data in the records, one on each line of the printout.

Use the Pack Database option when you want to remove records from the database permanently. As your database grows, you may approach the maximum record limit. If you have a large number of deleted records marked, pack the database to recover space.

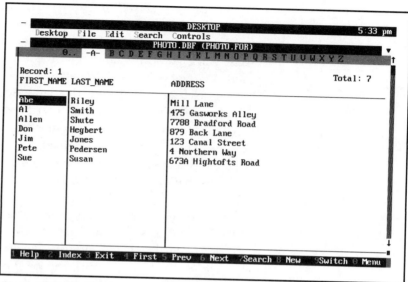

Figure 16.2: The Photo database shown in Browse mode

You can change the name of any field but you cannot change its size or type, nor can you add new fields to the database.

Finally, you may decide to change the name of one or more of the fields in your database. To do this, choose Edit Fields from the Edit menu. This brings up the Field Editor that you used to create the fields when you first created the database. Enter the new field name and select Save to record the changes into the .DBF file. Editing the field name takes care of the changes to the .DBF file. However, since the field now has a new name you must also use Notepads to make a corresponding change to the form file.

TRANSFERRING AND APPENDING RECORDS

You may want to create a new database that contains a specific group of records from an existing database. One way to do this is to reenter all the data into the new database by hand. A better way is to use the Transfer function from the File menu—that way it's done automatically. Transfer allows you to move records from one database to another. To transfer a group of records from one database to another, follow these steps:

1. Start Desktop Database and open the database that contains the records you want to transfer.

2. Choose the records you want to transfer with Select Record from the Edit menu.

3. Choose Transfer from the File menu. This opens the Transfer dialog box. Enter the name of the destination database into which you want to move the selected records. This database must already exist, as Transfer cannot create a database.

4. If the destination database contains a field that does not exist in the original database, the Field Defaults dialog box opens, asking you to enter a default value for this field. Type in the value you want to use for this field, or leave it empty if you don't want anything in the field.

If the original database contains fields not found in the destination database, they will not be transferred.

When you have confirmed the last default entry, the transfer is made. The records are sorted according to the order in the Sort Database selection in the Edit menu.

The Append command from the File menu allows you to add all the records in a database to the current database. For example, if you buy a mailing list from a photography magazine, you can add it to your newsletter mailing list with the Append command. To join two databases together, follow these steps:

1. Start Desktop Database and load the file containing the database to which you want to add records.

2. Choose Append from the File menu. This opens the Append dialog box. Enter the name of the database you want to append to your original database and click the Select button.

3. If your original database contains fields not found in the database you are appending, the Field Defaults dialog box opens so you can enter a value for that field.

If the database you are appending contains a field that your original database does not, it is ignored and not appended.

When you have confirmed the last entry, the new database is appended to your original database. The new records are sorted according to the order in the Sort Database selection in the Edit menu.

You now know how to select a set of records in a database and transfer them to another database, and also how to join two databases together. In the next section you will learn about sorting and searching your database.

SORTING AND SEARCHING THE DATABASE

The Desktop Database has the ability to reorganize your data. For example, if you have a bulk mailing permit, the post office accepts mail sorted into groups of zip codes. With Database, you can easily arrange your mailing labels into zip-code order.

To sort the address list for the photography newsletter into zip-code order, select Sort Database from the Edit menu. You will see the screen shown in Figure 16.3. The screen displays the name of the current sort field and contains several options:

- **Next** selects the next field as the sort field.

- **Prev** selects the previous field as the sort field.

- **Sort** performs the sort using the selected field.

- **Cancel** cancels the sort and closes the dialog box.

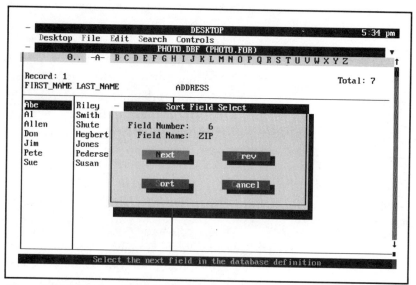

Figure 16.3: The Sort Field Select screen

As the database records are sorted into the requested order, a message asks you to wait for the sort to finish—except when the database is small. Database can only sort on one field at a time, using the first 12 characters in the field.

You can also use Database, for example, to determine how many subscribers you have in the 95819 zip-code area. Choose Select Records from the Edit menu; you will see the screen shown in Figure 16.4. You can specify up to eight fields for the selection process. Record selection is made as follows:

- **Field Name.** Enter the name of the field(s) you want to use as the basis for the selection.

- **Field Criteria.** Enter the actual criteria you want to use as the match for the field you selected.

To find out how many subscribers you have in the 95819 zip-code area, enter **ZIP** as the Field Name and **95819** as the Field Criteria. Choose Select to search the database for all the fields that match the

You must type in any underscores. Spaces are not allowed in select or search field names.

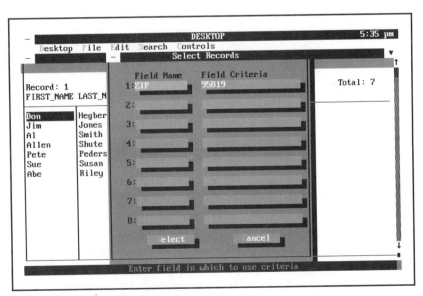

Figure 16.4: The Select Records screen

There is no equiva-
lent of the DOS *
wildcard.

field criterion. All records that do not match the criteria will be hidden. You can now use this information to make a direct mailing to this specific zip code.

Since you can specify up to eight field names as selectors, your selection criteria can grow quite complex. Additionally, Database allows you to enter a *wildcard*. The character represents any single character. For instance, the zip code 9581? matches all zip codes from 95810 to 95819.

You can specify ranges of numbers. For example,

95000..95999

matches all zip codes from 95000 to 95999. Similarly, you can select zip codes greater than a particular number. For instance,

95..

selects all zip codes whose first two digits are greater than or equal to 95. By the same token, you can select zip codes that are smaller than a particular number. For example,

..19

which selects all zip codes with the last two digits less than or equal to 19.

You can also specify a range with letters, which is useful for names, cities, and states. To select all last names from *A* to *C*, enter

A..C

To make the selection more specific, enter

A..CAT

which matches fields from A to CAT. In these range selections, the case of the letters is ignored.

You can view the data in your database in other ways by using the commands in the Search menu, which is shown in Figure 16.5.

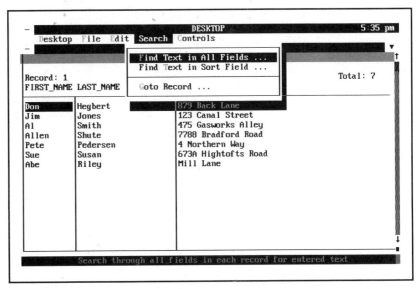

Figure 16.5: Search menu selections

These commands search through your database, looking for particular text:

- **Find Text in All Fields** searches all the fields in your database for the search string.

- **Find Text in Sort Field** restricts the search to the field that was last used as a sort field. In many situations, Find Text in Sort Field will be faster since the search is restricted to the sort field. Use the Sort Database command in the Edit menu to change to different sort criteria.

Both of these options have the following suboptions:

- **Search All Records** starts the search at the beginning of the database and includes all records, even hidden and deleted ones.

- **Search Selected Records** searches for the specified text in previously selected records.

- **Search from Current Record** begins the search with the current record.

You now know how to sort your database by any given field and how to search for specific occurrences of text.

The next section shows how to make address labels from your subscriber database. Then you will learn how to make form letters for people whose subscriptions have not been renewed.

CUSTOMIZING THE FORM FILE

The form file used for data entry into your database must contain an entry for each of the fields in your database. The same is not true of other form files, however. You can make as many form files as you want for your database. Each can present a different view of your data, and some can take advantage of just a portion of the data. When you design the form, remember to enclose the field names in square brackets. For example, to insert a person's name into the form file, type

[FIRST_NAME] [LAST_NAME]

When you load your database, the information from the database replaces the field names in the form. An example will make this clearer.

PRINTING ADDRESS LABELS   Suppose you want to make a form file in a notepad that produces address labels for your newsletter, assuming that your printer can handle adhesive address labels. First, open a notepad and create a new file called ADDRESS.FOR. Then enter the field names into the notepad, as shown in Figure 16.6. In this example, the only field from the database that you are *not* using is the subscription status field, SUB_STATUS. Be sure that the entries in the notepad file match the field names in the database exactly; otherwise, no records will be retrieved from the database and nothing will appear on the form.

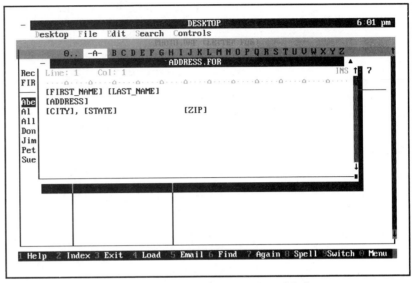

Figure 16.6: Entering the field names for an address label

You must provide any punctuation required in the address, including underscores, because the Desktop Database only provides the data themselves; the rest must come from the Notepad. Leave a space between [FIRST_NAME] and [LAST_NAME] in the notepad so that the names are written with a space between them. Also add a comma and a space between [CITY] and [STATE]. The position of the abbreviation for the state on this line of the label depends on the length of the city name, as you can see here:

Todmorden, MA

Rochdale, MN

Cleckheaton, PA

Macclesfield, IA

Huddersfield, MA

Giggleswick, CA

Golcar, CA

To see this, click back into the database and choose Select Load Form from the File menu and ADDRESS.FOR from the Load Form menu. If you want to fix the position of a field, place a tab where you want it. Open ADDRESS.FOR in the notepad and use a tab with the [ZIP] field. The example addresses just shown will look like this, with the zip codes aligned:

Todmorden, MA	07381
Rochdale, MN	09876
Cleckheaton, PA	13254
Macclesfield, IA	50312
Huddersfield, MA	71542
Giggleswick, CA	95819
Golcar, CA	96678

As you leave the notepad where you made the change, the results are reflected on the screen.

To print the database onto small adhesive address labels, you must first define the size of the page with Page Layout from the Controls menu. Set the page size to a length suitable for your labels (say six lines), set the left margin to an appropriate setting, and set the top and bottom margins to zero. Finally, choose the Save Settings option in Notepads so that you can use these settings when you print the data in your database the next time you use Desktop.

To print the address labels, return to Desktop Database, load the PHOTO.DBF database file, and then choose Load Form from the File menu. Load the form file you have just created in the notepad, ADDRESS.FOR, and see the record on the screen displayed in the new format. Now load the labels into your printer and choose one of the options from the Print selection in the File menu. You can choose which device you want to print to from the usual Desktop list of device names, or write to a file for printing later. Make the appropriate choices from the lists and start printing the address labels.

If you want to enter more data into your database or edit existing data, first make sure that you reload the original form file from the notepad. This lets you see all the data in your database as well as all the field names. The form file used for data entry has the same name as the database file but has the .FOR file-name extension.

PRINTING FORM LETTERS   In the next example, you will write a form letter reminding subscribers that you have not received their dues. Then you will merge the names and addresses from the database into the form letter based on the setting of the logical field SUB_STATUS.

First, prepare the text of the letter in a notepad, as shown in Figure 16.7, and call the file LETTER.FOR. The letter is a short reminder that $17 is due for subscription renewal. Remember to use square brackets around the database field names and to add any necessary punctuation between fields.

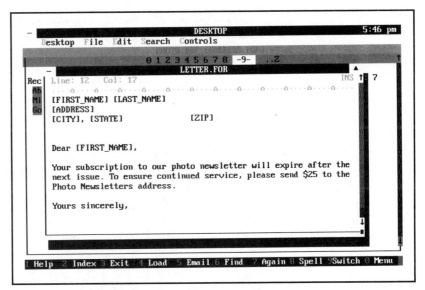

Figure 16.7: Form letter prepared in a notepad

Now open Desktop Database and load the file LETTER.FOR. Your screen will look like Figure 16.8, where the data from the database replace the field names.

Next, divide the database into two parts based on the field SUB_STATUS. Choose Select Records from the Edit menu and enter **SUB_STATUS** into Field Name and **F** (for false) into Field

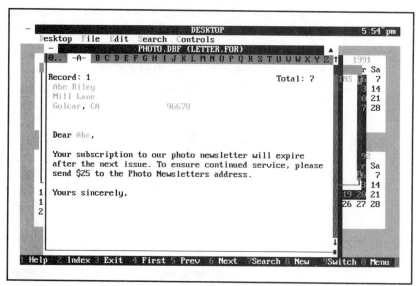

Figure 16.8: LETTER.FOR loaded into the Desktop Database

Criteria. In other words, use Sort Records to find all subscribers who
have not renewed their subscriptions by finding records in which the
subscription status field is set to false. In the example database, this
sort option isolates three subscribers—Pedersen, Shute, and
Hegbert—who will all receive copies of the form letter. Next, choose
Print from the File menu and run out the three form letters. Change
the page-layout information from the previous address-label settings,
since the reminder letter is going out on regular computer paper with
66 lines per page.

You might also load the ADDRESS.FOR form file into Desktop
Database and run off a set of address labels for these subscribers.
Both form files LETTER.FOR and ADDRESS.FOR use data from
the same PHOTO.DBF database file, but they use different fields
from the database and present the data in very different ways.

USING THE AUTODIALER

The Autodialer is a flexible Desktop Database feature that enables
you to make automatic phone calls using a Hayes-compatible modem.

You can make the call based on a Desktop Database record or according to a macro run by the Appointment Scheduler. If you have difficulty remembering certain telephone numbers, or are tired of dialing them repeatedly, use the Autodialer.

The Autodialer scans all the fields in a Desktop Database record for groups of numbers. It recognizes any group of three or more numbers as a valid telephone number, and can accept spaces, dashes, parentheses, or hyphens as delimiters within the number, as well as an *x* to signify an extension number.

If you want to use the Autodialer to dial a number from your Desktop Database, remember that the phone-number field must be the first field in the record to contain numbers. If you place the address or zip-code field before the phone-number field, the Autodialer may begin to dial those numbers rather than the phone number you wanted.

The Autodialer recognizes the following characters in a phone number:

- *P* indicates that you are using a pulse phone.

- *T* indicates that you are using a Touch-Tone phone.

- , (comma) inserts a two-second delay in dialing. This is very useful when dialing out through a switchboard. Use groups of commas to make longer delays.

- *, #, or *x* can be used to set off extension numbers.

- *W* waits for a dial tone before continuing. This is useful with long-distance services.

- *K* delays dialing until after you press another key from the keyboard. This is useful with certain online services such as banking, where you select the service you want directly from your phone. When you use *K* in a number, the Autodial Pause dialog box appears with two more options:

  Resume Dialing dials the remaining digits in the phone number.

  Cancel cancels the call.

- @ waits for a dial tone.

MODEM SETTINGS FOR THE AUTODIALER

Before you can use Autodial, you must set the transmission parameters for your computer and modem. Once set, these parameters remain constant until you change your modem. Choose the Configure Autodial selection from the Controls menu in Desktop Database to enter your modem parameters. The data-entry screen is shown in Figure 16.9.

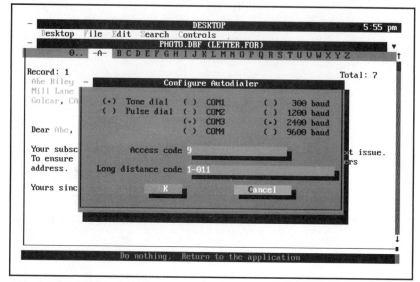

Figure 16.9: The Configure Autodialer screen

Select from the following configuration settings:

- **Tone Dial** selects the dialing procedure for Touch-Tone phones. A *T* in the phone number overrides this setting.

- **Pulse Dial** selects the dialing procedure for pulse phones. A *P* in the phone number overrides this setting.

- The **COM** port number indicates the number of the serial port to which your modem is attached.

- Set the baud rate according to the speed of your modem.

The Access and Long Distance Codes are applied for all numbers you dial.

- **Access Code** indicates the number you dial to get an outside line. The Autodialer recognizes this number and dials it for you. If you are working from home you probably don't need an Access code, so you can leave this entry blank.

- **Long Distance Code** indicates the long-distance code you use when making long-distance calls. The Autodialer dials this number after dialing the Access Code.

These settings are saved in the DESKTOP.CFG file. Once you have chosen your settings from the screen, select OK to set these new transmission parameters.

AUTOMATIC DIALING WITH THE AUTODIALER

To make a call using the Autodialer, select the Desktop Database record containing the phone number you want to call and choose Autodial from the Controls menu. The Database scans the record to find the phone number. When the number is found, the modem dials the number and a message is displayed, as shown in Figure 16.10.

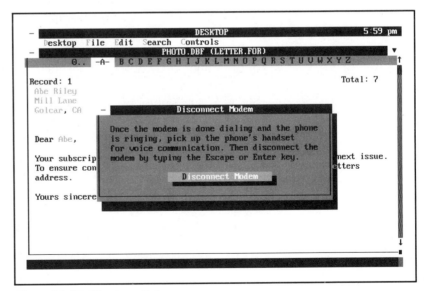

Figure 16.10: The Autodialer message

You must wait for the number to ring before disconnecting the modem. You cannot cancel an Autodial before the modem has dialed the number.

When the modem finishes dialing the number and the number is ringing, pick up the phone handset and disconnect from the modem by pressing Escape or the Enter key, or click on the Disconnect Modem button with the mouse. You can now talk to the person on the other end of the line.

When you are happy with the selections that you have made in the Desktop Database Controls and Window menus, you can save them for future use with the Save Setup option in the Controls menu.

USING THE AUTODIALER WITH DESKTOP

When you use Desktop in memory-resident mode, you can hotkey directly into the Autodialer by pressing Ctrl-O. Now you can automatically dial any number appearing anywhere on the screen with the Autodialer, provided that you have previously configured the Autodialer modem settings. The phone number can be in any Desktop document, in a word-processed document, in a spreadsheet, or even at the DOS prompt.

Enter the number to dial at the DOS prompt and press Ctrl-O. Do not press the Enter key after typing the number, since it is not a valid DOS command. The Autodialer opens a dialog box, as shown in Figure 16.11.

At the top of the dialog box you can see the number that the Autodialer is about to dial. If you click the Dial button, the Autodialer will use the modem to dial the number. Click the Next button if the number is not the one you want, and the Autodialer will search for another number. If there is no number on the screen, the Autodialer beeps. Finally, you can use the Cancel button to return to your application program. Remember that you must let the modem dial the number and the number must be ringing before you can disconnect the modem and pick up the telephone handset.

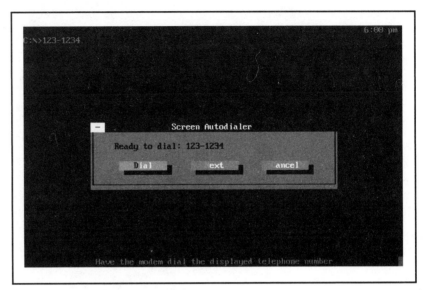

Figure 16.11: Autodialer dialog box

CHAPTER

17

*Telecommunications
Made Easy*

A modem is a device that allows computers to communicate over telephone lines. The modem generates an audible tone over which it superimposes the digital information from your computer.

PC Tools telecommunications allows you to connect your computer via a modem (or a null-modem cable) to almost any other computer capable of serial communications. You can transfer files between computers of the same or different type, or between micros and mainframes. If you have a Hayes-compatible modem, you can dial local bulletin boards or the large commercial services like Compu-Serve or Prodigy. Telecommunications supports up to four serial ports on your computer at baud rates from 300 to 19,200, and transfers files in ASCII or with the popular XMODEM error-correcting protocol. You can automate your sessions by using script files and you can use Telecommunications in background mode while you continue to work with your main application in the foreground.

If you have a fax card in your computer, you can send files directly from your computer to a facsimile machine or to another computer with a fax card. You can tell Telecommunications to whom you want to send the fax, as well as the time of day you want it sent. Telecommunications supports the following fax cards:

- Connection CoProcessor from Intel Corporation
- Satisfaxtion Board from Intel Corporation
- SpectraFax from the SpectraFax Corporation

If you work on a Novell network and have a fax card installed in one of the computers on the network, you can use it to send faxes, as well as use the fax log to check which files have been sent or received.

INTRODUCTION TO COMPUTER-TO-COMPUTER COMMUNICATIONS

After you have been using your computer for a while, you will want to move a file from one computer to another or download a file from a dial-up service such as a bulletin board. To get two computers to communicate successfully, you must pay special attention to many aspects of hardware and software.

HARDWARE REQUIREMENTS

Before your PC can communicate with another computer, both computers must have certain pieces of hardware. With computers in close proximity, you can establish a direct hardware link by using an RS-232 cable or a data-line facility built into your office phone system. If the computers are a long way apart, however, connecting them with a cable is obviously impossible.

The most common way of linking two computers that are far apart is by means of a standard telephone line and a modem. The modem may be internal (installed in one of the spare slots inside your computer) or external (connected to your computer by an RS-232 cable). Either type of modem is connected to the phone system by a modular telephone jack. You can either unplug your phone or find a voice/data switch that allows you to plug two jacks into the same line. Alternatively, you can install a dedicated modem line.

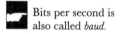 Bits per second is also called *baud*.

Modems vary in their speed. Currently, most modems used in PCs are either 1,200 or 2,400 bits per second (bps), although 9,600 bps modems are growing cheaper. Large mainframe computer installations use communications speeds far higher than these rates. Hayes Microcomputer Products has pioneered the use of a standard set of modem commands known as the AT set, and modems that conform to this command set are known as Hayes-compatible modems.

Versions of DOS up to 3.2 can address up to two serial ports called COM1 and COM2. DOS after 3.3 can address up to four serial ports and OS/2 can address up to eight. You usually set the port address by setting a hardware or software switch to configure the board as COM1 or COM2. Internal modems may have switches or jumpers to set the port address. External modems use the port address of the serial port to which they are attached.

Each device attached to your computer uses an interrupt request (IRQ) to tell the microprocessor when it needs attention. For example, IRQ1 is assigned to the keyboard, IRQ6 to the floppy disks, and IRQ7 to the printer. By default, COM1 uses IRQ4 and COM2 uses IRQ3. On 286 and 386 machines that conform to the AT architecture, you can use IRQ9 as a serial port if the other two are in use. On PS/2 computers, which have eight serial ports, the hardware automatically assigns a port number and IRQ to each.

DATA FORMATTING

The format you use to send a byte of data must also be used by the computer that receives the byte. Otherwise, you will receive garbage. The data format consists of

- Start bit
- Data word length
- Type of parity
- Number of stop bits

The start bit tells the receiving modem that what follows are data. There is always 1 start bit so you don't have to set it.

After the start bit come 7 or 8 data bits, depending on the word length in use. Since 7 bits can represent all ASCII values from 0 to 127 decimal, only 7 data bits are required to transmit text data. However, much of the data in computer-to-computer communications are in binary form and need all 8 bits. Program files are transmitted using 8 data bits.

The data bits are followed by the parity bit. Parity is a simple form of error checking and may be set to ODD or EVEN. When ODD parity is used, a 1 is placed in the parity bit if the sum of the data bits is even and a 0 if the sum is odd. When EVEN parity is used, the converse is true. ODD indicates that the sum of all the 1 bits in each transmitted byte plus the parity bit must be odd. That is, if the total is already odd, the parity bit is set to 0. If it is even, the parity bit must be set to 1. In EVEN parity, if the sum of the 1 bits is even, the parity bit must be set to 0. If it is odd, the parity bit must be 1. ODD and EVEN parity are the most common settings. In MARK parity, the parity bit is always set to 1 and is used as the eighth bit. In SPACE parity, it is set to 0 and used as the eighth bit.

No parity is used with 8 data bits, which you indicate by setting the parity to NONE. You can also use NONE with 7 data bits. Here the sending computer sets the parity and the receiving computer checks that the parity bit shows the correct relationship to all the other bits. If it does not, something went wrong during the transmission.

The end of the transmitted byte is defined by 1 or 2 stop bits. You use 1 stop bit with 8 or 7 data bits and parity other than NONE. With 7 data bits and NO parity, use 2 stop bits.

COMMUNICATIONS PARAMETERS

In addition to the data format, you must match several other settings before communication can begin: the transmission speed, whether your computer is the originator or the answerer, the direction of communication, and the communication protocol.

Transmission speed is measured in bits per second (bps). As mentioned, modern modems allow transmission speeds of 1,200, 2,400, or 9,600 bps. You must match transmission speed at both ends or you will receive garbage. Use the highest modem setting that both computers can handle. The higher the rate at which you can transmit and receive data, the lower your unit cost.

When two computers communicate, one is always considered the originator and the other the answering computer. The originator initiates the communications. When you log onto a bulletin board, set your computer to originate since the bulletin-board computer will always be set to answer.

Communications between computers can be *simplex* (one direction only), *half duplex* (both directions but at different times), or *full duplex* (both directions at the same time). Most communications between microcomputers are in full-duplex mode.

Communications protocols are methods of detecting transmission errors during the transmission. They usually divide the data into blocks, send the block, and then check that the block was received correctly. The sending and receiving computers must both use the same protocol.

The most common communications error is mismatched transmission speed between sending and receiving computers.

USING DESKTOP TELECOMMUNICATIONS

The last two options appear only if you have a fax card.

When you choose Telecommunications from the main Desktop menu, you will see a small submenu containing four entries:

- Modem Telecommunications

- Electronic Mail

- Send a Fax

- Check the Fax Log

I will describe how to use Modem Telecommunications first and then deal with facsimile transmissions and electronic mail later in this chapter.

When you choose Modem Telecommunications from the main Telecommunications submenu, you will see a screen like the one in Figure 17.1. As usual I have maximized the window to fill the whole screen. The default phone directory file, PHONE.TEL, is displayed on the screen.

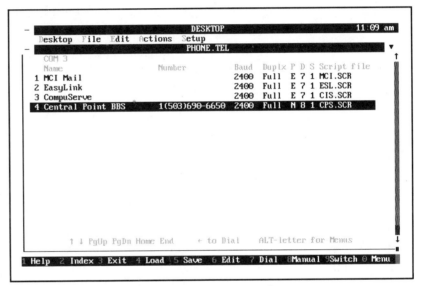

Figure 17.1: The Telecommunications main display

The main parts of the display are as follows:

- **COM port.** The number of the communications port that your modem is connected to is shown in the upper-left corner of the display.

- **File name.** The name of the current phone directory file is shown in the center of the window.

- **Name.** The name of the person or service to dial is shown in the far-left column.

- **Number.** The telephone number of the person or service to dial. If you leave this item blank, Telecommunications will ask you for the number when you try to dial out.

- **Baud.** The baud rate for this entry, usually 1,200, 2,400, or 9,600.

- **Duplex.** Defines whether the computers communicate as full duplex or half duplex.

- **P D S.** Defines the character format for communications, and is an abbreviation for Parity, Data Bits, and Stop Bits.

- **Script file.** In the far-right column is the name of the script file you want to use with this entry. Script files automate certain repetitive functions like entering your log-on sequence.

WORKING WITH PHONE DIRECTORY FILES

Instead of one large file, you might have several smaller files: one for work numbers, another for home numbers, and perhaps a third for bulletin-board numbers. Use the file name extension .TEL for Telecommunications configuration files.

When you start Modem Telecommunications from the Telecommunications submenu, the program loads the default phone directory file called PHONE.TEL. This file contains the names, numbers, and communications settings for the people and services you want to call. The file can hold up to 200 entries. If you need more entries, you can create an additional file.

To load a different phone directory file, select the Load option in the File menu and select the file name from the File Load dialog box, then choose Load. Telecommunications loads the file, replacing the original phone directory information with information from the new file.

Data communications can sometimes be difficult if the number you call is routed through an office PBX system. If a dedicated data line goes directly into the building, use it instead.

To change the information for a particular entry in the phone directory file, place the highlighted bar over the entry you want to change and select Edit Entry (F6) from the Edit menu. You will see the screen shown in Figure 17.2.

You can change any of the entries on this screen:

- **NAME** is the name of the person, company, or bulletin board. This entry can be as long as 50 characters.

- **DATABASE.** Enter the path and file name of a database file that has fields containing phone numbers or fax numbers.

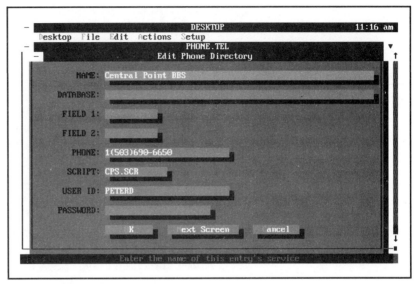

Figure 17.2: The Edit Phone Directory screen

- **FIELD 1** and **FIELD 2** are the fields in the database that actually contain the phone numbers or fax numbers you want to use.

- **PHONE** is the phone number that goes with the name you entered in the NAME line. This entry can be up to 50 characters, the first 25 of which you can see in this screen. You can enter the phone number as you are accustomed to because Telecommunications ignores spaces, dashes, and parentheses. (This is not true in most telecommunications software, which require pure number entries.)

- **SCRIPT** is the file name of the script file you want to use with this entry. Script files are described in detail later in this chapter.

- **USER ID** identifies you when you log on to an online service like CompuServe or MCI Mail. The user ID can be up to 25 characters long, and can contain upper- and lowercase letters.

- **PASSWORD** is a code known only to you that you enter when you access a bulletin board or other online service. The password can be up to 21 characters long, and again it can contain upper- or lowercase letters.

To see the rest of the phone directory parameters, select Next Screen:

- **BAUD** is the speed of data transmission, usually the number of bits per second (bps). The higher the number, the faster the data transmission rate. Baud rates of up to 9,600 bps are supported in all versions of DOS, and baud rates of up to 19,200 bps are supported in DOS 3.3 or later. Remember that this setting must match the setting on the remote computer. Modern modems can often operate at several different rates: they detect the speed of the transmission and change their baud rate setting as required to match.

- **PARITY** is used to help achieve correct communications. The sending computer adds an extra bit to the end of each data byte transmitted. You can set parity to NONE, ODD, EVEN, MARK, or SPACE. The parity setting must match the parity setting on the remote computer for successful communications.

- **TERMINAL.** Telecommunications can emulate several different terminal types found on mainframe computers. Choose from TTY (teletype, often used by computer services and bulletin boards), ANSI (American National Standards Institute), VT100, or VT52. If you are going to log on to a remote computer that requires terminal emulation, choose from one of these terminal types.

- **FLOW CONTROL** is used to prevent information from being transmitted faster than it can be received, which can sometimes result in data loss. There are two options:

    XON/XOFF. With XON/XOFF flow control, the receiving computer sends an XOFF to stop the sending computer temporarily from transmitting.

This gives the receiving computer time to catch up. When the receiving computer is ready to start again it sends an XON, and the transmission resumes. Most systems use XON/XOFF, but the settings must match on both computers.

NONE. With Flow Control set to NONE, there is no flow control of any kind.

- **END-OF-LINE PROCESSING, RECEIVE** selects the characters used to mark the end of a line when receiving an ASCII file transfer or when you press the Enter key during an online communications session:

    ADD LF. If the remote computer only uses a carriage-return character to mark the end of a line, use ADD LF to add a line feed during the incoming transmission, giving a carriage-return/line-feed pair at the end of each line.

    ADD CR. If the remote computer only uses a line-feed character to mark the end of a line, use ADD CR to add a carriage return during the incoming transmission, giving a carriage-return/line-feed pair at the end of each line.

    NONE. The remote computer expects a carriage-return/line-feed pair at the end of each line. Since this is what Telecommunications uses, there is no need to modify the data.

- **END-OF-LINE PROCESSING, SEND** selects the characters used to mark the end of the line in an outgoing ASCII file transfer:

    STRIP LF. The receiving computer only expects a carriage return at the end of the line, so Telecommunications removes all line-feed characters.

    STRIP CR. The receiving computer only expects a line-feed character at the end of the line, so Telecommunications removes all carriage-return characters. The Enter key sends a line-feed character.

NONE. The receiving computer expects a carriage-return/line-feed at the end of each line. Since this is what Telecommunications sends, there is no need to modify the data. The Enter key sends a carriage return.

- **DATA-BITS.** Select SEVEN or EIGHT data bits for the number of bits in the transmitted character. Most systems use eight data bits.

- **STOP-BITS.** Select ONE or TWO stop bits to indicate the end of the transmitted character. Most systems use one stop bit.

- **DUPLEX.** Select FULL for simultaneous two-way transmission or HALF for transmission of data one way at a time. If you cannot see what you are typing, change to half duplex, or if you see two of every character, change to full. Most systems use full duplex.

If you want to create a new entry in your phone directory, choose Create New Entry from the Edit menu. The screen used for creating new entries is identical to the one just described for editing entries. Choose OK to save the information you have just entered or edited.

To remove an entry from your phone directory, place the highlighted bar over the entry and select Remove Entry from the Edit menu. Be careful with this selection because it does not ask you to confirm your choice and deletes the entry immediately.

When you have finished entering your data, you can save your work by clicking on the close box or selecting OK. If you want to keep your entries in a different file, select Save from the File menu and specify the new file name.

SETTING MODEM PARAMETERS

Mismatched baud rates are often the cause of communications errors.

The final step you must complete before transferring files is to check the modem parameters in Modem Setup from the Setup menu. When you select Modem Setup, you will see the screen shown in Figure 17.3, which shows the modem initialization sequence for 300/1,200, 1,200/4,800, and 9,600/19,200 baud modems.

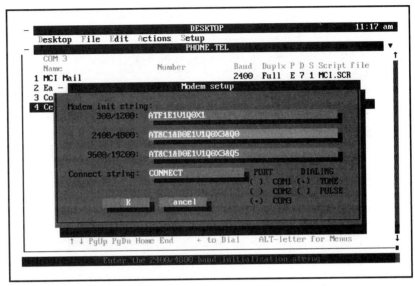

Figure 17.3: Modem Setup screen

You often hear the phrase "Hayes-compatible," but there is no absolute modem standard. Even different models of Hayes modems are not entirely compatible with each other. This is why communications programs have separate options for the Smartmodem 300, 1200, and 1200B and for the 2400 and 2400B. More modern modems have codes that older software will not recognize, but this is not usually a problem. Your main concern is whether the modem will work with your communications software. Table 17.1 lists the most frequently used AT commands for Hayes modems. You can also consult your modem reference manual for more information.

Table 17.1: Summary of the AT Command Set Used by Hayes Modems

COMMAND	EXPLANATION
AT	Command prefix
A/	Repeat last command
ATB	Use CCITT V.22
ATC	Assume carrier signal is always present

Table 17.1: Summary of the AT Command Set Used by Hayes Modems (continued)

COMMAND	EXPLANATION
ATD	Dial: go into originate mode, dial number that follows, go to online state
ATDT	Tone Dial: go into originate mode, dial number that follows, go to online state
ATDP	Pulse Dial: go into originate mode, dial number that follows, go to online state
ATDR	Reverse Mode: go into originate mode, dial number that follows, go to online state
ATE	Controls character echo
ATH	Controls modem hang-up
ATI	Requests modem ID information
ATL	Controls speaker volume
ATM	Controls speaker response
ATO	Go to online state
ATQ	Controls result codes
ATS	Sets modem S registers
ATV	Displays result codes
ATX	Controls features represented by result codes
ATY	Disables long space disconnect
ATZ	Modem hang-up, restores all default settings
AT&C	Controls modem based on DCD (data carrier detect)
AT&D	Controls modem based on DTR (data terminal ready)
AT&F	Restores factory settings as active configuration
AT&G	No guard tone
AT&J	RJ-aa/RJ-41S/RJ-45S jack
AT&P	Pulse dial make and break ratio = 39/61
AT&Q	Operates in asynchronous mode

Table 17.1: Summary of the AT Command Set Used by Hayes Modems (continued)

COMMAND	EXPLANATION
AT&R	Tracks CTS (clear to send) according to RTS (ready to send)
AT&S	Assumes presence of DSR (data set ready) signal
AT&T	Terminates presence of DSR signal
AT&V	Views current configuration
AT&Z$n = x$	Stores phone number x in location n

Hayes-compatible modems issue the string

    CONNECT

to inform your communications program that a connection has been established. If your modem is not Hayes-compatible, you may need to use a different connect string; enter the correct string into the Connect string text box. Consult your modem manual for more information.

The remaining items on this screen are PORT and DIALING:

- **PORT.** This is the serial port you want to use with your modem.

- **DIALING.** Select either Touch-Tone or pulse dialing.

DIALING A NUMBER

Make sure that your modem is attached and turned on before dialing a number, especially if your modem is external.

Before you can send or receive files, you must know how to use Telecommunications to dial a number. The simplest way is to position the highlighted bar over the entry you want to dial and press the Enter key. If you use a mouse, just double-click on the entry to dial the number. If your modem makes dialing and ringing sounds, you will hear the number being dialed. If the entry you selected did not contain a phone number, a dialog box opens for you to input the number to dial.

The options available in the Actions menu change when you are connected to a remote computer.

Alternatively, you can dial the number by selecting the Manual option from the Actions menu. Use this method if you want to use a different phone number without changing the other parameters you have already selected.

In either case, once a link has been established to the remote computer the screen displays the online window shown in Figure 17.4. What you see in the communications area in the center of this window is being received from the remote computer. In Figure 17.4 you can see the log-on screen for Central Point's bulletin board.

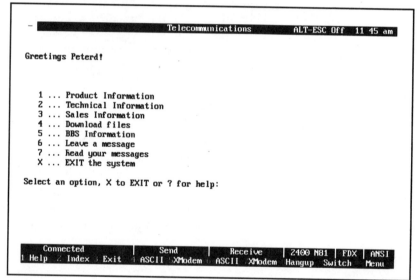

Figure 17.4: Telecommunications online window

The communications settings in use are shown on the right side of the message line. In Figure 17.4, the baud rate is 1,200, parity is set to none, there are 8 data bits and 1 stop bit. Duplex is set to FULL and the computer is in ANSI terminal-emulation mode. The short-cut function keys are shown on the next line. When sending a file, choose F4 to send the file in ASCII or F5 to send it using the XMODEM protocol. When receiving a file, choose F6 to receive it in ASCII or F7 to receive it in XMODEM. Use F8 to hang up the phone at the end of your session. If you press the Escape key from the online window, you will return to the Telecommunications window inside Desktop. Sometimes you need to send an escape character to the remote computer. To do this, press Shift and Escape simultaneously.

THE XMODEM PROTOCOL

XMODEM is one of the most popular communications protocols around. It is included in most microcomputer communications packages and is used by almost all DOS-based bulletin boards.

XMODEM divides data into blocks. Each block consists of the start-of-header character 01h, a 1-byte block number, the one's complement of the block number, 128 bytes of data, and a 1-byte checksum, as you can see in Table 17.2.

Table 17.2: XMODEM Protocol Block Format

LOCATION	CONTENTS
0	SOH (start-of-header character, ASCII 01)
1	Block number (starts at 1 and goes to 0 after FFh)
2	One's complement of the block number (255 – block number)
3–130	128 bytes of data
131	Checksum: add all data bytes and ignore any carry

The block number starts at 1 and is computed modulo 256. In other words, after 255 (FFh) it goes back to zero. You determine the one's complement by complementing all bits in the number (changing the zeros to ones and the ones to zeros) or by subtracting the block number from 255. You calculate the single-byte checksum by adding the ASCII values for all 128 data bytes and ignoring any overflow.

The 1-byte checksum does not always detect all errors. For this reason, an extension to XMODEM incorporates a 2-byte figure called a *cyclical redundancy check* (CRC-16). The CRC detects at least 99.99 percent of all errors. Table 17.3 shows the CRC-16 format.

XMODEM offers two types or error checking: a checksum and a cyclical redundancy check.

Table 17.3: XMODEM Protocol Block Format with CRC-16

LOCATION	CONTENTS
0	SOH (start-of-header character, ASCII 01)
1	Block number (starts at 1 and goes to 0 after FFh)
2	One's complement of the block number (255 − block number)
3–130	128 bytes of data
131	High byte of CRC
132	Low byte of CRC

There are many other communications protocols. YMODEM, YMODEM batch, and WXMODEM are variations of XMODEM. Kermit, developed at Columbia University, is often used between PCs and mainframe computers. Many communications software packages such as Crosstalk or SmartCom include excellent proprietary protocols of their own. Just remember that both computers involved in the transfer of a file must use the same protocol.

HOW TO RECEIVE FILES

Remember that Telecommunications changes the entries in the Actions menu when you go online.

Using Telecommunications, you can receive (download) files from a remote computer. For example, you can download a program file from a service like CompuServe or from your local PC user group's bulletin board. You can even download files from the office computer to work on at home. To receive a file, select the communications protocol that the computers in the transfer must both use. Telecommunications offers two choices:

- The ASCII file-transfer protocol does not check for errors caused by interference on the phone lines. However, you can use it to transfer text files if you have no other choice. If the remote computer supports the XMODEM protocol, use it rather than ASCII.

- XMODEM is probably the most well-known microcomputer file-transfer protocol. It checks for and corrects transmission errors, so you should use it for all file transfers, even though it is slower than ASCII.

When you register with a computer service, you will receive an explanation of how to use the service.

To transfer a file, call the number and establish a connection. The remote computer will ask you questions or give you a menu from which to select. Answer the questions or enter the commands. Make your choice of protocol from the options in the Receive menu. You can also use the Receive shortcut function keys on the keyboard: F6 for ASCII or F7 for XMODEM. Be sure that your choice matches the protocol in use on the remote computer. The Save dialog box appears. Enter the file name you want to use with the file and select the Save button to capture the file. If you select the ASCII protocol, the contents of the file are shown on your screen as the transfer takes place. If you choose XMODEM as the file-transfer protocol, the Receive box opens, as shown in Figure 17.5.

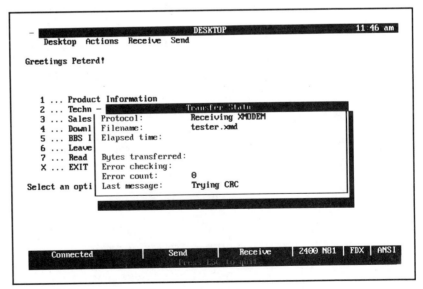

Figure 17.5: The Receive box

If you use the ASCII file-transfer protocol, you must use the End Transfer option in the Actions menu to let Telecommunications know that the transfer is complete.

The Receive box contains the following information:

- **Protocol** is the name of the communications protocol in use.

- **Filename** is the name you gave to the file.

- **Elapsed time** is the time the transfer has taken so far.

- **Bytes transferred** is the number of bytes transferred so far.

- **Error checking** is the error-checking method. XMODEM uses a checksum or a cyclical redundancy check to detect communications errors during the transmission. Telecommunications automatically selects the method that the remote computer is using.

- **Error count** is the number of errors encountered on a block of data. If there are more than ten errors on one block of data, Telecommunications stops the file transfer. If this happens, or if you see a large number of errors, try dialing the number at a different time of day—or even at night—to get a cleaner phone line for the transfer.

- **Last message** shows the text of the last message.

You can use End Transfer from the Actions menu to stop a transfer if you are seeing too many errors or decide that you do not want the file you are downloading. Finally, you should log off the remote computer before choosing the Hangup Phone selection (F8) from the Actions menu to end your session.

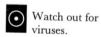 Watch out for viruses.

When you have completed the transfer, don't forget to check for viruses in your new files before you run them. Most of the big bulletin boards are very good at screening for infection, but you just never know. It is better to be safe than sorry.

HOW TO SEND FILES

Sending files is easy once you know how to use Telecommunications to receive files. Sending a file to a remote computer is often called *uploading:* you dial, establish the link, and communicate with the remote computer just as you did to receive files. Again, the choice of file-transfer protocol is important: the selection must be the same on both computers. This time, make your choice from the Send menu or press F4 for ASCII or F5 for XMODEM. Next, the File Load dialog box appears. Select the file you want to send and choose Load to send the file to the remote computer. A Send box, identical to the Receive box, appears on the screen to show the progress of the transfer.

COMMUNICATING BETWEEN YOUR PC AND AN APPLE MACINTOSH

PC Tools is available for the Apple Macintosh, where it is known as Central Point MacTools.

You can use Telecommunications to transfer files from your PC to an Apple Macintosh, either via a modem as already described or by using a *null-modem cable*. (A null-modem cable is a short length of serial cable with the appropriate connectors on either end to take the place of the two modems.) Several of the individual wires inside this special cable are changed from their normal pin connections in order to convince the two computers to communicate with each other properly. The two computers must be physically close together for this to work because if the cable is too long, voltage levels may fall below the accepted levels.

TRANSFERRING ENCRYPTED FILES

If you have encrypted a file using PC Secure, you can send the file to another computer running PC Tools for decryption. Remember that you cannot decrypt the file without knowing the key, so you must arrange a safe method for transferring the key before the file can be used. You should not give your key to the recipient over an ordinary phone line. Consider using a trusted courier or a scrambled phone to transfer the key. Once you have solved this part of the problem, the transfer proceeds like any other file transfer:

1. Use PC Secure to encrypt the file using the agreed key. All of the PC Secure parameters are stored in a special location in the file header.

2. Dial the number, establish a link, and transfer the file using the XMODEM file-transfer protocol.

3. End the Telecommunications program and decrypt the file using the prearranged key. PC Secure uses information encoded in the file header to recreate all the original program settings.

You can now use the file at both ends of the communications link.

WRITING A SCRIPT FILE

If you use online services regularly, you will find yourself entering the same information—your log-on information, for example—each time you link up with a bulletin board. You can automate this process if you use a script file containing this information. Script files use a simple programming language to start or stop a file transfer, to send comments to the remote computer, or to hang up the phone.

Telecommunications script files are text files, so you create them in a Notepad in Desktop. Several script files, all with the .SCR extension, are provided on the PC Tools distribution disks. The commands in a script file perform actions after you have made a connection with the other computer. Script files are not case-sensitive. The commands you can use in your script files are as follows:

- * indicates that what follows is treated as comments and not used as commands. It is a good idea to include comments in your script files to remind you what the script is doing.

- :*label*. A label is the destination for the GOTO command. Only the first eight characters in a label are used.

- **BACKTALK** tells Telecommunications to run the rest of the script file in background mode. This allows your computer to run an application program while continuing with the communications in the background. BACKTALK must be loaded memory-resident before this command will work. Remember, if you do run your script file in the background, commands that require input like INPUT or DATABASE will be ignored if they occur after the BACKTALK command. Be sure that they occur before BACKTALK in your script file.

- **DATABASE** combined with one or two of the variables (v1, v2, or v3) allows you to send the contents of up to two fields in a PC Tools Desktop database. The DATABASE command is used with the Database and Field 1 and Field 2 entries in the Edit Phone Directory screen. The contents of Field 1 are stored in v1, and the contents of Field 2 are stored in v2; if you only want to send one field, just use one of the variables.

- **DOWNLOAD** *protocol variable* or *file name* initiates a file transfer from the remote computer. The remote computer must be ready to send the file using the ASCII or XMODEM protocol.

- **ECHO** displays the characters received from the remote computer during a WAITFOR command. The first ECHO command in a script file turns on the display for all subsequent WAITFOR commands. This command is very useful if you are troubleshooting a new script file, but you should remove it once the script is working correctly.

- **GOTO** :*label* transfers execution of the script to the commands following the label. Only the first eight characters of a label are used.

- **HANGUP** hangs up the phone.

- **IF** *variable* = < >**CONTAINS** *string* provides the means for a conditional branch in your script when used with the GOTO command. The contents of *variable* are evaluated against *string* and may be equal to (=) or not equal to (< >) *string*. Also, you can use CONTAINS to see whether the variable contains *string*.

- **INPUT** *variable* allows entry of up to 80 characters from the keyboard, ending in carriage return or line feed, into one of the four named variables: v1, v2, v3, or v4.

- **PAUSE** *number* pauses the script for a specified number of seconds. PAUSE without a number pauses the script file for one second.

- **PRINT** *variable* or *string* prints the contents of a named variable or the contents of the string on the screen. Use a semicolon to suppress the return character at the end of the line for continuous printing. Does not send anything to your printer.

- **RECEIVE** *variable* captures up to 80 characters from the remote computer into one of the three named variables: v1, v2, or v3. The character string is terminated by the first carriage return or line feed sent by the remote computer. If nothing is received within ten seconds, the variable is set to null.

- **SEND** *variable* or *string* or **USER ID** or **PASSWORD** allows you to send a message to the remote computer. The message can be contained in one of the named variables or in a *string*. Use a ^ to indicate a control character (as in ^M for carriage return) and use a semicolon at the end of the sequence to suppress the return character at the end of the message.

  The SEND command has two other parameters, USER ID and PASSWORD. You can add USER ID or PASSWORD to your script file rather than having to put your bulletin board user identification or password into a variable or quote string. These entries are used with the corresponding entries of USER ID and PASSWORD in the Edit Phone Directory screen, and they are used when the script file is processed.

- **TROFF** turns trace mode off and execution of the script file continues normally.

- **TRON** turns on trace mode, which displays the commands in your script file in the message line at the bottom of the screen. When the command is displayed, the script stops executing until you press the spacebar. This is especially useful if you are troubleshooting a new script. However, you should remove the command once the script is running correctly. Press the Escape key to terminate the script.

- **UPLOAD** *protocol variable* or *file name* initiates a file upload from your computer to the remote computer, using either the ASCII or XMODEM protocol. The remote system must be ready to receive the file.

- **VARIABLES** allows you to use up to three named variables in your script: v1, v2, and v3.
- **WAITFOR** *string* compares the characters coming from the remote computer with the characters in *string*. Script execution is paused until a match for *string* is found. The case of all characters is ignored.

To use a script file in your communications, first make sure that it is in the PC Tools directory. Otherwise, Desktop will not be able to find the file and you will see the message

Unable to open file

Then choose the phone-number entry you want to use the script file with and select Edit Entry from the Edit menu. The Edit Phone Directory screen opens and you can add the name (and extension) of the script file into the SCRIPT FILE box in the center of the window.

Make sure that all the other information on the screen is correct and select OK to confirm your entries. To run the script, call the number. When the remote computer answers, the script will run. Figure 17.6 shows a simple script file for logging on to an imaginary system. You can make script files that are much more complex than this simple example. Be careful, however, not to make them too long in case something unexpected happens, such as the *sysop* (system operator) changing the start-up procedures. If the sysop changes the start-up sequence that your script file is tailored to, your script file may not work as intended.

USING BACKGROUND TELECOMMUNICATIONS

If you use Desktop in memory-resident mode, you can make file transfers in background mode. In other words, you can start a file transfer, load an application like Lotus 1-2-3, and work with Lotus while the transfer continues unattended in the background.

```
*Comment: My User ID Number is 12345
*Comment: My Password is TIRED MOOSE
*
WAITFOR "ENTER USER ID"
SEND    "12345"
WAITFOR "ENTER PASSWORD"
SEND    "TIRED MOOSE"
*
*30 October 1991
```

Figure 17.6: A script file for logging on to an imaginary bulletin board

⊙ Do not use the COM port selected for background communications from your foreground application program when a file transfer is taking place. You will interrupt the transfer.

If you selected background communications when you installed PC Tools with PC Setup, you are already configured for background communications. If you did not, add the line

BACKTALK /2

to your AUTOEXEC.BAT file before the line that loads Desktop. This designates COM2 as the serial port for background communications. You can choose any COM port (COM1 to COM4).

Backtalk occupies approximately 64K of memory.

To select COM 3 or COM 4 on an AT-style machine, you must specify the IRQ and the base port address.

To initialize COM 3, you must use

BACKTALK /3 = 4,3E8

See the discussion of System Information in Chapter 8 for more information on IRQs and their uses.

and to use COM 4, use

BACKTALK /4 = 3,2E8

If your phone has call waiting, you should disable it before starting an important communications session. Otherwise your session may be interrupted by the noise that signals an incoming call.

Computer-to-computer links are prone to interruption, and if you use background mode you will not see any of the communications error messages that may be generated during a transfer. To overcome this problem, Telecommunications creates a file called TRANSFER.LOG when you start a background file transfer using the XMODEM protocol. Any communications errors reported during the transfer are stored in this file. The first line of TRANSFER.LOG contains the name of the file you sent or received and the last line contains the word COMPLETED if the transfer was successful. If the transfer was not successful, the last line contains an error message such as **Time Out**, **CRC Error**, or **Too Many Retries**.

Telecommunications creates a TRANSFER.LOG file each time you start a background session using the XMODEM protocol, so you can delete the file if you want to save space once the file transfer has been successfully completed. You can look at TRANSFER.LOG with Notepads.

Start the file transfer as you would start a normal transfer, and then press Alt-B to invoke the background mode. Once you are in background mode, you can return to the main Desktop menu or go back to your foreground application program to continue working. A blinking *B* is displayed in the upper-right corner of your screen as the transfer proceeds. When the transfer is complete, you will hear a beep. If you are using a script file, however, you must stay in Telecommunications until the script file has executed.

USING YOUR FAX CARD WITH TELECOMMUNICATIONS

A fax card is an add-in board that allows you to perform many of the functions of a facsimile machine right from your computer. You can send files to any remote facsimile machine, or to other computers that have fax cards installed. If you work on a Novell network and you have a fax board, anyone on the network can send or receive faxes.

SOME HISTORY OF FACSIMILE TRANSMISSIONS

Facsimile transmission has been available over telephone lines for a long time. Fax standards were first established in the 1960s by the European-based CCITT (Consultative Committee for International Telephony and Telegraphy), and machines based on the group 1 standard took about six minutes to transmit one page. Group 2 fax machines cut this transmission time in half by the mid 1970s.

Modern fax machines are known as group 3 fax machines, and follow a standard introduced in the early 1980s. Group 3 machines use a 9,600 baud half-duplex modem to transfer data over standard telephone lines, and they use a data-compression technique to make the transfer as fast as possible. Transmission times vary a great deal, but a typical page of text takes from 30 to 60 seconds. On poor phone lines the fax machine's modem will drop back to 7,200 bps at first, then down to 4,800 bps, and finally down to 2,400 bps in an attempt to get the fax through.

As well as increases in speed, there have also been improvements in readability. Group 1 and group 2 fax machines had a resolution of about 100 dots per inch (dpi). Group 3 machines have a resolution of either 100 by 200 dpi in normal resolution or 200 by 200 dpi in fine-resolution mode.

There is a group 4 fax standard, and these machines can send a page in 5 to 10 seconds at a resolution of up to 400 dpi. However, they require an all-digital telephone system, not expected to be commonly available until after the end of this century.

Telecommunications offers the additional feature of sending binary files in non-fax mode to another computer using a similar fax card. This is done by using the 9,600 bps modem (usually reserved for the fax transmission) as a regular modem. As there are no standards for 9,600 bps modem transmissions, each manufacturer uses its own file-transfer protocol. This is why you have to have the same manufacturer's board at both ends of the link.

All the fax examples in this book were made using Intel Corporation's Connection CoProcessor fax card. The heart of this full-length card is a 10 MHz 80186 processor that allows true background fax transmission via the 9,600 bps fax modem. The board also contains 256K of RAM so it doesn't need to use as much of the computer's main memory.

The menu items concerned with fax management only appear in the Desktop menu if you installed them with the Install program.

There are two entries from the Telecommunications menu concerned with fax transmissions:

- **Send a Fax** allows you to send faxes, as well as to add, edit, or delete fax entries.

- **Check the Fax Log** allows you to look at the fax transmission you have set up and review fax statistics.

You can review information on up to 99 faxes; you can even keep them and reuse them at a later time.

SENDING A FAX

From the Telecommunications menu, select Send a Fax and you will see the Send FAX Directory screen shown in Figure 17.7. Before seeing how the Send FAX Directory screen works, take a moment to look at the selections in the Configure menu. This is where you set up some of the basic information for your fax transmissions:

- **FAX Drive.** Enter the path and directory name you specified when you installed Fax Telecommunications with PC Setup. See Chapter 2 for a complete description of PC Setup.

- **Page Length.** Enter the length of the page you want to use, in inches. Normally this will be set to 11 inches to represent a normal 8½-by-11-inch page. If you will be sending very short faxes, you might consider making this entry smaller to save paper.

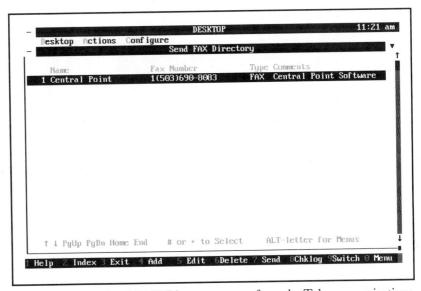

Figure 17.7: The Send FAX Directory screen from the Telecommunications menu

- **Cover Page.** Create your own cover sheet in a notepad before you send the fax. If you don't want to use a cover page, deselect this item. You can include a personal or company logo at the top of your cover page if you wish. The logo is kept in a file called PCTOOLS.PCX. You can customize this file with a graphics editor like PC Paintbrush, CorelDRAW, or any other graphics program that supports the .PCX file format. If you make a new logo file, be sure to name it PCTOOLS.PCX and copy it into your PC Tools directory; otherwise it will never be used.

- **Time Format.** Select the time format you prefer from the 24-hour clock or the AM/PM setting.

- **Sent From.** Enter your name or company name here, and the information will be used whenever you create a new fax.

Now that you have configured your system, we can look at how to send a fax. The Send FAX Directory screen is divided into four columns:

- **Name.** This is the name of the person or organization you want to send the fax to. The entry also has a sequence number that allows up to 99 entries.

- **Fax Number.** This is the number of the phone line to the fax machine.

- **Type.** You can send a file in fax or in non-fax or file mode. In fax mode, the file you send is translated into a form that all group 3 fax machines and fax cards can understand. If you send the file in non-fax mode, the file is not converted, but is sent in much the same way a normal modem would send the file. You can send any type of file by this method, including .EXE files, but the files can only be received by another fax card supported by PC Tools. They cannot be received by stand-alone group 3 fax machines.

- **Comments.** You can add information about a given fax entry.

To add a fax, select Add a New Entry from the Actions menu (F4), or click on Add in the message bar, and the FAX Details dialog box opens as shown in Figure 17.8.

You can edit or change all the entries in this screen:

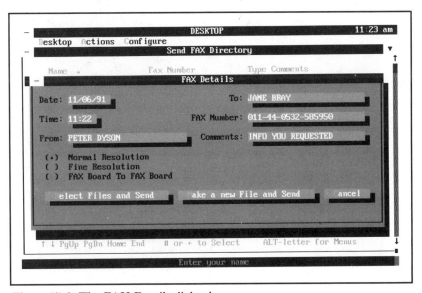

If you enter the current date and time into these two boxes, the fax will be sent immediately.

- **Date.** Enter the date you want your fax sent. Usually today's date appears in this box, but if you want to delay sending your fax until a future date, enter the new date into this box.

- **Time.** Enter the time you want your fax sent. The current time usually appears in this box, but you can use a later time if you want to delay the fax transmission until the rates are cheaper.

- **From.** Enter your name or company name here. If you have already entered this information into the Sent From dialog box in the Configure menu, there is no need to enter the information again.

- **To.** Enter the name of the person or company you are sending the fax to.

Figure 17.8: The FAX Details dialog box

- **FAX Number.** Enter the phone number of the fax machine you are transmitting your fax to.

- **Comments.** You can add descriptive comments to the fax entry to remind you of the fax contents.

- **Normal Resolution.** Select this setting if you are sending a text fax. This mode is faster than the Fine Resolution mode, so it is cheaper too.

- **Fine Resolution.** Use this setting if you want your fax to appear especially sharp, or if you are sending a fax containing graphics. This mode is slower than the Normal Resolution mode because more information is actually sent. Thus it is slightly more expensive.

- **FAX Board to FAX Board.** Use this mode if you want to send binary files to another computer with a PC Tools-supported fax card installed. You cannot send binary files to a facsimile machine. In this mode you are actually using the high-speed modem on the fax card to transfer your files from your computer to another identical modem in the receiving computer.

- **Select Files and Send.** Use this choice to open the Files to Select dialog box, and choose the files you want to send as faxes. Click the Add button to add these files to the list of files to be sent. When you have finished your selection, click the Send button to actually send the files you selected. You can use the Cancel or Delete buttons at any time to stop selecting files or to remove a file you have added to the list.

    A new dialog box opens to ask if you want to include a cover page with your fax, or send it without one. If you requested a cover page in the Configure menu, you can select the OK button to open a notepad and create your cover page. Choose No Cover Page This Time to send the fax without a cover page. The same Notepads file, COVER.TXT, is always used for the fax cover page. The file contents are automatically erased each time you send a fax. Press the Escape key or click on the close box to save the cover page, and a dialog box appears telling you that your fax has been sent. Select the OK button and you will return to the Send FAX Directory screen where you will see the fax you just created.

- **Make a New File and Send.** Use this selection if you want to open a new fax file now using a notepad. The Create A File dialog box opens for you to enter a new file name, and then a notepad opens for you to type in the text of your fax. Press Escape when you have entered the text for your fax; the next screen you see is the Cover Page Selection dialog box. The procedure for creating the cover page is exactly as I just described above. Finally, when you return to the Send FAX Directory screen, you will see all your faxes listed in order.

CHANGING AND DELETING FAX ENTRIES

After you have set up and sent a fax, you can use several of the selections in the Actions menu to edit the fax control information.

For example, if you want to send the same fax to several different people, just select the appropriate entry from the Send FAX Directory screen, enter the new fax number into the FAX Details dialog box, and select or click on Send.

Alternatively, if you have to send a fax to the same number on a regular basis—say a report you have to send to the same fax number each week—use Edit the Current Entry (F5) from the Actions menu, leave the FAX Details intact, select the new file that includes this week's report, and send the fax.

To delete an entry from the Send FAX Directory when you have no further use for it, select the entry you want to delete with the arrow keys or with the mouse, and use Delete the Current Entry (F6) from the Actions menu, or click on Delete on the message bar. Use these options carefully, as they delete the fax entry immediately, without first asking for your confirmation.

CHECKING THE FAX LOG

When you want to check on the status of a fax, you can select the fax log from two different menus:

- Select Check FAX Log (F8) from the Actions menu in the Send FAX Directory screen.

- Select Check the Fax Log directly from the initial Telecommunications submenu.

Either way, you will see the screen shown in Figure 17.9. If there are no entries in the fax queue, you will see the message

Nothing in FAX Queue.

as the only entry on this screen.

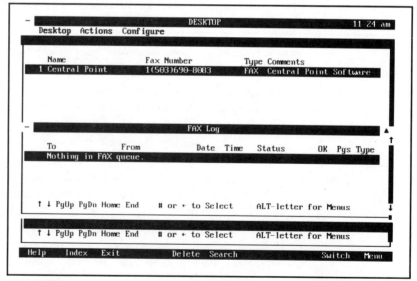

Figure 17.9: The Fax Log screen showing all the fax transmissions in the fax queue

This screen is divided into eight columns, as follows:

- **To** shows the name of the person the fax was sent to. This entry includes an index number listed on the left for each transmission.

- **From** indicates the name of the person sending the fax.

- **Date** and **Time** show the date and time the fax was sent—or if the date and time are in the future, the date and time that the fax will be sent.

- **Status** shows you the state of each fax transmission. Status can be one of the following:

    Aborted shows that you canceled the transmission.

    Dialing indicates that the number is being dialed now.

    Sending shows that the fax is being sent now.

    Sent indicates that the fax has been successfully sent.

    Receiving indicates that a fax is being received now.

    Received shows that the fax has been successfully received.

    An error message shows that the fax card is experiencing problems sending or receiving a fax, or that there are problems with the phone line. Errors include *Non CCP,* which indicates that one of the fax cards in the link is not compatible with PC Tools Telecommunications. *Bad Phone, Drop* points to the phone line as the problem.

- **OK** displays YES if there were no problems with the fax, and NO if problems were encountered.

- **Pages** tells you how many pages the fax was, including the cover page.

- **Type** tells you if you are using fax mode or non-fax mode for file transmission.

The selections in the Action menu change when you enter the fax log. There are now two selections: Delete the Selected Entry (F5) and

Search (F6):

- To delete an entry from the fax log, select Delete the Selected Entry (F5) from the Actions menu, or click on Delete on the message line. Delete removes the entries without asking for confirmation, so be careful when you use this option.

- To search for a Fax Log entry, choose Search (F6) from the Actions menu, enter the text you want to search for, and select OK. All the fax log entries that meet the search criteria are shown on the screen.

You can also set the rate at which the fax log is updated with the AutoUpdate option in the Configure menu. Enter a number in seconds to specify the time period between updates of the fax log.

USING ELECTRONIC MAIL

Telecommunications allows you to send and receive mail messages via MCI Mail, CompuServe, or EasyLink. You can send and receive messages on a regular basis, or you can send them immediately when they are ready. You can mail messages directly from Desktop Notepads and Outlines, as well as from inside Telecommunications, and if you are set up for background communications, you can send and receive messages without interrupting your foreground application program.

SETTING UP YOUR ELECTRONIC MAIL SYSTEM

When you select Electronic Mail from the Telecommunications menu for the first time, the Electronic Mail window is blank. If, after you have set the system up, you have mail when you open Electronic Mail, you will see a dialog box which indicates that messages are waiting to be read.

Before you can use Electronic Mail, you must first establish several important parameters, which you do with the Setup menu. Choose Mail service to select which of the three services you will be using, as shown in Figure 17.10. Choose from MCI Mail, CompuServe,

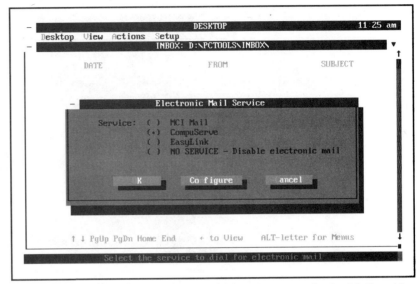

Figure 17.10: Select the online service you want to use in the Mail service dialog box

EasyLink, or choose NO SERVICE to disable Electronic Mail. Next, select Configure from this dialog box to establish telephone numbers, user ID numbers, and to enter your password, as Figure 17.11 shows.

You must enter the following:

- **Phone Number.** Type in the telephone number of your service. Parentheses, spaces, and dashes are ignored, so you can enter the number as you like.

- **User ID.** Enter the user-identification number supplied to you by the service. Upper- and lowercase letters are treated as different characters, so be careful to observe the correct case.

- **Password.** Enter the password supplied to you by the service.

- **Baud Rate.** Select the baud rate you want to use. Remember, the higher the number, the faster the transmission. Most services have different charges for different speed modems.

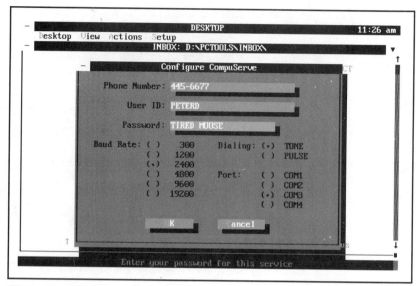

Figure 17.11: Enter communications parameters into the Configure dialog box

- **Dialing.** Choose pulse or tone dialing.

- **Port.** Select the COM port that your modem is connected to.

When you have made your selections, choose OK. The remaining communications parameters are already configured for you and stored in the file PHONE.TEL.

The next step in setting up your Electronic Mail is to establish a schedule for sending and receiving your mail. Choose Send Mail Schedule from the Setup menu to establish an automatic transfer. Figure 17.12 shows the Send Mail Schedule dialog box.

You must enter the following into this dialog box:

To send or receive mail automatically, remember to run Desktop as a memory-resident program.

- **Every.** Select the interval you want to use to send your mail; the default setting is 2 for every two hours.

- **Start.** Enter the start time; add "a" to indicate AM, or "p" to indicate PM. Alternatively, use a 24-hour clock without the "a" and "p" indicators; so 10:00p is equivalent to 2200 (the default setting is 09:30a).

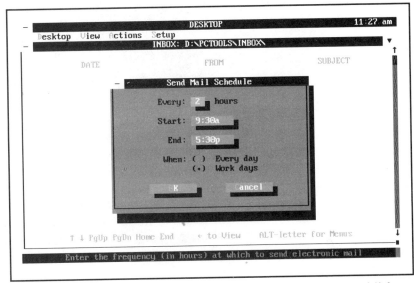

Figure 17.12: Use the Send Mail Schedule dialog box to establish an automatic mail schedule

- **End.** Enter the time after which mail should not be sent. The default setting is 5:30p.

- **When.** Specify when mail is to be sent; either every day, or only on work days. Work days are established from your settings in the Appointment Scheduler, described in Chapter 15.

As an example, if you enter 4 into Every, with a Start time of 10:00a, and an End Time of 6:00p, messages will be sent at 10:00 a.m., 2:00 p.m., and 6:00 p.m.

To read your mail automatically, use the Read Mail Schedule selection from the Setup menu; it works just like the Send Mail Schedule dialog box, and uses similar Every, Start, End, and When settings.

Electronic Mail stores three sets of messages, and the next step is to create directories on your hard disk to contain them. Messages fall into one of three categories:

- Incoming messages sent to you by other people are kept in an inbox.

- Outgoing messages to other people are kept in an outbox until you send them.

- After messages have been sent, they are kept in a sent box.

Use Mail Directories from the Setup menu to establish three directories for these three sets of messages. The Electronic Mail Directories dialog box opens, as shown in Figure 17.13. Enter the complete path names for the three directories into the dialog box. The default names are PCTOOLS\INBOX, PCTOOLS\OUTBOX, and PCTOOLS\SENT. It makes good sense to stay with these names.

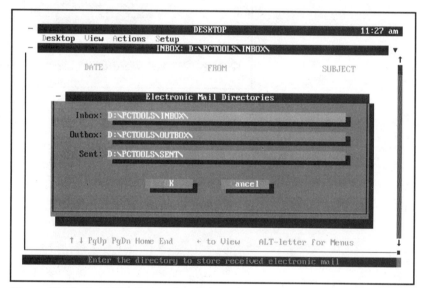

Figure 17.13: Establish directories on your hard disk for outgoing, incoming, and sent messages

CREATING A MESSAGE

Now you are ready to create a message. Select Create mail message from the Actions menu, or press F8. A notepad opens with the mail-header information already filled in for you. Exactly what you see in this header depends on the service you are using. For example, MCI Mail and EasyLink do not use a FROM line in their headers.

A CompuServe header is shown in Figure 17.14. Complete the entries in the header and then type in the body of your message. All the editing capabilities of Desktop's Notepads are available to you, including Find, Find and Replace, and the Spelling Checker. Electronic Mail chooses the file name for each message; it is important that you do not change this file name once it has been created.

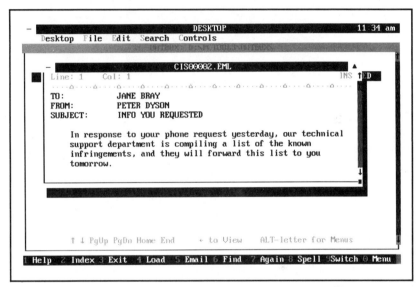

Figure 17.14: Fill in the header information, then type in your text for electronic mail

> **Electronic Mail** Notepads files have the file-name extension .EML.

When your message is complete, choose Send Electronic Mail from the File menu, or if you change your mind and decide not to send the message, choose Exit Without Saving to return directly to Electronic Mail. Finally, select when the message should be sent, from Send Immediately to Send the Message Now, or Send At Scheduled Time to send the message at a normally scheduled transmission. As soon as you select the method, Electronic Mail places your message file into the outbox directory you have specified.

VIEWING MESSAGES

Your message is now shown on the main Electronic Mail window, along with any others you created. You can check the contents of a message. Place the highlight over the message you want to check, and select View highlighted message from the Actions menu. A notepad opens, showing you the contents of your message. If you make any changes to messages in the outbox directory, you must choose Send Electronic Mail from the File menu, then Send at Scheduled Time, and, finally, select OK to save the changes. If you do not do this, the file in the outbox directory will not be updated with your changes and your original, unaltered message will be sent.

If you change your mind about sending a message, just highlight the message and select Delete Highlighted Message from the Actions menu. Be careful with this, because you are not asked to confirm your choice of message to delete. As soon as you choose it, the message under the highlight is gone.

You can also use the three selections in the View menu to look at your mail: View InBox (F4), View OutBox (F5), or View Sent (F6). To read a message on demand, use Read Mail Now from the Actions menu, or press F7.

CHAPTER

18

Using DeskConnect and the Desktop Utilities

This chapter describes the computer-to-computer communications program called DeskConnect, as well as the Utilities section of the Desktop.

USING DESKCONNECT

Imagine that you are leaving on a business trip, and that you want to load your important files onto your laptop computer so you can take them with you. At the end of your trip you will want to load these (edited) files back onto your regular computer again. If the two computers use differently sized disks, this can be a real problem, and if you have many large files, disk swapping rapidly becomes tedious. DeskConnect allows you to access your laptop's disk drives from your desktop computer and copy files from one machine to the other easily and safely.

INSTALLING DESKCONNECT

For DeskConnect to work, both computers must be connected by a null-modem cable. This is a special serial cable with sending and receiving wires crossed over, so that the wires used for sending by one computer are used for receiving by the other computer, and vice versa.

DeskConnect is really a pair of programs; one is a memory-resident program running on your desktop computer, the other is a stand-alone program running on your laptop computer. Once the two programs are running, your laptop computer's disk drives appear on PC Shell's drive line as networked drives. You can now copy files from one drive to the other, just as you would if they were in the same computer. There are several PC Shell functions that you cannot use—for instance, you cannot format a floppy disk on the laptop or use Directory Maintenance—but these are minor limitations usually designed with safety in mind.

Use the PC Tools Install program to configure and load DeskConnect, or configure it yourself from the DOS command line.

You must start DeskConnect running on your laptop *before* you start it on your desktop machine. To start DeskConnect on your laptop, type

DESKSRV

and to run DeskConnect on your desktop computer, type

DESKCON

or place the following command in your AUTOEXEC.BAT file:

DESKCON

If you do not use any of the command-line parameters, DeskConnect will use COM 1. This is the default method of starting DeskConnect. There are several optional commands you can use to configure DeskConnect to your own requirements, but if you do use any of them, remember that you may also need to change some of the settings on your laptop computer.

If you place the DESKCON command in your AUTO-EXEC.BAT file, DeskConnect will be loaded automatically every time you start your computer.

See Chapter 20 for a complete list of DeskConnect command-line parameters.

CONNECTING YOUR LAPTOP

When you load DESKSRV on your laptop, you will see the display shown in Figure 18.1. As you work with DeskConnect from your desktop computer, you will see the highlight in this display move from Waiting to Receiving and Sending as information passes

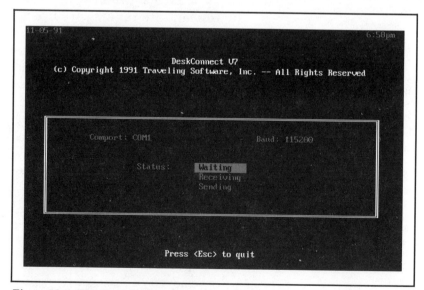

Figure 18.1: The DeskConnect screen on your laptop

between the two computers. There are no menus and no commands in DESKSRV, the program just acts as a buffer between the disks on your laptop and the DeskConnect program running on your desktop computer. The time and date, COM port in use, and baud rate are also shown in this screen.

When you start DESKCON on your desktop machine, a brief identification message appears on the screen. It is now safe to start PC Shell and choose DeskConnect from the Special menu. A check mark appears opposite the DeskConnect menu selection to show that DeskConnect is enabled. A small dialog box opens informing you of how the drives on your laptop have been remapped to drives on your desktop computer, as shown in Figure 18.2. If the connection fails for some reason, PC Shell displays an error message reminding you to start the software on both computers, and to check that the cable is installed securely.

In this example, the desktop computer has two floppy disks, drives A and B, and three hard-disk partitions, drives C, D, and E. The laptop has one floppy disk, drive A, and two hard-disk partitions, drives C and D. As you can see from Figure 18.2, all the drives on the laptop have been remapped to new drive letters on the desktop system,

DESKCON must be installed before you start PC Shell.

PC Shell treats laptop drives as network drives, so it may take longer to read them than normal.

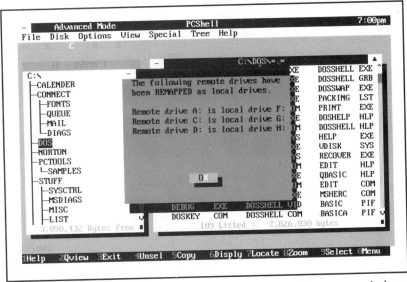

Figure 18.2: The disk drives on your laptop remapped onto your desktop system

so drive A on the laptop becomes drive F on the desktop system, drive C on the laptop becomes drive G, and drive D on the laptop becomes drive H. Now select OK, and you will see all these drives represented as icons on the PC Shell drive line. To look at the files on drive G, just press Ctrl-G or click on the drive icon, and you will see the usual PC Shell tree listing on the screen.

TRANSFERRING FILES

Once the two computers are connected, you can use all the capabilities of PC Shell to select files and copy them from one to the other. First select a directory, then highlight the files that you want to copy. Use Copy from the File menu to copy the files to the correct disk on your other computer. The first dialog box asks you to choose the destination disk and the next dialog box asks for the target directory to copy the files into. If the files you have selected already exist on the laptop, you may have to use one of the following selections:

- **Replace All** replaces all duplicates on the target directory.

- **Replace File** replaces the current file in the target directory with the same name as the current file.

- **Next File** skips this file and moves on to the next file.

- **Skip All** skips all files and returns to the PC Shell main screen.

As the files are copied across, you will see a dialog box showing the name of the file being copied. When all files have been transferred, you are returned to the PC Shell screen.

ENDING A DESKCONNECT SESSION

When you are ready to end a DeskConnect session, make sure that you are not logged on to one of the laptop computer's disk drives. If you are, change to one of the drives on your desktop computer, then choose DeskConnect from the Special menu. In the subsequent dialog box, choose Disconnect. The check mark next to the DeskConnect menu item disappears, and you can exit PC Shell safely. If you want to remove the DESKCON memory-resident program from memory, type

DESKCON /U

and you will see the message

DeskConnect V7 successfully uninstalled

on the screen. You can also type **KILL** to remove DESKCON, but remember that KILL also removes PC Shell, Desktop, CPSCHED, and BackTalk, if they were the last memory-resident programs loaded.

To halt just the laptop part of the link, press the Escape key and type **Y** to confirm that you want to stop using DeskConnect.

USING THE DESKTOP UTILITIES

There are three entries in the Utilities menu in Desktop: Hotkey Selection, Ascii Table, and Unload PCTOOLS Desktop.

HOTKEYS AND DESKTOP

If you want to hotkey into PC Tools Desktop from Microsoft Windows, you cannot use Ctrl-Shift, Ctrl-Alt, or Shift-Alt because Windows reserves these hotkeys for its own special purposes.

If you use Desktop in memory-resident mode, you can hotkey into it using the special hotkey combination. You can change these defaults by choosing Hotkey Selection from the Utilities menu. When you choose Hotkey Selection from the Utilities menu, the PCTOOLS Desktop Hotkey Selection window opens. Choose the program whose hotkey you want to change from the list on the screen and enter your new hotkey combination. The keys that you press are shown on the screen in angle brackets next to the program name. These new keys are put into operation as soon as you leave this screen.

EXAMINING THE ASCII CODES

ASCII (pronounced *ass'-key*) stands for the American Standard Code for Information Interchange. ASCII codes represent letters, punctuation symbols, numbers, mathematical symbols, and so on. When you type a character, what the computer actually reads is the ASCII code for that character. You can also employ ASCII codes to control devices (such as monitors and printers).

In ASCII, each character is represented by a unique integer value, commonly referred to as a *decimal value*. The values 0 to 31 are used for control codes, and the range from 32 to 127 is reserved for the letters of the alphabet and common punctuation symbols. The entire set of 0–127 is called *standard* ASCII. All computers that use ASCII characters can understand the standard ASCII set, although not all can work with the *extended character set*, which are the values 128 to 255. These values encode uncommon symbols and punctuation marks, for example, Greek letters. (We'll examine this set shortly.)

ASCII CONTROL CHARACTERS   The *control code* characters (0 to 31) are reserved for special purposes that usually have to do with controlling devices or communications.

Codes 1 to 4—which stand for SOH, STX, ETX, and EOT—are used in communications to indicate the start and end of both the transmission (codes 1 and 4) and its text (codes 2 and 3). Other codes are used to control the flow of transmitted data: for example, ACK (acknowledge) and NAK (negative acknowledge) indicate whether data were received successfully, and ENQ (enquire), SYN (synchronize), ETB (end-of-transmission block), and CAN (cancel) are also used to control the flow. Additional codes punctuate the flow of information: FS (file separator), GS (group separator), RS (record separator), and US (unit separator) all fall into this category.

Several codes are used to control peripheral devices, particularly printers. The CR (carriage return), LF (line feed), FF (form feed, which is sometimes referred to as new page), HT (horizontal tab), BS (backspace), and VT (vertical tab) sequences all find uses in device control.

Ctrl-S and Ctrl-Q are often used as pause and restart commands, and Ctrl-[produces the Esc character. An escape sequence, comprising the Esc character followed by one or more other characters in a set order, is a common way of controlling complex devices such as terminals and printers that have more capabilities than can be controlled by the

---

The standard ASCII codes use 7 of the 8 bits in a byte.

Codes 1 to 4 are generally not used in modern microcomputer communications.

The VT sequence is rarely used to control devices.

Ctrl-S is often called X-OFF, and Ctrl-Q is often called X-ON.

individual ASCII control-characters alone. See your printer manual for more details.

THE EXTENDED CHARACTER SET   The IBM extended-character set starts where the standard ASCII set leaves off. The next available decimal code is 128, and the extended set runs from 128 to 255. Its characters—which include the PC line-drawing set, mathematical symbols, and graphics characters—are not standard on computers that are not compatible with IBM's microcomputers. Word-processing programs have different ways of allowing you to use the characters in the extended ASCII set. In WordStar, for example, you can display these characters by simultaneously pressing the Alt key and typing the decimal value of the appropriate character on the numeric keypad (you cannot use the regular number keys for this purpose). Moreover, printers vary in their ability to print these characters.

Because different languages (for example, Norwegian and Portuguese) use different characters and keyboard layouts, there are a number of language-specific ASCII tables. These tables use decimal codes 128–255 for necessary characters that are not provided by the standard ASCII set. Each of these tables is called a *code page*.

LOOKING AT THE ASCII TABLE   Desktop contains a complete extended ASCII character set table, available from the Utilities menu. When you select Ascii Table from the Utilities menu, you will see the screen shown in Figure 18.3.

The ASCII characters are displayed on the screen in two columns of 16 characters each. The ASCII character is shown in the center of each column. The hexadecimal code for the character is shown on the left and the decimal code is shown on the right. If you look at the first 32 ASCII characters, this display changes slightly: the left side of the display still shows the hex codes, the characters, and the decimal codes, but the right side now shows the control codes for these characters and their abbreviated names.

To find a character in the table, just type the character from the keyboard and the display scrolls to the right part of the ASCII table. If you type **E**, the display changes to include the *E* character. If you enter a control sequence like Ctrl-J, the display moves to the first part

ASCII 255 is the largest decimal value that can be represented by using all 8 of the bits in one 8-bit byte.

If you have an EGA or VGA monitor, you may see nonstandard symbols in some parts of the ASCII table.

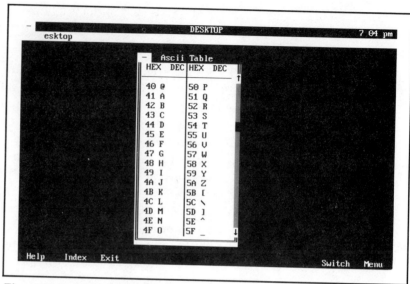

Figure 18.3: ASCII Table from the Utilities menu displays the full ASCII extended-character set

of the ASCII table that includes all the control characters. You can access the extended ASCII character set if you hold down the Alt key and type a number between 128 and 255 from the ten-key pad. This is especially useful when you are working with the PC line-drawing set or other special symbols (for instance, Alt-129 is the German ü).

UNLOADING DESKTOP

If you are through using Desktop, or you want to recover memory space to run a large program, you can remove Desktop from your computer's memory. Choose Unload PCTOOLS Desktop from the Utilities menu, and you will see the screen shown in Figure 18.4.

You cannot remove Desktop if you hotkeyed into it from inside an application program. Also, if you are using several memory-resident programs, you must remove them in the opposite order from which you loaded them. Otherwise, you may not be able to recover the memory they occupied without rebooting your computer. Choose Unload when you are ready to remove Desktop, or select Cancel to return to Desktop.

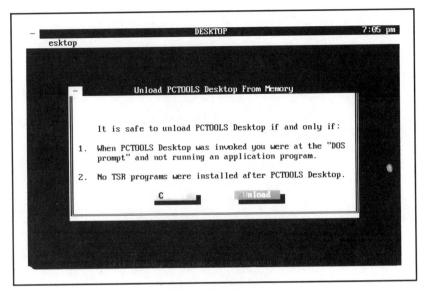

Figure 18.4: The Unload PCTOOLS Desktop warning screen

You can also remove Desktop if you type

KILL

from the DOS prompt. Remember that Kill also removes PC Shell, BackTalk, DeskConnect, and the Scheduler if they were loaded.

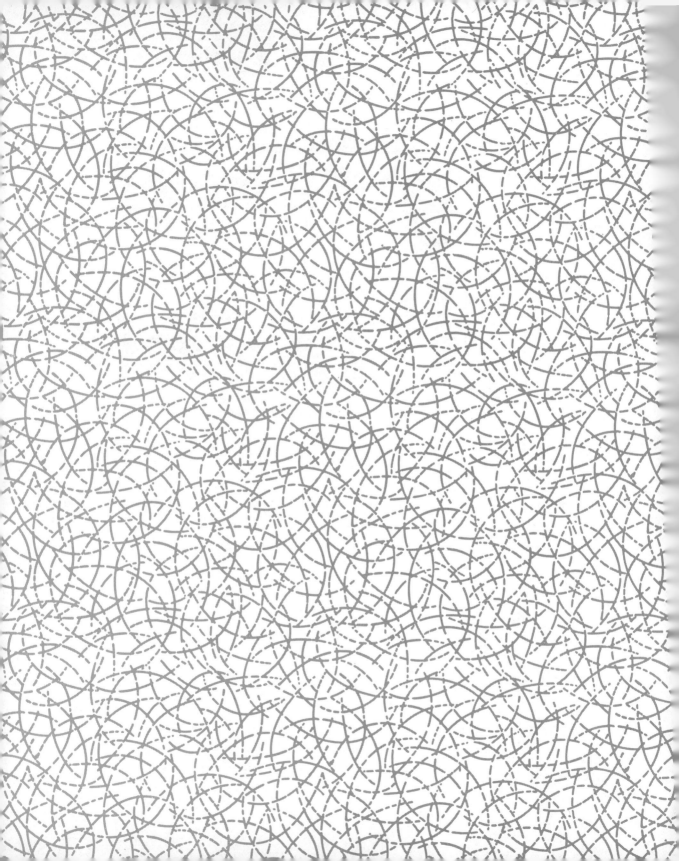

PART V

Reference Tools

CHAPTER

19

Troubleshooting

Most of the chapters in this book have dealt with a specific utility, describing how to use it in detail. This chapter is a little different in that it describes how to benefit from the troubleshooting facilities available in the DiskFix program to help understand and solve your disk-related problems. It also describes memory-resident programs and some of the common problems associated with them.

USING THE DISKFIX ADVICE MENU

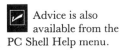
Advice is also available from the PC Shell Help menu.

The selections in the Advice menu work in much the same way as the context-sensitive help that is available in the rest of the PC Tools programs. You select one topic from the list with the up and down arrow keys and then press Enter, or click on the item to see a more detailed explanation. This lower-level window often includes specific suggestions about which of the PC Tools programs to use to help solve your problem. If DOS reports an error that you are unfamiliar with, you can learn more about the error message from the selections available through Advice and then run the appropriate program to fix the problem. The selections in the Advice menu are divided into categories, each defining a different group of problems. In the following sections, I describe how to use each of these groups.

First load the DiskFix program and choose Advice from the list of options.

GENERAL PROBLEMS

Let's assume that you are having disk problems. Select General Problems; this opens the window shown in Figure 19.1.

You think the problem has something to do with read errors. Move the highlight until it is on the Error Reading (or Writing) Drive X selection, then click the mouse or press Enter. Another window opens to display a more complete description of the proposed solution, as shown in Figure 19.2. Press F5 (GoBack) to return to the list of errors and press it again to return to the main list of DiskFix help topics.

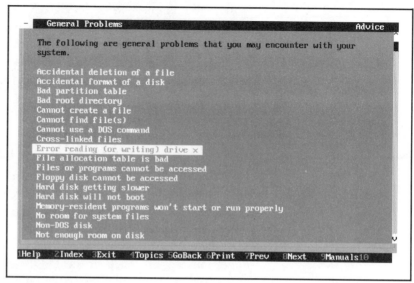

Figure 19.1: The first General Problems window

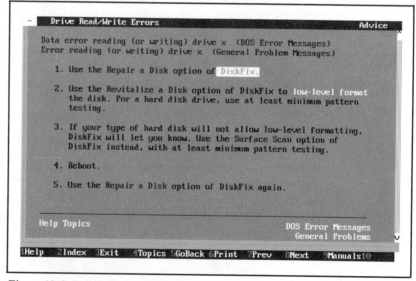

Figure 19.2: Advice lists the PC Tools programs you can run to solve your disk problems

DOS ERROR MESSAGES

The second selection from the Advice screen displays a list of the common DOS errors you might see from time to time. The list includes many disk-related error messages, but it is by no means a complete list. Some of the error messages are relatively insignificant, such as

Abort, Retry, Fail?

which often results if you try to read a drive before you have inserted a floppy disk. However, some of the other errors can panic even the most seasoned computer user—such as

Invalid drive specification

which can mean that your partition table has been corrupted or that the boot track has been destroyed. This sort of message should not be ignored because it can indicate a deteriorating hard disk.

If you ever *do* see the error message Invalid drive specification and you know that you used to be able to access that drive, choose the Invalid drive specification error message from the list of DOS Error Messages. This displays the window shown in Figure 19.3, which offers several suggestions on which PC Tools programs you can run to fix the problem.

CHKDSK ERROR MESSAGES

The DOS command CHKDSK checks the formatted size and the amount of free space on a disk. It also reports the amount of space used by hidden files, directories, user files, and bad sectors, as well as details the memory size and amount of free memory available in your computer. CHKDSK tests for logical errors in the file-allocation tables and the directories, and can output a series of error messages depending on what it finds.

If you are using DOS 3.3 or later, you can also use CHKDSK to give you a report on the fragmentation of a file. CHKDSK will report that the file contains a number of non-contiguous blocks if the

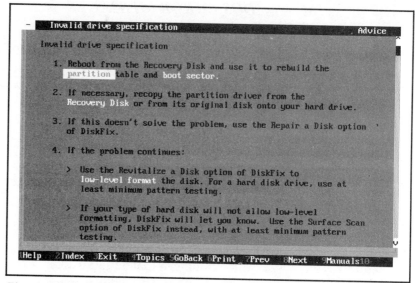

Figure 19.3: Choose the appropriate error message from the list on the screen

file is split into pieces. If you should see this error, press ↓ to scroll a bit and highlight the Contains xxx non-contiguous blocks message, as Figure 19.4 shows. Press Enter.

The next window advises you to run the Compress disk-optimizer utility, because the CHKDSK error message tells you that the file is fragmented or broken up into several pieces that are spread over the disk. Because the file is in several different areas of the disk, it will take longer to load all the pieces than it would take to load the file if it were in only one piece. Compress will fix this file fragmentation.

DATA PROTECTION GUIDELINES

The Data Protection Guidelines selection offers specific suggestions to fix specific problems: running Undelete to recover accidentally deleted files, for example, or using DiskFix if you have disk-related problems. This selection also offers you the good advice of backing up your system regularly to ensure effectively against the loss of data.

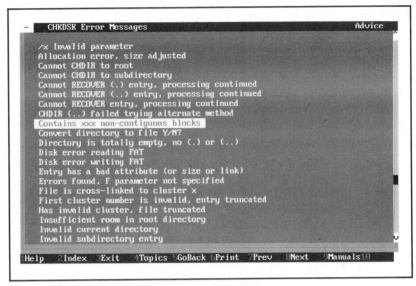

Figure 19.4: Choose the appropriate CHKDSK error message

IF ALL ELSE FAILS

This heading contains a last-resort suggestion: if all else fails even after you have followed all the suggestions contained in Advice, you should back up your entire hard disk (all partitions), perform a low-level format of the disk, and reload your program and data files back onto the disk. This is a time-consuming operation and should only be performed when you have exhausted every other way to solve your disk-related problem.

If you go this route, use CP Backup to back up all your files and directories. Then use Revitalize a Disk in the DiskFix program to perform a low-level format without destroying the data on the disk. Revitalize a Disk copies the data in each track, reformats the track, and then rewrites the original data back again.

If your disk is of a type that does not allow DiskFix to perform a revitalization, your options are slightly different, and rather more complex:

1. Make a backup of all the partitions on your hard disk before doing anything else.

This low-level format differs from the operation performed by Revitalize a Disk because it *does* destroy all the data on the disk.

2. Use a program like Disk Manager or a diagnostics program like QA Plus to perform the low-level format.

3. Partition the disk using the DOS FDISK command or a program like Disk Manager.

4. Format each of the partitions on the disk using PC Format or the DOS FORMAT command.

5. Use CP Backup to restore the complete backup you made in step 1.

If you do not feel comfortable about performing this series of complex operations, get help from a friend, your computer dealer, or from the members of your local PC Users Group. If your disk problems persist after reformatting, consider replacing the disk.

MEMORY-RESIDENT PROGRAMS

In this section, I describe terminate-and-stay-resident (TSR) programs and memory-resident programs. I detail the problems that they can cause and include some possible solutions.

WHAT IS A MEMORY-RESIDENT PROGRAM?

One of the major problems of MS-DOS is that it does not support more than one program running at a time. DOS is a single-user, single-tasking operating system. In contrast to this, OS/2 is single-user multi-tasking and UNIX is multi-user multi-tasking. The TSR program is an ingenious method that at least partially overcomes this limitation in DOS.

A TSR program loads itself into memory and returns control to DOS, but waits in the background. When you press a certain key combination from the keyboard (the *hotkey*), the TSR interrupts the application you were running and gives instant access to its services. When you are finished with the TSR program, you return to your application program. You can run PC Shell, Desktop, or both programs in this TSR mode.

Other memory-resident programs in the PC Tools package work in a slightly different way. They attach themselves to the operating system and remain in memory, working constantly in the background, much like the DOS PRINT utility. Indeed, PRINT is often cited as the first real memory-resident program. PC-Cache is a program in this category, as is the small portion of the Data Monitor program that performs delete protection. These programs work all the time, unlike PC Shell or Desktop, which are activated only when you press their respective hotkeys.

There are several major benefits to using TSR programs rather than programs loaded from the DOS command prompt (often called *transient applications*):

- Speed. You can access Notepads or Outlines to make a note to yourself, or use the calculators without leaving your main application. If you are using a large and complex application, this can save you a significant amount of time.

- Configuration. Loading a selected set of utilities allows you to configure your own computing environment exactly as you want it, rather than having to work with several different large foreground applications that may contain features you never use.

- Data Exchange. You can capture data from your foreground application and paste it into the clipboard for later use in a word processor.

- Convenience. You have several programs accessible at virtually the same time.

PROBLEMS WITH TSR PROGRAMS

Microsoft has published preliminary guidelines for writing reliable TSRs, but they have not been universally accepted.

One main advantage of memory-resident programs is that they can be used together. However, these programs are often distributed by different manufacturers and there are no universally adopted standards for writing TSRs. Not surprisingly, conflicts occasionally arise between different TSR programs and between TSR programs and the main application.

COEXISTING WITH OTHER TSR PROGRAMS

If you use several TSRs, problems may arise because they do not coexist properly, even though they share the same hardware and operating system. One delinquent TSR can disable your whole system, even causing you to lose data. Ideally, TSRs should be loaded into memory in sequence and should form an unbroken structure in which control is passed from program to program with no one being bypassed.

If you install a new TSR and one of your other TSRs stops working, the second program is probably interfering with the first. Loading order is often critical for certain TSR programs.

The recommended loading order for PC Tools (from first to last loaded) is as follows:

1. DOS internal commands (PROMPT, PATH, etc.)

2. DOS external commands (MODE, PRINT, etc.)

3. Network drivers such as IPX.COM and NETx.COM on a Novell network

4. Mouse drivers

5. Print spoolers

6. Mirror

7. PC-Cache

8. Data Monitor

9. Keyboard enhancers such as SuperKey or ProKey

10. Any TSR program that does not fit into any of the categories listed here

11. Commute

12. PC Shell

13. Desktop

To determine where programs are located in your computer's memory, select the Memory Map option in the Special menu of PC

Shell. This loads the System Information program and lists the memory areas in use, the number of bytes (or kilobytes) in use by a program, and the name of the program using the memory.

Most TSRs are automatically loaded with the AUTOEXEC.BAT file. Some TSR installation programs change the contents of this file without telling you, which can sometimes lead to unexpected results. If you experience conflicts between programs after adding a new TSR to your system, you can start tracking down the culprit by executing the commands in your AUTOEXEC.BAT file one at a time from the DOS prompt.

To isolate the problem:

1. Make sure that you don't load any TSR programs at all. You can do this by booting your computer from the Recovery Disk made by the Install program, because that disk does not contain an AUTOEXEC.BAT file.

2. Make drive C the current drive.

3. Enter the statements from your AUTOEXEC.BAT file that load the first TSR program.

4. After loading the TSR, run it to test it.

5. When it performs as desired, type in the next entry from your AUTOEXEC.BAT file to load the next TSR. Test this program and also test the TSR you loaded previously.

6. Continue this process until you have loaded and tested all of your TSR programs.

This method should help you find out which program is causing the problem.

You can also have hotkey conflict, where two programs are looking for the same key combination at the same time. The result is that the first program responds to the hotkey every time and the second program never sees the hotkey and therefore never runs. In both PC Shell and Desktop, you can change the hotkey specification to avoid this kind of conflict.

Memory space is always at a premium, and well-designed TSR programs should allow you to decide how much memory to allot to a particular application. Some TSR programs require that large areas of memory be permanently allocated for their use, but PC Tools uses only a small area of memory while dormant. When you use the hotkey, PC Tools saves the contents of your computer's memory into a temporary disk file. In this way, PC Tools occupies the smallest amount of space in memory when it is dormant and can use all the memory needed when you activate it with the hotkey.

If you have expanded memory installed in your computer, PC Desktop uses it to store the image of the foreground application. This memory is cleared when you hotkey out of Desktop. With the optional parameters available for PC Tools programs, you can configure the PC Tools memory allocations to be optimum for your system.

Finally, well-designed TSR programs should check for double installation, and refuse to install themselves if they are already installed. This way, you avoid having multiple copies of a program in memory.

CONFLICTS WITH
THE MAIN FOREGROUND APPLICATION

The main areas of conflict between TSR programs and foreground application programs are the same as those between TSR programs themselves. Key conflicts can arise with your foreground application, too. Some programs use esoteric key combinations to perform various functions and sometimes these key combinations can interfere with or prevent the proper working of your TSR programs. For example, in WordStar you use the Ctrl key in combination with many other keys to perform text-manipulation commands. Your TSR program may require that same key combination for correct operation. Again, a well-designed TSR program that lets you customize the hotkey has the advantage here.

Memory can continue to be a problem, and you may find that you cannot load a particular application and its data file if you have too many TSR programs installed in your system. You may have to uninstall a TSR so that you can load your application and its data.

Use the TSR Manager to communicate with DOS TSRs if you are running Microsoft Windows.

Many PC Tools programs will show you a message indicating that there is not enough memory available for them to run. You can always use the System Information program or the DOS CHKDSK command to check whether you have sufficient available memory.

Restoring the correct video mode as you exit from the TSR can be a problem, too. The screen may fill with garbage characters. There can also be conflicts between programs running in text mode and in graphics mode returning the screen correctly.

REMOVING TSR PROGRAMS

Well-organized TSR programs can remove themselves from memory or uninstall themselves. In PC Tools, you can use a program called Kill to uninstall DeskConnect, Desktop, PC Shell, CPSCHED, and Backtalk, as long as they were the last memory-resident programs you loaded.

You can also remove a TSR program from your computer by removing the commands that load the program from your AUTOEXEC.BAT file and then rebooting your computer. This is a brutal approach, but with programs that don't have a removal mechanism, it is the only way to stop them from being loaded.

Another approach for releasing memory used by TSR programs is to use one of the TSR management-utility programs, such as Mark or Release, available as shareware from TurboPower Software. These programs manage multiple TSR programs (even programs from different vendors) and release them from memory in the correct order.

CHAPTER

20

*The PC Tools Complete
Command Reference*

In this last chapter, I list all the PC Tools programs in alphabetical order and detail the parameters that you can use when you load them from the DOS command prompt. You can set many of these optional parameters when you install PC Tools; others are extremely useful in batch files.

The parameters are optional unless otherwise noted. If you don't use them, the program will start up in the usual way.

To see a list of the command-line options for any particular program, type the program name followed by /? and the program will display its command-line parameters onscreen. For example, to see a list of the parameters available in PC Tools Desktop, type

DESKTOP /?

and you will see a list of options on the screen.

VIDEO AND MOUSE MODES

Many of the PC Tools programs let you specify video or mouse parameters on the command line. Each program that does so lists these parameters on the screen when you type the program name followed by **/VIDEO**. To look at the video and mouse parameters available in Commute, type

COMMUTE /VIDEO

at the DOS command prompt.

Use PC Config to set most of these switches for all PC Tools programs.

You can choose from the following video switches:

/25	Sets the screen to 25 lines; this is the default
/28	Sets the screen to 28 lines, VGA only
/43	Sets the screen to 43 lines, EGA and VGA only
/50	Sets the screen to 50 lines, VGA only
/60	Sets the screen to 60 lines, for use with the Video 7 VGA
/BF	Uses the computer's BIOS to manipulate screen fonts; the programs do not write directly to the screen

/BW	Starts the program in black-and-white mode
/FF	Does not suppress "snow" on CGA monitors; you can make your system work faster by using this switch if you don't mind snow on the screen
/LCD	Use this option if your laptop computer has a liquid crystal display
/IN	Uses the original default color scheme rather than the current configuration
/MONO	Selects the IBM monochrome mode
/NF	Disables the use of special graphics characters on the screen; the mouse cursor becomes a square character and other special characters are removed

And choose from the following mouse switches:

/IM	Disables the mouse in PC Tools programs
/LE	Swaps the left and right mouse buttons to make a left-handed mouse
/NGM	Turns off the graphical mouse cursor and uses a square character instead
/PS2	Resets the mouse hardware

BACKTALK

Backtalk is the memory-resident program that performs Desktop background communications.

Syntax

To run Backtalk, add the following line to your AUTOEXEC-.BAT file:

    BACKTALK switch

Description

/1	Installs Backtalk using COM1
/2	Installs Backtalk using COM2
/3 = *irq, address*	Installs Backtalk using COM3, where *irq* specifies the interrupt request and *address* specifies the base port address; for example, on a PC AT or clone, specify COM3 with /C3 = 4,3E8
/4 = *irq, address*	Installs Backtalk using COM4, where *irq* specifies the interrupt request and *address* specifies the base port address; for example, on a PC AT or clone, specify COM4 with /C4 = 3,2E8

COMMUTE

Commute is a communications program that lets you run another computer over a modem, network, or null-modem connection. You can run programs, transfer files, even take control of the remote computer.

Syntax

COMMUTE *script name list name user name switch*

Description

script name	Starts the Commute program using the specified script file; it is not necessary to include the .CSF file extension with this parameter.
list name	Specifies the name to call from the names in the Private Call List; use quotation marks to enclose text that includes spaces
user name	Specifies the user name to call via local-area network from the names in the LAN User List; enclose multiple words in quotation marks

You can specify the communications parameters to use from the following list:

/BR = *n*	Sets the baud rate to the value specified by the number *n*, where *n* is one of the following: 1,200, 2,400, 4,800, 9,600, 19,200, 38,400, 57,600, or 115,200
/CP = *n*	Sets the COM port to the values specified by *n*, where *n* is 1, 2, 3, or 4
/CT = M, D, or L	Sets the connection type to modem (M), direct (D), or LAN (L)
/MA = *string*	Specifies the modem answer string; if this string includes spaces, enclose the complete string in quotation marks
/MD = *string*	Specifies the modem dial string
/MH = *string*	Specifies the modem hang-up string
/MI = *string*	Specifies the modem initialization string

Choose from the following security parameters:

/BT = ON or OFF	When set to ON, allows the controlling PC to reboot your computer
/DPW = *password*	Sets the default password to the text contained in *string*, up to 10 characters; if you do not enter a string after the /DPW parameter, you turn off the Default Password option
/DR = A, B, AB, or N	Specifies which floppy-disk drives the controlling PC can use during a Commute session; use a single letter for one drive, AB to allow both, or N for none

/IA = n	Specifies the inactivity timeout for automatic disconnect to the value n, where n is a value from 1 to 60 minutes; set the value to 0 for no automatic disconnect
/L = A or M	Selects the Auto-Login method (A) or the Manual Login method (M)
/LK = ON or OFF	When set to ON, allows the controlling PC to lock your keyboard
/PR = ON or OFF	When set to ON, lets the controlling PC use your printer

Specifies the configuration parameters from the following:

/NE	Does not use expanded memory, if it is available
/NL	Does not load the LAN portion of Commute, to save memory space
/NU	Does not use the upper memory blocks available with DOS 5; this option allows a different application to use the upper memory blocks
/NX	Does not use extended memory, if it is available
/R or /RL	Loads Commute memory-resident to wait for a call from another PC, equivalent to using Wait for Any Caller in the Call Manager. Using /RL is the same as using Wait From Call List in the Call Manager
/RG or /RGL	Loads Commute memory-resident to wait for a call, ready to give control to the calling PC. Using /RGL waits only for callers on the Give Control List

/RT	Loads Commute memory-resident to wait for a call, ready to take control of that calling PC
/U	Stops waiting for a call and unloads Commute from memory

Finally, choose from the following list of general parameters:

/8250	The Intel 8250 UART (Universal Asynchronous Receiver-Transmitter) is a communications chip used on the IBM Asynchronous Communications Adapter card, on many third-party communications and multifunction cards, and in many modems. With the PC AT, IBM upgraded to the 16450 UART, and in the PS/2 they used the 16550 UART. There are slight performance differences between these chips. If you have one of these earlier 8250 UARTs in your system, use this switch to make Commute emulate the later, more modern UART in software
/AL = ON or OFF	When set to ON, turns on the activity log file
/CF	Forces Commute to go through the configuration process when starting, as though the program were starting for the first time
/NA = *name*	Sets the Commute user name

COMPRESS

Compress improves your hard-disk performance by unfragmenting your files.

Syntax

COMPRESS *drive switch*

Description

    drive   The drive letter of the drive you want to compress; if you don't enter a drive letter, Compress assumes that you want to use the current drive

Specify your choice of compression selections with the following options:

    /CC   Performs a full compression and clears all unused clusters

    /CD   Optimizes directories, but does not unfragment files

    /CF   Performs a full optimization

    /CS   Optimizes the free space on your disk, but does not unfragment files

    /CU   Unfragments files, but does not collect the free space into a single piece

Specify the physical file ordering from the DOS prompt or from a batch file with the following options:

    /OD   Places files close to their parent directory

    /OF   Positions select files at the front of the disk; program files do not normally grow in size once you have installed them, so placing them at the front of the disk prevents them from becoming fragmented again in the future

    /OO   Places all directories first, followed by all files arranged by directory

    /OS   Directories are located at the beginning of the disk and files are placed where it is most convenient for the program; this is the fastest ordering option and is the one you will use most often

Select the type of sort from the DOS prompt or from a batch file with the following options:

/SE	Sorts by file extension
/SF	Sorts by file name
/SS	Sorts by file size
/ST	Sorts by file-creation date and time

Specify the sort order from the DOS prompt or from a batch file with one of the following parameters:

/NM	Stops Mirror from running automatically when Compress completes the disk optimization; you should always run Mirror once Compress has finished the optimization
/SA	Performs an ascending sort
/SD	Performs a descending sort

CONVERT

Convert finds setup files made by other hard-disk backup programs and changes them into a format that CP Backup understands.

Syntax

CONVERT *drive switch*

Description

/DEST =	Specifies the directory where you want to put the converted setup files
/CPBACKUP	Searches for CP Backup setup files
/FASTBACK	Searches for FastBack setup files
/NORTON	Searches for Norton Backup setup files

/PROMPT	Asks for confirmation from you before completing each conversion
/QUIET	Does not write anything to the screen during the conversion process

CPBACKUP

CPBackup gives you several fast methods of backing up your hard disk to floppy disks or another medium.

Syntax

CPBACKUP *drive set name file name switch*

Description

drive	You can specify the drive to be backed up from the command line. This is useful if you are working on a network and want to back up a station hard disk rather than the network-server drive. This will also save you time, since the server drive will be large and will contain perhaps hundreds of directories and files
set name	When you use CPBackup from the DOS command line or in a batch file, you can use a default set of backup options that you have previously saved in a file. Suppose you want to make a backup that will save all WordStar files that have changed since they were last backed up. Use the Options selection in CPBackup to select the method of archive and then use the Save Setup command to save these settings in a file called WORDBACK. Include the line **CPBACKUP WORDBACK** with no file-name extension in your batch file. This will start CPBackup, load the settings you saved in WORDBACK, and ask you to insert a disk. When the backup is complete, you return to the next command in the batch file

file name   Specify the file(s) that you want to back up. You can use the DOS wildcard characters to include groups of files

There are several powerful file-selection switches you can choose from:

/COPY	Makes a full copy backup
/DATE = *mmddyy – mmddyy*	Backs up or restores all files with file dates between the two specified dates
/DIF	Makes a differential backup
/EXATTR = *shr*	Excludes files with the specified attributes: *s* for system, *h* for hidden, or *r* for read-only; do not leave spaces between the letters
/FULL	Makes a full backup; this is the default setting
/FULLERASE	Makes a full backup to tape, after first erasing the tape
/INC	Makes an incremental backup
/SEP	Makes a separate incremental backup

Select hardware parameters from the following:

/ADDR = *base-i-d*	Specifies the address to use or the tape drive, where *base* is the address of the controller card, in hex; *i* is the single digit for the interrupt request (IRQ); and *d* is the single hex digit representing the DMA (Direct Memory Access) channel number
/DOB	Turns on the automatic detection of the COPY II PC Deluxe Option Board when making a backup to unformatted disks; do not use this parameter with a tape drive

/DRIVE = *d:n*	Selects the drive and media type for the backup, where *d:* is the drive letter to use and *n* defines the disk-media type, which can be one of the following: 360, 720, 1,200, or 1,440, representing 360K, 720K, 1.2MB, or 1.44MB floppy disks, respectively
/DRIVE = TAPE	Specifies a tape drive as the device for the backup
/NO	Prevents simultaneous hard-disk and floppy-disk DMA, or direct-memory access (/NO is short for "no overlap"). If you use this parameter, your backups will be slower but will work on computers that cannot perform these operations simultaneously due to hardware limitations. Try this option if your computer hangs up during the backup or restore process
/RATE = *rate*	Specifies the data rate for the tape drive, where *rate* is 1, 2, or 5, representing 1,000 Kbps (kilobits per second), 250 Kbps, and 500 Kbps, respectively. The rate must be one that the tape controller can support; see your tape drive manual for more details

Finally, choose from the following general parameters:

/ECC	Uses error correction
/NOECC	Does not use error correction
/NONSF	Uses non-standard formatting
/NOSAVE	Does not save backup history file to the hard disk
/SAVE	Saves the backup history file to the hard disk
/SF	Uses standard formatting

/R   With this parameter, starts CP Backup in
           restore mode and asks you to insert a backup
           disk; CP Backup does not read the hard disk's
           directories and files, so it starts up much faster

CPBDIR

CPBDIR is a stand-alone application program used to look at
backup disks made in CPBackup's proprietary format. The Install
program locates CPBDIR in the PCTOOLS\SYSTEM directory
on your hard disk.

Syntax

CPBDIR *switch*

Description

/d: Specifies the drive letter to use with CPBDIR; you
           must include the colon after the drive letter

/X   Lists extended information about the backup,
           including disk number, time and date of the
           backup, the backup format used, and the com-
           pression setting used

/V   Verifies the backup disk by checking the parity
           information on each track

CPSCHED

CPSCHED, the PC Tools scheduler program, does not use any
command-line parameters.

DATA MONITOR

Data Monitor is a memory-resident program that prevents unauthorized writes to your hard disk, installs delete protection, and displays the drive letter of the disk being accessed.

Syntax

DATAMON *switch*

Description

/ALL + or –	Enables or disables all options except Delete Tracker
/DATALOCK + or –	Enables or disables Directory Lock
/LIGHT + or –	Enables or disables Disk Light
/SENTRY + or –	Enables or disables Delete Sentry
/SCREEN + or –	Enables or disables Screen Blanker
/TRACKER + or –	Enables or disables Delete Tracker
/WRITE + or –	Enables or disables Write Protection

The following general parameters are also available:

/LOAD	Loads Data Monitor in memory-resident mode, using the settings in the DATAMON.INI file
/LOW	Does not use DOS 5 upper memory blocks, even if they are present in this computer
/STATUS	Shows a list of the current Data Monitor settings on the screen; this parameter can be abbreviated to simply /S
/UNLOAD	Unloads Data Monitor when the program is loaded memory-resident; this can be abbreviated to /U

DESKCONNECT

DeskConnect lets you connect two computers together, usually your main desktop computer and your laptop, so you can transfer important files before and after a business trip. DeskConnect is really two programs: DeskCon runs on your desktop machine and DeskSrv runs on your laptop. When the two computers are connected via a null-modem cable, these two programs talk to each other, allowing you to transfer files backwards and forwards.

Syntax

On your laptop computer:

DESKSRV *switch*

On your main office computer:

DESKCON *switch*

Now start PC Shell and initiate a communications session by selecting DeskConnect from the Special menu. The drives on your laptop are mapped onto your office computer and appear on the drive line at the top of the PCShell window. You can now move files backwards and forwards between the two computers by copying files from one drive to another. At the end of the session, choose DeskConnect in the Special menu a second time, then choose Disconnect from the message box to break the software connection between the two computers.

Description

Both DeskCon and DeskSrv use the same command line switches, as follows:

/B:*n*   Sets the baud rate for the communications between the two computers. Make sure you set the baud rate to the same value at both ends of the link. The baud rate can be any of the following rates: 300, 600, 1,200, 2,400, 4,800, 9,600, 19,200, 38,400, 57,600, or 115,200

/C:*n*   Specifies the COM port for communications, where *n* represents COM ports 1 to 4; if you use COM3 or COM4, you must also use both the /I and the /P switches

/I   Specifies the interrupt request (IRQ) to use with COM3 or COM4; refer to your hardware manual for more information

| /P | Specifies the port address for COM3 or COM4 |
| /U | Unloads DeskCon from memory |

DESKTOP

Desktop provides an easy-to-use desktop manager including word processing, database, calculators, an appointment scheduler and a to-do list.

Syntax

DESKTOP *switch*

Description

/C3 = *n* or /C4 = *n*	Specifies that your modem is on COM3 or COM4 by setting interrupt request, Base Port Address. See your modem manual for details. Not needed if you are using a PS/2, since the hardware automatically assigns a port number and interrupt request to each
/CS	Clears the screen and displays the calender when you run Desktop in memory-resident mode
/DQ	Specifies that you will hotkey into Desktop from the DOS prompt rather than from inside another application. If you use this selection, the state of the computer memory is not saved into a file and Desktop consequently starts up much faster
/MM	Allows you to run Desktop without loading any applications that were on the stack last time Desktop was run in memory-resident mode.
/O*drive*	Forces Desktop to use another drive for building the overlay files. If you use a RAM disk, you will speed up program operation but must have at least 400K of memory. If you want to run both

	PC Shell and Desktop from a RAM disk, you need a minimum of 1,000K of memory
/R	Loads Desktop in memory-resident mode
/RA	Loads Desktop in memory-resident mode, starts the program, and the Appointment Scheduler displays today's schedule and to-do list. If you use this parameter in your AUTOEXEC.BAT file, make sure that it is the last command in the file; any subsequent commands will only run after you exit Desktop

If Desktop is memory-resident and you want to run background communications, use Backtalk /2 for COM2.

After you have run PC Desktop as a memory-resident program, you can remove it from memory with Kill, which also removes PC Shell and other PC Tools programs from memory if they were the last memory-resident programs loaded.

DISKFIX

DiskFix diagnoses and repairs disk and file problems quickly and automatically.

Syntax

> DISKFIX *drive switch*

Description

drive	The drive for DiskFix to analyze. If you want to test more than one drive, separate the drive letters by a space. Defaults to the current drive
/HCACHE	Use this parameter if you have a HardCache card installed in your computer
/HCARD	Use this parameter if you have a HardCard installed in your computer

/RO:*file name*	Used after the /SCAN or /TEST parameters, this option generates a DiskFix report, overwriting an existing DISKFIX.RPT file
/RA:*file name*	Used after the /SCAN or /TEST parameters, this option generates a DiskFix report, appending this new report to an existing DISKFIX.RPT file
/SCAN	Performs a surface scan with no pattern testing on the specified disk, using the selected DiskFix options
/TEST	Performs the Repair a Disk selection on the specified drive, without making any repairs

DIRECTORY MAINTENANCE

Directory Maintenance lets you manage the directory structure on your hard disk, no matter how complex the structure or how large the drive.

Syntax

DM *drive directory switch*

Description

drive	Changes to the specified drive
directory	Changes to the specified directory
/CO *source directory destination directory*	Copies a directory; include the complete path name
/DD *path*	Deletes the directory, including any files and subdirectories; include the complete path name
/MA *path* HSRA	Changes the specified attributes of the directory. Type the complete path name. Use the attribute letters as follows: H for Hidden, S for System, R for Read-only,

	and A for Archive; any attributes not specified will be removed
/MD *path*	Makes a new directory; be sure to type the complete path name
/PG *prune directory graft directory*	Moves the *prune directory* and makes it a subdirectory of the *graft directory*. Be sure and type both path names in full, including any drive letters, as needed
/R	Rereads the directory tree for the current drive and updates the TREELIST file
/RN *old name new name*	Renames the *old name* directory to the *new name;* enter the complete path for *old name*, but just the directory name for *new name*
/RV *name* ⁻	Changes the volume label of the current drive to *name*

FILEFIND

FileFind locates missing files or groups of files, searches for text, and searches by date, file size, or attributes.

Syntax

> FF *drive file name search text switch*

Description

drive	Selects the drive to search
file name	Specifies the files to locate; use the DOS wildcard characters * and ? when appropriate, and enclose multiple words in quotation marks
search text	Specifies the test to search for; remember to enclose multiple words in quotation marks

The following switches are optional:

/ALL	Searches all drives for files
/CB	Searches the current directory and any subdirectories for the file(s)
/CO	Restricts the search to the current directory only
/CS	Makes the search case-sensitive
/WW	Restricts the search to whole words only

To set a file attribute, use one of the following switches with a plus sign. To turn an attribute off, use the same switch followed by a minus sign:

/A+ or /A–	Sets or clears the archive bit
/H+ or /H–	Sets or clears the hidden attribute
/R+ or /R–	Sets or clears the file's read-only bit
/S+ or /S–	Sets or clears the file's system bit
/CLEAR	Clears all attributes from the located files

The following general parameters are also available:

/CURRENT	Sets the file's date and time to the current system date and time
/D*date*	Sets the file's date to *date*, in mm-dd-yy format
/T*time*	Sets the file's time to *time*, in hh:mm format
/F:*file name*	Saves a list of the located files in *file name*

FILE FIX

File Fix repairs damaged Lotus 1-2-3, Lotus Symphony, or dBASE files.

Syntax

    FILEFIX *file name switch*

Description

    file name   Specifies the file for File Fix to work on

The other command-line switches that File Fix accepts are the video and mouse parameters described at the start of this chapter.

INSTALL

Use Install to load or reconfigure the PC Tools package, or to make a Recovery Disk.

Syntax

Place PC Tools disk number 1 in drive A before using Install.

    INSTALL *switch*

Description

/BPD:*n*	Specifies the duration of the beep prompt, where *n* is the value in milliseconds; the default is 100
/BPF:*n*	Specifies the frequency of the beep prompt, where *n* is the frequency in Hertz; default in 1,000
/FC	Forces Install to copy applications even if they have already been installed
/RD	Creates a Recovery Disk

KILL

Use Kill to remove several of the PC Tools memory-resident programs from memory. Kill removes PC Shell, Desktop, Backtalk, CPSCHED, and Deskconnect.

Syntax

> KILL

Description

Kill does not support any command-line arguments.

MI

MI is a memory-mapping program that lists the type, size, and location of areas of memory, and the application programs using them.

Syntax

> MI *switch*

Description

/A	Lists all blocks of memory
/F	Filters out unprintable characters
/N	Does not pause a long screen listing
/O	Uses alternative display format
/Q	Quick summary only; does not show information for individual TSR programs
/V	Lists hooked vectors

MIRROR

Mirror saves a copy of the system area of your hard disk for use in recovering files after an accidental erasure or reformatting of the disk.

Syntax

> MIRROR *drive switch*

Description

drive	The drive letter for Mirror to protect; use multiple drive letters to protect several drives
/1	Specifies that Mirror should save only the latest FAT and directory information
/PARTN	Saves a copy of your hard-disk partition table information, boot sector, and CMOS information to a floppy disk
/NOCMOS	Used with /PARTN, directs Mirror to save partition table information and boot-sector data, but no CMOS data; this is for use on older computers that do not use CMOS memory

PARK

Park is a stand-alone hard-disk, head-parking program. Be sure to run it before you move your computer.

Syntax

    PARK

Description

There are no command-line parameters for Park.

PC-CACHE

PC-Cache creates a disk cache in your computer's memory to speed up disk accesses.

Syntax

    PC-CACHE *switch*

Description

/EXTSTART = nK	Specifies the start of the cache buffer in extended memory. EXTSTART must be larger than 1MB (1,024K). PC-Cache is compatible with VDISK.SYS
/FLUSH	Empties the cache
/Idrive	Specifies the drives that should not be cached
/NOBATCH	Reduces the amount of time that the interrupts are disabled between transferring sectors. Sectors are handled one at a time. Used when caching in extended memory
/OFF	Turns PC-Cache off
/ON	Turns PC-Cache on
/PAUSE	Acts as a troubleshooting option by pausing at the PC-Cache status window
/QUIET	Disables the startup message for use in batch files
/STATUS	Displays statistics about the current state of the cache; this parameter can be abbreviated to /S
/WRITE = ON or OFF	Controls whether disk write operations are cached

The PC Tools 6 switches /PARAM, /PARAM∗, /INFO, and /MEASURES have been replaced by the single parameter, /STATUS.

You can specify the size of the cache with one of the following parameters. You may use only one SIZE parameter and you cannot mix conventional, expanded, and extended memory:

/SIZE = nK	Specifies the amount of standard memory for the cache; the default is 64K and the maximum is 512K

/SIZEXP = nK	Specifies the amount of expanded memory for the cache
/SIZEXT = nK	Specifies the amount of extended memory for the cache; this can only be used with computers using Intel's 80286 or later microprocessors
/UNLOAD	Removes the cache; this can be abbreviated to just /U
/WIN	Resizes PC-Cache automatically when Microsoft Windows starts
/X	Use this parameter if you use NEC or WYSE 3.3 DOS and have a single partition of larger than 40MB

PC CONFIG

Use PC Config to select the screen colors and the display, mouse, and keyboard options for all the PC Tools DOS programs.

Syntax

    PCCONFIG switch

Description

/S	Sets the keyboard speed and exits back to DOS. Use this if you changed the keyboard speed but forgot to check the Enable Keyboard Speed box.

PC FORMAT

PC Format is a safe formatting alternative to the DOS FORMAT command.

Syntax

    PCFORMAT drive switch

Description

drive	Specifies the letter of the drive you want to format
/1	Specifies the single-sided format
/4	Formats a floppy disk as a 360K disk in a high-capacity drive. This means that you can format a low-capacity floppy disk (360K) by using a high-capacity (1.2MB) disk drive. If you format 360K floppy disks in a high-capacity floppy-disk drive, you may not be able to read them with a 360K floppy-disk drive
/8	Formats a disk with eight sectors per track, for use with versions of DOS before DOS 2.0
/DESTROY	Formats the disk and erases all data on the disk
/F	Specifies a full format
/F:nK	Selects the size of the floppy disk. Valid entries are 160, 180, 320, 360, 720, 1,200, or 1,400. Size 2,880 is available in DOS 5 for 2.88MB floppy disks
/N:n	Specifies the number of sectors per track for the format; valid entries are 8, 9, 15, or 36
/P	Copies the information from PC Format to the device connected to LPT1
/Q	Specifies a quick format for a previously formatted disk; this erases the data in the FAT and the root directory
/R	PC Format reads and then reformats every track on the disk; the FAT, root directory, and data on the disk remain intact
/S	Copies the operating system files to the floppy disk to make it a bootable disk

/TEST	Simulates the format without actually writing to the disk
/T:*n*	Specifies the number of tracks for the format; valid entries are 40 or 80
/V	Causes PC Format to ask you to input a volume label for the disk when the format is complete

When you run PC Format on a hard disk, the following options are available in addition to the /Q, /P, and /TEST parameters just explained:

drive	Indicates the drive letter of the hard disk that you want to format
/S	Copies the operating system files to the hard disk to make it a bootable disk; first boot your system with the version of DOS that you want installed on your hard disk
/V	Allows you to add a volume label

PC SECURE

PC Secure compresses, encrypts, and hides your files.

Syntax

PCSECURE *switch file name*

Description

/C	Turns compression off when encrypting a file
/D	Decrypts the file specified in *file name*
/F	Performs a full DES encryption on the specified file
/G	Specifies full Department of Defense procedures: the file is encrypted and the original file is over-written seven times and verified for complete

erasure; the /G parameter is not available outside the United States.

/K*xxxx*	Specifies that the characters defined by *xxxx* are used as the key for encryption/decryption
/M	Allows the specified file to be encrypted several times
/P	This parameter allows you to enter a new password after pressing the Escape key
/Q	Performs a quick encryption on the file specified in *file name*
/S	Turns on silent mode, so that the only messages sent to the screen are error messages. This mode is particularly suited to batch-file use
file name	File name of the file for encryption or decryption; you can use the DOS wildcard characters in the name to specify several files

PC SHELL

PC Shell is a DOS shell program that provides disk, file, and applications support.

Syntax

PCSHELL *switch*

Description

/A*n*	Specifies the amount of memory PC Shell uses when it is active in memory-resident mode and after you have hotkeyed into it. The default size is 235K. The largest amount of memory you can specify is approximately 200K less than the total memory in your computer
/DQ	Specifies that you will hotkey into PC Shell from the DOS prompt rather than from inside another

application. If you use this selection, the state of the computer memory is not saved into a file and PC Shell consequently starts up much faster

/F*n*   Changes the default hotkey from Ctrl-Escape to Ctrl and a function key, where *n* is the number of the function key, from 1 to 10

/O*drive*   Forces PC Shell to use another drive for building the overlay files; if you use a RAM disk, this speeds up program operation

/R   Specifies the amount of resident memory that PC Shell uses when it is not active

/TR*n*   Specifies that PC Shell do a tree rebuild every *n* days; the default setting is 1, which indicates a daily tree rebuild

REBUILD

Use Rebuild to recover CMOS data, a copy of your partition table, and the boot sector saved on the Emergency System Recovery Disk.

Syntax

REBUILD *drive switch*

Description

drive   Specifies the drive where Rebuild will find the PARTNSAV.FIL file

/ICHK   When you initially collect CMOS data, the Mirror program creates an internal program checksum that characterizes the data as coming from a specific computer. This is to prevent you from loading the CMOS data back into the wrong computer by accident. If you use this switch, Rebuild ignores the checksum and loads the CMOS data anyway

/LIST	Lists the existing hard-disk partitions; no data are changed
/N	Does not pause at a full screen; this parameter is only used with /LIST
/TEST	Simulates the rebuild process, showing what will happen without writing anything to the disk; CMOS and partition-table information are not changed

SWAPSH AND SWAPDT

Swapsh moves the resident portion of PC Shell into expanded (EMS) or extended (XMS) memory, or onto your hard disk, to decrease the amount of conventional memory needed to load PC Shell in memory-resident mode. Swapdt performs the same function for the Desktop. Load Swapsh or Swapt in AUTOEXEC.BAT after all other network drivers, your disk-cache program, and any other programs that require background processing or hook the device driver chain have been loaded.

Syntax

    SWAPSH *switch*

or

    SWAPDT *switch*

Description

Both programs use the following general switches:

/N	Does not load memory-resident; instead, Swapsh waits for a PC Shell command and Swapdt waits for a Desktop command
/U	Removes both Swapsh and PC Shell or Swapdt and Desktop from memory

/D*path*	Specifies the full path name for the swapped files; the default is C:\
/S*x*	Specifies the swap type, where 0 specifies automatic, 1 selects swap to disk, 2 uses extended memory, and 3 uses expanded memory. If the selected type is unavailable or fails, the switch defaults to /S0
/P*x*	Sets the pasting buffer size for the clipboard, where *x* is a number between 0 and 9; each increment adds 256 bytes to the clipboard buffer
/T*x*	Sets the clipboard pasting speed, where *x* is a number between 0 (slow) and 3 (fast)

There are also several PC Shell hotkey parameters:

/A	Selects the Alt key as PC Shell's hotkey
/C	Selects the Ctrl key as PC Shell's hotkey
/L	Uses the left Shift key as PC Shell's hotkey
/R	Uses the right Shift key as PC Shell's hotkey
/K*xx*	Specifies *xx* as PC Shell's hotkey, where *xx* is a two-digit hexadecimal code from Table 20.1.

Table 20.1: Two-Digit Hexadecimal Codes for PC Shell Hotkey

KEY	CODE	KEY	CODE
A	1E	B	30
C	2E	D	20
E	12	F	21
G	22	H	23
I	17	J	24
K	25	L	26
M	32	N	31
O	18	P	19

Table 20.1: Two-Digit Hexadecimal Codes for PC Shell Hotkey (continued)

KEY	CODE	KEY	CODE
Q	10	R	13
S	1F	T	14
U	16	V	2F
W	11	X	2D
Y	15	Z	2C
0	0B	1	02
2	03	3	04
4	05	5	06
6	07	7	08
8	09	9	0A
–	0C	=	0D
F1	3B	F2	3C
F3	3D	F4	3E
F5	3F	F6	40
F7	41	F8	42
F9	43	F10	44
F11	57	F12	58

SYSTEM INFORMATION

System Information lets you look in all the dark corners of your computer to see much complex information that is not normally available without some complex programming.

Syntax

SI *switch*

Description

/DEMO	Starts System Information running in demonstration mode, where each screen is shown automatically for a few seconds, in sequence; to exit from the demonstration, hit Escape
/MEM	Goes directly to the conventional memory display; press Escape to return to DOS
/NOVID	Disables extended video checking
/RPT	Prints a full System Information report to a disk file

UNDELETE

Undelete recovers erased files and directories.

Syntax

UNDEL *drive file name switch*

Description

drive	The drive letter of the drive containing the deleted files; if you don't specify a drive, Undelete assumes the current drive
file name	File name and path name where the deleted files are found. If you don't specify a path, the current path will be used. You can use the DOS wildcard characters * and ? if you wish
/ALL	Specifies automatic recovery of all deleted files. Undelete will use different characters in a file name if there is a chance that it will create duplicate file names when files are recovered
/DOS	Uses the DOS method for recovering files
/DT	Uses information from the Delete Tracker file

	to help reconstruct the original file name; used in DOS 5
/LIST	Lists all the deleted files available for recovery in the specified directory
/M	Undeletes DOS-protected files using Mirror in DOS 5
/NC	Undeletes all files without asking for confirmation on each file
/S	Undeletes files protected by Delete Sentry

UNFORMAT

Unformat recovers data and program files from a hard disks after it has been reformatted by the DOS FORMAT command.

Syntax

UNFORMAT *drive*

Description

The only parameter it makes sense to use with Unformat is the drive you want to unformat.

VDEFEND

VDefend is a small memory-resident program that can protect your system against over 400 computer viruses.

Syntax

VDEFEND *switch*

Description

/N	Use this switch if a network driver will be loaded after VDefend is loaded
/U	Unloads VDefend from memory

─────── **VIEW** ───────────────

View lets you look at data files made by many popular applications programs, without loading the application program or even knowing which program created the file.

Syntax

VIEW *file name switch*

Description

file name   Specifies the file to view

View accepts the video and mouse parameters described at the beginning of this chapter.

─────── **WIPE** ───────────────

Wipe completely obliterates deleted files so that they can never be recovered, not even by PC Tools.

Syntax

WIPE *drive file name switch*

Description

drive	Specifies the drive letter for a disk wipe
file name	Specifies a file for wiping; use the DOS wildcard characters * and ? to broaden the specification to include several files
/DELETE	Deletes files but does not wipe them
/DISK	Wipes the entire disk
/GOVT	Uses the Department of Defense rules for file obliteration
/HIDDEN	Deletes or wipes hidden files in addition to specified files

/MODIFIED	Deletes or wipes files that have been modified since they were last backed up
/NOCONFIRM	Deletes or wipes files without pausing to confirm the operation with you; use this selection with care
/READONLY	Deletes or wipes read-only files as well as the selected files
/REP:*n*	Repeats the wipe operation *n* times; the default is 3
/QUIET	Suppresses prompts: Wipe just gives status information; use this selection with care
/SUB	Extends the delete or wipe operation to subdirectories
/UNMODIFIED	Deletes or wipes files that have not been modified since they were last backed up
/UNUSED	Wipes only the unused data space on the specified disk
/VALUE:*n*	Uses *n* as the wipe value; it can be any number from 0 to 255

INDEX

FREE CATALOG!

SYBEX ®

Mail us this form today, and we'll send you a full-color catalog of Sybex books.

Name _____

Street _____

City/State/Zip _____

Phone _____

Please supply the name of the Sybex book purchased.

_____

How would you rate it?

_____ Excellent   _____ Very Good   _____ Average   _____ Poor

Why did you select this particular book?

_____ Recommended to me by a friend

_____ Recommended to me by store personnel

_____ Saw an advertisement in _____

_____ Author's reputation

_____ Saw in Sybex catalog

_____ Required textbook

_____ Sybex reputation

_____ Read book review in _____

_____ In-store display

_____ Other _____

Where did you buy it?

_____ Bookstore

_____ Computer Store or Software Store

_____ Catalog (name: _____)

_____ Direct from Sybex

_____ Other: _____

Did you buy this book with your personal funds?

_____ Yes   _____ No

About how many computer books do you buy each year?

_____ 1-3   _____ 3-5   _____ 5-7   _____ 7-9   _____ 10+

About how many Sybex books do you own?

_____ 1-3   _____ 3-5   _____ 5-7   _____ 7-9   _____ 10+

Please indicate your level of experience with the software covered in this book:

_____ Beginner   _____ Intermediate   _____ Advanced

Which types of software packages do you use regularly?

_____ Accounting _____ Databases _____ Networks

_____ Amiga _____ Desktop Publishing _____ Operating Systems

_____ Apple/Mac _____ File Utilities _____ Spreadsheets

_____ CAD _____ Money Management _____ Word Processing

_____ Communications _____ Languages _____ Other _____
                                                   (please specify)

Which of the following best describes your job title?

_____ Administrative/Secretarial _____ President/CEO

_____ Director _____ Manager/Supervisor

_____ Engineer/Technician _____ Other _____
                                        (please specify)

Comments on the weaknesses/strengths of this book: _____

_____

_____

_____

_____

_____

PLEASE FOLD, SEAL, AND MAIL TO SYBEX

SYBEX, INC.
Department M
2021 CHALLENGER DR.
ALAMEDA, CALIFORNIA USA
94501

SYBEX ®

SEAL

Task	Utility	Chapter
Look up ASCII characters	Desktop Utilities	18
Make appointments	Desktop Appointment Scheduler	15
Make disk bootable	PC Shell	4
Make new directory	Directory Maintenance	8
Mark bad cluster	DiskFix	7
Obliterate files	Wipe	9
Optimize hard-disk file organization	Compress	8
Optimize interleave factor	DiskFix	7
Park hard-disk heads	Park	4
Password-protect files	PC Secure	9
Perform calculations	Desktop Calculators	14
Prepare outline	Desktop Outlines	13
Prevent unauthorized disk writes	Data Monitor, VDefend	9
Print system information	System Information	8
Protect deleted files from being overwritten	Data Monitor	9
Rearrange directories	Directory Maintenance	8
Rearrange files	Compress	8
Recover accidentally deleted file	Undelete	9
Recover accidentally formatted hard or floppy disk	Unformat	10
Remove directory	Directory Maintenance	8
Remove memory-resident program	Kill	20
Rename directory	Directory Maintenance	8
Rename file	PC Shell	4
Repair disk	DiskFix	7
Repair Lotus, Symphony, or dBASE file	File Fix	7
Repair media defects	DiskFix	7